A Search for Justice

A Search for Justice

JOHN SEIGENTHALER

Contributors:
JAMES SQUIRES
JOHN HEMPHILL
FRANK RITTER

Aurora Publishers, Inc.
Nashville/London

Copyright © 1971 by Aurora Publishers Incorporated
Nashville, Tennessee 37219
Library of Congress Catalog Card Number 73-108293
Standard Book Number: 87695-003-9
Manufactured in the United States of America

• CONTENTS •

•

73664

This book is dedicated
to the memory of
John F. Kennedy, Martin Luther King
and Robert F. Kennedy,
who sought justice
and died in the pursuit of it.

Acknowledgments

The authors are indebted to many individuals for assistance in the preparation of this book. We would like to express our thanks to Warren F. Nardelle of the New Orleans *Times Picayune*, Romera Carraro of the *Los Angeles Times*, Annette Corkan of the Memphis *Press-Scimitar*, Gene Brady of the Memphis *Commercial Appeal* and Madonna K. Miller of *The Nashville Tennessean* for searching the files of their newspaper libraries for facts and information. We would like to acknowledge a special debt to Byrd Douglas Cain whose dedicated research work was invaluable to us, and to Wayne Murphy for his design suggestions.

We deeply appreciate the legal advice and assistance of Alfred H. Knight.

We are aware of the peculiar difficulties that confront editors and we acknowledge the special problems that must be confronted in a book where there are four separate contributors. The editorial suggestions of Dominic de Lorenzo and Valerie de Lorenzo were most helpful to us and the final editing of Susan Van Riper substantially improved the continuity of our presentation.

For typing and retyping the manuscript we are grateful to Edna Gardner, Alice Sloan and Carolyn Evers Cockrell.

During the preparation of "a search," conversations with

many practicing lawyers led to sharp disagreements which often resulted in a searching reexamination of our own conclusions. We demonstrate our appreciation to them for their cooperation and willingness to debate various points of view by protecting their anonymity.

During and after the three trials discussed in this book, we were aided by the insights and reportage of Bill Crider and Bernard Gavzer of the Associated Press, Henry Leiffermann formerly of the United Press International and Martin Waldron of the *New York Times.*

At times we interrupted the busy schedules of a number of people, authorities who patiently allowed us to probe their knowledge in particular areas. Some of them challenged assumptions, offered specific fact data, or suggested other source material. We are indebted to Justice Stanley Mosk of the California Supreme Court, Justice Robert K. Dwyer of the Tennessee Criminal Court of Appeals, Fred P. Graham, Archibald Cox, Alan Dershowitz, Dr. Otto Billig, and to the members of the staff of the offices of attorney general in Connecticut and Massachusetts.

We would like to pay tribute to Charles Edmundson of the Memphis *Commercial Appeal* and Roy Hamilton of the Memphis *Press-Scimitar* and to Walter Sheridan of NBC News and Richard Townley of WDSU-TV, New Orleans. These reporters were victims of injustice dispensed by the system of justice.

Finally, but most importantly, we would like to express our heartfelt thanks to Amon Carter Evans, publisher of *The Nashville Tennessean,* for his tolerance and generosity to us during the period we were working on "a search."

Chapter 1

Justice Under Law...
And Order

*"Trial by jury, instead
of being a security to persons
who are accused,
shall be a delusion,
a mockery, and a snare."*
**Lord Denman,
O'CONNELL vs. THE QUEEN**

This book was born one summer noon in 1969 when three newspaper reporters, just home from covering three criminal trials of national significance, sat down to lunch with their editor to discuss their recent assignments. Each of the three trials had involved the same crime—political assassination. Frank Ritter had recently returned from the trial of Clay Shaw in New Orleans. Jim Squires was recently back from the James Earl Ray hearing in Memphis. John Hemphill had just come home from the Sirhan Bishara Sirhan trial in Los Angeles.

All three correspondents were deeply disturbed over basic flaws they had found in the American system of justice as demonstrated in these three separate trials. Now, away from the pit of legal conflict and removed from courtroom spectacles, they were discussing with their editor, John Seigenthaler, a former official of the U. S. Department of Justice, their convictions about the injustice that seemed, to them, inherent in the American legal system. They were distressed by the blind confidence an apathetic public seemed to place in this system, which they felt was pockmarked with imperfections.

Each of these three separate criminal cases had drawn the full attention of the public in the United States and around the world. So astounding were the crimes charged, so speculative were the possibilities that each killing had been part of some hidden conspiracy, so controversial were the fallen leaders—loved and despised by millions—that it is not surprising that the trials attracted world-wide speculation and interest.

The outcome of the three trials is well known. Shaw was cleared of the charge that he conspired with Lee Harvey Oswald to plot the murder of President John F. Kennedy. Ray pleaded guilty to the charge that he murdered Martin Luther King. He was sentenced to ninety-nine years in prison. Sirhan was convicted of murdering Senator Robert F. Kennedy. The same jury that found him guilty sentenced him to die in the gas chamber.

Many volumes have been written in the recent past exploring the possibility of conspiracy in each of the three assassination cases. Some of the books have sought to offer new insights, additional evidence, even novel theories about conspiratorial plots in the deaths of President Kennedy, Dr. King and Senator Kennedy.

It is not the purpose of this book to do so. This work is designed to study the assassination trials of Shaw, Sirhan and Ray for the purpose of pointing out obvious defects in the administration of justice, shown to exist in the course of these cases.

Where the question of conspiracy confronts the writers—as it sometimes does, particularly in the case of James Earl Ray—it is dealt with. But none of the authors here is attempting to show that he found solutions or clues heretofore unknown. We did find serious problems in the system of justice. And here there are obvious solutions. To point to these is an adequate achievement for us.

Notoriety naturally confronted those who were on trial for crimes involving the cold-blooded murders of national leaders. But beyond the heinous character of the offenses and the prominence of the victims, each of these three trials had some intriguing personalities as principal participants: the defendants, the judges, the prosecutors, and the defense lawyers. How these personalities reacted in the face of crisis; how they talked, even walked; what they said and did not say—all became part of the human drama that captivated the public.

It was ironic that during the first five months of 1969 there would be three criminal trials involving political murder—a crime which, until the 1960's, had been uncommon in American history. Thus it was with a sense of developing history that these three aggressive, young but mature journalists went to three far-removed cities to report to their readers the day-to-day developments in the trials of Shaw, Ray and Sirhan.

The good reporter is trained to perceive the human equation in every story situation; to look for and report on the impact of happenings on the lives of people caught up by time and events. But the good reporter looks, too, beneath the surface display of human emotion to scrutinize the subsurface mechanics of the system—in this case the court system—which so often works its impersonal will on individual destinies.

These three reporters looked separately and independently at the court system. What they saw shook them.

In retrospect the verdicts rendered in each of these cases can be rationalized as evidence that the American system of justice works. It is simple to accept the following conclusions: (1) The evidence against Shaw was scant and questionable—and he was acquitted. (2) The evidence against Ray was strong, if circumstantial—and he was sentenced to prison for the rest of his life. (3) The evidence against Sirhan was strong, and direct—and he was sentenced to be executed.

A lawyer may say that the weight of evidence balances almost perfectly in these cases with the severity of the sentence. Therefore justice works and works well.

Such a syllogism is false. And despite the "logic" of spokesmen of the bench and bar who support the system of justice if not the ideal of justice, three reporters, operating in different courtrooms, before different judges and different opposing lawyers and different juries, each independently reached the conclusion that American justice works accidentally, if at all.

Despite what seemed to be a consistency in the verdicts, vis-a-vis the weight of evidence, these newsmen felt that the administration of justice was mired in inconsistency. None of them felt that the administration of justice functioned well in New Orleans, Memphis or Los Angeles; none of them felt he would have much confidence in his own chance to get a fair verdict were he to be put on trial in those same courts, before the same judges.

It has been said that a love of justice is in reality no more than a fear of injustice. This fear perhaps provides some of the safeguards which have made the American system of justice a "model" in the eyes of the professional lawyers who practice under the system. Woven into that fear of injustice is the thread of political prosecution that ran such a jagged pattern through the fabric of early Anglo-American jurisprudence.

It is possible that the political overtones built into these assassination cases affected the views of these three correspondents, if not the jurors.

The reporters' views and the views of their editor leaned, however, toward the sentiment that the American system of justice has not moved to keep pace with the space-age environment of the 1960's and 1970's; that the system has been left too long to the lawyers. As a result it has come under the control and dominance of a legal profession which is satisfied with the status quo because it serves and profits members of the profession well enough; that the system is devoid of meaningful public scrutiny and thus devoid of meaningful public criticism; that it is thus sorely lacking long-overdue reform; that in the absence of such reform the administration of justice is in serious trouble and often, on a day-to-day basis, may actually be more inclined to thwart justice.

These three newspapermen had gone to court with their eyes and ears attuned primarily to the dramatic stories that they knew would unfold as three men went on trial with life and liberty at stake. They came away with the strong belief that more than three men were on trial; American justice was on trial.

The search for justice, as Clarence Darrow once said, is as old as the conscience of man. That search, he might have added, is as unstable, as unreliable, as enigmatic and as haunting as the conscience of man.

In the first six months of 1969 that search for justice in the American criminal court system focused on the crime of political assassination. Three national leaders, John Fitzgerald Kennedy, Martin Luther King and Robert Francis Kennedy, had been slain by assassin gunfire. King and Robert Kennedy had fallen within a seven-week period in 1968. Now three men were accused before the American bar of justice, each in one of these three murders.

In New Orleans, Clay Shaw, a cultivated and soft-spoken gentleman of the old South, was about to go on trial for conspiring to murder President Kennedy.

In Memphis, James Earl Ray, a professional criminal, a fugitive from prison, a loner who had lived by his dull wits, was about to go on trial for murdering Dr. King.

In Los Angeles, Sirhan Bishara Sirhan, a volatile, profane young Arab immigrant who imagined himself an anti-Israeli guerilla, was about to go on trial for killing Senator Kennedy.

It was appropriate to the national mood that these criminal cases should come at the exact moment in history when the people of the land seemed preoccupied with violence. Average Americans yearned for "law and order" and were beginning to sense a shocking fact about themselves: they were afraid. Public opinion polls indicated many people were afraid to walk down the streets of their hometowns after dark. Others suffered a gnawing dread that the forces of evil were grasping control of affairs from the forces of good.

The vast majority of people considered themselves "law abiding citizens" and they felt they had become the unprotected, forgotten folk of a society wracked with turbulence, demonstrations, riots and talk of revolution.

Many varied factors washed together to color the cloth of this public fright. In the background was an awareness of the mounting crime statistics J. Edgar Hoover was publishing through the Federal Bureau of Investigation. The FBI kept winning its battle against the lawless each Sunday night on the American Broadcasting Company's television network. But in real life Mr. Hoover kept telling the nation that the war with the underworld was being lost.

For a long time these empirical FBI statistics had seemed almost as unreal as the violence in television shows: something to be aware of, to tolerate, even to enjoy talking about. The "Mafia" and the "syndicate" and the "Cosa Nostra" were as chimerical as the "communists." They were at least one step removed from the lives most people lived, and to many they were romantic fantasy.

Then came the urban riots of 1967 and 1968. As city after city was ravaged by ghetto disorder the public began to realize that this was not fantasy—it was real life. The news pictures on front pages and on TV screens were now real: looting, arson, assault, even guerilla warfare. Suddenly crime was on the front doorstep. Photographs told the disturbing story of vandals looting shattered

store windows, hauling away clothing, whisky, television sets—
sometimes while armed policemen stood nearby and watched.
Cities were in flames and some city officials were telling police
not to bother the ghetto rioter who was screaming "burn, baby
burn." Then there was that long string of Supreme Court decisions which police felt shackled them and freed the robber.[1]
Ironically, the Warren Court which produced these decisions was
situated in the nation's capital where crime seemed most ramp-
ant.

In the Washington, D.C. area, there were nightly street mug-
gings by roving gangs of youth intent on crime and destruction.
All this led Senator Herman Talmadge, the Georgia Democrat, to
comment: "My wife would be safer in the jungle wilds of the
Belgian Congo at midnight than she is on 'M' Street in the District
of Columbia at high noon."

The call for "law and order" was becoming a plaintive wail
as the presidential primary election campaigns began in early
1968. Suddenly "Support Your Local Police" was more than a
slogan on a John Birch Society bumper sticker. It was a national
anthem. "Law and order" was a dominant theme of the presidential political dialogue of 1968.

Ramsey Clark, the attorney general of the Johnson Administration, became a key target of Richard Nixon, the Republican
candidate. The Republicans claimed that the attorney general
was "soft on crime." Clark, the chief law enforcement officer
of the nation, was a civil libertarian—and it was not a year when
it was politic to be in favor of the Supreme Court guidelines protecting the rights of the accused. The presidential campaign of
George Wallace, the former Alabama governor, was still another
factor that helped condition the nation to a mood of insecurity.

The shots that took Dr. King's life so suddenly in April in

---

1. Mallory versus U.S. (354 US 449; 1957) held invalid a confession by a man detained at
police headquarters for a period of hours during which he was interrogated; Mapp versus
Ohio (367 US 643; 1961) held a police raid without a search warrant where "lewd" books
were confiscated violated the constitutional rights of a defendant and was an unlawful search
and seizure; Gideon versus Wainwright (372 US 335; 1963) held that a state was required to
provide a defense lawyer for an indigent; Escobedo versus Illinois (378 US 478; 1964) held that
the police could not refuse to allow a suspect held for questioning the opportunity to consult
his lawyer at any time during interrogation; Miranda versus Arizona (384 US 436; 1966) held
that police were required to advise a suspect of his right to remain silent and his right to
counsel before he made any statement.

Memphis and those that killed Senator Kennedy in June in Los Angeles served to build on that mood.

Then, in the burning heat of the summer of 1968, there was the brutal clash at the Democratic National Convention in Chicago between demonstrators and the police force of Mayor Richard J. Daley. As the nation sat transfixed before its television sets all the random feelings of fright were crystallized as police shock troops smashed into demonstrators. Policemen were caught by news cameras in the act of clubbing, manhandling, and mauling demonstrators, in what was later to be called a police riot. Many newsmen found themselves caught under the flailing barrage of police billy clubs. Reporters, many of whom had covered social conflict all the way from the Little Rock desegregation crisis to the Poor People's March on Washington, at once sharply criticized the police.

But in many homes the police assault was viewed as a long overdue counterattack on the anarchist street-criminals who had been intent upon raping the social order and disrupting "decent, established institutions." Many who demonstrated had not engaged in provocative acts, but were there to protest, peacefully, the war in Vietnam and the seemingly impenetrable wall of psychological resistance the political establishment had thrown up to ward off anti-war sentiment. But when the police charge came, the night sticks fell on the heads of the washed as well as the unwashed, and numerous reporters and photographers took their lumps while trying to cover the charge.

If there was a point in time when a majority of voters began to think "law and order" was as serious an issue as the war in Vietnam, the conflict in the shadow of the Democratic Convention hall was precisely that moment.

The dangers posed to the administration of justice by the temper of the times were several. The "law and order" mood in the nation might motivate unscrupulous prosecutors to bring preposterous actions. Defense lawyers, aware of the mood and fearful that it might infect juries, might urge defendants to plead guilty rather than risk trial by jury. Judges, under the glare of the public spotlight that turned on cases of unusual violence, might react with harsh, arbitrary, extreme rulings from the bench. The uniform fear of public violence might lead some juries to "smell blood" and recommend maximum sentences as a lesson to other offenders when, in other times, conviction for the same crime might receive more temperate sentences. The fibre of the judicial system, supposedly insulated against popular winds and partisan fires, might bend or melt under the pressure and heat of public sentiment.

The year 1969 presented three classic studies of how a violent society deals with crimes of violence. There might never be a better time in this country to analyze and compare the defects and deficiencies in the system of justice than during this five-month period in 1969 when three political assassination trials confronted the criminal courts in three different state jurisdictions.

Law, as administered by the judicial system, holds civilized society together. There must be consistency and substance to the law if it is to be effective in a free, open, violent society. In the trials of Clay Shaw for conspiracy to murder John F. Kennedy, James Earl Ray for the murder of Martin Luther King, and Sirhan B. Sirhan for the murder of Robert F. Kennedy, the nation had an opportunity to test the substance and consistency of the law. Was its application effective, efficient, intelligent, honest? Was it a search for truth? Was it a search for justice?

Some lawyers may contend that it is not fair to test the entire system of criminal justice on the basis of three trials. Some will argue that under the stress and duress of trials such as these the courts are "incident prone" and that the potential for "reversible error" is high in cases where there is a great deal of public attention attracted to the courts.

But if the courts cannot function well when the whole world is watching, the malfunctioning will magnify in the shadows of routine when concern is limited to an obscure defendant, his lawyer and family; or, on the other side, to the victim of the crime, his relatives and friends and the prosecutor.

The notorious nature of the offenses charged, and the prominence of the victims slain in these cases very well may have made judicial test tubes of the courtrooms at New Orleans, Memphis and Los Angeles.

A reading of the accounts of the trials of Shaw, Ray and Sirhan leaves basic negative impressions about the system of justice. These three trial-tragedies, the characters who assumed leading roles in them, the manner in which the trial-productions were "staged" and the way the personalities performed, all served to give a "theater" quality to the administration of justice. A criminal trial can become more than anything else a theatrical production. It is produced for an audience of twelve jury-spectators and, quite often, offers a double feature: the case for the prosecution and, then, the case for the defense. Defendants, witnesses, lawyers, even the judges, costume themselves in a manner to befit the roles they must play. Actually they are expected to perform as actors. The lawyers and key witnesses hope to sway the jurors to the "truth" of their side. Parts and speeches by the players—lawyers and witnesses—are rehearsed and practiced to give a "stage presence" quality to the performances. Attorneys work to achieve a "jury presence" even as actors work to develop a stage presence.

Is this artificial stage-play environment conducive to the sound administration of justice? Surely not. And yet it has been, almost from the beginning, the nature of the system of criminal justice in this country. And the lawyers who are thought of as legal "legends" almost invariably have been accomplished performers.

Another negative impression e m e r g e s from these three cases: there is no "one" system of justice. There are fifty-one administrations of criminal justice. There is the federal court system, and then there are fifty different administrations of justice—each state having its own with different procedures, different rules, different precedents, different methods of dealing with crime.

Some lawyers, even some legal reformers, argue that the diversity that exists in fifty-one administrations of justice reflects the genius of the system; that the court system has developed in a natural way to meet differing needs of people in different regions and states; that what faults there are with the contradictions and conflicts that exist from state to state are the blame of the legislatures which enact statutes, and that the courts themselves are helpless in doing anything but following laws the legislatures pass.

Most legislatures are made up of substantial numbers of lawyers, who almost invariably are members of the American Bar Association. Most proposals for court change come from bar association recommendations and the organized bar, largely through the bar associations, holds massive influence over state courts.

There is great public apathy about the courts. Actually, the public knows very little about how the courts function. A man-on-the-street survey conducted in Tennessee during the James Earl Ray trial indicated that more than six out of every ten persons interviewed thought Ray was being tried in federal court in Memphis for a federal crime, rather than in state court. Two out of ten did not know whether the trial was in state or federal court. Only two out of ten answered correctly that Ray was being tried in a state court.

In addition to the federal system and the state systems, there is another duality in the administration of criminal justice: the rule of law as it is understood by individuals in their home states and the practice of the rule of law as it is in fact implemented in the various states. Many citizens have come to think of the entire system of criminal justice as the law as it is enforced in their own regions, at least in their own states. The fact that a crime in one state may not be a crime in another state does not register on most Americans. For example, many do not know that prostitution, gambling, the purchase and sale of liquor, or abortion may be a crime in one jurisdiction and perfectly legal in another. Nor does it register on most Americans that a defendant may get a six-month sentence in one state and twenty years in another state for the same crime; that the jury, in one jurisdiction, will set the defendant's sentence while the judge will set the sentence in another jurisdiction. The fact that a rule as regards jury selection, or even the selection of judges, in one state is not followed in another state is not known. The fact that insanity in one state may not be judged insanity in another state has not been explained to or thought out by most citizens. But these are the most basic facts of the administration of justice. The evils apparent in the conflicts in the methodology of the system of criminal justice—both the administration of justice in a given area and the administration as it in fact exists in the fifty states— are built into the main-stream of court procedures and go beyond the specific cases of Shaw, Ray and Sirhan.

But in these three cases there were glaring examples of basic wrongs in the system. Suddenly in 1969 the "search for truth" was on in New Orleans, Memphis and Los Angeles. A review of those searches leads to some disquieting conclusions concerning the discharge of criminal justice:

1. The administration of justice in these three states, Louisiana, Tennessee and California, and in many other states, is a procedural hodgepodge. There are, built into the system, conflicting, confusing, contradicting practices which are maintained from state to state—practices which argue against "uniform fairness" and actually stand in the way of finding truth.

2. The adversary system in which lawyers take diametrically opposing points of view can be a farce, insofar as a search for truth is concerned. It can seek and find falsity as easily as it can find truth. As it is applied today, the adversary system is no more than a battle of wits.

3. The jury selection system is a device, not to find a group of impartial peers to seek truth but to allow adversary lawyers, through a nonsensical game of legal musical chairs, to find jury members partial to their points of view.

4. The judiciary protects men whose temperament, judgment and understanding are at least questionable and who, because of age or personality, are not suited for the job of judge.

5. The "cop out," or the deal by which the defendant is allowed to plead guilty to a crime, is a tool of the legal trade which can work against the welfare and protection of society and against the welfare and rights of the accused.

6. "Expert" witnesses are often less than expert. They are likely to work for either side that pays in a criminal case. As it is with the employment of counsel, such factors as the courtroom demeanor, depth of voice, attractiveness of physical appearance and warmth of personality may count far more with the jury than the witness's actual knowledge of his field.

7. The district attorney, by virtue of the power resident in his office, has a life-or-death grip on accused persons and can literally ruin the lives of innocent people.

8. The organized bar, perhaps aware that the courts are imperfect, has seized on imperfections in the press and has directed its major "reform" attention to the "free press versus fair trial" question. The emphasis on the "need" to control press coverage of criminal cases has diverted criticism away from the courts and their administration. Adverse comments about the operation of the courts have been buried under an avalanche of

legal sentiment favoring the Warren Commission report critical of the press handling of the assassination in Dallas, the ruling of the Supreme Court in the Sam Sheppard case and the "press-control" report of the American Bar Association Committee headed by Justice Paul C. Reardon of Massachusetts. All of this has delayed further the exposure of weaknesses in the administration of justice. The Reardon Report is a "ghost story" whose solutions are designed to intimidate, not reform.

9. Lawyers are almost uniformly satisfied with the system as it now works and feel no sense of urgency to bring about dramatic, immediate change.

There are various bar groups now involved in updating procedures. Some of the efforts in such areas as providing adequate representation for indigent defendants have been positive. But most of the talk of reform has been lip service that came too late to help straighten out long established defects.

Of all the reforms considered in recent years by the American Bar Association, for example, none has been pursued with nearly as much vigor as the effort developed by the Committee headed by Justice Reardon on the free press-fair trial question.

Too often "court reform" has meant little more than additional salary for judges (which is important), and studies aimed at modernizing civil court procedures, where the real money is made in the practice of law.

In seeking real reform the bar is going to have to look inward to the confusing practices in the criminal system and is going to have to *invite* the press to put the spotlight of publicity on the total deficiency in the way the courts are run. Much would already have been accomplished if the bar had been as self-critical as it has been inclined toward criticism of the press. The attacks on press coverage have been helpful in that many newsmen have had second thoughts about how to cover criminal trials. There have been some (not yet enough) moves toward moderation in covering crime and the courts. But if the system of justice is to be upgraded over the long term of history it will have to begin soon with an honest admission by the bar that the courts are now basically constructed to serve *the legal profession,* not the people.

These are strong words. Are they the rantings of four emotional, angry journalists over-reacting to assaults on their profession's integrity and performance? The authors are aware that many lawyers will contend that we have overstated our case. But we have limited our conclusions to a consideration of the three cases at hand: New Orleans, Memphis and Los Angeles. We *do not* dwell on the many chronic complaints against the system, such as overcrowded dockets, overcrowded penal institutions, the contrast between a rich man's chance for justice compared with the poor man's chance, the complex panoply of problems that range from bail requirements to parole techniques.

It is our view that, if anything, we have understated the case. Much more is wrong with the administration of justice than was demonstrated in the three cases here considered. But these three cases stand as symbols of basic evils in the system.

Chapter 2

The State of Louisiana Versus Clay Shaw:

Justice...
Through The Looking Glass

1.

"And they shall see
what is ere long
Not through a glass,
but face to face."

Thomas Hardy,

"A FANTASY"

The public trial of Clay Shaw began, in fact if not in court, on February 17, 1967—the day the New Orleans *States-Item,* in a copyrighted story, announced on the front page that district attorney Jim Garrison was investigating the assassination of President John F. Kennedy.

The name "Clay Shaw" was not mentioned in that story. But in light of the actions of Jim Garrison in the days and months that followed, everything that was said and written then and later about the Kennedy assassination in Dallas became a part of the ordeal Clay Shaw was to endure in New Orleans until his acquittal March 1, 1969. Even then, it was not to end. Between publication of the first story of the New Orleans probe by the district attorney, until the jury cleared Shaw, over two years later, Jim Garrison himself was responsible more than any other individual for the mass of public attention given the case.

Clay Shaw was innocent.

But district attorney Garrison, through every facet of the public media—from Johnny Carson's "Tonight" show to *Playboy Magazine*—actively campaigned to show that a massive conspiracy had occurred. Garrison implied repeatedly that Shaw was somehow part of the conspiracy. Everything he said in the days before he charged Shaw could only have the cumulative effect of adding to the question of Shaw's guilt in the public mind. All the weird contentions and wild accusations Garrison made in interviews in print, or radio or television, local or national, made Shaw the often unnamed target—but a real target nonetheless. In retrospect, Garrison's charges seem far-fetched because the evidence he finally produced against Shaw seemed so ludicrous, so insulting to human intellect, that the jury rejected it out of hand. At the outset, Garrison's claims seemed not so outlandish. After all, the very idea of political assassination was, in itself, far-fetched. The findings of the Warren Commission seemed cursory, superficial, and inadequate. Books attacking the Warren Commission had been written and had even made best seller lists. Many people wanted to believe in a conspiracy.

The nature of the evidence Garrison produced and the character of the witnesses he brought into court will be dealt with in the account of the actual trial which follows. As that account will show, the evidence was flimsy, and many of the principal witnesses were unreliable.

But long before the case was called to be tried in court, Garrison was campaigning publicly to convince newspaper readers, radio listeners, and television watchers that somewhere there was a conspiracy that had started in New Orleans and had ended in Dallas. Shaw could not escape the implications of that campaign which predated the criminal conspiracy charge against him.

Whatever caused Jim Garrison to act as he did, the impact on the administration of justice was such that those who followed the case closely could only come away from it with their confidence in the court system badly shaken.

The problem in the beginning was that Garrison spoke with such authority and self-assurance about this conspiracy he was going to prove. He is an impressive man—garrulous, aggressive, outspoken, a physical giant. He stands six feet six inches and weighs 240 pounds. His size fourteen shoe falls heavily in the courthouse corrider in Orleans parish. Like many big men he has a "big" voice and like many good lawyers, he modulates it well. The press reports were that Garrison, chief law enforcement officer for his county, carried a snub-nosed pistol holstered under his left arm beneath a well-tailored suit coat, for the purpose of self protection against criminal elements in vice-ridden New Orleans.

After his election as district attorney in 1962 Garrison had been almost constantly engaged in public controversy, and somehow the conflict always pitted his own popularity and his own word against some other public official, agency or institution: the mayor of New Orleans, the Metropolitan Crime Commission, the city police department.

He even attacked the home-grown judiciary. He took on the eight district Criminal Court judges before whom he practiced and won out against them. He told the public that the judges were blocking his efforts to clean up vice in the shadowy precincts of the city's French Quarter. The judges smarted under Garrison's assault on their integrity, then filed a defamation suit against him. But the U.S. Supreme Court—presided over, ironically, by Chief Justice Earl Warren—ruled that criticism, such as Garrison's, of public officials in the performance of their duties, is justifiable if the charge is made without malice. The irony is that subsequently the commission headed by Chief Justice Warren, which investigated the assassination of President Kennedy, was to come under severe criticism from Garrison.

And so Jim Garrison had fought his hometown battles and, in the arena of community understanding, had come through it all with public support in his community, the community in which Shaw was to be tried.

As a prosecutor he had been successful, but not spectacular. His record of convictions was adequate. The office he held was probably the most powerful in his area of local government. It was an office that by its very nature commanded widespread press attention and notice.

When Garrison spoke, reporters in New Orleans listened. Some newsmen thought he had his eye on higher political office— the mayor's seat, or even the governor's chair. At any rate, his mammoth physical dimensions, the power of his office and his bold personal approach to public issues had made him something of a demiurge in the eyes of his constituents. He had captured more than attention—he even held a degree of respect in the eyes of those who had elected him.

Most reporters who covered the courthouse beat liked him. He made good copy. He could be personable—particularly when taking some newsman into his confidence about a pending case. He had a way of opening a conversation with, "Now it is quite obvious from what we know about it . . .," and suddenly it was

obvious to the reporter that Garrison knew even if the press and
public did not yet know. He had received a substantially good
local press.

All of this worked to make Jim Garrison, at forty-four, something of a local legend when word broke that he had run across
some dramatic new facts in his investigation of the assassination
of President Kennedy. Overnight Garrison had at his call representatives of the national news wire services, television newsmen
of national prominence, and reporters from the major daily papers
all across the nation. Newsmen in New Orleans knew before the
States-Item broke that first story on February 17, 1967, outlining
some of the points in the Garrison investigation, that the probe
was underway.

For a time the New Orleans press kept it secret, trusting
Garrison. Then the *States-Item* became convinced that Garrison
planned to leak his story through a national news magazine.
At that point the newspaper published the story of the probe.

In typical style, Garrison counterattacked. He denied the
paper's claim that he had planned to release the story through
a national publication. Beyond that he said the news stories
were "irresponsible." He denounced the local newspapers.

And then, as if to impropriate his own word—"irresponsible"— in the weeks and months that were ahead, Jim Garrison
made some of the most preposterous statements any prosecutor
had ever uttered in or out of court.

To comprehend the full import of the statements by Garrison,
it is necessary to understand some of the eccentric personalities
whose names became involved in this case.

First there was David William Ferrie, forty-nine, a former
airline pilot who had been dismissed because of an arrest record
on charges that he was a homosexual. An unstable, unreliable
soldier of fortune, Ferrie was given to weird, egoistic exaggera-
tions. His very appearance was grotesquely distorted. The victim
of a flash fire, he wore a wig and painted on his eyebrows.

Once a student for the Roman Catholic priesthood, Ferrie
was expelled from the seminary as "unfit." His presence in the
case gave Garrison a sort of "phantom at the opera" villain. Ferrie
could only serve to convince a gullible public and press that
Garrison had in fact found out a plot.

Ferrie figured in Garrison's investigation as a would-be villain because shortly after President Kennedy had been assassinated, a New Orleans private detective named Jack S. Martin, a bishop in an obscure and malcontent Catholic religious group into which he had once ordained Ferrie, swore that the former airline pilot had had a hand in killing Kennedy.

"Bishop" Martin, who was fifty-one, two years Ferrie's elder, had said that Ferrie had known Lee Harvey Oswald, and that both had been members of the same Civil Air Patrol unit where Ferrie had trained Oswald to use a rifle with a telescopic sight. The Warren Commission had taken Martin's original statement. But scarcely had "the bishop" made the charge against Ferrie to the Commission staff than he admitted that the charge was false. He told agents of the Secret Service and the FBI that it was all "a figment of my imagination." He had invented the stories about Ferrie and Oswald, he said. But the old charge by Martin against Ferrie was a fact around which the prosecutor could play on the theory that some unknown conspiracy was behind Kennedy's death.

It was not that Martin's story was believable; it was simply that when Garrison mentioned Ferrie's name, Martin's old repudiated charge triggered questions about why Martin had made the claim in the first place; why had he changed his mind and his story?

Some of those on whom Garrison was to rely—a drug addict and thief, admitted liars and even some psychiatric cases—proved as unreliable as Ferrie and "Bishop" Martin.

And there were other random circumstances which Garrison indicated were far more than coincidentals as he sought to create a background pattern for his "plot":

1. Oswald had been in New Orleans for several months before Kennedy was assassinated.

2. He had been seen in front of the New Orleans International Trade Mart where Shaw worked as director.

3. While standing in front of the Trade Mart, Oswald handed out leaflets supporting the cause of Premier Fidel Castro of Cuba. He represented the "Fair Play for Cuba" Committee.

4. Oswald tried to go to Cuba from New Orleans by way of Mexico. When he failed he went back to Dallas.

5. A group of anti-Castro Cuban exiles were training as

guerillas and planning a Cuban invasion before federal agents broke up their training camp and ended their plans.

6. Ferrie reportedly had claimed that he had been a pilot in the ill-fated invasion of the Cuban Bay of Pigs.

For a public still intensely concerned about the Kennedy assassination here was enough to stimulate considerable speculation about a plot. All Garrison had to do was find witnesses who would pull together these "coincidences;" and this is what he sought to do.

In private, "off the record" conversations with newsmen, Garrison strongly implied to some reporters that the Cuban guerillas had planned to kill Castro in Cuba and that when their plans were thwarted by the government, they decided to kill President Kennedy. Oswald, Ferrie, and Shaw, it was implied, were part of this.

Proving this theory was to become something of a problem because there was no indication that Oswald had any plans in concert with the guerillas; he was pro-Castro while the guerilla group despised the Cuban dictator; Ferrie told some weird tales about himself—the "I was a pilot for the CIA at the Bay of Pigs" was only one of them—but there was no indication that he ever knew Oswald. "Bishop" Martin confirmed that he had lied when he claimed Ferrie knew Oswald; finally, there was no indication that Oswald's presence in front of the Trade Mart had anything to do with Clay Shaw who ultimately said under oath that he never had seen Oswald and had never spoken to him.

Garrison, still, was to infer that he had links that forged together a chain that stretched Oswald, Ferrie and Shaw from New Orleans to Dallas. He never really got around to producing any evidence of that and ultimately he was to say that it was not really necessary to prove Shaw had anything to do with the death in Dallas for him to be guilty of conspiracy to kill President Kennedy. In an effort to make his chain of evidence hold together, Garrison produced some of the most bizarre witnesses ever to be subpoenaed in court. In addition to the drug addicts, liars, convicted criminals and psychiatric cases, some of these witnesses said that they were victims of the art of hypnosis. They all were brought forth to testify against Shaw.

Shaw was to be the unfortunate victim of some unlikely happenstance. Just six short days after the *States-Item* story broke

the news on Garrison's investigation, the nude body of David
Ferrie was found dead in the pilot's apartment with a note which
read: "To leave this life is, for me, a sweet prospect. I find nothing
in it that is desirable and on the other hand, everything is loath-
some."

Immediately speculation flared that Ferrie was the victim
of either murder or suicide. The Orleans Parish coroner, Dr.
Nicholas J. Chetta, said Ferrie died of a ruptured blood vessel in
the brain. It was not a violent death. There were some fifteen
bottles of pills in Ferrie's apartment when the body was found,
but Dr. Chetta said that even an overdose would not have caused
the blood vessel hemorrhage. He found the death to be from
"natural causes."

An autopsy was performed. Dr. Ronald A. Welch, a pathologist from Louisiana State University who conducted the autopsy,
told the *New York Times:* "Ferrie died from natural causes and
not as a result of suicide." The dead man, it was determined, had
suffered for years from the weak blood vessel at the base of the
brain. He had told friends he had high blood pressure and also
had said he had suffered from "sleeping sickness."

It could not be determined when the note, which seemed to
be a suicide letter, had been written. But the doctor said there
was no evidence of suicide. Garrison ignored this, however, and
said that Ferrie was a suicide and a prime suspect who would
have been arrested within a few days. Ferrie's death and
Garrison's claims of suicide gave a sense of substance to the
district attorney's theory, at least for a time.

Nobody who knew much about Clay Shaw would have considered him a suspect likely to plot the death of any man, much
less President Kennedy. Shaw was soft-spoken, mild-mannered
and introspective. He was tall, gaunt and angular with a near
ascetic presence and an almost athletic carriage. Clay Shaw
had been a supporter of John F. Kennedy in 1960 and had worn
a "Kennedy button" when it was not the popular political thing
to do in Louisiana. He was said to be a man who had admired
John Kennedy in the president's approach to both national and
international problems.

Many who had done business with him at the Trade Mart
thought, despite the fact that he had been decorated in war,
that it would have been impossible for him to commit a violent

or vicious act, or even to condone one. Some even said he was effeminate.¹ Gray-haired attractive, walking with a slight limp, he was considered a peaceable person: a good man, perhaps not the typical "man on the street," but surely law-abiding. He had been an officer in World War II and had been honored by the French government in both war and peace. He had been paid tribute by leaders in his own community as head of the Trade Mart.

Jim Garrison accused such a man of participation in a plot to murder the President. But Jim Garrison said far more than that. His long string of statements had significance even beyond the question of whether Shaw conspired to kill the President.

A major controversy had been raging in the nation since the death of President Kennedy over an issue called free press versus fair trial. Garrison's continuing discussion of his investigation of the Kennedy assassination seems quite profoundly to run against a principal point raised by the American Bar Association in seeking to curtail press coverage of the courts. The legal profession, insofar as it speaks through the American Bar Association, had been insisting that extra-judicial statements about a pending criminal case by a prosecutor or a policeman prejudiced the rights of the accused.

If a prosecutor spoke out to newsmen about a case, beyond mentioning the barest facts regarding the charge, he violated American Bar Association guidelines and could be held in contempt. This had been the long-held rule outlined in Canon Twenty of the ABA Code of Professional Ethics. Even as the Shaw case developed, the American Bar Association House of Delegates proposed and subsequently passed a new section of the Canons of Professional Ethics for lawyers: "It is the duty of the lawyer not to release or authorize the release of information or opinion for dissemination by any means of public communication, in connection with pending or imminent criminal litigation with which he is associated, if there is any reasonable likelihood that such dissemination will interfere with a fair trial or otherwise prejudice the due administration of justice." This new proposal was the result of a study and report by an ABA committee headed by Justice Paul Reardon of the Massachusetts Supreme Court.

---

1. In his book **American Grotesque,** James Kirkwood tells of interviews, after the trial of Shaw, in which members of the prosecution team and even Judge Edward Haggerty spoke of Shaw's alleged homosexuality.

The Reardon report included a provision for holding this press in contempt for reporting on "prejudicial" statements by lawyers. Various associations of newsmen would protest the thrust of this language. But the Reardon report which proposed this language was prepared and presented and voted on while Garrison's media campaign was underway.

According to Garrison's fellow lawyers, speaking through the American Bar Association House of Delegates, it would be improper for a prosecutor to keep up a running random commentary about a case in which a defendant was to stand trial. Strangely, the American Bar Association and its official membership never once challenged Garrison for what he said while Shaw awaited trial.

Noted in the paragraphs that follow are some of the assertions attributed to Garrison which could only serve to "interfere" with "the due administration of justice" for which the Bar claims such concern.

The Associated Press, immediately after the *States-Item* broke the news of the Garrison probe, quoted a spokesman for Garrison as saying: "There is no basis for the story."

The next day, February 18, Garrison called a press conference to say there was indeed a basis for the *State-Item* story after all. He said that the Warren Commission report was inaccurate in concluding no conspiracy was involved in this case.

"There were other people besides Lee Harvey Oswald involved."

Garrison said his investigation dated back to October, 1966— four months earlier—and that it had shown that the conspiracy had its genesis in New Orleans.

"Arrests will be made, charges will be filed and convictions will be obtained."

He said that the New Orleans newspapers were irresponsible for breaking the story of his investigation. The *States-Item,* smarting a bit under Garrison's charge of irresponsibility, said in an editorial that ran February 18, that the newspaper broke the story because Garrison had planned to gain national attention and personal exposure through a deal to leak the news of his investigation in a national magazine.

Garrison called another news conference to answer the editorial. This time he barred the local press. By now news media from all over the world had felt the shock waves of the initial story in the *States-Item* and were pouring into New Orleans to see this colorful, dynamic giant of a man.

At the outset there seemed to be some hesitancy on Garrison's part to attack specific agencies of the federal government. But gradually his position hardened until he was accusing the Central Intelligence Agency of concealing evidence and of actual participation in the assassination. Garrison gave the CIA top billing, but the FBI and the Warren Commission were close behind as his statements continued to attract space in the public media.

Implicit in much of what he said was that he had a wealth of secret information.

"We already have the names of the people in the initial planning."

It might be argued that Garrison, in calling a news conference excluding the local press, did so to save the local community from his views which might ultimately have been prejudicial to prospective jurors. But he had been dealing with the press for some time, now, as a public official. He knew that when he talked to the national press about this matter that the television networks, all with local affiliates, broadcast his words into his home community where the case would ultimately be tried. He knew too that local papers, the *States-Item* and the *Times-Picayune,* subscribed to national wire services and had direct access to his words through these services, even though local newsmen were kept out of one of his early press conferences.

By barring local reporters he gave most newsmen the idea that he was piqued and acting out of spite toward the New Orleans newsmen because they were needling him for seeking national publicity. In the press conference—with hometown newsmen kept out—he attacked them:

"Arrests probably were just a few weeks away until the disclosures of the investigation by the local newspapers. Now they are most certainly months away." This was Febuary 20. Clay Shaw was charged on March 1. Garrison was given to positive, clearcut statements which were easy for a public, suspicious of the Warren Report, to believe:

"A plan was developed in New Orleans which culminated in the assassination of President John F. Kennedy."

"The Warren Commission report is inaccurate in stating Oswald acted alone in the assassination of Kennedy November 22, 1963 . . . We are not wasting time and we will prove it. Arrests will be made, charges will be filed, convictions will be obtained."

The FBI and the Warren Commission had "inadequate evaluation machinery" in the Kennedy assassination investigation.

Leaks from Garrison's office resulted in reports appearing in the New Orleans press that Kennedy had been shot by a group of Cubans who fired on the President from behind a billboard. A source "close to the investigation" was quoted as saying that the plot to kill Kennedy grew out of an original plan to assassinate Castro.

After Ferrie's death Garrison seemed to become bolder in his public statements. Dr. Chetta, the coroner, said Ferrie's death came from natural causes. Dr. Welch, the Louisiana State University pathologist who conducted the autopsy, said: "Ferrie died from natural causes and not as a result of suicide."

On February 22 Garrison held another press conference, in which he stated:

"The apparent suicide of David Ferrie ends the life of a man who, in my judgment, was one of history's most important individuals. Evidence developed by our office had long since confirmed he was involved in events culminating in the assassination of President Kennedy. We had reached a decision to arrest Ferrie next week. Apparently we waited too long."

He gave no details as to how Ferrie was involved in a conspiracy and he made no explanation of why he thought the death—despite medical evidence—was suicide.

His statements had shock appeal:

"I have no reason to believe Lee Harvey Oswald killed anybody in Dallas November 22, 1963."

On February 24 Garrison announced his office had "solved" the assassination.

"We know what cities are involved, how it was done in the essential respects and the individuals involved."

But it still might take him months or years to work out the "details of evidence," he said

Reporters now were asking Garrison if he would seek federal aid in his probe of the president's assassination:

"What would be the purpose of seeking federal aid? To delay the investigation another three years? We have done more in three months with a small staff than the government did in three years with 5,000 men."

Of the late "suicide" Garrison said:

"The only way people involved can get away from us is to kill themselves."

Then Garrison added a mystical strain to what had become almost a running commentary:

"The key to the whole case is through the looking glass. White is black and black is white. I don't want to sound cryptic, but that is the way it is."

That describes the Garrison investigation—justice through the looking glass.

On March 1, Garrison charged Clay Shaw with participation in a conspiracy to murder John F. Kennedy. In a search warrant application Garrison gave Shaw an alias, "Clay Bertrand." (Police and newsmen in New Orleans confided to out-of-town reporters that the "alias" was a name commonly used by homosexuals in New Orleans.) In this same application for a warrant to search Shaw's home Garrison charged that Shaw, Ferrie and Oswald had met there to plan Kennedy's death. This incidental intelligence had come to Garrison, the district attorney contended, in the request for a search warrant, from a "confidential informant" who had taken sodium pentothal, "a truth drug."

The search of Shaw's residence turned up five whips, a black hood and cape—but nothing in the way of evidence of any conspiracy.

Shaw said he was innocent. His bond was set at $10,000. He made it and was released. Garrison seemed to think things were going well:

> "Former employees of the Central Intelligence Agency" were suspected of the conspiracy to kill Kennedy. "We managed to get the names of some of them in a way I can't describe here. But we cannot find out through any government agency where they are located now and we have a stone wall as far as identification of other individuals. But I can say the rest of them are Cubans who were trained in New Orleans. It will be some time before all arrests are made but there is no doubt about that."

The trial of the Shaw case was assigned to Judge Edward A. Haggerty—whitemaned, testy, outgoing—a man who didn't work very hard to dodge photographers. At fifty-five he had been on the bench thirteen years and he thought he knew his way around a courtroom. It had become the vogue at the criminal bar to set down guidelines for the press in criminal trials, which in general sought to parallel the recommendations in the first draft of the Reardon Report. Judge Haggerty came through with his guidelines, including an admonition to lawyers about commenting on the case.

In late March, Mark Lane, the author of the book *Rush to Judgment,* who had become a perennial critic of the Warren Commission, came to New Orleans to lend his moral support to Garrison. The two met the press for pictures and Lane told reporters that Garrison would "perk up the eyes and ears" of the world with his investigation. When Garrison was asked about his probe, he replied:

> "I have nothing to say, not because of the court guidelines but because I have had nothing to say for weeks. My comment is no comment."

In early March Garrison had issued a challenge to the CIA to produce a photograph which he said had been taken of Oswald and some unnamed Cuban companion leaving the Cuban embassy in Mexico City. He claimed in a statement that the CIA had suppressed this photo and had given a phony picture to the Warren Commission:

> "It is perfectly obvious that the reason the true picture of Oswald and his companion was withheld and a fake picture substituted was because one or both of these men were working for agencies of the United States government in the summer of 1963."

These statements by Garrison were only one facet of the public dialogue which kept the press drumbeat going about the case. On March 12, a three-judge panel opened court for a hearing which gave an idea of the sort of evidence Garrison was compiling against Shaw. This hearing was to determine, in the opinion of the judges, whether there was adequate evidence to try Shaw without a grand jury indictment, since Louisiana law allows prosecution on the complaint of the district attorney alone. For the first time at this hearing the public had a glimpse of what could be expected in the way of evidence. The "key" witness Garrison was to produce turned out to be a young insurance salesman, Perry Raymond Russo, who claimed he was present at a party and heard a conversation among Shaw, Ferrie and Oswald about killing the President. He contended he knew Oswald as "Leon Oswald" and Shaw as "Clem Bertrand." He had allowed himself to be placed under hypnosis by Garrison's agents three times to improve his memory of events, he testified. He had been administered sodium pentothal, the "truth serum," and he acknowledged that he had, in the past, been under the treatment of a psychiatrist.

A second witness who tied Shaw to Oswald was Vernon Bundy, a narcotics addict facing c r i m i n a l prosecution by Garrison's office who swore that he saw Oswald and Shaw together one day in the summer of 1963. At the time he saw them, he was preparing to inject two capsules of heroin into his arm.

The three-judge panel ruled there was sufficient evidence to try Shaw and five days later the grand jury indicted him.

There were other developments, most of which stemmed from action by Garrison's office which kept interest high in the case against Shaw. A young woman named Lillie Mae McMaines, formerly known in New Orleans as Sandra Moffett, was named by Garrison's office in a "fugitive from justice" warrant. Perry Raymond Russo had earlier claimed that she attended the party at Ferrie's apartment in 1963 where the plot to kill the President was discussed by Shaw, Oswald and Ferrie. At Shaw's trial he was to say he could not be sure she was at the party.

Mrs. McMaines was taken into custody March 28, in Omaha, Nebraska, where she then lived. She said she had never attended such a party and had not met Ferrie until some time in 1965.

Garrison issued a warrant for a former New Orleans night club operator, Gordon Novel, seeking that he be arrested as "a most important witness" in the case against Shaw. Novel appeared April 1, in court in Columbus, Ohio—the fugitive warrant technically claimed he had conspired to commit burglary—and was released on $10,000 bond. He said he could prove the whole Garrison investigation was "a fabrication."

Then on April 5, Shaw appeared at his formal arraignment and entered a plea of not guilty.

All of these events kept Garrison "alive" in the press. But more than actions stemming from Garrison's office, his personal comments kept interest building in his case:

"Purely and simply it's a case of former employees of the CIA, a large number of them Cubans, having a venomous reaction from the 1961 Bay of Pigs episode. The name of every man involved and the names of the individuals who pulled the triggers are known to the CIA."

On May 8, Garrison's office reported the FBI and CIA were

withholding evidence on the Kennedy assassination and that an investigation of these two agencies would be initiated.

J. Edgar Hoover, the director of the FBI, who for years has been praised for the integrity and effectiveness of his organization and for the efficiency of the bureau's "evaluation machinery" somehow escaped a Garrison subpoena before his grand jury. But John McCone, former CIA director and his successor, Richard Helms, the current director of the CIA were subpoenaed and so were FBI agents Regis Kennedy, stationed in New Orleans, and a former agent named Warren DeBrueys. McCone and Helms ignored the subpoenas. Regis Kennedy appeared before the grand jury. Kennedy, who of course was not related to the late President, claimed executive immunity and refused to divulge to Garrison's grand jury the inside details of the FBI's investigation.

This, said Garrison, was "a fifth amendment coverup."

But the CIA, not the FBI, bore the brunt of Garrison's anger:

"What the CIA is doing is a criminal act and if the director of the CIA and the top officials of the CIA were in the jurisdiction of Louisiana, I would charge them without hesitation."

"Naturally they (the CIA) are paying lawyers involved. There is no question about that."

He named two members of the New Orleans bar he said were being paid by the CIA to thwart his investigation. They were Burton Klein and Steven Plotkin. Klein's crime was a grievous offense.

"We have reason to believe that Mr. Klein has recently been to Washington, D.C."

Both Klein and Plotkin immediately denied they were employed by the CIA. Garrison continued his attack on the agency.

"Its criminal activities (began) in my judgment immediately after the assassination when they failed to reveal in its entirety what its activities were in New Orleans when Lee Harvey Oswald was working for it."

Some six weeks after Shaw was charged, Garrison revealed a startling development. The unpublished phone number of Jack Ruby, the Dallas night club operator who had slain Lee Harvey Oswald was listed in separate address books which had belonged to Shaw and Oswald.

There was a code that had to be broken before this could be discerned, Garrison told newsmen. But the code had been broken by Garrison's office. An address book belonging to Shaw had been confiscated on the day he was arrested when Garrison's men, armed with a search warrant, had invaded the accused man's residence.

"It contains a unique address which also exists in the address book of Lee Harvey Oswald."

It took only a matter of hours for the press to explode the myth of Garrison's code which had been developed, undoubtedly, with that master "evaluation machinery" he maintained his office possessed and the FBI and Warren Commission lacked.

And so went Garrison's statements: bizarre, unanswerable.

"No, Lee Harvey Oswald did not shoot President Kennedy. He did not fire a shot from the Book Depository Building."

"Oh, I can say who did it without question . . . . We know the group and we know some of the names of the group, but we don't know which one was standing where. And we can't find out with the CIA keeping its vaults locked."

There came a gradual but certain sentiment among many newsmen covering Garrison's case that he was indeed "through the looking glass" and in fact, trying to make it seem that "black is white and white is black."

The uncertain feeling reporters began to have about the case grew as many persons who had been close to Garrison's side of the case began to desert him.

The most dramatic in a series of defections came from Dean

Andrews, the pudgy, jive-talking lawyer and part-time assistant
district attorney from adjoining Jefferson Parish. In the early
days after President Kennedy's death, Andrews had told the
Warren Commission there was a link between Oswald and Shaw.
But he recanted and said his statement about the two men was
false.

Garrison apparently got from Andrews' statements that a
man he identified as Clay Bertrand had contacted him in behalf
of Oswald and asked him to represent Oswald after the President
was killed. Garrison's theory was that Clay Shaw and Clay
Bertrand were one and the same. Andrews testified before the
grand jury. But then, as it became clear that Garrison's
grand jury investigation was going to lead to a trial, possibly to
a conviction, Andrews decided not go along with his fabrication.
Once again Andrews went back on his story. He said that it had
never happened.

Garrison didn't like defectors. Andrews' case was taken to
the grand jury. He was indicted for perjury, convicted and sentenced to eighteen months on each of three counts. But he would
not go along with Garrison's claims that Shaw and Oswald were
involved in any conspiracy or any other matter.

Then there was a young man named Alvin Beaubouef who
had given Garrison an affidavit about David Ferrie, which was
supposed to "fill in the facts" about Ferrie's relationship to the
assassination of the President.

A story appeared in *Newsweek* which quoted Beaubouef as
saying Garrison's office had offered him $3,000 to testify against
Shaw and swear that he overheard the planning of the assassination. According to *Newsweek,* Beaubouef tape-recorded the
conversation with Garrison's men. When they found out what had
been done, the district attorney's men then tried to get Beaubouef
to sign a statement saying he did not consider the $3,000 a bribe,
Newsweek said. When the m a g a z i n e broke the story that
Beaubouef was not going to go along with Garrison—if indeed
he ever had thought of it—Beaubouef and his lawyer called a
press conference and declared the story *Newsweek* had printed
was factual. Beaubouef said Garrison's office had threatened
him if he tried to make trouble with their investigation.

In answer Garrison released a copy of an affidavit Beaubouef
had given his office in which he said he had not been threatened

or coerced or bribed. And a lawyer-friend of the district attorney, Clyde Merritt, told reporters he notarized the statement Beaubouef gave Garrison's men and that Beaubouef had not seemed under any threat or coercion. But Beaubouef, like Dean Andrews, was not going to be a part of Garrison's conspiracy case.

The key defection came from inside Garrison's intimate staff. William Gurvich, the chief investigator in the case who had been so prominent in the early days of the probe and who had first announced to newsmen that Clay Shaw was to be charged with the conspiracy, quit Garrison outright and in disgust.

There was "no truth" to the claim Garrison had made of a conspiracy involving Shaw, Gurvich said. He urged the Orleans Parish grand jury to begin an immediate investigation into the conduct of the district attorney.

He had evidence, he contended, of "travesties of justice on the part of the district attorney in the case of Louisiana versus Clay Shaw."

According to Gurvich, the investigation had become an obsession with the district attorney. Gurvich claimed that at one point Garrison had even considered raiding the New Orleans office of the FBI. No Bar group, apparently, took note of Gurvich's statement. Garrison's office said Gurvich had not played a major role in the case anyway.

Amazingly, the organized bar did not seem to be upset with Garrison, despite his repeated sensational statements about the case. There were a few exceptions. A Detroit lawyer, Sol Dann, who had represented the late Jack Ruby, called upon the Louisiana and American Bar Associations to investigate Garrison. "This fraud has gone on long enough," the Michigan lawyer said of the investigation. There was a need to "put an end to any further exploitation of this horrible tragedy and prevent a repetition of the carnival proceedings that prevailed . . . in Dallas."

At home in New Orleans, Garrison's old foes, at the Metropolitan New Orleans Crime Commission urged State Attorney General Jack Gremillion to probe Garrison's methods of investigation. Gremillion replied by letter that he had no jurisdiction to do so.

The bar, in effect, was to lay off Garrison and let him try to work his will on a jury. As the quotations noted above indicate,

Judge Haggerty's guidelines had been repeatedly insulted by Garrison.

But neither the judge, nor the state attorney general, nor the local, state or national organized bar was to take Garrison on. Finally, when twelve jurors rendered a verdict which made Garrison appear stupid, the president of the American Bar Association issued a statement critical of the New Orleans district attorney. It was too little and too late to save Clay Shaw the cost of a lawyer, the humiliation of indictment, the emotional strain and physical ordeal of a criminal trial.

More than that, it was much too late to cut off the repeated prejudicial statements that came from Jim Garrison as Shaw's trial date approached:

"A team of at least seven men, including anti-Castro adventurers and members of the paramilitary right participated in the assassination of President John F. Kennedy."

"Members of the Dallas police department were involved in the assassination and the protection of the assassins." He contended that the assassins were "big business, Texas style—a handful of tremendously oil-rich psychotic individuals."

"Senator Robert F. Kennedy has done everything he could to obstruct the investigation . . . Development of the truth about the assassination . . . would interfere with his political career."

"President Kennedy was killed by a bullet from a .45 calibre pistol that was fired by a man standing in a sewer manhole that connected with the drainage system under Dealey Plaza."

"All the screaming and hollering now being heard is evidence that we have caught a very large fish. It is obvious that there are elements in Washington which are desperate because we are in the process of uncovering their hoax."

On NBC television, July 15, 1967 Garrison said that at least three men had shot President Kennedy and that the Warren Commission's contention that Oswald had been a lone assassin was a "fairytale."

"Oswald was a decoy for the real assassins, who hoped he would be killed by the Dallas police . . . When this failed it was necessary for one of the people involved to kill him."

In a television interview January 31, 1968 Garrison said Ruby was near the scene of the assassination of Kennedy an hour before the President was killed. Here Garrison said Ruby had been seen driving a truck from which a man carrying a rifle emerged, according to a woman resident of Dallas, Mrs. Julia Ann Mercer.

"A military ally of the United States penetrated the forces involved in the assassination. The President was assassinated by elements of the Central Intelligence Agency."

When the time came for Clay Shaw to stand trial it had to be expected that most of those who would be called as prospective jurors to try the case would have read or seen or heard, through the public media, some statement which Garrison had made about the case.

No overt effort had been made by the bench or bar to silence Garrison. His fellow district attorneys from across the country had made a defensive gesture. It cost them their supper. While meeting in convention at New Orleans on March 16, 1968, the National District Attorneys Association declined to give the microphone to Garrison at their dinner meeting when they learned that Garrison planned to take the place of Hubert Humphrey, the principal speaker who could not appear.

The "Jolly Green Giant"—as Dean Andrews was to call Garrison—wanted to tell his fellow prosecutors at dinner about his great investigation. But program officials of the organization of district attorneys, having listened to Garrison briefly at brunch, apparently recognized the impropriety of making their convention a platform for him to further argue his case before it was to come to trial. When Garrison found out that he was to be denied the speaker's spot, he had the Monteleone Hotel, where the convention was being held, lock the convention delegates and their wives out of the dining hall. The dinner was cancelled. All of this put an even greater spotlight on Garrison and his case. Still, the organized bar gave him his lead and let him proceed against Shaw.

The accused defendant, during all this period, was a picture of solemn dignity. He did not appear to be self-indulgent about his plight. After he was charged he appeared briefly on television to say, in his soft, deep voice, that he was completely innocent. He granted few interviews and accepted his attorney's advice to say nothing about the charges against him.

In one rare interview he told a newsman: "I do not understand Jim Garrison's motives at all. A man's mind is a labyrinth. And Jim's mind is more labyrinthian than most."

In the light of all that has been said by the American bar about the so-called Reardon report being intended to provide a means to punish lawyers and perhaps police who made prejudicial statements to the press, it is shocking that Garrison was never disciplined. The author of that report, Justice Paul C. Reardon, of the Massachusetts Supreme Court, insists that the principal meaning of his bar committee's work was not to punish the media but to provide a way to control lawyers and police.

"The main thrust of these recommendations," he said, "is against the lawyers and the law enforcement agencies, the people over whom we have some control who can be subject to some professional discipline within our own house."

There isn't much doubt that Garrison falls within the purview of Judge Reardon's intended target. But Garrison talked while Shaw suffered and while the organized bar continued to look the other way—through the looking glass.

2.

"O! It is excellent
to have a giant's strength . . .
but it is tyrannous
to use it like a giant."
William Shakespeare,
MEASURE FOR MEASURE

On January 20, 1969 at nine o'clock in the morning the clerk in Section C of the Criminal District of New Orleans called the case docketed for trial: The State of Louisiana versus Clay Shaw.

Judge Edward A. Haggerty, Jr., robed in judicial black, his hair white-thatched, peered down at the array of lawyers on opposing sides of the counsel table before his bench. At fifty-five, with a dozen years of judicial experience, Judge Haggerty considered himself ready for a trial which would run just after the New Year celebration through Mardi Gras time.

The judge was known as a feisty, jocular man. His words were sometimes wry, sometimes witty, usually newsworthy.

For almost two years the nation and the world—not to mention all New Orleans—had listened to the words of District Attorney Jim Garrison, the "jolly green giant," who spoke of a massive conspiracy he claimed had started in Louisiana and culminated in the assassination of President Kennedy in Dallas.

Garrison charged that those involved in a conspiracy to kill Kennedy were Clay Shaw, the defendant present in court; Lee Harvey Oswald, the man the Warren Commission concluded killed Kennedy; and David Ferrie, an itinerant, former airline pilot who had died a strange but, doctors said, natural death just after it was revealed that Garrison was investigating the Kennedy assassination.

That is what Garrison charged.

Now as Judge Haggerty looked down on the courtroom from his bench above the lawyers, someone was missing: it was Jim Garrison, the outspoken prosecutor. He was not in court. At the counsel table, ready to go to trial, were four of Garrison's assistants: James L. Alcock, Alvin V. Oser, William Alford and Andrew J. Sciambra. Across the room sat Shaw's defense team headed by F. Irvin Dymond, who was assisted by the Wegmann brothers, Edward and William, and by Salvatore Panzeca.

As Judge Haggerty banged his gavel opening court the lawyers looked placid, calm, reserved and unemotional.

Before the trial was many hours old the opposing counsel would be tearing into each other with a vengeance, each accusing the other of bad faith, bad motives and bad judgment.

Newsmen, that first day and throughout the early days of the trial, asked themselves, the court officers and the lawyers: where is Garrison? He had been so dominant a personality in the pre-trial preparation of the case that his absence created a disappointing void. There were some who said he would wait for the most dramatic moment to put in an appearance. Others intimated that since evidence in his case was not to be as strong as he had claimed in his public statements, he would not show up in court, but would leave the prosecution to his assistants.

Without Garrison in court, much of the drama was drained from the case. After all the pre-trial lightning from Garrison there was no instant thunder in court without him. And as the tedious task of jury selection began—a process that was to take more than two weeks—some of the tautness slipped from the courtroom as Garrison, the man who had started this whole chapter in legal history, stayed away.

Security the first day of the trial was tight. A sheriff's deputy, armed with a shotgun, patrolled the roof of the courthouse. Other officers were stationed throughout the court building.

Everyone who wanted to enter the courtroom where Shaw was being tried—and this included newsmen as well as spectators—had to have an identification card supplied in advance by the sheriff's office.

Court officers and deputies frisked everyone who sought to enter the courtroom in the initial stages. But as the trial moved slowly on, the searches became less and less thorough. Perhaps it was the tedious jury-picking process that transmitted to the court officers a lethargic spirit. Perhaps it was the knowledge that Shaw, free on bond, was a more likely target out of court than inside.

Actually, if anyone had wanted to get inside the court with a weapon or any kind of contraband, it would have been easy—primarily because the routine searches were conducted, as a rule, only in the morning and after the noon lunch break. After the first few days persons returning from court recesses were not searched.

Inside the courtroom there was ample room for the press corps attending the trial. There was sufficient room most days, too, for all the spectators, after extra benches had been installed at Judge Haggerty's orders.

There would be times when the courtroom would become filled with spectators. This was true in the latter stages of the trial, or on a day when an exciting witness was expected to testify. It was then that the identification cards the sheriff's office issued became valuable. At those times the armed deputies in court seemed more concerned about getting seats for the important spectators—friends of the principals in the case—than they were concerned about security for Shaw. As interest began to build in the case, more reporters came in from across the nation and some were shocked at the lax security. The searches became less and less a part of the daily routine. The armed guard on the roof went away after the first day. The number of deputies assigned to court dwindled. "Security" became a myth.

For Clay Shaw the tiresome early days of the trial, devoted to the business of jury selection, were vital. In Louisiana, the law provides for a bobtailed jury verdict. Twelve jurors would finally retire from this courtroom to decide on Shaw's guilt or innocence. But under this state's unusual law it would take only nine of the twelve votes of the jurors to convict, or acquit, Shaw. As confident as he seemed, the defendant had to be afraid.

As each potential juror took the witness stand, Shaw's eyes studied the face of the man or woman who might have to help decide his fate. It was Clay Shaw's freedom at stake and his attorneys were naturally cautious.

And the lawyers for the prosecution were alert as each side sought a favorable position in the first two weeks which were taken up with the time-consuming process of choosing the jury.

Many who had been summoned for prospective jury service had read or heard of the case and had already formed opinions about it. These people were excused by Judge Haggerty as soon as they said they could not try the case with an open mind. Still others said the long service on the jury would adversely affect their jobs.

But there were some—a relative few—who said they had

formed no opinions about Shaw's guilt or innocence and that the jury service would not work a financial hardship. It was to such veniremen as these that the opposing attorneys put to work their legal skills in searching the minds of the potential jurors to try to discover what, if any, prejudices they had and how these feelings would benefit or hurt one side or the other. The prosecution and the defense had twelve challenges each. This meant that each side could arbitrarily and without any announced reason excuse this number of prospective jury members.

In two weeks more than a thousand veniremen were called to the courthouse to appear and be examined for jury service.

On Saturday, February 1, with the lawyers' nerves on edge, Judge Haggerty as hale and hearty as ever, and out-of-town newsmen gaining weight on New Orleans cuisine, a panel of twelve jurors was finally selected. But two alternate jurors had to be picked still, in the event one or two of the regular jurors became ill. And so Judge Haggerty announced that on Monday the jury search for two alternates would go on. He summoned 150 more prospective jurors for appearance on Monday. Hopefully, two acceptable jurors could be found among them. Both sides were running low on challenges. When they had exhausted their remaining challenges, Judge Haggerty would have to try to decide whether a juror would fairly try the case.

On Monday, before the jury-selection procedure was renewed, chief defense lawyer Irvin Dymond rose to make a motion. It was the nearest thing to a moment of drama the case had known during two tiring weeks.

Dymond told Judge Haggerty that Lillie McMaines, also known as Sandra Moffett, was a potential witness for the defense, but was afraid to come back to Louisiana because she was fearful that Garrison would bring some charge against her.

Mrs. McMaines, now married to a part-time preacher in Omaha, had been arrested there previously on a warrant sworn out by Garrison which identified her as a material witness in the case.

Dymond simply was asking the judge to give her the protection of the court if she would return to take the witness stand for the defense, not the state.

Judge Haggerty, anxious to move on with the effort to pick two alternate jurors, said he would delay a decision until after the full jury panel had been picked and sworn. When that time came he turned Dymond down.

Of those 150 citizens of Orleans Parish called that Monday as the trial's third week started, only one was seated as a jury alternate during a long, nerve-racking day. John Joseph Beilman, Jr., twenty-six, an employee of a film manufacturing firm who said he rarely read any newspapers and only then to see what movies were playing, was seated. He said he had heard some people express to him their opinions about the Clay Shaw case, but this had not influenced him personally. He thought he could serve as a good juror and give Shaw a fair trial, he told the Court.

But, like most people called into court as strangers to the proceedings, he was not too certain about some aspects of the law. He wasn't clear, for example, on the difference between "probable guilt" and "guilt beyond reasonable doubt." His confusion on this point brought the opposing lawyers into a wrangle.

Defense lawyer Dymond challenged Beilman's right to sit on the jury after the man expressed his difficulty about the difference between "probable guilt" and "guilt beyond any reasonable doubt." Under the law, a juror may not find a defendant guilty if there is reasonable doubt in his mind about the defendant's guilt.

"In other words," Dymond said to Beilman, "You cannot conclude that a man is probably guilty, or possibly guilty. Before you convict, you must decide he is guilty beyond any reasonable doubt." He asked Haggerty to dismiss Beilman.

The prosecution objected to Dymond's effort to dismiss Beilman as an alternate juror. It was typical of the sort of infighting that had gone on for two weeks. Judge Haggerty sustained the State's objection after explaining in detail to Beilman what the law meant by "reasonable doubt" as regards the duty of jurors.

"It's a little difficult," the judge conceded, "to give a course in the law in five minutes. Sometimes it's difficult to do it in four years." Monday's session ended with one alternate seated and one more still to be chosen.

On Tuesday morning, Garrison's office issued a subpoena for slides of the color film of President Kennedy's assassination. It was another break in the routine of jury picking. Judge Haggerty granted the subpoena and directed Time, Inc., the national news magazine which had purchased the film slides from Abraham Zapruder, to make the film available to Garrison. The Judge directed that the film would be used solely as evidence to protect *Time's* publication rights and copyright.

Spokesmen for Garrison said the film would be used in support of the claim that Kennedy was fired on from more than one direction. Garrison already had possession of the film itself, under a 1968 court order, but Prosecutor Alcock said color slides of the films also were requested. These frames showed Kennedy as he was hit by gunfire.

With the subpoena for Time, Inc. out of the way, nearly 150 more prospective jurors were questioned during the day. But the effort to choose the second alternate juror failed. During the effort both the defense and prosecution exhausted all their peremptory challenges. The defense used its last peremptory challenge to reject Ulysses Simpson Porter, forty-nine-year-old post office foreman who said he knew of no reason why he would not make a fair juror. "I have only a very vague knowledge of the case because I don't do much reading," he said. But the defense would not seat him. Now Judge Haggerty would make the final decision as to the fitness of the final alternate juror who would serve as second alternate.

The case had received so much notice that many would-be jurors did not feel they could give Shaw a fair trial. That is why more than a thousand persons had been questioned as prospective jurors—a record for any trial in New Orleans' history. Most of those who were rejected said they had fixed opinions about the case. As one prospective juror, Robert Higgins Baillio, Jr., explained: "As far as having an opinion about Mr. Shaw, I don't have a fixed bias. But as far as the publicity surrounding the district attorney's investigation, I can't help but be influenced to some extent."

Harold Charles Wiltenmulth told the court that "due to the great amount of publicity, I'm afraid I do have feelings."

Sheriff's deputies assisting at the trial continued to express hope that the jury selection would be completed as quickly as possible. They were tired of standing around the courtroom all day, listening to the trying, repetitive process of attempting to choose jurors.

But it was not until the following morning, Wednesday, that

the second alternate was chosen. He was John Burlet, forty-six. The Judge told him before noon to take a seat in the jury box.

Less than an hour after the final juror was chosen, Haggerty confided to newsmen: "I'm glad that game of mental chess is over. Both the state and the defense have been picking those jurors' brains. And it finally got so bad they were asking if anyone knew cousins of the cousins of the policemen."

This was the jury selected to try Clay Shaw: Irvin Mason, fifty, a machine operator; Oliver M. Schultz, thirty-nine, a New Orleans Public Service Inc. employee; William Ricks, Jr., twenty-six, a teacher at Booker T. Washington High School; Charles D. Ordes, thirty-nine, a supervisor for American Can Co.; Herbert J. Kenison, twenty-eight, a microfilm printer; James G. O'Quinn, thirty, a petroleum engineer; Larry D. Morgan, twenty-four, an aircraft mechanic; Sidney J. Hebert, fifty-five, a retired Fire Department captain; Harold W. Bainum, Jr., a credit manager; Warren E. Humphrey, fifty-two, a postal employee; David I. Powe, twenty-eight, a credit manager; Peter M. Tatum, forty-three, a maintenance mechanic. The two alternate jurors were Joseph Beilman, Jr., a Kalvar Co. employee and John Burlet, president of CNT Crane Service Inc.

Newsmen now turned their attention to the man who had scarcely been inside the courtroom—Jim Garrison. He was the man who had brought reporters from all over the nation and around the world to New Orleans for this trial of Clay Shaw. He had said he knew what had happened at Dallas on November 22, 1963.

His statements about the Shaw case had made Jim Garrison a national celebrity and an international figure. For two years he had courted the spotlight—and now that the case had opened he seemed to be dodging it. What had happened to his zest for center stage?

During the first week of trial, Garrison had appeared only once in the courtroom. He stayed eighteen minutes, said not a word, and only observed the preliminary work being done by his assistants. During the trial's second week, the district attorney did not appear in court at all. He issued no public statements and gave no interviews to reporters covering the trial. Newsmen's telephone calls to him, for the most part, were not returned.

There were reports, as the third week of trial got underway, that Garrison was waiting until testimony began before starting his own participation. None of his assistants said so for certain, but it was generally acknowledged that Garrison would make the opening address to the jury.

For if he did not make the opening argument—which, under New Orleans law gives the state the opportunity to outline what it expects to prove with the evidence that follows—it would be assumed that Garrison was running away from the battle; that all his charges so loudly expressed were lacking in substance.

His assertions that he had the secrets of what happened at Dealey Plaza in Dallas when Kennedy was killed, expressed in every public forum imaginable, from Johnny Carson's Tonight Show to *Playboy Magazine* had brought the attention of the world to New Orleans.

Had the United States Government—as Garrison repeatedly charged—really lied to the world about the murder of President Kennedy? Had there been a government conspiracy of silence to cover up "the real truth" about the death of the president? Had the CIA, the FBI, the executives of those two agencies and even President Lyndon Johnson all known and hidden the facts from the world? Had the Warren Commission, the Dallas police, even Robert Kennedy, brother of the slain president, obscured the truth about Dallas? These were Garrison's contentions.

The time was very near when Jim Garrison would have to substantiate his claims before a court of law. He had offered no solid evidence to back up his claims. His proof, it was anticipated, would come in court. For now Clay Shaw, a man more at ease with antiques and good books than the hostilities of the adversary legal system and the ambiguities of Louisiana law, was on trial.

But the idea that Garrison would "hit and run" began to diminish when he subpoenaed the Zapruder film. His office, even as the jury was being selected, was moving on other fronts. He was seeking to obtain the autopsy photographs and X-rays of President Kennedy's body. He was calling witnesses who were on the scene in Dallas, including Texas Governor John Connally, who had been riding in the car with Kennedy and who had been sorely wounded by gunfire.

Garrison's barrage of press statements over two years had

the nation expecting him to bring his theory of what happened in Dealey Plaza into the open in court.

Still, the district attorney and his men would not have to rely on evidence of what happened in Texas as a basis to convict Shaw. The law Shaw was accused of violating did not require proof that he plotted the actual murder of the President. This may not have been understood by the public. Garrison's legal theory was based on a noose in the Louisiana criminal code—not unlike the conspiracy statutes in most states—which held that it was not necessary for the conspirators to succeed in their plot to be found guilty of conspiracy.

Louisiana law defines a criminal conspiracy as: "The agreement or combination of two or more persons for the specific purpose of committing any crime: provided that an agreement or combination to commit a crime shall not amount to a criminal conspiracy unless, in addition to such agreement or combination, one or more of such parties does act in furtherance of the object of the agreement or combination."

In other words, the crime of conspiracy consists of two elements. First, the agreement to commit the criminal act. Second, one act by one of the conspirators in furtherance of the conspiracy. That act need not be criminal; it could be perfectly innocent, such as the legal purchase of a rifle, or Shaw's trip to the West Coast during November, 1963, on business, or the alleged lakefront meeting in New Orleans between Shaw and Oswald. It could have been the taking of a rifle by Oswald to the Texas School Book Depository Building.

Louisiana law further specifies that if the intended crime in a conspiracy is consummated, "the conspirators may be tried for either the conspiracy or the offense, and a conviction for one shall not bar a prosecution for the other." In other words, assuming that Garrison was correct in his allegations against Shaw, then the defendant could, under the law, have been tried for the murder of the President. But murder, obviously, is more difficult to prove than conspiracy.

Garrison's chief assistant, Jim Alcock, during the examination of jurors, repeatedly explained to veniremen: "In order to convict Mr. Clay Shaw we aren't legally required even to prove that John Kennedy is dead."

Under the law he was correct. But if this was to be the limit of the proof, why was Garrison going to such great lengths to subpoena evidence and witnesses that would perhaps shed some light on what occurred at Dallas: the autopsy photographs, the Zapruder film, the witnesses at the scene?

What Garrison would be allowed to try to prove in court would rest, ultimately, on the decision of Judge Haggerty. The judge had established guidelines for lawyers to follow in dealing with the press—but he had ignored how Garrison had abused those guidelines in the period prior to the trial.

Judge Haggerty himself seemed to enjoy the press. He went out of his way to "cooperate" with reporters. He would hold impromptu sessions with the press in his chambers and regale newsmen with anecdotes and jokes as he discussed their questions about the trial.

During one such session he got into an exchange about the unique Louisiana law requiring agreement of only nine of the twelve jurors on the question of guilt or innocence. He acknowledged some reservations about the constitutionality of it. But it was the law. And in order to satisfy reporters' curiosity he had looked up the jury law in all other states so he would know just how unique the statute was in his state. Again, during this impromptu meeting with reporters, he was asked about the defense motion concerning Mrs. McMaines. He had only one copy of the motion and he was besieged by reporters to relate exactly what was in it. He balked at reading the document. It was too long, he said. He tried to summarize it, then simply handed it over to a reporter and told him to copy it and make it available to other newsmen. He would rule on it when the full jury panel was picked, he said. In high good humor, he departed, advising reporters that if they wished they could view the quarters where the jury would deliberate over the evidence. (Some newsmen took his offer. It was a grim, dusty room at the top of a winding staircase, with a single window at the end and dusty law books stacked in the corners.)

Just how cooperative Judge Haggerty was to be with the press would not come to light until the jury selection was completed and the jurors sworn. It was then that he agreed—to the amazement of some newsmen who asked him—to allow a picture-taking session with members of the jury.

It was a remarkable moment in American jurisprudence when

Judge Haggerty appeared with reporters and photographers beside the swimming pool at the Rowntowner Motor Inn, some ten blocks from the courthouse, where the jurors would be sequestered during the trial.

With newsmen clustered around him while they awaited the appearance of the jurors for the "formal" photographing session, the judge chatted about the hazards of being a jurist. He commented about how the case had inconvenienced him. He had been forced by the trial to turn down invitations to at least four Mardi Gras balls. He explained: "I couldn't be out until 4:00 or 5:00 a.m. every morning and then come into court all bright eyed and bushy tailed."

The judge told reporters he did not know how much the state intended to prove about Kennedy's assassination. But, he added: "If the state wants to overprove its case, then I can't prevent them from doing it. If that's what they want to do, I'll just have to call a ball or a strike when the time comes."

With a judge like this, it is not surprising that Garrison had been able to get away with his pre-trial statements without censure by the court; or that he would later be allowed to "overprove" his case by repeatedly showing the jury the Zapruder film.

The actual photographing of the jurors began. Dressed smartly in suits and ties, the jurors came out of the motor inn, accompanied by sheriff's deputies, and marched briskly to the pool area where Haggerty and members of the press waited. Haggerty had ordered the suits and ties because, as he put it, "We're not going to have any repetition of the monkey trial." Presumably, he meant by this that the press would not have the opportunity to picture the Shaw trial jurors as bumpkins.

Haggerty directed the jurors to sit in chairs placed beside the pool, against a backdrop of palms and ferns. Stiff-backed and solemn-faced, the jurors watched fascinated as the judge darted back and forth, giving directions about how the picture-taking session should proceed.

"No one talks to the newsmen—I want that understood," the judge shouted as he strained to be heard above the noise of the photographers jostling and scrambling for position. Then, with all the jurors seated the judge said: "I don't want anyone else in the picture. And that includes the sheriff."

Sheriff Louis Heyd, who had been edging into the right side of the picture, backed away.

"All right," Haggerty shouted, "fire away!" And with that, at least seven television cameras began to grind and some twenty other newsmen with an assortment of photographic gear moved in.

Five minutes later, the judge asked, "Is everyone finished?" A clutch of TV cameramen on a balcony overhead clamored vigorously and yelled down that they were not through. "I know," the judge said, ruefully shaking his head. "You never get enough."

But, finally, everyone did get enough and Haggerty directed that the jurors be taken to lunch. But first, he said, the jurors would walk around the pool a couple of times for the newsmen. "To get a few action shots," the judge confided. And so, the jurors trudged obligingly around the pool, under the hot sun, while the television cameras hummed and the photographers hustled back and forth to get a favorable "angle."

Before leaving, Haggerty once again talked freely with newsmen who gathered around him. He gave on-camera interviews to a few television reporters. The judge seemed impressed when Gerold Frank, author of *The Boston Strangler,* came up, introduced himself and shook the judge's hand. Frank explained that he was in New Orleans just to observe. He said he planned no book about the Shaw trial.

Haggerty informed reporters that Garrison himself was indeed expected to make the opening address to the jury. In fact, the judge added, Garrison's staff had confided it would be a fifteen-page address. This would be mimeographed, Haggerty said, and copies of it would be passed around to members of the press.

The next day, Haggerty's information proved to be correct. For Jim Garrison, calm and deliberate, stood before the all male jury—a rare courtroom appearance in the trial against Shaw—and delivered an opening statement which declared President Kennedy was killed in a crossfire from guns wielded by "a number of men."

Shortly after the courtroom began filling up that morning, the district attorney strolled through the crowd, pushed through the gates separating the press and spectators from the inner court area, and sat down at the glass-topped table for the prosecution. Looking up briefly, his eyes met those of Shaw, who was seated about ten feet away at the defense table. The opening statement—as the judge had forecast—was fifteen pages long. Garrison read the document slowly and with little emphasis, almost in a monotone, enlivened infrequently by a raised voice which a few reporters starved for action described as a burst of passion.

Garrison told the jury that the state would prove Kennedy's fatal wound "was received from the front." Speaking with measured emphasis, he added: "The eyewitness testimony will also show that the shooting came from a number of directions and that, therefore, the President was murdered, not by a lone individual behind him but as the result of a conspiracy to kill him."

With this statement, the district attorney served notice that the Warren Commission was on trial also. For the Warren Commission concluded that Kennedy was killed by Oswald, acting alone, and that there was no evidence of a conspiracy. The commission had found that Kennedy was shot from behind only, and that the bullets came from Oswald's rifle. Garrison claimed evidence to the contrary.

Every newsman had suspected, but no one knew what the unpredictable Jim Garrison might say in court. Now that he had disclosed his intentions in the opening statement, the trial course was charted.

As he spoke, Garrison stood before the crowded, hushed courtroom and apologized for subjecting the jury to the lengthy reading. Dressed in a dark suit with matching vest and tie, he bent over a microphone in the high domed, dark paneled courtroom and outlined the state's case against Shaw: "It is the position of the state of Louisiana that regardless of the power which might bring about the execution of a President of the United States, whether it be initiated by a small group or the highest possible force, neither the planning of his murder or any part of it will be regarded as being above the law."

Reading for nearly three-quarters of an hour, Garrison touched on the testimony which he said the prosecution would put on the stand.

"With David Ferrie now dead and Lee Oswald now dead," Garrison said, "the state is bringing to trial Mr. Shaw for his role—as is revealed by evidence—in the conspiracy to murder John F. Kennedy." Turning to the events in Dallas the day Kennedy was killed, the district attorney said: "As to the planning—the conspiracy—our jurisdiction is limited to New Orleans, although we will later offer evidence concerning the assassination in Dealey Plaza in Dallas because it confirms the existence of a conspiracy and because it confirms the significance and relevance of the planning which occurred in New Orleans.

"With regard to the assassination itself, the state will establish that . . . President John F. Kennedy and Governor John Connally . . . were wounded as a result of gunshots fired by different guns at different locations—thus showing that more than one person was shooting at the President.

"The evidence will show that he was struck in the front as well as in the back—and that the final shot which struck him came from in front of him, knocking him backwards in his car. Once again, since Lee Oswald was in the Book Depository behind the President, this will show that a number of men were shooting and that he was, therefore, killed as a result of conspiracy."

The district attorney said he would seek to link Oswald, Ferrie and Shaw by proving that they met several times in New Orleans to plan the President's murder, and that on one occasion Shaw met Oswald on the lakefront and gave him what appeared to be money.

Shaw, seated at the defense table, sat quietly while Garrison was giving his statement. Occasionally, he wrote with a blue pen on a yellow legal pad. He chain-smoked constantly.

Only once was Garrison's presentation interrupted. That was when Irvin Dymond, Shaw's lawyer, objected to Garrison's mention of events in Dallas. The defense attorney said the assassination itself had nothing to do with the alleged conspiracy in New Orleans. Alcock argued that "the sole issue is whether we (the state) are going to be circumscribed, in presenting our case, by the defense counsel's wishes." Dymond replied heatedly: "We do not want them to be bound by our wishes—but by the law." Haggerty, in overruling Dymond, said: "I cannot tell the state how to run its case—if it wants to overprove its case, it can do so." It was a statement he had made to reporters previously and it now left a clear indication that all the "facts" relating to Dallas would be admissable in court here.

Garrison, as he continued, said the state would prove, as required by the definition of criminal conspiracy, the following overt acts:

Oswald, Ferrie and the defendant Shaw met in the apartment of Ferrie in New Orleans during September, 1963.

Oswald, Ferrie and Shaw discussed means and methods with regard to the assassination of John F. Kennedy—particularly the selection and use of rifles to be fired from multiple directions simultaneously to produce a crossfire; they established and selected the means and routes of escape from the assassination scene; they discussed possible alibis for those involved.

Shaw traveled to the West Coast of the United States in November, 1963.

Ferrie made a trip from New Orleans to Houston on the day of the assassination, November 22, 1963.

Lee Harvey Oswald took a rifle to the Texas School Book Depository in Dallas, Texas on or before November 22, 1963.

Earlier, prosecutor Alcock had pointed out that it was necessary only for the state to prove, first, that Shaw agreed with someone to assassinate Kennedy and, second, that one overt act was made in furtherance of the conspiracy. But the state would seek to prove much more.

It was now Irvin Dymond's turn to give his opening address to the jury on behalf of Clay Shaw. He quickly went to what he termed the heart of the prosecution's case. He asserted that the defense would prove the state's star witness, Perry Raymond Russo, "a notoriety seeking liar, whose name does not deserve to be mentioned with honor and justice."

Dymond added: "It is our intention to prove to you not only that Clay Shaw did not engage in a conspiracy to kill the President but that he never knew or laid eyes on either Oswald or

Ferrie." The lawyer said he was not there "to defend the findings of the Warren Commission—we have neither the inclination, the desire or the money to do that. We are not trying the Warren Commission in this case."

The defense intended, Dymond said, to "strike at the very core of the state's case—that is, the alleged conspiratorial meetings of Oswald, Ferrie and Shaw." It was remembered that Russo, in the 1967 preliminary hearing, had testified that he overheard Shaw, Oswald and Ferrie planning the President's murder. But Dymond now called Russo a "liar" and said he would prove that Russo told a reporter he did not know the difference between fact and fantasy; that Russo wanted to get out of the case but was scared. "If I stick with my story," Dymond quoted Russo as saying, "Shaw and his lawyers will get me. If I change my story, Garrison and his staff will ruin me." Shaw's defense, then, would be an attack to discredit the state's key witnesses. It was a strategy that would succeed.

The evidence began. Jim Alcock called five quick witnesses during three hours of testimony in the afternoon. All five gave statements for the prosecution designed to show that Shaw and Ferrie were seen in Clinton, Louisiana—about 120 miles north of New Orleans—with Oswald. They testified that Shaw drove up before the registrar's office in Clinton in a black, late model Cadillac. Ferrie was in the front seat with Shaw. Oswald, who got out and went into the voting registrar's office, was in the back seat, the witnesses said.

It was important testimony. Shaw was contending that he had never known either Ferrie or Oswald. Clinton town marshal John Manchester testified that he saw Shaw in his town in late August or early September of 1963, and that Shaw was driving a large black Cadillac. Manchester said he checked Shaw out because the Congress of Racial Equality was conducting a voter registration drive at the time and "it was my job to keep law and order and keep out outside agitators." That last statement drew chuckles from the spectators.

Dymond drew a vigorous outburst from the prosecution table when he asked Manchester: "Isn't it true that you were doing everything in your power to keep the Negroes from being registered?" Alcock objected strenuously to the question and Haggerty sustained the objection.

Later, Dymond and Manchester had this exchange:

Q. "Did you have occasion to report this to the Warren Commission?"

A. "I figured if they wanted it, they could come to me."

Q. "Didn't you think it your duty as a law enforcement officer to give them the information?"

A. "I felt it was my duty if they came and asked me for it."

Q. "Can you tell us how they were supposed to know about it if you did not tell them?"

Later, Henry Earl Palmer, registrar of voters of the east Louisiana parish, testified that Oswald came into his office, seeking to register to vote, but was turned down because he couldn't prove that he had lived long enough in the parish.

Corrie C. Collins, former chairman of the CORE chapter in Clinton, testified he saw Shaw and Ferrie in the Cadillac and that Oswald got out and went into the registrar's office. Collins was cross-examined by Dymond:

Q. "You were aware that the Warren Commission was conducting an extensive investigation into the assassination of President Kennedy, were you not?"

A. "I was aware that there was an investigation."

Q. "You knew you had seen Lee Harvey Oswald in Clinton?"

A. "I did."

Q. "Did you report this to the Warren Commission or any federal authorities?"

A. "No one asked me."

Q. "You didn't consider it your duty to tell them."

A. "I figured if they wanted to know they would ask me."

Q. "Do you think they were supposed to guess that you had information?"

Collins was not permitted to answer this question.

Collins, Manchester and Palmer all testified that they identified Oswald, Shaw and Ferrie later from pictures they saw on television and in the press. However, although Collins said he recognized Shaw from a picture that ran in the press after Shaw's arrest, the state's witness could not recall what day it was that he had seen Shaw in Clinton, whether the sun was shining, where exactly the car was parked, or whether he was standing to the car's right or left.

Edwin Lea McGee, a Clinton barber, particularly remembered

Oswald from the day he came into his shop in the late summer of 1963 for a haircut.

Former State Representative Reeves Morgan remembered the time Oswald came to his home to seek help in getting a job at East Louisiana State hospital. "He was a very well-appearing fellow," Morgan testified.

The next day, the prosecution turned from Clinton to New Orleans and began putting on testimony designed to link Shaw directly with Oswald. A number of witnesses, including several city policemen, testified that Oswald distributed "Fair Play for Cuba" handbills in New Orleans during the summer of 1963. They said that he stood in front of the building where Shaw had his office.

A heroin addict and convicted thief told the court that he saw Shaw pass what appeared to be a sum of money to Oswald during a meeting in the summer of 1963 on the city's lakefront. The witness, Vernon William Bundy, Jr., thirty, touched off a shouting match between defense and prosecution attorneys, and caused Haggerty finally to plead: "Gentlemen, don't scream! You'll have me screaming!"

Bundy, once a pressman at a New Orleans laundry, testified he was at Lake Pontchartrain in June, 1963, preparing to give himself a heroin injection, when Shaw drove up in a black limousine and met Oswald.

"This man (Shaw) gave Oswald what looked to me was a roll of money—most likely it was money," Bundy testified. Speaking in staccato fashion as he slumped in the witness chair, Bundy gave this testimoney to prosecutor Alcock:

Q. "Is this the man (pointing to Shaw) who drove up to the lakefront?"

A. "Yes, this is the man who got out of the car."

Q. "I'm going to show you a picture. Do you recognize this man?"

A. "Yes, I saw him meet Mr. Shaw at the lakefront. I know him now to be Lee Harvey Oswald."

Q. "Did you hear any words pass between these two men?"

A. "I heard Oswald say, "What am I going to tell her?"

Q. "Did you hear any other words passed between these two men?"

A. "The gentleman here (Shaw) tried to make this small fellow, Oswald, quieten down. They were staring at me."

Q. "Why were you looking at them?"

A. "Well, I had heroin on me and I didn't know if they were police officers or what. I just hoped I had time to dispose of the heroin before they got to me."

Q. "Did they do anything else?"

A. "This man (Shaw) gave Oswald what looked to me was a roll of money. Oswald put it in his back pocket and as he did some leaflets fell out."

Bundy testified that later, after Oswald and Shaw left, he gave himself a heroin injection. He added: "After I shot my heroin, I was looking around for something to wrap my 'fix' equipment in. And I walked over and picked up one of these leaflets. It had something written on it like 'Help Cuba,' or 'Free Cuba'—I don't know what it was."

Under cross-examination by Dymond, Bundy testified he had been a drug addict, off and on, since he was thirteen. Now he was trying to kick the habit, he told the jury. Asked if it was true that he stole to support his habit, Bundy replied it was not. He then went on to explain: "I can't state that never have I stolen. If I saw something laying around with nobody nearby, I picked it up—sure, to support my habit."

"So," Dymond persisted, "You testify that you did steal on occasion to support your heroin habit?"

"Yes," Bundy replied.

At one point, Bundy told the court he was sure it was Shaw he had seen at the lakefront in 1963, and that he could prove it if he could get Shaw to walk about in the courtroom. Getting up from the witness chair just inside the railing, he asked Shaw to walk behind him.

After Shaw had made the trip twice, Bundy got up and did an imitation of the way the defendant walked, turning outward his right ankle. (Shaw favors his right foot because of a weak right ankle.) "I remember him twisting that foot," Bundy testified, "because it frightened me."

During the last part of the day, the prosecution called an unexpected witness to the stand: a self-styled New York tax specialist, Charles I. Spiesel. The fifty-year-old New Yorker was to spark some stimulating exchanges with Dymond. He testified for Alcock that he attended a party in New Orleans in June, 1963 at which Shaw, Ferrie and others discussed the proposed assassination of Kennedy. In the most explosive, and surprising, testimony so far in the trial, Spiesel told the hushed courtroom he was invited by Ferrie to a party hosted by Shaw in the city's French Quarter.

While at the party, which was attended by about ten other men, the conversation turned to Kennedy and quite a few people began criticizing the President, Spiesel said. He added: "The conversation went around the table and, finally, someone said, 'Somebody ought to kill the sonofabitch.' A man standing next to Shaw, with a splint on one hand, said, 'Yes, I'd like to do it myself, but how would they kill the President,' and after five or six minutes the consensus was that it would have to be done by a high-powered rifle and that the one who did the shooting would have to be about a mile away."

At this point, Alcock interrupted to ask if Shaw had contributed anything to the conversation. With the courtroom audience straining to hear, Spiesel tapped his right hand against the witness chair as he said: "Mr. Shaw, during the course of the conversation, seemed to be amused at it. After one of the men asked if the President could be assassinated, I said, 'Yes, it could be done, but how would the man who did it get away?' Shaw turned to Ferrie and asked, 'Couldn't you fly him out?' Mr. Ferrie hemmed and hawed around and finally said it could be done."

Spiesel said someone else at the party asked the man with a splint on one hand how he would be able to shoot anyone since his arm was wounded. "The man replied, 'In a week or two, this is coming off and I'll be able to do what I said I'd like to do.' "

Spiesel's testimony came as a shock because the state had not previously disclosed that it had any witnesses except Perry Raymond Russo to any alleged conspiratorial meetings. Spiesel sounded reliable during direct examination by Alcock. He wilted considerably during a cross-examination by Dymond. The defense lawyer tore into his story.

During Dymond's cross-examination, Spiesel acknowledged that he had tried to charge officials for CBS Television two thousand dollars for his story but was turned down. In another exchange with Dymond, the witness testified this way:

Q. "Isn't it a matter of fact that you once claimed in a law-

suit that the New York police had hypnotized you and followed
you around and harassed you out of business?"
A. "No, not in that terminology."
Q. "Are you not the same Charles I. Spiesel who filed a suit
in New York City, based on the allegations I cited to you?"
A. "Yes, but you've pulled something that sounds bad."
Q. "The suit was dismissed, was it not?"
A. "It was."
Q. "Is it true that you claimed you recently have been sub-
jected to a Communist conspiracy?"
A. "What do you mean by that?"
Q. "Haven't you recently been followed about, according to
you, had your phone tapped, and so forth?"
A. "Not particularly recently."
Q. "Well, when?"
A. "In a period around 1964 and 1965."

Under further cross-examination, D y m o n d elicited from
Spiesel the disclosure that he has—without the benefit of an attorney—filed other lawsuits against other defendants, charging
them with keeping him hypnotized, off and on, over a period of
years.

The next day, Saturday, Dymond continued his cross-
examination of Spiesel, drawing from the witness his explanation
of why he brought a suit for $16 million against the Pinkerton de-
tective agency, a psychiatrist, business competitors and others.

Spiesel testified that the defendants in the lawsuit, which
was still pending, used "a new police technique" to torture him.
He said the torture included instances where people opposed to
him conspired to disguise themselves as "friends and relatives"
of his and then passed him quickly in the street. He alleged that
he was hypnotized, off and on, against his will, by various persons from 1948 until 1964, causing him to suffer "hypnotic illusions" and lose the power to perform "normal sexual relations."

He also believed that competitors of his conspired to ruin
his business by tapping his telephone, harassing his customers
and by stationing someone beside his fuse box to turn out the
lights in his office at inopportune moments.

His credibility—and sanity—were strenuously challenged by
Dymond, who sought to show that the witness could not be be-

lieved. The accountant, nervous and uncomfortable, seemed near collapse at times.

Then Dymond asked the court to direct the witness to search in the French Quarter for the brownstone building where he had claimed he heard Shaw discuss the shooting of Kennedy. Haggerty granted the request and said the search would start at the corner of Dauphine and Esplanade.

It was one of the oddest developments in the trial. What happened can only be described as carnival. Representatives of the press were the first to arrive at the corner of Dauphine and Esplanade in the French Quarter. More than one hundred newspapermen, a covey of court officials, policemen, sheriff's deputies, and various others, including a vendor for "Icee Frozenated Fun Drinks," were there for the spectacle.

Children on bicycles, followed by yapping dogs, romped through the huge crowd which, by noon, had blocked the intersection. Then Shaw drove up in his blue Continental. Immediately, dozens of TV cameramen and newspaper photographers ran into the street and began taking pictures. Shaw, looking slightly amused at the whole affair, took it in good grace, saying little and smiling frequently.

As the tallest man in the crowd, Shaw towered over those who crowded about him. Puffing on a cigarette as he stood on the street corner, he suggested casually: "Let's move to a neutral corner." And, leading the pack of newspaper men and curiosity seekers, he walked over to the grassy median strip on Dauphine and stationed himself under a shade tree. There he stood for perhaps fifteen minutes, entertaining those who could get close enough with an anecdote-filled history of the French Quarter. (Shaw has restored several historic residences in the Quarter, including one which once was occupied by John James Audubon in 1821.)

By now, the crowd had grown to some two hundred people. Others were hanging out second and third-story windows to see what was going on in the streets below. Automobile traffic jammed and impatient drivers blew their horns loudly.

Then, Judge Haggerty and Spiesel drove up. Shaw was left alone as the reporters and photographers rushed to record the arrival. One newsman, pushing through the crowd to reach the judge, almost upended a hefty TV cameraman who threatened to punch him in the nose if he did it again. Bystanders separated the two before any damage was done and the rush to the judge continued.

Standing with his back against a two-story brick apartment building, the judge puffed a cigarette and shouted to be heard above the tumult in the street. "Don't anybody talk to the witness. I don't want you guys talking to the witness at all."

All was in readiness—but the jurors had not arrived. As it turned out, they had been delayed in their special bus. A policeman explained that the jury was in a traffic jam. Traffic had been terrible that day in New Orleans because it was the first day of the Mardi Gras celebration. There were six parades in various parts of the city.

But the best carnival was at Esplanade and Dauphine where one woman bystander, who had been in court practically every day as a spectator, commented: "If they would just pass out popcorn and balloons, we'd be all ready, wouldn't we?"

The jury arrived and Haggerty instructed the jurors to follow Spiesel anywhere he wanted to go. The witness first went into the Dauphine apartments, 1323 Dauphine St. Newsmen and the public were kept out of the building by deputies who instructed them to wait outside. (However a mailman, not to be deterred from his duly-appointed rounds, pushed past the deputies and went inside.)

Minutes later, Spiesel and the jury came out of the building and went into another apartment house around the corner, the Esplanade apartments at 906 Esplanade Ave. When they emerged from this apartment, the judge adjourned court until the afternoon.

When court convened again, Spiesel testified that he believed the Esplanade apartments was where the party was held where he heard the conversation to which he had testified. He added, however, that it was only "similar" and that he could not be certain it was the same place. It had been so long ago, he explained, that he could not remember the address. Since he had not been to the building before or since, it was not easy to say whether the Esplanade apartment was the scene of the party.

During the afternoon, Shaw became faint at one point and was prevented from falling by sheriff's deputies. Dymond said

Shaw had a chronic back problem and "going up and down the stairs got to him."

Throughout the third week of trial, Shaw seemed at times virtually untouched by the scenes around him. During recesses, he talked quietly with friends. He was quick to smile, quick to exchange greetings with reporters and spectators who spoke to him. But through it all, he remained an enigma. You could learn more about Shaw by going down to the corner drugstore and buying a book about the Garrison investigation than you could by watching Shaw in the courtroom and listening to the testimony of prosecution witnesses.

It was obvious that he would have preferred to be elsewhere; this was especially true when he stood inside the railing during recesses and watched silently as groups of curious onlookers clustered together in the spectators' section to discuss the case and "Mr. Shaw." It was not a good feeling to see the man trapped in the gaze of the curious who flocked to see a spectacle.

In many ways, although he was not physically present in the courtroom, the most important man in the conspiracy trial seemed to be Lee Harvey Oswald. In fact, the first two witnesses in the case—a barber and a former state representative—did not mention Shaw at all. They had never seen the defendant, and testified solely about the activities of Oswald.

The testimony by the first two witnesses seemed to set the trend for witnesses who followed. In fact, fourteen of the first fifteen witnesses testified, in part at least, about Oswald. Nine of the fourteen testified solely about Oswald and never mentioned Shaw's name.

Garrison, in his opening address to the jury, gave an early indication of the importance Oswald was to play in the case. In that fifteen-page address, of r o u g h l y four thousand words, Oswald's name was mentioned fifty-eight times. Shaw's name was mentioned twenty-six times.

Witnesses during the first week of testimony were not kind to Oswald. Most pictured him as a publicity seeking young man, a devotee of Castroism who was filled with an apparent hatred of his own country. The witnesses placed Oswald in New Orleans in the summer of 1963 promoting the pro-Cuban cause, distributing leaflets, getting himself arrested and scuffling with those he angered because of his pro-Castro views.

The fourth week of trial began February 10, with the testimony of the man around whom the attorneys for both sides had said the state's case would either rise or fall: Perry Raymond Russo. The twenty-seven-year-old salesman's testimony consumed the whole day. Russo testified to the prosecution that he heard Shaw, Oswald and Ferrie discuss the proposed murder of Kennedy. For the defense Russo said that the alleged discussion had "every characteristic" of an inconsequential "bull session" and that he did not know if the three men were serious.

"You could believe what David Ferrie said or not believe him," Russo said. "He was prone to the spectacular."

"Do you mean to infer," Dymond asked Russo, on cross-examination "that Mr. Ferrie was a little on the crazy side?"

"I always thought so," the witness replied.

Russo related essentially the same story he told during a preliminary hearing in the Shaw case in March, 1967. As a result of that earlier testimony, a three-judge panel ruled that there was sufficient evidence to require Shaw to stand trial on charges that he conspired with Ferrie and Oswald to assassinate the President.

While telling the court that he heard Shaw, Oswald and Ferrie discuss killing Kennedy during a party at Ferrie's apartment in September of 1963, Russo had this exchange with Prosecutor Alcock:

Q. "What conversation transpired in the presence of the defendant (Shaw)?"

A. "Well, Ferrie generally monopolized the conversation. There was a lot of talk. I seem to recall a record being played—something of Cubans talking. It was probably a speech."

Q. "Did anyone say anything unusual?"

A. "Ferrie said, 'We're going to kill the President.' But he had said that before."

Q. "He had said it on previous occasions?"

A. "Yes. During the summer of 1963 he had become obsessed with Kennedy and the Cuban thing."

Q. "Do you recall any conversation in which the defendant Shaw participated?"

A. "Yes."

Q. "Who was present at the time the defendant participated in the conversation?"

A. "David Ferrie, Oswald and the defendant—and myself."

Q. "What conversation took place at this time?"

A. "Well, it seemed to be a continuation of the conversation before. Ferrie had said before how Kennedy should be killed and how easy it could be done."

Q. "Can you explain this?"

A. "Ferrie carried around a bunch of clippings with him. I saw Kennedy's name on some of them and I suppose most of them were about Kennedy."

Q. "What happened then?"

A. "Ferrie paced back and forth, talking about the projected assassination and how there could be a triangulation of cross-fire."

Russo testified that Ferrie said there would have to be at least three people shooting at the President to kill him. One person, who would be the scapegoat or "patsy," would fire a diversionary shot.

"Ferrie said the diversionary shot would have to be shot first," Russo testified, "and then, the other two people would shoot for the kill. There would be a slight lull, but the shots would be almost simultaneous."

Q. "What else did Ferrie say?"

A. "He said that as soon as the assassination was performed there would be an escape flight. And they discussed Brazil and Cuba, but to go to Cuba would mean stopping to refuel. Ferrie then mentioned Mexico."

Q. "Did the defendant say anything?"

A. "He said that was not possible. There would have to be a stop for refueling and there would have to be some friends to give them assistance to fly out and the police would be everywhere."

Q. "What else was said?"

A. "Oswald told Shaw to shut up. Ferrie knows what he is doing. He's a pilot."

Russo testified that when he first went to Ferrie's New Orleans apartment the night of the alleged conspiratorial meeting, Ferrie introduced Shaw to him as "Clem Bertrand." He added that he knew the man only by that name and had never before heard of Clay Shaw. Oswald, Russo said, was introduced to him as Ferrie's roommate, and Oswald used the name "Leon Oswald." Russo's direct testimony took about an hour. The cross-examination would last a day and a half. When Dymond began to question him, Russo's memory seemed to falter. He could not remember what he had been doing just prior to going to Ferrie's apartment. He could not recall whom he went there with, the day or date, or who left the "party" first. Earlier, at the 1967 preliminary hearing, Russo testified that he "definitely" could say that two of his friends, Niles (Lefty) Peterson and Miss Sandra Moffett (now Mrs. Lillie McMaines) were present for a while but left before the alleged assassination discussion took place.

During cross-examination, Russo insisted that he had been "forced" by defense counsel into testifying that Peterson and Miss Moffett were at a party, and that now he couldn't really be sure who was there except for Ferrie, Oswald and Shaw.

Russo acknowledged that he had given at least three interviews to newsmen during 1967—after Ferrie's death—and had never mentioned the alleged conspiratorial meeting, Lee Oswald, "Clem Bertrand" or Clay Shaw. In those interviews, Russo detailed his long friendship with Ferrie and told how Ferrie had frequently said the President ought to be killed.

Dymond questioned Russo at length about a 3,500-word memorandum which Assistant Prosecutor Andrew Sciambra had written after interviewing Russo for the first time. Sciambra went to Baton Rouge in early 1967 to talk to Russo, in response to a letter written by Russo, who was attending college at the time. Russo acknowledged that he did not tell Sciambra, the Garrison staff man, about the conversation he said he overheard, although he and the DA representative talked more than an hour. Under cross-questioning by Dymond, Russo testified in this way:

A. "I thought a big deal was Ferrie's philosophy. I thought that was the important part."

Q. "You knew President Kennedy had been assassinated, did you not?"

A. "When I spoke with Mr. Sciambra? Yes."

Q. "You say you also knew at this time that you had heard three people plan the assassination of the President?"

A. "I don't understand the question."

Q. "When you were talking to Mr. Sciambra in Baton Rouge, did you not know you had overheard this talk of conspiring to assassinate Kennedy?"

A. "Well, I don't know whether I had heard a discussion

about any conspiracy. I heard a discussion about killing the President."

Q. "When you heard this, you didn't take it seriously?"

A. "I knew that with Mr. Ferrie's philosophy, you wouldn't know whether to take him seriously or not."

Q. "With all this, you knew the district attorney was investigating the case, you knew you heard three men talking of killing the President, and yet you thought the important thing was Ferrie's philosophy."

A. "That's what I thought was important."

Later, Dymond asked Russo again if he thought the three men were serious when they talked of killing Kennedy and the witness replied:

"You could believe what David Ferrie said or not believe him. He was prone to the spectacular."

Q. "Did this conversation not have every characteristic of a bull session?"

A. "Every characteristic of it."

Q. "Did David Ferrie ever ask you to leave the apartment before the discussion about the proposed assassination began?"

A. "I was in and out. In the very beginning, there were a couple of remarks as to why I was there."

Q. "Did anyone ever swear you to secrecy or say what they would do to you if you told?"

A. "No."

Q. "Never did? Actually, you left the premises that night not knowing if it was a bull session or what. Right?"

A. "That's right."

The next day, as the cross-examination of Russo continued, Dymond became more stern. He attacked the witness's credibility and emotional stability. At times, the questioning brought outbursts from Russo, and counsel for both the defense and prosecution yelled at each other. At one point, when Russo, Dymond and Alcock were all shouting at the same time, Haggerty broke in: "Cut this screaming out! We can proceed as well by keeping our voices down."

"Your honor," Dymond replied, "when someone tries to talk while you're asking a question, you have to raise your voice to be heard."

The chief defense lawyer began to probe Russo's mental state.

Q. "Mr. Russo, have you ever undergone psychiatric treatment?"

A. "Yes Sir."

Q. "When was that?"

A. "During my first year of college."

Q. "And what year would that be?"

A. "1959."

Q. "How long did you remain under a psychiatrist's care?"

A. "Well, I went to him for consultation for about twelve to eighteen months."

Q. "How often did you consult him?"

A. "Initially, on a consultation basis, about twice a week."

Q. "After your active consultation period ended, is it not true that you later had lengthy talks with the psychiatrist on occasion?"

A. "Not lengthy talks. I called him on the phone whenever anything was bothering me, or when I had something to discuss with him."

Q. "When was this?"

A. "In 1963 and 1965, I'm sure of that."

The questions about Russo's treatment by a psychiatrist were part of a concentrated assault on his credibility and sanity by the defense and succeeded in raising considerable doubt about whether Russo's testimony should be seriously considered. More damaging than the fact that he had undergone psychiatric treatment, was his sworn testimony from the stand. He acknowledged the following to various people during 1967:

The investigation by Garrison was "the most blown-up and confused thing I've ever seen."

He "did not know the difference between fantasy and reality" and wished he "had not ever gotten involved in this mess."

If Garrison knew what he had told his priest about his (Russo's) testimony in the 1967 preliminary hearing, the district attorney "would go through the ceiling."

He did not think the alleged conversation among Shaw, Ferrie and Oswald "sounded like a legitimate plot;" it actually sounded like the men were "just shooting the breeze."

The alleged conspiratorial conversation at Ferrie's apartment was "vague" in his mind and he could not "truthfully say who said what."

He would like to sit down alone with Shaw and resolve his doubts about whether the defendant was the same man he had heard talking with Ferrie and Oswald.

He was not sure whether the three men were plotting to kill Kennedy or Castro.

This was Garrison's principal witness.

Russo made these admissions after intense questioning. Only rarely did he answer "yes" or "no" to a question, unless directed to do so. Instead, he would answer, when asked if he had made certain prior statements, with such phrases as: "In essence," "perhaps," "maybe," "if I could qualify my answer," "yes, with an explanation." At one point, when asked if he had made certain statements, the witness replied: "I don't know. Maybe. That's hard to say. Perhaps." Repeatedly, when asked questions which should have required a simple yes or no answer, Russo launched into long, discursive explanations that strayed. At times, he talked rapidly and loudly, cutting sentences in half and repeating phrases and fragments.

At least twice, the court secretary making a verbatim account of the testimony asked Russo to "slow down" so his answers could be recorded accurately.

Russo testified that he was hypnotized on three occasions by Dr. Esmond Fatter, a private physician, with the assistance of coroner Dr. Nicholas Chetta. But, he added, hypnosis was induced only so he could better recall events of September, 1963.

Dymond attacked Russo's credibility strenuously. It was generally acknowledged that the state's case was wrapped up in what the young man had to say. The defense attorney built his attack around these points:

Russo was unable to remember details about who went with him to Ferrie's apartment the night of the alleged conspiratorial conversation; what day it was; what date it was, or who else was at the party prior to the time of the conversation.

There were discrepancies between testimony given by Russo during this trial and testimony he gave during the preliminary hearing in 1967.

Statements indicating he thought Shaw innocent made by Russo to newsmen, Ferrie's former roommate, Layton Martens and a New Orleans police captain.

Russo failed to report to anyone that he had overheard any conspiratorial conversation until a few days after Ferrie died in 1967.

By day's end, when Dymond finally announced that he had finished his cross-examination, Russo looked tired and slumped visibly in the witness chair. He frequently glanced at the clock on the wall in the rear of the courtroom and compared the time with his own wristwatch.

During Dymond's cross-examination, the defense attorney announced to the court that experts would prove that Russo's testimony was "planted" in his mind during a hypnotic trance induced by prosecution representatives. Dymond said the experts in psychiatry and hypnosis would show that Russo's testimony was "planted in his mind by suggestive questions put to him while he was hypnotized."

"These experts will testify," Dymond told the court, "that to put Russo in such a trance destroyed his credibility as a witness."

The following day, the prosecution read a dead man's testimony into the record in an attempt to rebut Dymond's inferences that Russo was insane. The testimony had been given by Dr. Nicholas J. Chetta, the coroner who died in 1968, about a year after giving the testimony during the 1967 preliminary hearing.

Shaw's lawyers objected to the reading and declared it was "the rankest kind of hearsay." But Alcock said Dymond "opened the door" for the late coroner's testimony when the defense delved into psychiatric treatment received by Russo. Dymond denied he was questioning Russo's sanity by asking him about his visits to the psychiatrist. But Judge Haggerty said: "To the layman, a person who goes to a psychiatrist has something wrong with him. Whether he's goofy or nuts is something else."

The state was then allowed to read sixty-seven pages of testimony given by the late coroner, Dr. Chetta. In that testimony, the coroner said that Russo met "all the requirements of legal sanity." The coroner defined "legal sanity" as being able to meet requirements of the McNaghton rule, which states a person may be held accountable for his crimes if he knows the difference between right and wrong and is competent to consult with counsel.

The cross-examination of Russo had been effective. Now Assistant District Attorney Sciambra took the witness stand to testify about the memorandum he wrote in 1967 after interviewing Russo in Baton Rouge. That seven-page memo loomed larger and larger as the trial progressed, because nowhere in it did Sciambra mention that Russo gave him the key information that there had been a meeting between Shaw, Oswald and Ferrie when the assassination was plotted.

In the memo, written about a week after Sciambra interviewed Russo for the first time, the assistant district attorney quoted Russo as saying that he had seen Shaw on two occasions—once at the Nashville Avenue wharf and again at a New Orleans service station. Nowhere in the memo did Sciambra mention a third time Russo claims to have seen Shaw—at the alleged "party" where the witness claimed he overheard the conversation concerning the murder of Kennedy.

Sciambra, the assistant prosecutor, testified that Russo told him about the party but that he neglected to put the information in his memorandum. The memo, Sciambra said, was "incomplete, inaccurate, filled with errors and had numerous omissions."

Now the state turned to the question of whether Shaw had an alias. During the fast-paced day, postal workers for the New Orleans Post Office testified that Shaw ordered his mail, which normally went to 1313 Dauphine St., to go to 1414 Chartres St. during six months in 1966. During this time, mail carrier James Hardiman testified, he delivered several letters to the Chartres Avenue address to a "M. Clem Bertrand." The state claimed

Clay Shaw marches from Garrison's office in handcuffs

District Attorney Jim Garrison talks with newsmen

Garrison wears a pistol as he directs the investigation

Judge Edward Haggerty directs a photographing session for newsmen for the Shaw jury

Judge Haggerty covers his face when arrested at a stag party some months after the trial

Shaw used the alias "Clay Bertrand" while at the party to which Russo referred.

"It was nice handwriting, very nice," said Hardiman, the twentieth prosecution witness. When asked if he delivered mail addressed to anyone other than Shaw, he replied: "Yes, I delivered letters addressed to quite a few people . . . I can say I delivered mail addressed to Clem Bertrand at that address."

Hardiman could not recall how many Clem Bertrand letters he delivered. "But I handled enough letters that when the name came out in this case, it came back to me," he added.

Another witness that day, R. Charles Roland, former owner of Winterland Skating Rink in Houston, testified that Ferrie and two young male companions came to his rink the day after Dallas, introducing himself loudly several times, as if he were interested in making sure everyone knew he was there.

In the opening statement to the jury, the state had said it would show by Roland's testimony that Ferrie was trying to establish an alibi for himself on the day Kennedy was killed. However, since Roland testified to events which he said took place the day after the assassination, the relevance of his story could not be discerned.

Dymond attacked Roland's credibility by asking him questions about when he first came forward with his story. The lawyer asked Roland whom he first talked with in the district attorney's office about Ferrie's visit to Winterland.

"I talked to Mr. Sciambra about it," he testified. "He called me about a year after Mr. Ferrie was in my place."

Q. "That would have been about 1964?"

A. "That's right, about 1964. I can't be sure of the exact date, but it was about a year later."

Sciambra had testified earlier that he did not join the district attorney's staff until 1966. The assistant district attorney also said the Garrison investigation into Kennedy's assassination did not begin until 1966.

"Would you consider it unusual," Dymond asked Roland, "that you got a call from Mr. Sciambra two years before the district attorney started his investigation of this case?"

"So I was off on the time," Roland snapped back.

The trial's most dramatic moment occurred the next day

when Abraham Zapruder, a Dallas dress manufacturer, took the witness stand for the prosecution.

Zapruder was the man who had made a home movie of the assassination. He had left his office the morning of November 22, 1963, to see the President's motorcade and, stationed on the grassy knoll in Dealey Plaza, he had filmed the event.

With Alcock asking the questions, part of the exchange with Zapruder went this way:

Q. "What did you see as you were taking the movie film?"

A. "I saw the approaching motorcade of the President, coming from Houston Street, turning left on Elm Street and then coming down toward the underpass. As the car approached where I was standing, I heard a shot. The President grabbed toward his throat. Then I heard a second shot, which struck Kennedy in the head. There was a lot of blood."

Q. "Were you able to see the President's reaction?"

A. "As I said, he grabbed himself, his hands toward his chest and throat, and leaned toward Jacqueline."

Q. "What happened when the second shot struck?"

A. "I saw his head practically explode. The back seemed to open up. There was blood all over, brains, everything came out."

Q. "At this time, what did you do?"

A. "I started toward my office. I was screaming, 'They shot him, they shot him!' Some of the people, they didn't know what had happened. I kept telling them, 'They've killed the President.'"

Zapruder's testimony set the stage for showing in the courtroom the color film. There were strong objections by Dymond. The film had been viewed many times, of course, by various officials, including the Warren Commission. Still photos of certain frames in the film had appeared in *Life* magazine. Never before, however, had the film been viewed by the public. Dymond feared, obviously, that the film, with its impact of the death of the President, could only hurt his client. But the judge ruled the film relevant.

The courtroom was packed with spectators and newsmen when the judge admonished the jury: "Okay, gentlemen of the jury, pay close attention to what you're about to see." Necks craned, chairs scraped, spectators crowded to one side of the courtroom.

The projector cast a picture about two feet square on the

screen, which was placed twenty feet from the jury in the front of the courtroom. The film began rolling.

It was a sunny day in Dallas and people lined the sidewalks as President Kennedy's motorcade turned right off of Main Street onto Houston Street. Heading north, the parade traveled perhaps two hundred feet before turning left on Elm Street, facing the Texas School Book Depository building.

Motorcycle officers preceded the President's limousine. Texas Governor and Mrs. John Connally sat in the jump seats behind the driver. The President and Mrs. Kennedy were in the back.

Kennedy, his brown hair making him clearly distinguishable, waved to the crowds to the right and left as the motorcade advanced down Elm toward the triple railway underpass. Jacqueline, in the pink suit she wore that day, sat at her husband's left side.

There is a road sign on the grassy knoll where Zapruder stood to shoot his film and, for a brief moment, the view of the President's car was blocked. Then the car came into sight again.

At that time, it could be seen that the President seemed to be reaching for his throat. As he slumped downward, he seemed to turn slightly to his left toward Jacqueline.

Mrs. Kennedy leaned forward to help her husband. A second, maybe two, maybe three, passed. Then, suddenly, another shot came. The President's head jerked violently. A pink spray erupted from his skull.

There was no sound accompanying the film, but it seemed as if one could hear the shot as it smashed viciously into the President's head.

"Oh, my God!" a newsman in the courtroom whispered. A woman spectator to his right cried, "Jesus, he's hit!"

After the fatal shot, it appeared that Mrs. Kennedy rose to her knees in the seat. There was a sudden flash of brilliant red— probably the roses she had been given that morning when she arrived at the Dallas airport. And then she clambered onto the trunk of the car reaching backward.

A Secret Service man leaped to the back of the car and caught her, pushing her back. And then the view of the car was blocked again, this time by a tree with white blossoms, and the motorcade moved toward the underpass and disappeared.

The lights in the courtroom came back on. Several spectators wiped tears from their eyes. Others sat quietly, as if struck speechless. There was for a moment absolute silence.

"If it is requested by the jury," Haggerty said, breaking the stillness, "we will show the film again." Dymond, who felt showing the film over prejudiced Shaw's defense, seemed stunned.

And then there was a recess. When court resumed, the judge announced that some of the jurors had requested that the film be shown again.

It was shown again. And then a third time—this time showing each frame individually, a process that took nearly forty minutes. Dymond, fearing the film's impact and noting the jury's interest, objected without success.

As the last frames were being shown, one of the jurors, Larry D. Morgan, stood up in the jury box and addressed the court: "Your honor . . . could we see the last half of the film again at regular speed?"

The entire film was shown again. In all, the film was shown five times that day. The first time, it was shown out of the jury's presence. At that time, Dymond objected to the showing on grounds that the film was irrelevant to the Shaw case, and that the film had not been under the constant control of Zapruder since it was taken.

Zapruder testified that the film he had was a copy of the original. He added that the copy had been in Garrison's custody until that day.

Garrison had told the jury in his opening address that he would attempt to prove with the film that Kennedy's fatal shot came from the front, and not the rear. He said the Zapruder film would show that Kennedy fell backward when he received the fatal shot. Those who viewed the film in the courtroom, however, differed as to whether the President fell forward, backward, or sideways.

Zapruder was not asked his opinion about where the shots came from.

In other testimony from witnesses who were in Dealey Plaza the day of the assassination, Garrison's assistants sought to buttress the allegation that bullets aimed at Kennedy came from more than one direction. These witnesses included Buell Wesley Frazier, the man who drove Oswald to the Texas Book Depository the day of the assassination. Frazier testified that he thought the shots came from the direction of the triple underpass in front of Kennedy.

Another was Robert H. West, county surveyor for Dallas County, who testified that he thought the shots came from the direction of the grassy knoll to the President's right front.

Frazier, a co-worker of Oswald, testified that he regularly drove Oswald to Irving, Texas every weekend so that Oswald could visit his wife, who was staying at the time with Mrs. Ruth Paine. Frazier said that on Thursday before the assassination on Friday, Oswald asked if he could travel with Frazier to Irving to pick up some curtain rods for his Dallas apartment. Frazier was surprised that Oswald wanted to go to Irving a day early, but he agreed to drive him.

The next morning, Friday, November 22, Oswald rode with Frazier back to the depository building. Frazier said Oswald carried with him a package wrapped in brown paper.

"Wnen I asked him what it was," Frazier added, "He told me it was the curtain rods. When we got to the depository building, Oswald got out and went inside, taking with him the package."

West, the surveyor, testified about the topographical features of Dealey Plaza and identified three state exhibits which were admitted into evidence. These included an aerial photograph of the plaza, a scale drawing of the parade route, and a mock-up model of the plaza.

West said he was in the plaza the day of the murder. He added that after the shots were fired there was a "commotion" in the area near the grassy knoll. He added, on cross-examination, that he did not know whether the commotion was caused by people scrambling to get out of the line of fire.

For the first time since he gave the opening address to the jury, Garrison appeared in court, but he stayed only twenty-eight minutes and left before the Zapruder film was shown.

The Zapruder film continued to play a large part in the trial. The very next day, for example, it was shown to the jury for the fifth, sixth and seventh times, and its reshowing brought the most raucous outbursts from attorneys for both the defense and the prosecution. At one point, several attorneys, the judge, and a number of bailiffs were all shouting and screaming at the same time.

The prosecution chose to show the film again during the

testimony of Lyndal Shaneyfelt, a photographic specialist with the FBI, and again when Dallas motorcycle officer Billy Joe Martin was on the stand. State's attorney Alvin Oser told the court the reason for showing the film during Shaneyfelt's testimony was so the agent could identify it as being similar to the film he worked with during his investigation of the assassination.

"There is no excuse for showing this film again," Dymond complained. "The jury has already seen it four times."

"I can't control how the state is going to present its case," Haggerty replied in overruling the defense objection.

Later, during Martin's testimony, the prosecution announced that it wanted to show the film again, so the jury could see that the officer was, in fact, in the Presidential motorcade the day Kennedy was killed. Martin's testimony centered around his version of what happened when Kennedy was fired upon.

"You mean they want to show it again?" Dymond asked, incredulity in his voice.

"You can't object now," Oser shouted.

"We can make our objections anytime we wish," defense attorney William Wegmann shouted back.

Bailiffs shouted for order as the courtroom erupted in near pandemonium with several lawyers and the judge shouting to be heard. Finally, Haggerty prevailed and told the court. "Now, let's not have a circus and all this confusion."

But it did resemble a circus. Spectators crowded into the aisles to see the viewing screen. Others stood on seats. "Down in front, you with the hat," a reporter hissed at a woman wearing a huge black hat, who knelt beside the prosecution table.

Chairs and tables rasped loudly on the courtroom floor as they were pulled or pushed by deputies and others straining to see the film. Candy and gum wrappers littered the floor where spectators and newsmen had thrown their refuse. One woman casually sipped from a can of soft drink as she watched the President being murdered.

And so, the film was shown again—the sixth time for the jury and the eighth time in all. Twice, up to that point, the film had been shown out of the jury's presence.

About halfway through the film, at the point where Kennedy received the fatal shot, Oser stopped the projector. The picture, showing a halo of blood around Kennedy's skull, remained on the screen. Dymond and Wegmann jumped to their feet, both objecting loudly.

"Conduct yourselves like gentlemen," Haggerty shouted. "Wait a minute, shut up this screaming."

Dymond cried that the prosecution was stopping the film for prejudicial purposes. He pointed out that Oser had insisted on showing the film again merely to determine the position of officer Martin in the motorcade. However, the frame in the film showing the halo of blood around Kennedy's skull—the most gruesome picture in the film—did not have Martin in it. Dymond argued that there was no legitimate reason for the state to stop on that particular frame.

For a few minutes, the jury was taken out while the attorneys argued over the objection. When the jurors came back into the courtroom, Oser announced that he wanted to run the film again.

"Run it again?" Dymond asked as if he could not believe it.

Dymond: "We object to another rerunning of this film and base our . . ."

Haggerty: "They (the prosecution) can show it a hundred times if they wish."

Dymond: "Your honor, may I reserve my bill for exception? You asked us not to interrupt you."

Dymond went on to object on grounds that the film was irrelevant and that its continual reshowing to the jury was prejudicial to Shaw. Haggerty overruled the objection and the film rolled again. Shaneyfelt and Martin were state witnesses. But the state did not ask their opinions on the question of the direction from which the shots were fired. The defense did ask.

Attorneys for the state then attempted unsuccessfully to keep FBI man Shaneyfelt from giving his views about where the shots came from. The prosecution had the agent testify at length about the FBI investigation of the murder, but did not ask him his opinion about where the shots originated.

Shaneyfelt's testimony on this point was important because it was in direct conflict with what Garrison said he would prove about Kennedy's assassination—that the fatal shot came from the front, from a rifle wielded by someone other than Oswald.

Martin testified that he could not tell from which direction the bullets which struck Kennedy came, but that they seemed to come from behind the President. He later found splotches of what appeared to be blood on his motorcycle and uniform.

FBI agent Shaneyfelt, a photographic specialist, testified that it was his opinion that President Kennedy received his fatal shot from the rear. He said his opinion was based on extensive and minute scrutiny of the Zapruder color film.

In other testimony during the day, former Dallas Sheriff's Deputy Robert D. Craig testified he saw Oswald run down a "grassy knoll" in Dealey Plaza fifteen minutes after Kennedy was shot and jump into a station wagon driven by another man. Craig said the driver appeared to be a Latin, with a muscular neck. He said he later went to police headquarters and, in the presence of Police Captain Will Fritts, identified Oswald as the man he had seen. He added: "Oswald said, 'That station wagon belongs to Mrs. Ruth Paine (a friend of the Oswalds), and don't try to get her involved in this.' He then leaned back in his chair and said, 'Now everyone will know who I am.'"

Craig had told his story in 1964 to the Warren Commission's attorneys. However, at that time, Police Captain Fritts testified to the commission that no sheriff's deputy ever identified Oswald as being the man who jumped into a station wagon after the assassination.

Craig was employed by the Dallas County sheriff from 1959 until 1967. He moved to New Orleans from Dallas after he quit the law enforcement profession and went to work for a car dealer named Willard Robertson. Dymond ask Craig if it was not true that Robertson was a member of "Truth and Consequences"—the group of New Orleans businessmen who contributed money to pay expenses incurred by Garrison in his investigation of the assassination.[2] Craig replied that he did not know, and denied inferences by Dymond that he had ever worked in New Orleans under an assumed name.

A number of other witnesses testified they were in Dealey Plaza the day of the murder. They told what they said they saw, or thought they saw. One witness, Mrs. Phillip L. Willis, said it was her opinion the fatal shot came from the front. Another witness,

---

2. Willard E. Robertson, one of the organizers of Truth and Consequences testified in January, 1971 that the fund raised $99,488.96. He said Garrison made no accounting as to how the money was spent. Governor John McKeithen contributed $10,000 from the state's "law enforcement fund," according to Garrison.

Mrs. Elizabeth Carolyn Walther of Dallas, said she saw two men, one of them holding a rifle, standing in a window in the Texas School Book Depository Building shortly before Kennedy's motorcade passed. She added that one of the men held a rifle and the other stood beside him.

Several other witnesses testified that there was considerable activity, after the fatal shot was fired, in the area of the grassy knoll to the President's right front. They added, however, that they were not sure whether the activity was caused by people running toward the shooting or away from it.

The fourth week of trial closed on a Saturday with the showing, for the third day in a row, of the Zapruder film. Whispers of "Oh, no, not again!" were heard in the press section as the prosecution announced that it wanted the jurors to witness the film for the eighth time.

Again, Haggerty overruled objections by defense attorneys and said he would allow the film to be seen again during the testimony of Mrs. Mary Moorman. Mrs. Moorman testified she took a picture of the presidential limousine as it passed through Dealey Plaza. State's attorney Alvin Oser said the Zapruder film would show clearly where Mrs. Moorman stood.

Dymond objected and pointed out that another picture, taken by someone else in Dealey Plaza, had already been shown to the jury and that it revealed where Mrs. Moorman was standing at the time. "Your honor," Dymond continued, "It has already been shown where Mrs. Moorman stood. We can see her in this photograph. There is no need to run the film again to find that out."

Again, it was like a circus in the courtroom as some spectators scrambled to get to a place where they could see the film as it was projected on the screen. There were loud cries of "down in front," as some spectators blocked the view of others. Through it all Clay Shaw was scarcely noticed.

By Saturday of the fourth week a total of fifteen state witnesses had been presented who did not even mention Shaw's name. In fact, Shaw's name had not been mentioned in testimony since early in the morning of Thursday, two days before.

He had faded into the background—as had the other major personality, Jim Garrison.

The state, in presenting witnesses to the assassination itself, argued that their testimony tended to corroborate the story told by Russo about the alleged conversation involving Shaw, Oswald and Ferrie. But actually, about all Garrison's men proved with his Dealey Plaza witnesses was that pandemonium reigned that November day in Dallas, and memories fade considerably with time and circumstance.

As the fifth week of trial began, the prosecution—in an abrupt unexplained change in strategy—delayed calling former Texas Governor John Connally as a witness. Connally, who had been wounded in the same burst of gunfire which killed Kennedy, and his wife were scheduled to testify for the state on Monday. However, on Sunday the Connallys disclosed that they had been advised by the state they would not be needed on Monday. As it later turned out, the Connallys were not called at all. Connally had said that while disagreeing with the Warren Commission's finding that he was wounded by a bullet that first hit Kennedy, he had agreed on the findings as they related to Oswald being a lone gunman who fired from the depositiory. Now, said Garrison's office, Connally had become a hostile witness. He would not be called.

The week opened with testimony from a pathologist for the prosecution who testified it was his "expert opinion" that Kennedy was killed by a shot from the front. Dr. John Nichols, a professor at the University of Kansas, said Kennedy's reactions to the shot—as recorded in the Zapruder film—were "comparable with a gunshot from the front."

The doctor's testimony was in direct conflict with that given by Shaneyfelt, the FBI agent, who said the fatal shot came from behind. Whereas Shaneyfelt had been qualified by the state as an expert in photography, Nichols was qualified by the state as an expert in pathology and forensic medicine.

Dymond objected to Nichols giving his opinion on the basis merely of looking at the Zapruder film. "Dr. Nichols is not a photographic expert," the Shaw attorney said. "He has been qualified as an expert in pathology. How can he look at a picture and say where the fatal shots came from?" The objection was overruled and the Zapruder film was shown—for the ninth time to the jury—so Nichols could identify it as being "similar" to the one he examined in making his judgment about the assassination.

The doctor, whose testimony extended over into the next day's proceedings, said he was suing the federal government for access to autopsy photographs of the President to "confirm" his opinions. He was also seeking to obtain the clothes Kennedy was wearing the day of the murder, but the federal government had refused to cooperate. On cross-examination, he admitted that his acquaintance with ballistics was limited.

"I want to know the truth, the whole truth, and nothing but the truth," Nichols said.

Also on Monday, the jury heard testimony by retired FBI agent Regis L. Kennedy, who testified that he searched unsuccessfully after Kennedy was slain for a man known only to him as "Clay Bertrand." The state, of course, alleged that this was an alias frequently used by Shaw.

Agent Kennedy's testimony was delayed for more than an hour while he consulted with U.S. Attorney General John Mitchell by phone.

On the day after the assassination, the erratic, hipster lawyer, Dean Andrews, had told the FBI he received a call from a "Clay Bertrand" shortly after Oswald was arrested in Dallas on charges of killing the President. He had then talked with FBI man Kennedy.

Andrews had told Kennedy that "Bertrand" asked him to arrange a legal defense of Oswald. Andrews later said he made this claim seeking personal notoriety—that it never occurred.

Kennedy had not been authorized by Attorney General Mitchell to answer questions about Andrews' call. He apparently relied on a federal statute which says no FBI agent or former agent may testify in state courts unless authorized to do so by the U.S. attorney general. Now Mitchell gave his permission. After returning to the stand Kennedy testified that he had indeed been investigating the assassination and his search for "Clay Bertrand" was in furtherance of that probe. He added, however, that he was never able to locate "Bertrand."

Testimony about Dealey Plaza witnesses then continued. One state witness, an electrical engineer, said he thought the gunfire which killed Kennedy came from the "grassy knoll" area to the President's right front.

"I was standing not more than ten or fifteen feet from the President when the fatal shot struck him in the head," said William Eugene Newman, Jr., of Dallas. Newman said it appeared that two shots struck Kennedy, the first one passing through his throat. The witness added: "When the car approached us, I saw that Kennedy had been shot. The President seemed to be looking about in the crowd to see where the shots were coming from. It was a cold stare as if he were looking right through me."

"The final shot struck him in the head, it looked like right above the ear. His ear came off. The wound turned white, then blood red. He seemed to stiffen up just like a board and fall over Mrs. Kennedy's lap."

For the first time since the trial began, Garrison participated in questioning of witnesses. Before this, his visits to the courtroom had been limited to about one a week. Edward F. Wegmann, one of Shaw's lawyers, criticized the district attorney for his infrequent appearances. "It's just to keep up his public image as superstar." Garrison, for his part, still withheld comment to the press.

It was the next day that Garrison's office confirmed rumors that he would not call Governor Connally to testify as a state's witness. "I understand Governor Connally has been giving interviews to television stations changing testimony he gave the Warren Commission," state's attorney Alvin Oser said. "We must now regard him as a hostile witness." He did not say what testimony Connally had repudiated. Reporters could find none.

There was another Dealey Plaza witness. Richard Randolph Carr of Dallas testified that three men, one of them a Latin, left the despository building minutes after Kennedy was shot, and fled in a station wagon. A fourth man, he testified, fled on foot. Carr said the FBI told him to keep his mouth shut about what he had seen.

The rest of the day's proceedings were taken up with efforts by the state to prove that Shaw had frequently used the alias "Clay Bertrand." Mrs. Jessie Parker, a hostess at the VIP Room at New Orleans International Airport, testified she saw Shaw sign the guest register as "Clay Bertrand" in December, 1966. She said this occurred when Shaw and a friend came into the VIP Room one day. The guest register was brought to court and exhibited to the jury.

The afternoon's proceedings were conducted out of the jury's presence. During the four-hour session, the court heard testimony from two more witnesses to try to show that Shaw had used an alias. The defense presented six witnesses—including Shaw, himself, in an unusual move—to rebut the prosecution's contention.

The state wanted to present testimony that would show Shaw had admitted, while being booked on charges of criminal conspiracy, that he used the alias "Clay Bertrand." New Orleans policeman, Aloysius J. Habighorst, testified while the jury was out that Shaw signed an arrest record which listed "Clay Bertrand" under the space reserved for aliases.

Shaw, dressed again in a dark blue suit with red tie, took the witness stand during the jury's absence to testify about circumstances surrounding his arrest and booking. He gripped his hands tightly in front of him as he answered questions put to him by the defense.

"Were you at any time asked whether you had an alias or any name other than Clay L. Shaw?" Dymond asked Shaw.

"I was certainly not," Shaw replied.

"Did you at any time tell anyone at Central Lockup (where the booking occurred) that you had an alias?" the lawyer asked.

"I did not," Shaw answered.

Dymond then offered into evidence a copy of the arrest record, which Shaw testified had been supplied to him by the booking clerk. The copy did not list any aliases. The state introduced the "original" record and it listed "Clay Bertrand" in the space for aliases.

Under the cross-examination by Prosecutor Alcock, Shaw testified that he had not been mistreated, threatened or intimidated in any way by representatives of the district attorney's office or the police department. At one point, he smiled broadly when asked if anyone in the district attorney's office had physically abused him, and answered:

"No one abused me. Certainly not."

At another point, Shaw evoked laughter from the crowded courtroom when he answered, in response to a question about whether he had trouble seeing over the three-foot high booking desk at Central Lockup: "No. That wasn't a problem for me."

Shaw, who is six feet four inches, was the tallest man in the courtroom except on the rare occasions when Garrison entered.

Shaw gave quick, crisp replies to Alcock's cross questions. Once, when asked repeatedly the same question—"Did you testify that officer Habighorst never asked any questions?"—he replied firmly: "That is my testimony."

Officer Habighorst's allegation that Shaw used the alias

"Bertrand" stirred a legal conflict. Judge Haggerty ruled that he would not permit the policeman's testimony to be admitted as evidence before the jury. The judge said he was ruling the testimony inadmissible on grounds that Shaw had not been allowed to have his attorney present at the time Habighorst allegedly asked Shaw if he had an alias. That was legal reason enough, the judge said. He went beyond that, however: "Even if officer Habighorst's testimony is true, and I doubt it very seriously, it would be violative of the defendant's rights because the officer did not advise Mr. Shaw that he had a right to remain silent."

Alcock, on his feet, objected strongly to Haggerty's expressed doubt about the truth of the officer's statement.

"I am asking for a mistrial," he said, his voice high-pitched, "because of the court's unsolicited, gratuitous remarks about the reliability of the state's witness."

"Take a writ," Haggerty shouted, denying the mistrial motion.

"I'll do that," Alcock shouted back, flushing red.

The clash came during the closing ten minutes of the day's session. Both the judge and Alcock lost their tempers.

"You're passing judgment on the state's witness, before the press, before the world?" Alcock asked, as if he could not believe his ears.

"The world can hear it," Haggerty replied. "I do not believe officer Habighorst."

Alcock announced he would apply at once to the Louisiana Supreme Court for the writ of certiorari. That meant, in effect, that the state would ask the high court to review Haggerty's refusal to grant a mistrial and to rule if the Judge was correct in his refusal. Such an application by the prosecution is usually done whenever the state feels a judge has abused his authority. However, in practice, such writs have rarely been granted by the Louisiana Supreme Court.

In effect, what the state was asking was that the Louisiana high court order Haggerty to declare a mistrial, on the basis of the judge's comments on Habighorst's testimony. This would mean that this trial would end at once and that the prosecution could bring a second trial at a later date. The jury, of course, had not heard Haggerty's words.

The next morning, the Supreme Court refused the state's request. Six of the seven high court justices signed an order rejecting the prosecution's application for a review of Haggerty's action.

After Haggerty announced receipt of the appellate court's ruling, Alcock asked the Judge to reconsider his ruling on Habighorst's testimony. Haggerty replied: "I have reconsidered and I've made my decision. The evidence is still inadmissible."

The state rested its case, and by doing so left no doubt that it had decided not to present testimony relating to the autopsy photographs and X-rays of President Kennedy which Garrison had claimed was so vital.

Garrison had waged a long fight to get access to the autopsy material from the National Archives in Washington. And a Washington judge had ruled earlier in the week that the material should be shown to state experts who would appear at the Shaw trial. Garrison had put on all the direct proof the jury would hear.

Now it was Shaw's turn.

The defense issued a subpoena for Governor Connally. But he was never called.

The first action in court by the defense was to move for a directed verdict of not guilty. The lawyers for Shaw asked the judge to declare Shaw innocent, rather than asking a jury to decide. In arguing for a directed verdict, Dymond said the state had failed to prove its charge that Shaw conspired with Oswald and Ferrie to kill Kennedy. The defense attorney dealt at length on the testimony of Russo, and explained: "On cross-examination of Russo, I asked him if it was his testimony that he sat in on a conspiratorial meeting where the assassination of President Kennedy was discussed. His reply was, 'No, I never said anything about any conspiracy. I didn't sit in on any conspiracy.' I asked him if he heard anyone agree to do anything unlawful and he said he did not. Russo testified he wasn't sure who was the object of the conversation he heard—Castro or Kennedy.

"In the words of the state's own witness, this alleged discussion was nothing but a 'bull session', such as he had heard Ferrie conduct on many occasions.

"Now, your honor, President Kennedy was on certain occasions extremely unpopular because of some of his policies. And there were many bull sessions across the country where people expressed violent disagreement with the President. But it would be ludicrous and ridiculous to brand each of these bull sessions an unlawful conspiracy to commit an assassination."

Dymond argued that the state is required by law to prove that Shaw and at least one other person had an agreement to commit the murder of Kennedy. This he said, the prosecution failed to do.

"Your honor," Dymond added, "this strikes at the heart, the very core of what the state is required to prove. We have come to the absolute void, the absolute failure of the state."

Alcock responded that the state acknowledged the complexity of the conspiracy law and realized it must prove an agreement existed between Shaw and his alleged co-conspirators. The state's attorney added: "The law of conspiracy is complicated and somewhat broad—very, very broad. But the words which Perry Raymond Russo used to characterize the meeting he attended are irrelevant to the court. The fact that he called it a 'bull session' is something, of course, which may not be irrelevant to the jury.

"Russo's personal appreciation of what transpired at the meeting is not material at this point. And in any event, a meeting of the minds can be demonstrated in many ways—not just verbally, but in actions." It was a critical argument between prosecution and defense, and yet Garrison was absent.

Haggerty announced that he would consider the defense motion for directed verdict and rule the next morning. If granted, the trial would end right there, with Clay Shaw free.

But the trial did not end right there. The next morning, Haggerty denied the motion. There was a smattering of applause and a chorus of "yeas" from a few people in the spectator's section. Haggerty did not comment on the brief demonstration but immediately recessed the court. The judge explained that he wanted to give the press a chance to report his decision.

Now Dymond and his associates had Clay Shaw's liberty in their hands. After the recess, the defense began presentation of its case. Marina Oswald Porter, widow of Lee Harvey Oswald, was the first witness called for Shaw. Mrs. Porter, twenty-seven, a native Russian, had remarried since Oswald's death. Her husband, Kenneth Porter, accompanied her as she arrived at the Orleans Parish Courthouse to give her testimony.

All eyes in the courtroom turned toward the door when

Dymond announced that the first witness for Shaw would be Mrs. Porter—wife of the man the Warren Commission said killed Kennedy. Garrison had said Shaw and her husband were co-conspirators in Kennedy's death.

Marina, walking beside a deputy, came hesitantly down the courtroom aisle. After taking the oath, the slightly built young woman paused to take off a blue raincoat and drape it across the railing around the witness chair. For a moment her hands fluttered about the collar of her gray dress and smoothed her hair. Then, suddenly, her face brightened in a broad smile directed at no one in particular and Dymond's examination began.

Speaking in a quiet voice and with a slight accent, Marina told of her life with Oswald while they lived in New Orleans. She said that so far as she knew her late husband had never known Shaw.

With a shy smile from time to time, she contradicted testimony by Russo in regard to his allegation that Oswald was a roommate of Ferrie's. Oswald spent his nights at home—except for one night in jail—during the months the family lived in New Orleans during the fall of 1963, she swore.

At one point, she asked for a drink of water and drank from a paper cup. She paused frequently, a finger pressed to her lips, to search for the correct word to answer a question. She did not understand many of the words used by the attorneys and once evoked laughter when Alcock told the court he was trying to test the witness's credibility.

Marina asked, laughing, "You're trying to test my what?"

Under Alcock's cross-examination, she said that Oswald treated her badly while they were married, that he seldom told her what he was doing or talked with her about anything. She said he threatened her physically on several occasions.

With Dymond asking questions on direct examination, she testified this way:

Q. "Did you and Lee Harvey Oswald have any friends in New Orleans?"

A. "No sir, just his relatives. His aunt and uncle and their children."

Q. "Was he absent from home any nights?"

A. "Just one night when he was in jail."

Q. "Did you ever know, or were you familiar with the name 'Clay Shaw'?"
A. "No."
Q. "When did you first hear that name?"
A. "When this trial began."
Q. "Did you hear the name 'Clay Bertrand' or 'Clem Bertrand'?" (These were the names the state alleged Shaw used as aliases).
A. "No."
Q. "When did you first hear of either of these Bertrand names?"
A. "From the newspapers."

Mrs. Porter, easily led into conflicting testimony at times, corrected herself on several occasions, explaining that she had not understood the questions. She responded many times by saying she didn't know or couldn't recall answers to questions.

She testified that her husband had used aliases on at least two occasions, once when he ordered his rifle and once when he rented an apartment in Dallas, shortly before Kennedy's assassination.

At times, Mrs. Porter seemed ill at ease in the witness chair. She squirmed and fidgeted and tugged at the hem of her skirt. When a recess was called, she sat quietly and smiled at the jurors as they filed past her chair on the way out of the courtroom. During the recess, she chatted with bailiffs as she sat in one of the jury seats.

Marina testified that her late husband had owned a rifle and that she had seen him clean it numerous times while they lived in New Orleans. She added that she did not see the weapon again after they moved to Irving, Texas, just outside Dallas.

Testifying in response to questions by Prosecutor Alcock, she said Oswald admitted to her that he once attempted to shoot former General Edwin A. Walker. Speaking of her husband's political activities she said he had frequently passed out leaflets in support of Castro. "He was quite excited," she said. "He liked to shout about how brave they were."

Also during the first day of the defense's case, an FBI agent testified that the bullet fragments recovered from the presidential limousine the day Kennedy was killed came from Oswald's rifle. Afterwards, business associates of Shaw's testified he was busy during the fall of 1963, when the state alleges he conspired to kill Kennedy, obtaining leases for the proposed new International Trade Mart, of which Shaw was managing director until his retirement.

The FBI agent, Robert A. Frazier, testified he made extensive ballistics tests in connection with his part in the assassination probe. He added that these tests proved that bullets recovered in the limousine came from the Mannlicher-Carcano bolt-action rifle found in the Texas School Book Depository the day of the assassination. The Warren Commission concluded that Oswald had ordered the rifle from a mail order house, under the name of Alek Hidell. Garrison, in his opening address to the jury, had promised Frazier would be qualified by the prosecution as an FBI expert in ballistics and would testify for the state. However, Frazier was never called by the prosecution and Garrison gave no explanation. The defense called him to give his expert testimony.

What the special agent had to say was a blow to the state. He struck at the prosecution's contention that more than one person was shooting at Kennedy and said there was no evidence that shots were fired at the President from in front.

Frazier testified that three empty cartridge cases were found in the depository and that ballistics tests showed these were fired from the bolt-action rifle owned by Oswald. The cartridges were found on the sixth floor of the book depository building, in the spot where the Warren Commission said Oswald stood to fire at Kennedy.

Shaw's business associates, including his former secretary and the president of the International Trade Mart, Lloyd J. Cobb, testified for the defense about a trip Shaw made in November, 1963, to the West Coast. It was this trip that the state alleged Shaw took to establish an alibi for himself on the day of the President's assassination.

The defense witnesses testified that there was nothing unusual about the trip, that it was made at the invitation of a Portland, Oregon, firm, and that it had been planned for several weeks prior to November 22, the date of the President's murder.

Cobb testified that during August, September and October of 1963, he was in constant touch with Shaw because they were trying to arrange for financing of the proposed new International Trade Mart building, which had since been constructed.

The testimony from business associates was designed, in part, to contradict that from prosecution witnesses who claimed they saw Shaw in Clinton, Louisiana in late August or early September of 1963 with Oswald and Ferrie.

The next day Frazier, of the FBI, continued his testimony about his part in the assassination investigation and told the court that shots which turned Kennedy's Dallas motorcade into a nightmare of blood and horror came from the rear.

In general, the agent's testimony buttressed the conclusions reached by the Warren Commission. With the testimony, Shaw's lawyers began what they had said originally would be unnecessary—a defense of the conclusions reached by the Warren Commission. Dymond continued to argue throughout the trial that what happened in Dallas November 22, 1963, and what the Warren Commission concluded about those events, was irrelevant to the Shaw case. But he knew that the showing of the Zapruder film made it relevant.

Garrison, of course, had contended from the first that the President was shot by several persons, and that the fatal shot came from the front. This, in fact, was the way Shaw, Oswald and Ferrie planned it, Garrison was contending.

The defense now felt that if it could show that Garrison was in error about how the President was shot, this one contradiction could help disprove the district attorney's entire theme.

Because of this, Shaw's lawyers had to defend the same conclusions reached by the Warren Commission—something they had hoped to avoid. They had to show that Kennedy was killed by Oswald, acting alone, and that there was no evidence to indicate a conspiracy.

During the second day of the defense's case, Mrs. Ruth Paine, a kindergarten teacher, also appeared. It was she who started the chain of events which led to Oswald's being hired as a file order clerk at the Texas School Book Depository. Mrs. Paine, of Irving, Texas, had befriended Marina Oswald during the summer and fall of 1963. Marina was living in the Paine home at the time of the assassination. Oswald, who was estranged from Marina at the time, lived in a Dallas rooming house but commuted to Irving on weekends.

A tall, slender, dark-eyed brunette, Mrs. Paine wore a blue suit with matching blue coat and a single strand of pearls as she testified about her acquaintance with the Oswalds.

"Lee found it difficult to get a job," she said, "because he could not drive and my efforts to teach him failed."

Mrs. Paine, thirty-six, added that she learned that the depository building might be hiring workers and placed a call to the firm's management to confirm this. She said she then told Oswald about a job opportunity at the depository and he went the next day to apply.

The state had intimated that Oswald got the job at the depository in the furtherance of a conspiracy to shoot at Kennedy from the building as the President rode by.

The defense, on the other hand, sought to show that Oswald got his job weeks before it was known Kennedy was coming to Dallas, and that Oswald chose the depository job by chance, not design.

But it was FBI man, Frazier, whose testimony gave the defense's second day its greatest drama. The FBI agent said there was not a shred of physical evidence to indicate the shots came from anywhere but above and behind the President. He added that his part in the exhaustive federal probe of the murder convinced him that the shots which killed Kennedy came from the sixth floor of the Texas School Book Depository building, to the right rear of the Presidential limousine. The acoustical characteristics of the high-speed bullets used to shoot the President could have convinced witnesses that shots were being fired from Kennedy's front. The shots would have been "relatively easy" to make, although they would have been complicated somewhat by the fact that the target was moving. This movement could have been compensated for, however, by "leading" the target by six inches.

He also said that one bullet passed through Kennedy's body, from back to front, nicking the knot of his necktie. This bullet could have been the same one which struck Governor Connally who was riding in the jump seat in front of Kennedy.

Frazier added that it was virtually impossible to prove beyond all doubt the conclusions he reached. But there was no physical evidence, he declared, to indicate anything to the contrary. There was considerable evidence, he added, to support his conclusions. The agent, who had twenty-six years of experience with the FBI, testified under direct examination by Dymond:

Q. "Do the bullets used to shoot the President have any acoustical characteristics of a high-speed projectile that travels faster than sound?"

A. "Yes, these bullets travel about 2,600 feet per second, and sound travels about 1,100 feet per second. As a result, when a person stands in front of the gunfire, he will hear a report— a sort of sonic boom—made by the bullet itself, before he hears the explosion of the gunpowder."

Q. "Would you say this sonic noise can be confused with the gunpowder explosion?"

A. "Yes, it is easily confused unless you are listening particularly for it and unless you have been specially trained to hear it."

Q. "Would you say it was a difficult shot to make from the sixth floor window of the Texas School Book Depository building?"

A. "It would not be a difficult shot with the Mannlicher-Carcano rifle."

Q. "Why is that?"

A. "The effect of the scope of the rifle would be to reduce the distance by about three-fourths or about eighty feet in this instance. It would be a relatively easy shot."

Q. "Did you find anything inconsistent with the theory that all the shots fired at the motorcade came from the sixth floor of the Texas School Book Depository Building?"

A. "No sir. There was nothing inconsistent that I found to indicate that the shots came from anywhere but above and behind."

When the sixth and final week of trial began, the first witness for the defense was Lieutenant Colonel Pierre A. Finck, one of three doctors who performed an autopsy on President Kennedy's body. Finck, an Army pathologist, was aided by two Navy doctors when the autopsy was performed the night of November 22 and the morning of November 23.

Finck testified that Kennedy was definitely shot from behind—once in the back and once in the head. The first bullet, Finck told the jury, entered through the President's back, near the top, and nicked his necktie as it passed through the throat. The second shot, the pathologist said, entered Kennedy's head in the lower center portion and blew out the top right half of his skull, leaving a hole about five inches in diameter.

"It was the second shot, fired from above and behind," which killed the President, Finck added.

With the testimony from Finck, who was the only witness presented during the day, the state and defense continued to wrangle over conclusions reached by the Warren Commission.

Finck testified this way, with Dymond asking the questions:

Q. "Do you have a definite opinion as to whether the projectile which exploded the skull came from the front or the back?"

A. "I have a definite opinion. My firm opinion is that the bullet entered the back of the head and exited at the right top of the head."

Q. "Was there any evidence that the President was hit by more than one shot in the head?"

A. "No, there was not."

Q. "What is your opinion as to the direction of the bullet?"

A. "The bullet definitely struck in the back of the head, disintegrated—which is often the case when a bullet of high velocity goes through bone. This caused many fragments which we found in the President's brain."

Q. "Is this your honest, professional opinion, or have you been influenced, in any way, by the supposed desires or wishes of anyone in government?"

A. "My opinion is an honest, professional opinion."

Finck performed the autopsy on the President, along with Dr. J. Thornton Boxswell and Dr. J. J. Humes, at the National Naval Medical Center at Bethesda, Maryland about seven hours after the assassination. At that time, the President's widow, his brother Robert F. Kennedy, and several advisers were waiting in another part of the hospital.

The direct examination of Finck lasted only about an hour and a half. But cross-examination by Oser lasted the rest of the day. The prosecution attorney's examination largely concerned details of the autopsy procedure. Several times, Haggerty admonished: "Move on to something else—you covered that."

By day's end, the jurors were obviously tired. Several dozed in their chairs as Oser, Dymond and the Judge swapped angry comments. Once, Oser told Dymond: "Now you're getting cute."

"Control yourself, Mr. Oser!" Haggerty shouted.

Finck, a graduate of the University of Geneva in Switzerland, spoke with an accent and testified in a precise, deliberate and pedantic manner, frequently spelling words and breaking dates down into individual numerals.

Under cross-examination, the doctor said he had not seen photographs taken of the President while the autopsy was being made, until some time after he had made his report. He added that he did not have the photos in his possession at the time he testified before the Warren Commission in 1964.

"Why didn't you?" Oser asked.

"I was told," Finck replied, "that it was the wish of the attorney general, who was then Robert F. Kennedy."

At one point, during a close examination by Oser, Finck asked Haggerty if he could make a statement. The Judge, flushing red, replied: "No sir, you're not running the show. You may answer the question. You can't volunteer information. You can only give an answer to a question and then explain."

Time and again, Oser asked the court to instruct Finck "to answer yes or no and then explain."

Finck rarely gave a "yes" or "no" answer and told Oser once that he had been "forced" to answer in a certain way. "I'd like the record to show," Oser told Haggerty, "that the witness was not forced to do anything."

On the next day, hip-talking attorney Dean Andrews, Jr., whose conflict with Garrison led to his conviction on perjury charges, testified that he lied about being asked to represent Oswald because he thought he saw a chance to become famous. Andrews, a former Jefferson Parish assistant district attorney, was called by the defense to rebut prosecution inferences that Shaw—as Clay Bertrand—called Andrews to obtain counsel for Oswald. It was a pathetic performance. Andrews was the man who first introduced the name "Clay Bertrand" into the Kennedy assassination probe. On the stand, Andrews said the story he told the FBI in 1963, just after Kennedy's death, was a "lot of bull."

"I can't give you any explanation for it," the portly lawyer told the jury. "I might have believed it myself at the time but it was just a figment of my imagination. I thought that whoever went to Dallas (to defend Oswald on charges of murdering Kennedy) would be a famous man." Then, somewhat sadly, he added:

"I might have been famous, too—as something other than a perjurer."

Wearing dark eye-shades and wiping perspiration from his brow, he told the jury he had been living a lie since he first concocted the story in 1963 that a "Clay Bertrand" called him, seeking legal counsel for Oswald.

"I started it and I couldn't quit," he added. "I was carrying on a farce and I've been continuing the fiasco up until now."

FBI agent Regis Kennedy had testified earlier that after the assassination Andrews told agents the story that he had been called by a man known only to him as "Clay Bertrand" and asked to go to Dallas to defend Oswald. That same day Oswald was shot to death in Dallas by Jack Ruby. Agent Kennedy had told the court the FBI conducted an unsuccessful search for a "Clay Bertrand" but finally dropped the search after questioning Andrews again.

In lengthy, disjointed testimony before the Shaw jury, Andrews said that he did receive a call, while in a New Orleans hospital, the day after Kennedy's death. That call, he said, was from a French Quarter tavern owner and had nothing to do with Kennedy or Oswald. Later, Andrews said, he convinced himself that the call did involve Oswald and he summoned FBI agent Kennedy to tell him about it.

Andrews said he had another purpose in calling the FBI—to tell them about the times he had in fact done legal work for Oswald when the accused assassin lived in New Orleans. Before he realized what was happening, Andrews testified, he had involved the tavern owner, although he had not given the FBI the tavern owner's name.

Andrews had told his story to the Warren Commission and testified twice before the Orleans Parish Grand Jury. It was in connection with his grand jury testimony that Andrews was later indicted and convicted for perjury.

"I've never identified anyone as Clay Bertrand," Andrews now told the jury. "I used the name 'Clay Bertrand' as a cover name for Eugene Davis (the tavern owner who had called him in the hospital). I didn't deliberately lie. I might have overloaded my mouth with the feeling that I was important because I was a witness. The only explanation is that my mouth went ahead of my brain."

Andrews said that when the FBI asked him to name the man who called him to represent Oswald, "It suddenly dawned on me that I was about to involve an innocent man (Davis) in a lot of bull. So, I used the cover name 'Clay Bertrand'. Remember, I was in the hospital at the time, under sedation, and I elected a course that has been whiplashing on me ever since. I can't stop it. No matter which course I take now, I either get indicted or charged."

With Alcock asking the questions, on cross-examination, Andrews answered this way:

Q. "Then your testimony before the Warren Commission (which investigated President Kennedy's death) was not true?"

A. "It was page after page of bull."

Q. "You mean page after page of lies, don't you?"

A. "If you want to put it like that, okay."

Q. "You were under oath at that time, were you not?"

A. "I elected not to involve an innocent person (Davis) in a matter like this. I did the best I could with what I had. And here I sit."

Later, when asked where he got the name "Clay Bertrand," Andrews testified that Davis had once been introduced facetiously to him as Bertrand. This took place, the witness said, at a wedding between two homosexuals many years ago.

"I knew Gene Davis at the time, had known him for a long time," Andrews said. "But he was at this reception for these fags (homosexuals) who were getting married.

"Everyone was already there when I arrived, eating those sandwiches, getting all that booze. I was walking around, taking it all in, when this girl, Big Joe, says to me, 'meet Clay Bertrand.' She meant Gene Davis.

"Well, I knew he wasn't Clay Bertrand. I knew him as Gene Davis. I had been introduced myself as 'Algonquin P. Calhoun,' but people knew me as Dean Andrews and they knew it was a joke.

"Of all the names I could have picked out of the air to give the FBI, I had to pick 'Clay Bertrand'. If I had it to do over again, I'd pick the name 'John Jones.' "

Andrews, who was on the stand most of the day, was accompanied by his attorney, who sat by the witness chair as his client testified. Andrews testified under direct examination by Dymond that Shaw definitely did not call him in November, 1963, requesting legal counsel for Oswald.

Q. "Have you ever received a call from Clay Shaw?"
A. "No."
Q. "Have you ever known Clay Shaw?"
A. "No."
Q. "When was the first time you ever saw Mr. Shaw?"
A. "When I saw his name in the papers as a result of the investigation."

Andrews added that he saw Oswald about four or five times in the fall of 1963 when Oswald came to his office seeking representation in legal matters.

"The first time I saw him (Oswald), he was in the company of this mex (a person of Mexican descent) and these three swishes, uh, that is these three people," Andrews testified.

At this point, Judge Haggerty admonished Andrews to "use the legal term for swishes instead of trying to make a comedy out of your testimony."

Chastened, Andrews added, "They (the three swishes) appeared to be homosexuals from the way they walked."

The attorney said he never did any legal work for Oswald because "the man never could raise the twenty-five dollar fee that was required."

"He'd make promises," Andrews said. "One day I saw him downtown (in New Orleans) handing out chits—you know, leaflets, having something to do with Cuba, help Cuba or something.

"I picked one of the leaflets up and then dropped it like a hot potato. I wasn't interested in helping Cuba. I asked him if he had my fee and he said he didn't."

Andrews added that there was nothing unusual about Oswald, explaining: "I didn't pay any minute attention to Oswald because I didn't know he was going to kill the President. He was just a walk-in client to me. The only oddball thing was that the mex was always hanging around him every time I saw him."

Later, under cross-examination, Andrews declined to answer numerous questions about his testimony before the Warren Commission and the Orleans Parish Grand Jury. He repeatedly told the court: "I decline to answer that on the grounds that my answer might, could, would, may, somehow, someway, link me up with a chain of circumstances that could be used against me or tend to incriminate me."

Andrews said he was fearful that his answers might interfere with his appeal of the perjury conviction secured against him.

At first, Haggerty ruled that Andrews was within his legal rights to refuse to answer the prosecuting attorney's questions. Alcock complained bitterly, "The state is being handcuffed. The defense has already got what they wanted from this witness. Now the witness claims privileges and the state cannot show how this man has vacillated on previous occasions about his testimony."

Andrews' attorney, Michael Baron, replied that the state was "being handcuffed by the constitutional safeguards provided by the Fifth Amendment to the U.S. Constitution." After a recess, however, Haggerty reversed his previous ruling and said he would order Andrews to answer. It was then that the witness told the jury he had lied in his original story to the FBI, the Warren Commission and the grand jury.

"Would it be fair to say that we could take your entire testimony before the Warren Commission and dump it into the trash can because it is a lie?" Alcock asked Andrews.

"Some of it was square," Andrews replied. He had told the truth when it related to the incidents involving Oswald's visits to his office in the summer of 1963, he said. He then volunteered: "I was the first critic of the Warren Report. I got in there on the band wagon early. I said I didn't think this boy (Oswald) was capable of doing it (the assassination), nor was his instrument (rifle) capable."

During the early part of his testimony, Andrews sprinkled slang expressions right and left. Garrison, he said, "had the right ha-ha but the wrong ho-ho." And he evoked laughter from the spectators and jury, and joined in the laughter. But later, when he admitted living a lie since 1963, he seemed a sad and somewhat tragic figure.

When finally excused from the witness stand, he softly whistled "whew," wiped perspiration from his head with a forefinger and smiled broadly at the jury.

Then, stepping down, he patted a deputy on the back and walked out of the courtroom.

The defense now turned to the testimony by a handwriting expert, Charles Andrews Appel, Jr., of Washington, in an effort to prove it was not Shaw who signed the name "Clay Bertrand" to a guest register in 1966 at the New Orleans Airport.

Appel, who retired from the FBI in 1948 after twenty-four years with the bureau, testified that the writing in the register did not match the defendant's penmanship at all. His testimony was aimed at countering that of the state's witness who said it was Shaw who signed the book.

Under cross-examination, Appel—who years before had been credited with helping solve the case against Richard Bruno Hauptmann, the man convicted of kidnapping Charles Lindbergh's son in the 1930's—said he did not ordinarily testify for the defense against law enforcement agencies. But he added: "But there comes a time when I feel that an injustice would be done if I did not render my services. Therefore, I felt it my civic duty to testify in this case. I felt it was needful for me to intervene in this case."

Much of the defense testimony during the rest of the day was aimed at an attempt to discredit the prosecution's star witness, Perry Raymond Russo. Lieutenant Edward Mark O'Donnell, a seventeen-year veteran with the New Orleans Police Department, said Russo told him that he (Russo) was under "considerable pressure" from Garrison and that he was afraid Garrison would charge him with lying under oath.

"I told Mr. Garrison about Russo telling me that he had never seen Shaw in David Ferrie's apartment," the lieutenant testified, "but Russo denied he told me that."

Another defense witness, free-lance writer James R. Phelan, pictured Russo as a man fearful of telling the truth because of what Garrison might do to him.

"Russo told me he felt trapped," said Phelan, who wrote critically of Garrison's investigation in an article for *The Saturday Evening Post* in 1967. "He said he was sorry he had come forward as a witness. But he added that if he tried to change his story (and tell the truth) Mr. Garrison would probably charge him with perjury, clobber him, discredit him and cause him to lose his job."

Phelan said he interviewed Russo at length in preparation for an article which was published in *The Saturday Evening Post* in May, 1967, entitled "Rush to Judgment in New Orleans." In that article, Phelan said Russo had told contradictory stories— once in his first interview with assistant District Attorney Andrew

Sciambra, and another one in court, at the preliminary hearing for Shaw. The second story, Phelan said, was told only after Russo had been hypnotized by prosecution representatives and "shot" with a "truth serum."

Phelan said he questioned Sciambra about the memorandum which the assistant district attorney wrote for Garrison after interviewing Russo. Nowhere in that memo, Phelan said, did Sciambra mention the alleged conspiratorial meeting which Russo later claimed he overheard. With Dymond asking the questions, Phelan testified in this way:

Q. "Did you ask Mr. Sciambra why his memorandum on his interview did not contain any mention about an assassination plot? What was Mr. Sciambra's reply?"

A. "He said that I didn't know what the hell I was talking about. He stated that I was all wrong about there not being any mention of the plot."

Q. "Was there any other conversation between you?"

A. "Yes. I told him I would bet my job with *The Saturday Evening Post* against his job with the district attorney's office that no mention of the plot was included in the memorandum."

Q. "Was there any response to this proposal?"

A. "I didn't get a bet."

Q. "What else did you tell Mr. Sciambra?"

A. "I told him that if he had heard of an assassination plot, surely he would have put it into his notes. I found it absolutely incredible that he could interview Russo, while investigating the crime of the century, and then come back and write a thirty-five hundred word memorandum about it and not even mention the crime."

Phelan said Russo later told him that if Garrison knew what he (Russo) had told a priest, the district attorney "would go through the ceiling."

"Mr. Russo then told me," Phelan testified, "that he would like to sit down with Shaw and make sure of his identification of the man. I replied, 'For God's sake, you got up in court and testified that this is the man who talked about killing the President. Now you want to meet with him to see if he is the man.' "

Later, Phelan said, "Russo told me he was afraid to meet with Shaw because he felt such a meeting would convince him he was wrong, and he added: 'If I found that out, what could I do? I could go on the run. I could go out to California or San Francisco and become a beatnik, but I couldn't run from myself.' " Under cross-examination, Phelan acknowledged that he once told Russo that he would be a "patsy" if Shaw were acquitted of the charges against him. "I told Russo that Mr. Garrison had a way of busting those who didn't go along with his theories. Later, after my story appeared, I was advised by my lawyers not to come back to New Orleans because of the ruthless way Mr. Garrison had of dealing with people. But I did come down and the first thing I did was go around and tell Garrison's friends, 'Go tell Big Jim I'm in town and I'm not hiding from anybody.' "

In other testimony during the day, Arthur Jefferson Biddison, a long-time friend of Shaw's, contradicted a prosecution witness's testimony that letters addressed to a "Clay Bertrand" were delivered for Shaw at the Biddison home. A New Orleans realtor, Biddison said he took care of Shaw's mail in the summer and fall of 1966 while Shaw was in Europe and at no time did mail arrive for anyone named "Clay Bertrand."

Then, Shaw himself took the stand the following day. Dressed in a conservative business suit and holding black-rimmed glasses in his hand, Shaw directly faced the jury as he testified. Measuring the effect of his words, he denied having anything to do with plotting to kill the President. He said he had met Kennedy personally on two occasions and voted for him in the 1960 election.

Shaw said he had always been a Democrat and had never even joked about killing Kennedy.

"Did you ever at any time want President Kennedy to die?" Dymond asked Shaw.

"Certainly no," the defendant replied, looking straight at the jury.

Shaw, of course, had maintained all along that he was not guilty of the charges brought against him by Garrison. But it was still a dramatic moment when he took the stand as the last witness for the defense. Everyone already knew he would deny knowing Oswald and Ferrie but this did not detract from his saying it. A hush of expectancy settled over the courtroom.

Dymond asked the questions:

Q. "Have you ever known Lee Harvey Oswald?"

A. "No, I never have."

Q. "Have you ever had any conversation with him?"

A. "No, never."

Q. "I show you a picture which purports to be a photograph of the late David W. Ferrie and ask you if you've ever seen this man."

A. "No."

Q. "Have you ever been to a party with these men?"

A. "I have not."

Then, turning to the instances when Shaw contended he had met the President, Dymond asked:

Q. "Do you recall the day President Kennedy visited New Orleans?"

A. "Yes."

Q. "Did you have any special part in welcoming the President?"

A. "Yes. I was invited by Congressman Hale Boggs to be a member of the reception committee which met the President's plane when he came here in 1962 to dedicate the Nashville Avenue Wharf."

Q. "Did you accept the invitation to sit on that committee?"

A. "I did."

Q. "Prior to the President coming to New Orleans, had you ever met him?"

A. "Yes, I had."

Q. "And when was that?"

A. "This was in the spring of 1962 when former New Orleans Mayor Chep Morrison was appointed by President Kennedy as ambassador to the Organization of American States. Mr. Morrison was kind enough to invite me to come to Washington to be present when he was sworn in for that position and I met the President at that time."

Q. "Did you have any ill feeling toward President Kennedy?"

A. "Certainly not."

Q. "Were you a supporter of President Kennedy?"

A. "I was."

Q. "When you say you supported him, what do you mean?"

A. "I voted for him."

Shaw denied ever attending parties such as those described by prosecution witnesses Russo and Spiesel. He also denied that he had ever met either of the men and said he had never seen them before they appeared in court to testify against him.

Shaw denied every other allegation made against him during the trial. He had never been to Clinton, Louisiana. He had never used the alias "Clay Bertrand," and he had never signed his name as "Clay Bertrand." Asked if he had ever used an alias, Shaw replied that he had not but that he once used the pseudonym "Allen White" when he authored a play. The pseudonym combined the maiden names of his grandmothers, Shaw explained.

Now, the defense closed its case. The state began putting on rebuttal witnesses. A New Orleans couple testified that they saw Shaw and Ferrie together at the airport in the summer of 1964. Mr. and Mrs. Nicholas Tadin said they saw the men when they went to the airport to pick up their sixteen-year-old son, who was taking flying lessons from Ferrie.

Tadin acknowledged under cross-examination that he lied often but insisted that he was "telling the truth now." His wife said she had not wanted to appear in court to testify but did so because of her husband.

"I didn't want to get involved," Mrs. Tadin added.

Tadin, asked when he first approached Garrison's office with his information, replied: "I contacted them for the first time this morning."

"Why did you wait so long?" the witness was asked.

"I didn't want to get involved," Tadin replied. "But I was sitting at home last night, watching the news on television and they told about the Shaw trial. I said to myself, 'Hell, this ain't true—so I figure I'll call and tell what I know.' "

Once, while Tadin was testifying, a shouting match erupted between defense and prosecuting counsel. The state argued that Dymond was interrupting the witness but Dymond contended that Tadin was answering before the question was asked.

"I know your emotions get aroused at certain times," Haggerty admonished the lawyers, "But let's keep it cool."

"Do you think I'm misleading the court?" Dymond asked, his face flushing in anger.

"This seems to be much-to-do about little," Alcock muttered.

The state continued its rebuttal testimony the next day, again putting Dr. John Nichols on the stand to testify about his opinions of the President's wounds, although he had not examined them. Haggerty ruled out much of the doctor's rebuttal testimony on grounds that it was repetitious.

Peter Schuster, a photographer for the Orleans Parish coroner, testified about one of the Dealey Plaza photographs, claiming that it showed a man "holding something." However, he did not specify what the "something" was.

The final state rebuttal witness was a handwriting expert, Elizabeth McCarthy, who testified that it was her opinion that Clay Shaw did sign the "Clay Bertrand" signature to the guest register in the airport lounge.

The state concluded shortly before noon.

Dymond immediately renewed his motion for a directed verdict. Judge Haggerty, now apparently intent upon letting the jury decide, denied the motion. This drew a smattering of applause from the spectator section.

The trial of Clay Shaw was now nearing an end. There remained only the lawyers' arguments from opposing sides, the charge of the judge, the verdict of the jury. The state divided the chores of final argument among three members of the staff of prosecutors. Alcock was to argue first for the state. He would be followed by Oser. The final word from the prosecution would come from Jim Garrison himself, so strangely silent throughout this trial. Dymond took upon himself the burden of the argument in behalf of Shaw, and his jury argument was spliced in between Oser and Garrison.

The arguments began at 2:30 p.m. that Friday. They would go on until nearly midnight.

Alcock, standing before a capacity courtroom audience, but focusing on those fourteen men—twelve jurors and two alternates seated in the box—opened by thanking the jury members for their patience and their service.

The Shaw case, he said, was similar to a puzzle. It was the state's job in such a case, to put the pieces of the puzzle together so that the jury could see what had happened. He dwelt at length on the testimony from the Clinton, Louisiana witness. He said: "One promise made by the defense was that Shaw not only did not consort with Ferrie and Oswald, but that he never laid eyes on either of them. But within four hours of the opening of this trial that promise was broken and this defendant, this man (Shaw) was proven to be a liar."

Shaw, sitting quietly at the defense table, intently watched the jury. Occasionally, he scribbled notes on a yellow legal pad.

Rocking back and forth on his feet, Alcock's voice rose to a shout as he argued to the jury: "Clay Shaw is not the type of man you could easily forget because of his stature, his hair, his general physical appearance. And he was not easily forgotten by all the witnesses who placed him in the presence of Lee Harvey Oswald and David W. Ferrie."

Because it was apparently felt by the prosecution that Dymond had damaged the image of some state witnesses, Alcock now turned to the question of their reputations. One of those he now defended was the ex-convict and dope addict, Vernon Bundy, who claimed he had seen Shaw and Oswald together.

"Gentlemen, I want to make one thing clear," said Alcock. "I do not apologize for Vernon Bundy. You take your witnesses as you find them. It would be fine if you had some bank president before you to tell about how they overheard a conspiracy to assassinate the President. But you're not going to find many bank presidents around who associate with the likes of Lee Harvey Oswald and David Ferrie."

Alcock's argument was a preliminary for the state's closing words which would come from Jim Garrison. When Alcock finished, his associate Oser took over and discussed the testimony of the state witnesses who had talked about what they saw at Dealey Plaza. The assistant district attorney took issue specifically with the Warren Commission conclusions. "There were at least three people and three guns in Dealey Plaza that day, firing at Kennedy," he said. "The President, I submit to you gentlemen of the jury, was caught in a crossfire. Otherwise, it is mathematically and scientifically impossible for one person with one gun to do what was done in Dealey Plaza that day."

Oser crowded the courtroom with exhibits dealing with state testimony about the events in Dallas. These included two four-foot photographs of a page from the Kennedy autopsy report, and numerous color photographs showing the President's head exploding as he received the fatal shot.

The court was so crowded by exhibits that the assistant prosecutor was forced at one point to tack a huge photograph—

of a bullet recovered from the stretcher used to carry Connally —onto the judge's bench.

In addition, Oser used a slide projector to show enlarged pictures from the color film taken of the assassination by amateur photographer Abraham Zapruder. While the slides were being shown, the jurors leaned forward, watching closely. Several jurors once requested that some of the attorneys in the courtroom move so they could see better. One juror stood up to get a better view.

Garrison, who had not been present for much of the trial, was present while the Zapruder slides were being shown.

Dymond's closing argument for the defense began at 7:40 p.m., after the jury had been to dinner. He began his plea for Shaw by saying he did not think that a criminal trial was the place for "implications, veiled charges, hints of guilt or wrongdoing." He added: "If the state means to charge the federal government with fraud, dishonesty, deceit and unscrupulous conduct, let them come forward and say so."

Dymond said he wanted to make it clear that "the Warren Commission is not on trial in this court." He added, "This is a trial in which Clay Shaw is charged specifically with conspiring to murder President Kennedy."

Speaking for an hour and fifty-five minutes, Dymond told the jury that the only reason Shaw was brought to trial was to provide Garrison with a forum for an attack on the Warren Commission. "The world will be waiting," he told the jurors, "to see if a man can be convicted in a production where a patsy was picked for an attack on the Warren report. The Warren Commission did not know when it issued its report that it would be pounced upon by a group of vultures who would use it to climb to fame and fortune over the body of the late President."

The defense attorney said he could not accept the inference that the federal investigation into the Kennedy assassination was "one giant fraud." To be successful, such a deceitful attempt would have had to have the cooperation of the doctors at Parkland Hospital where Kennedy was taken, the Dallas police, the Secret Service, the FBI and even Robert F. Kennedy, Dymond said. He added: "I say 'how', and when I say 'how', I call upon you, as sane, sensible people to consider how it could be possible that this many people could be a party to a fraudulent scheme, and have five and a half years elapse and not one person come forward to say, 'I want to tell the truth.' That is absolutely beyond belief." Dymond was blunt. Russo was a liar, he said, and Spiesel was an obvious paranoid. "This is a court of law, it is a court of justice. You don't ask a jury to believe testimony of this kind." After Dymond's presentation, the state was allowed a final closing argument. Alcock took up a few minutes to rebut specific points raised by Dymond.

"It appears that the defendant led two lives—he was a veritable Dr. Jekyll and Mr. Hyde," said Alcock. "During the day he was a so-called pillar of society. During after hours, he consorted with the likes of Lee Harvey Oswald and David Ferrie."

Then, Alcock relinquished the floor to Garrison who made the final plea to the jury. He read for twenty-nine minutes from a typewritten address he had prepared. Speaking so softly he could hardly be heard, Garrison told the jury: "The government's handling of the investigation of President Kennedy's assassination was a fraud. It was the greatest fraud in the history of our country, probably the greatest fraud in the history of humankind."

Garrison charged that "massive power" had been brought "to prevent justice from ever being brought to this courtroom," and told the jury that the Warren Commission was just a cover-up for the real truth about Kennedy's death. He dwelt at length on what he termed the excessive use of big government power, but added "We don't have to accept this."

Mentioning the defendant for the first and only time during his talk, Garrison said: "You sit here in judgment of Clay Shaw. This is more than the ordinary case because of the victim. You represent, in a sense, the whole of humanity against great power—humanity which yet may triumph over excessive government power."

In a final emotional flight, Garrison put to the jury the words from President Kennedy's inaugural address in 1961. He said: "I submit that you should ask not what your country can do for you, but what you can do for your country."

His final argument concluded about 11:30 p.m.

Judge Haggerty launched immediately into the reading of the charge to the jury. For half an hour he explained the law of conspiracy. The two alternate jurors were excused. The panel retired to consider its verdict shortly after midnight.

While the jury was out, Haggerty and Garrison circulated

among the spectators signing autographs and accepting con-
gratulations. Shaw, chatting quietly with well-wishers, did not
betray nervousness. He did appear tense. Dymond, talking with
newsmen, was frank to admit his misgivings: "I'm worried, scared
and tired."

Finally, shortly before 1 a.m. on Saturday morning—after less
than an hour of deliberation—the court was notified that the jury
had reached a verdict. There was a flurry of activity as spectators
and newsmen rushed to their seats.

About ten deputies, under the direction of Sheriff Heyd, stood
behind the defense table, in a semicircle around Shaw and his attorneys. Garrison saw none of this. He was not present.

The jurors, looking tired, filed in. It was 1:02 a.m.

The jury foreman passed the panel's written verdict to the
court clerk who read from the paper to the crowded courtroom:
"We the jury find the defendant not guilty."

There were loud cries, both from the press and spectator
sections, some of joy, some of despair. There was shouting and
applause until Haggerty restored order.

Shaw, who had been ordered to stand while the verdict was
being read, smiled broadly. He continued to smile while the tumult continued around him.

Haggerty ordered the sheriff's deputies to accompany the
jurors out of the courtroom. They passed by Shaw, who shook
hands with each of them.

The trial of Clay Shaw was over.

Later, interviews with jurors disclosed that the panel took
only one vote. It was unanimous.[3] All found Shaw not guilty.

None of the jurors, apparently, was impressed with the
state's case. David I. Powe, a juror, explained: "Garrison has a
right to his opinion about the government and the Warren Commission. But I just don't feel his opinion is enough to convict a
man."

---

3. In his book **American Grotesque** (Simon and Schuster, 1970) James Kirkwood reports on
a series of interviews, conducted after the trial, with members of the jury. Several of those
interviewed said one juror voted "guilty" on the first ballot, but immediately switched his
vote before a second ballot was taken.

3.   *"The price of justice*
                               is eternal publicity."
                               Enoch Arnold Bennett

And so in the early morning hours of March 1, the first of the three assassination trials of 1969 came to an end. Clay Shaw was acquitted; his ordeal was over.

Jim Garrison's attempt to convict Shaw of a dark plot to murder President Kennedy was shown to be a search for a lie. The jury rejected Garrison's far-fetched theories about federal conspiracies, FBI coverups, crossfire at Dealey Plaza. A jury verdict had discredited Garrison; the New Orleans *Times Picayune,* in a front page editorial, criticized Garrison; from Detroit, the president of the American Bar Association rebuked Garrison. But, so what?

No bar action was brought against the district attorney by any member of the legal profession; no judicial action was ever taken against him; the informal censure by the ABA president was mild criticism and was short-lived.

So on the morning of March 3, forty-eight hours after the jury cleared Shaw, Garrison announced that he had "just begun to fight."

That day he charged Clay Shaw with perjury, claiming Shaw had lied under oath when he testified he never knew Oswald or Ferrie.[4]

Shaw was released without bond—but Garrison's hammer still was heavy over his head. The jury had believed Shaw, cleared him, declared him innocent. But Garrison had just begun to fight.

On March 4, Garrison struck again. He arrested Thomas Bethell, one of his former investigators, charging that Bethell had, in August, 1968, given one of Shaw's attorneys the trial strategy for the prosecution.

When he heard of it, Frank Ritter laughed, "What strategy?"

Two days later, Garrison struck again. This time it was Dean

---

4. More than a year later Jim Garrison published his book **A Heritage of Stone.** The book jacket described the work as "his full views of the assassination of John F. Kennedy . . ." The text of the book runs 239 pages. The name Clay Shaw is mentioned only three times and then merely in one-sentence footnotes unrelated to the charges Garrison had brought against Shaw.

Andrews, the luckless lawyer who had testified during the actual trial with such candor about his own sad shortcomings and hapless ambitions. Andrews, already convicted of perjury for lying to the grand jury—he admitted he lied—now was charged with giving inconsistent statements on the one hand at the Shaw trial and on the other to the grand jury.

To most newsmen who followed the trial closely the charges were outrageous. Shaw had testified in a direct and open manner. The prosecution had not shaken his testimony when he was cross-examined. The jury, obviously, believed him and doubted Garrison's witnesses—Russo, Spiesel, Bundy and the rest.

There can be no doubt that there was conflicting testimony given during the trial. But it was Garrison's own witnesses who had been shown to lack credibility.

Russo, the state's "star witness," who had let himself be hypnotized to "help" his memory, who admitted he had been under psychiatric care in the past, was made to look ridiculous by his own contradictory statements from the witness chair; Bundy, the ex-convict and drug addict, admitted on the witness stand that he was a thief; Spiesel, the New York "suprise witness" who had thought people were hypnotizing him against his will, was made, by his statements, to look bizarre. Another surprise witness, Nicholas Tadin, who came late to court with his wife with a story trying to tie Shaw and Oswald together, admitted he had lied in the past—although he claimed this story was the truth. These were only a few of Garrison's array of weak witnesses whose stories were challenged.

By their verdict the jurors had said they believed Shaw—not Garrison's confused assortment of witnesses.[5]

Still, it was Shaw Garrison charged with perjury. And a year later the charge was still pending, untried, still threatening Shaw.[6]

Clay Shaw should never have been required to stand trial. The evidence against him would have been considered comic had the charge not been so deeply serious. District Attorney Jim

---

5. Some jurors interviewed by James Kirkwood (author of **American Grotesque**) indicated they believed some of the prosecution witnesses. Obviously there was no pattern of believability to the state's sworn proof.

6. On January 25, 1971, as this book was being prepared for publication, Clay Shaw's attorneys asked the Federal District Court in New Orleans to block the state perjury prosecution by Garrison. During this hearing Shaw told the court that he feared that if he testified at a perjury trial and was acquitted he would then be charged again with perjury. "I see no end to this thing so I think my rights to express myself are severely restricted," he said. The Federal Court stopped the prosecution.

Garrison should have been challenged by the local or state bar association, or by the state attorney general or by the courts, or by individual attorneys in his state, or by some official spokesman for the American Bar Association long before Clay Shaw was ever required to employ expensive legal counsel to answer the charge that he conspired to murder President Kennedy.

Judges in Garrison's home state naturally were nervous about taking any action to censure him. After all, he had demeaned the eight district criminal judges before whom he practiced, in a dispute unrelated to the assassination case. In the fall of 1962 the judges had brought against the district attorney a defamation of character suit because he claimed publicly they were interfering with his drive to clean up vice in the New Orleans French Quarter. Garrison was fined $1000, sentenced to four months in jail, and this was sustained by the state Supreme Court. He appealed to the Supreme Court of the United States. The conviction was overturned and Garrison won the right to criticize the judiciary at will. In the face of that ruling, perhaps the Louisiana judges felt that rather than take Garrison on in another bitter fight in which it would be made to appear that they were trying to cover up some unknown truth about the assassination of President Kennedy, they would simply let a jury of citizens decide. At any rate a three-judge court somehow had ruled that there had been adequate evidence to take Shaw to trial. Judge Haggerty himself ruled twice during trial that Shaw was not entitled to a directed not-guilty verdict. It was not until after the trial—two years after Shaw had been placed under a shadow and burdened with a strain that hospitalized him for a brief period—that the president of the American Bar Association issued a statement questioning Garrison's methods.

William T. Gossett, of Detroit, president of the ABA, then called the trial a charade and said proceedings such as Shaw's case "tend to create doubt about our judicial process . . . our system of jurisprudence."

Gossett said he did not know what caused Garrison to act as he did. "He may have had unreliable information. Certainly his principal witnesses seemed to be wholly unreliable."

Asked if there would be disbarment proceedings against Garrison, Gossett said such action could be taken only if it could be shown that the prosecution was "malicious." "You can't disbar an attorney for incompetence," he said.

He suggested a course of conduct: Shaw could sue for damages. "He has had to pay attorneys' fees, he has lost two years of his life preparing for trial . . . he has had to endure the anxiety." Gossett thought that attorneys in Louisiana would "be compelled to investigate" and he thought the people of Louisiana would feel "a sense of outrage" over the case. The Louisiana bar never took any action but the "outraged" people of the state did. The following year they re-elected Garrison their district attorney for another four years. It was an overwhelming political victory: he received approximately 85,000 votes against a combined total of about 75,000 for three opponents in the Democratic primary, which in New Orleans assured Garrison of general election.

He had campaigned, among other things, by taking a full page advertisement in a weekly newspaper with heavy circulation in the black section of the city, aligning himself with the memory of the late President Kennedy and saying he had not forgotten the Negro people. He claimed his chief opponent, Harry Connick, a former assistant U.S. district attorney, was the federal government's candidate against him. He injected into his campaign the idea that the federal establishment had tried to suppress his probe of the assassination, including the trial of Shaw. He swept the black city wards and got a healthy-to-respectable vote elsewhere. Poor Connick, realizing on election night the liability of his former employment as a federal prosecutor, attributed his loss to "a strong anti-federal government feeling" in his region of the country.

The last thing Shaw wanted was to have to go back to court in New Orleans. Still, the president of the nation's bar association suggested his recourse was to sue Garrison for damages. This, of course, would only provide more legal expense, more loss of time and perhaps reputation, and more anxiety. In such a case Shaw's most intimate personal problems might be laid bare.[7] Obviously he didn't want to sue Garrison. And he didn't want to be persecuted in another meaningless trial on a perjury charge which should not have been brought.

---

7. On February 28, 1970, Clay Shaw filed a five million dollar damage suit against Jim Garrison. Due to a backlog of court cases, it was estimated that it probably would be more than a year before this suit was ever brought to trial.

There is another interesting after-the-fact postscript to the Shaw trial that involves Judge Haggerty. It will be remembered he told reporters he had cancelled his party-going activities during the Mardi Gras so he could give himself fully to the duties imposed by the Shaw trial. He couldn't stay out all night partying and come to court "bright eyed and bushy tailed."

On December 17, 1969, Judge Haggerty was arrested by New Orleans police in a raid on a motel during what His Honor called "a before-the-wedding bachelor party." Charges prepared by the office of the district attorney, Jim Garrison, accused him of soliciting for prostitution, obscenity and resisting arrest. When the raid occurred, officers said, Judge Haggerty tried to make his departure. Police said they restrained him.

At police headquarters he ducked his head, dodging photographers. It later came out—at his trial—that the police had a secret agent at the party who carried a miniature radio transmitter. This agent claimed in court that Haggerty brought three women and stag movies to the motel party.

The case was assigned to Judge Alvin Oser—who, as assistant district attorney, had helped Garrison prosecute Shaw before Haggerty and who since the trial had become a judicial officer himself. The Haggerty defense asked that Judge Oser be recused from trying the case, and he was. Haggerty was acquitted of the charge and returned to his bench February 2, 1970—a year after he had been sitting on the trial in the Shaw case.

There is no doubt that the "stag" party occurred in the Haggerty case. In the Shaw case the evidence that Shaw attended a party where Kennedy's assassination was plotted was unreal and unbelievable.

As Judge Haggerty went back to the bench, the Louisiana Judiciary Commission conducted a closed hearing on the matter in May 1970, and later recommended he be ousted from office.[8] No question was ever raised about Haggerty's conduct during the Shaw trial: permitting Garrison's statements out of court; allow-

---

8. Late in 1970, the Louisiana Supreme Court ordered Haggerty off the bench in a ruling stemming from the stag party arrest, unrelated to the Shaw trial. The judge said he would appeal, and would run again for election to the bench if the appeal failed. In another interesting post-trial development—unrelated in any way to the case—Perry Raymond Russo was arrested on August 22, 1970 on charges of theft and burglary. He and a companion were accused of stealing property valued at $8,000 from a New Orleans residence, and possession of a stolen safety deposit box key. Garrison's office declined prosecution in the burglary case. Russo was given a three month suspended sentence on the charge of possessing a stolen key.

ing repeated showings of the film; his "picture party" with the jury and press. And no bar action was taken against Garrison.

It is true there were rare instances in which lawyers spoke against him. A Chicago attorney who had represented the late Jack Ruby asked that Garrison be stopped. He, of course, might have been thought to have had a personal interest since his client killed Lee Harvey Oswald and since Garrison had involved Ruby himself in some of his serio-comic comments.

The New Orleans Crime Commission—a non-legal, citizen's group—spoke out against Garrison. But Garrison had long been a critic of the Commission and so this agency might have been prejudiced. When Garrison struck out at a few attorneys who represented persons he wanted to involve in his case, charging the lawyers were in the pay of the CIA, these members of the bar issued strong denials and defended themselves.

But by and large, Garrison did not receive serious criticism from the legal fraternity.

It was, in fact, only the press that made any effort to keep Garrison "honest." The traditional role of the press has been to serve as a critic of government—all branches of government, including the judicial branch. While a handful of reporters were taken in by Garrison, most were not. Many made a major effort to expose the sort of case he was preparing against Shaw.

Jim Squires, one of the contributors to this work, visited New Orleans and interviewed Garrison shortly after the original *States-Item* article appeared.

"This man is very convincing," was Squires' first impression. "He has made himself believe that he is on to something very hot."

Garrison's appearances on television left the same impression with large segments of the television audience. So much about the Kennedy assassination was in doubt in many minds. And Garrison's self-assurance, his ability to articulate his theories, his ready answers to questions put to him, carried a ring of conviction.[9]

---

9. Once the trial ended, Garrison went back on television. Shortly after the trial he appeared in a half-hour "meet the press" type interview with Alex Gifford, a New Orleans television newsman. His voice carrying its old ring of authority, Garrison said of the jury verdict: "We've been in office six and a half years and this is as far as I can recall, the first major public interest case that we have lost . . . We lost one in a goldfish bowl." To the suggestion made in local newspaper editorials that he should resign, Garrison said: "I did not fight the federal government for two and a half years to resign or leave this

As events were to prove, it was a smoke ring which was wafted away on winds of courtroom fact. Squires saw through Garrison's "case" early and reported that his theories were questionable. Many other newsmen, both in print and electronic media, saw through Garrison's techniques very early and tried to expose the misty nature of his evidence.

Within two weeks after Garrison's secret investigation was publicized by the New Orleans *States-Item,* the United Press International was to send its distinguished veteran reporter, the late Merriman Smith, dean of White House correspondents, to New Orleans to report on what was going on. Smith was a good choice for the assignment. He had been on the scene in Dallas, the reporter who got the very first report out that the President had been shot on November 22, 1963. He was toughened by years of Washington news management and news control. He had seen politicians from top level executives to low level bureaucrats propound phony theories for personal or political reasons.

His report on Garrison, filed March 4, 1967, ended with this: "With all respect to the hard-driving, forty-five year old district attorney, his case so far has to be described as flimsy. In his currently powerful position, he can arrest almost anyone for anything. But proof will come harder, particularly considering the credibility of some of his sources."

Hugh Aynesworth, in the May 15 issue of *Newsweek* magazine, wrote: "There has been a conspiracy in New Orleans—but it is a plot of Garrison's own making." Aynesworth called Garrison's investigation a "scheme to concoct a fantastic 'solution' " to the assassination.

James Phelan, writing in the May 6 issue of *The Saturday Evening Post,* outlined evidence which seemed to clearly discredit Garrison's "key witness," Perry Raymond Russo. Phelan, like many other newsmen, had gone to New Orleans and listened to Garrison's convincing fabrication. Garrison made available to Phelan certain documents connected with his big investigation, including some of the statements by Russo. These, Phelan found,

office simply because the newspaper thinks I should."

Of the charge of perjury he had brought against Shaw he said: "It's not a matter of persecution when we charge someone with committing perjury; its my duty to charge people if there is an indication that they lied under oath."

Of his initial case against Shaw he said: "It seems to me that this was an eminently fair prosecution."

revealed startling contradictions in statements Russo had made.

One document Phelan saw was a report to Garrison of the initial interrogation of Russo by Sciambra, the assistant in the district attorney's office.

"There was no positive identification of Lee Harvey Oswald as Leon Oswald," Phelan wrote. In addition, he reported, "when shown a picture of Clay Shaw, Russo said nothing whatever . . . about having known him as Clay Bertrand."

Phelan also reported that it was only when Russo was given a "truth serum" drug called sodium pentothal that he had said he recalled the party where he was supposed to have seen Shaw, Oswald and Ferrie. And, Phelan wrote, when Russo was placed in a hypnotic trance he was told by the physician who induced hypnosis to see "Bertrand, Ferrie and Oswald" on a television screen, "And they are talking about assassinating somebody."

Phelan was a journalist whose article ripped the credibility of the Garrison case.

There were other articles by other reporters which contributed to a body of fact that tore at Garrison's propositions. The *New York Times* documented the story that Ferrie's death was from natural causes—not suicide. That came from the pathologist who conducted the autopsy. George Lardner, a reporter from the *Washington Post,* who in fact had been with Ferrie shortly before he died, exploded the coroner's theory of the time of Ferrie's death, as it had been stated by Dr. Nicholas Chetta. The *Omaha World* reported that Garrison's efforts to get back to New Orleans the young woman known as Sandra Moffett, to get her to tell about attending the party with Russo, were based on false information. The *Dallas Times Herald* helped destroy the myth about Garrison's claim that he had found Jack Ruby's unlisted phone number in separate address books belonging to Shaw and Oswald. The *Chicago Tribune* reported in a copyrighted story, December 29, 1967, that Garrison himself had been under psychiatric care from 1950 until 1955, and "was discharged from the army as totally unfit for military service." Gene Roberts from the *New York Times* reported, June 11, 1967, that two Louisiana convicts had said that Garrison's men had offered to set them free if they would "cooperate" in the investigation of Shaw.

These were but a few of the attempts by various newsmen

from several publications to let their readers know that there were gaping holes in Garrison's evidence.

Perhaps the most concerted and extensive efforts to take apart the Garrison case and expose it for what it was were exerted, in separate reports, by two major television networks— the National Broadcasting Company and Columbia Broadcasting System.

The NBC program, telecast June 10, 1967, was a direct assault on the ethics of Jim Garrison.

The CBS report, televised on four consecutive nights, June 25-28, was not so direct but the sum of its factual conclusions had the effect of tearing Garrison's theories.

Both networks spared no expense to develop programs to try to penetrate the smoke screen which had been generated by the fire of Garrison's frequent statements.

NBC sent a team of news staff men to New Orleans, including Walter Sheridan, a crack investigator who had a background with the FBI, and who had worked in the U.S. Department of Justice under Robert Kennedy, heading the so-called "task force" that was assigned to delve into the machinations of Teamsters President James R. Hoffa. Sheridan had worked with Kennedy on the old McClellan Committee in the United States Senate, then had helped out in the 1960 presidential campaign as a coordinator in Pennsylvania. He was a friend of the late President, a closer friend of his brother, Robert, and a professional investigator who took pride in detail work. If there was some government conspiracy involved in the Kennedy assassination, Sheridan would have been a man committed to exposing it for NBC.

He had been in New Orleans only a few weeks before he became totally convinced that Garrison's investigation was a farce. In discussions with contributors to this book, Sheridan said of Garrison: "He isn't quite rational on the subject of this investigation. He seems almost like a fanatic. Justice is in real danger down here."

Sheridan worked closely in New Orleans with representatives of the NBC outlet there, particularly with Richard Townley, a member of the WDSU-TV news staff who knew Garrison.

The network called its program: "The JFK Conspiracy: The Case of Jim Garrison."

The program cast doubt on the investigation and sought to

show that Garrison and his investigators had threatened or offered "favors" to some witnesses to "cooperate" in his investigation.

In a series of filmed interviews persons stated that there had been efforts by Garrison's office to "frame" Clay Shaw. John ("The Baptist") Cancler, a convicted burglar, said Garrison's investigators had told him charges against him might be dropped if he would "put something" in Clay Shaw's house. A known drug addict, Miguel Torres, in prison for theft, said he had been promised a Florida vacation and access to heroin if he would say he had known Shaw.

A Turkish bath house operator, Fred Leemans, told Sheridan that Garrison offered him money to "remember" Shaw and a young man named "Lee" had visited his establishment.

According to the NBC findings, lie detector tests Garrison gave his most vital witnesses—Russo and Vernon Bundy, the narcotic addict—had cast doubt on their truthfulness.

Garrison knew of these "negative" reports, the network contended. Beyond that, the network said it had located Clay Bertrand, a New Orleans homosexual. Shaw was not Clay Bertrand, NBC said.

Garrison was quick to move against NBC. He charged Sheridan and WDSU-TV reporter Richard Townley with bribery and intimidation in connection with the probe they had conducted to gather material for the NBC special program. He also demanded equal time and received half an hour of prime time July 15, 1967, to give his reply to the NBC criticism.

Nobody with CBS was arrested. The principal attack of that network's presentation dealt with an examination of what happened in Dealey Plaza in Dallas. With veteran newsman Walter Cronkite serving as anchor man for the four programs, CBS took apart the Garrison case piece by piece, playing his claims off against the findings of the Warren Commission. At times CBS went to great lengths to re-create conditions as they were at Dallas that day. When it was over, CBS had given Garrison time to say that Oswald had been used as a decoy and that "it was necessary for one of the people involved (Jack Ruby) to kill him" when Dallas police failed to get Oswald after the assassination.

In its conclusions CBS discredited, for the most part, Garrison's claim about what happened when President Kennedy died. The network concluded that Oswald, acting alone, was the assassin.

Still, Clay Shaw was headed for a trial. And the bar did not join with the press to expose Garrison—despite growing evidence and mounting press concern that Garrison's case was essentially a farce.

The search for a lie continued, unchecked by the bar or the courts or the ABA guidelines, despite Judge Reardon's contention that "the main thrust" of his recommendations was "against the lawyers and law enforcement agencies . . . who can be subject to some professional discipline within our own house."

Chapter 3

The State of Tennessee Versus James Earl Ray:

Who Slew The Dreamer?

1.

*"It is acknowledged
that neither convict prisons,
nor the hulks,
nor any system of hard labor,
ever cured the criminal."*
**Feodor Dostoevsky,
CRIME AND PUNISHMENT**

Travelers did not notice, but as they walked through the bustling lobby of London's Heathrow Airport the morning of June 8, 1968, the place was teaming with Scotland Yard detectives. A fugitive from justice was about to walk into a police snare. The most intense international manhunt in history was minutes away from its end.

Cautiously the British plain-clothes officers kept under surveillance the mild, bespectacled man of middle years as he strolled casually on his way to board a commercial flight for Brussels. Then the men from the Yard moved in swiftly. They accosted, disarmed and took into custody James Earl Ray, wanted in Memphis, Tennessee, for murder: the assassination of Dr. Martin Luther King, the leading American disciple of Gandhian nonviolence and civil disobedience, and the man most people identified as the leader in the fight for equal rights for Negroes in America.

Thus ended the most extensive and expensive manhunt in history.

Thus began one of the most unsatisfactory and inconclusive criminal judicial proceedings in history.

James Earl Ray, alias Ramon George Sneyd, alias Eric Starvo Galt, alias John Willard, Harvey Lowmyer, W. C. Herron, James O'Connor, Paul Bridgman and James Walton, was a hardened, professional criminal. He had never been a successful one. The murder of Martin Luther King was the only crime he had ever been involved in that he had not bungled.

Once he had robbed a grocery store in Illinois, but fell from his getaway car when it made a sharp turn as he sped from the scene. Dazed, he was caught after the fall. On another occasion he stole a typewriter in Los Angeles, but dropped his bankbook at the scene and was captured. After a robbery in Chicago, he ran up a dead-end alley and was shot. He tried to escape from deputies in St. Louis once by jumping suddenly into an elevator. He forgot to close the door and they dragged him out.

Ray was the typical "born loser." A child of the leanest depression times, he was reared in the squalid poverty of a Missouri river town, and he always had the image of a poor boy grown up poor. He was a sickly youngster, accustomed to a life of poverty, branded a thief in school and regarded throughout his teenage years as a young hoodlum. He failed even to make it in the army, being thrown out as unfit for military service.

As a petty criminal, his specialty was poorly planned robberies which frequently aborted. He had spent most of his adult life in prison. So unimportant was he that when he escaped from the Missouri State prison in the spring of 1967 nobody bothered to look for him.

Now he had become a man of many names who had committed one of the most widely publicized criminal acts of the century: a murder which set off a chain reaction of racial violence across the land. He managed the execution of this crime with deadly perfection—quite out of character—then escaped the country without being traced. Until the Federal Bureau of Investigation realized the true identity of the man who fled Memphis, Ray had remained an unsought escaped convict.

The British warrant read to James Earl Ray after his apprehension was made out in the name of one of his aliases—Ramon George Sneyd. That was the name on the passport on which he was traveling. He had "borrowed" that name from a Toronto police captain he had never met.

The warrant against him officially charged that he was traveling on a false passport and was illegally in possession of a revolver. But as the British constabulary whisked the prisoner away to Cannon Row police station they were fully aware of whom they had captured and of the gravity of the real charge which would confront him.

Within a few hours after Ray was confined to Cannon Row station, Fred M. Vinson, Jr., the Assistant United States Attorney General in charge of the criminal division of the Justice Department and the son of the former Chief Justice of the U.S. Supreme Court, was on a flight to London to push into a motion the legal and diplomatic machinery to move James Earl Ray expeditiously back to the United States to stand trial in Memphis.

From the outset the British were completely aware of the importance of the criminal they had captured—and they were naturally nervous about keeping him safe and secure. They were aware that Ray was an escaped convict. A man facing a capital crime in America and with the proven ability to escape might try to flee. The authorities were equally alert to the dangers that might come to the prisoner should someone seek to harm James Earl Ray while he was in custody.

Ray was put under the strictest possible security. On the morning of June 10—two days after his arrest at the air terminal—Ray was arraigned in Bow Street Magistrates' Court on the charges that he was traveling on a false passport and was illegally carrying a dangerous weapon.

The British named a capable solicitor, Michael Eugene, to represent Ray to make certain that he was given all his legal rights. In Magistrates' Court that day the man in custody demonstrated recognition when asked to answer to the name "Sneyd." But he did not acknowledge that he was James Earl Ray. On the same day Ray appeared in Bow Street, the U.S. Embassy in London made the first official move on the part of Washington to initiate the return of Ray to Memphis. The embassy, working in cooperation with the U.S. Department of Justice, asked that a provisional extradition warrant be issued for Ray.

After arraignment Ray was moved to Brixton prison, again for safekeeping and then, on the next day, June 11, he was transferred to Wandworth prison where it was thought that even more effective security could be maintained.

The provisional warrant issued at the request of the U.S. Embassy was followed up by a specific extradition request from Washington asking for Ray's return to stand trial on murder charges. The wheels of justice were now beginning to grind in the United States. The "search for justice" was getting under way.

Ray began looking toward home, the United States, toward a criminal trial where he knew he ultimately would be confronted by evidence that he murdered Dr. King. And so he gave to his solicitor, Michael Eugene, a list of three names of American lawyers—attorneys he wanted ultimately to defend him when he was taken back to Memphis to stand trial. The three names on the list were F. Lee Bailey, a defender of unpopular clients who had represented Albert Disalvo, the Boston strangler; Arthur Hanes, a former mayor of Birmingham, Alabama, who had successfully defended two members of the Ku Klux Klan accused of murdering Mrs. Viola Liuzzo, a civil rights worker; and finally, Percy Foreman, the Houston lawyer who most recently had gained notice from his defense of Mrs. Candace Mossler, who had been charged, along with her nephew, Melvin Powers, with murdering Mrs. Mossler's wealthy husband in Miami.

How James Earl Ray went about compiling his list isn't known. He was familiar enough with the underworld and interested enough in lawyers involved in criminal cases to know who had success in defending those charged with murder. Bailey, Hanes and Foreman were not unusual choices for any man charged with the sort of crime Ray was going to face.

Michael Eugene was to say later that Ray was more interested in Bailey and Hanes as first choices than he was in Percy Foreman—the man who finally went to court with him.

Ray told Solicitor Eugene: "Try the first two"—Bailey and Hanes. If neither would accept his case, then he wanted Foreman as third choice.

Following the instructions of his client, Michael Eugene wrote letters to both Hanes and Bailey to determine if either was interested enough in Ray's case to take it on. Bailey replied negatively: he would not defend James Earl Ray. Hanes was interested.

Arthur Hanes subsequently told reporters that he never heard from James Earl Ray, personally or indirectly, before the letter arrived from London from Michael Eugene.

The case intrigued Hanes. Here was a chance for a Southern attorney, a states' righter, a segregationist, a son of the deep South and the old South, to take on the entire federal establishment which seemed to be involved in the case against Ray.

Hanes had represented Collie Leroy Wilkins and Eugene Thomas who had been charged with killing Viola Liuzzo. That had been back in 1965. Now here was a man charged with murdering the best known of all civil rights leaders: Martin Luther King. Of course James Earl Ray was entitled to counsel. But to Arthur Hanes, the ex-mayor of Birmingham, the Ray case seemed to fit his interests well as a lawyer, as a Southerner, as a politician, and as a man. Memphis was not Birmingham or Montgomery, he knew, as he weighed the ultimate question for the lawyer: what sort of jury he would confront. But Memphis was the capital of the cotton country, a town that had no love for King, had considered him an interloper. The tradition in Memphis, from reconstruction through W.C. Handy and the birth of the blues, through Boss Ed Crump's day to the present labor-strike environment, had been "keep them in their place." "They" broke out of bounds occasionally, on election day, when they would vote in a massive bloc. But, after all, "Uncle Ed" Crump taught them how to vote. Memphis was the home town of Aubrey James Norvell, who shot James Meredith down as Meredith marched into Mississippi. There was a big black population—but what about an all-white jury in Memphis? The prospect must have appealed to Hanes as he considered his role as defense attorney.

Those who knew Hanes told themselves when they heard the news that he had taken the case, that James Earl Ray had an able, aggressive, competitive lawyer who would provide the accused man with a viable defense, if one could be devised. Everyone wondered who would pay him just as they wondered whether Ray had been paid to kill King.

On June 19, Arthur Hanes flew to London to meet with his new client. To most British reporters, Hanes was the sort of Southern leader they had always read about and heard about—but rarely had an opportunity to see and interview. He had been mayor of Birmingham when the city's police chief Eugene "Bull" Connor was turning fire hoses and police dogs on the followers of Martin Luther King. When a citizens' committee in Birmingham sought to end peacefully a Negro boycott of downtown business in Birmingham in 1963, Hanes said of the effort: "They are a group of fuzzy-minded liberals, pinkos and Reds mixing in there with blacks and whites . . . it's all part of a Communist conspiracy to cause trouble in this country . . . . Birmingham will become a

Negro town where white people will cower behind barred doors."
When Hanes was questioned by the British press upon his arrival in London about how he would be paid for representing Ray,
his answer was taken to mean that some group, possibly co-
conspirators, would pay the bill for Ray's defense.
"He ain't gonna pay me with love. I can tell you that," Hanes
said.
Conspiracy rumors started the moment the news flashed from
Memphis that King had been murdered. One theory was that a
syndicate killer had accepted a "contract" from the Ku Klux Klan
to murder Martin Luther King. Another theory was that Black
Muslims or some black militant group had plotted King's
death. There were reports that the John Birch Society would pay
for Ray's defense. The States' Rights party of Georgia was said to
be initiating a "legal defense fund" for the accused fugitive.
For those who had never believed the conclusions of the report of the Warren Commission on the presidential assassination
there was even the idea that the same unseen, unknown conspirators who had arranged for President Kennedy's killing and for the
murder of Lee Harvey Oswald, now had struck again. As in the
killing of President Kennedy, there were enough "clues" and unanswered questions to feed the rumors of a conspiracy in the
case of Dr. King's slaying.
First of all, within minutes after Martin Luther King was shot
on the balcony of the Lorraine Motel, there was an inexplicable
short wave radio broadcast about an imaginary automobile chase
through the Memphis suburbs in which a white Mustang reportedly was pursued. Ray had escaped in a white Mustang.
A police car was parked at a Memphis intersection next to a
young man who had a short wave radio in his car. Over this short
wave radio the policeman, Lieutenant Rufus W. Bradshaw, heard
the voice of some unknown broadcaster telling of this mythical
chase which the voice claimed was already in progress. He mentioned the Mustang and said that shots were being fired by its
occupants. The officer at the intersection immediately reported
over police radio the short wave broadcast that he had heard so
that the police department would be aware that the chase was on.
Already a white Mustang had been observed at the crime scene.
Undoubtedly police cars turned immediately toward the section of the city where the chase reportedly was under way. Police

officials in Memphis were reluctant to say that this broadcast, whatever its origin, hindered their manhunt for James Earl Ray.

Later, police would contend that the broadcast had been made by a teen-ager in a Memphis suburb—a ham radio operator who was "playing around" with his set. The white Mustang was believed to be pure coincidence. The police were convinced there was nothing to the broadcast. Still, it was made.

A year later, the teen-ager, Eddie Montedonico, now a college student away from Memphis, would say privately that he knew nothing of the broadcast and had nothing to do with it.

But Ray, nonetheless, slipped away from Memphis in a white Mustang immediately after the killing.

Could one man, even a professional criminal, succeed in such a daring, broad daylight murder and make his getaway completely unaided? How could a fugitive flee from state to state, and country to country without funds? Who was providing his funds? The theory of a conspiracy became a natural assumption.

There were many factors other than the unexplained short wave broadcast which fed the rumors of a conspiracy. There was a federal warrant issued in Birmingham, April 27—twenty-three days after the murder—charging that Eric Starvo Galt, thirty-six, had conspired with a man "whom he alleged to be his brother" in the assassination of King. The same day a first degree state murder warrant was sworn out in Memphis charging Eric Starvo Galt with the killing.

So Galt, whoever he was, had conspired, federal authorities were charging, with another man whom he apparently had identified at some point as his brother. At this point the federal authorities seemed to believe in a conspiracy.

Those who were trying to read something into every piece of fact that developed remembered quite well that on April 5, immediately after King was slain, U.S. Attorney General Ramsey Clark had said during an impromptu news conference that there was no evidence of a "widespread plot." He added: "This appears to be the act of a single individual." Two days later the attorney general said: "We have evidence of one man on the run. There is no evidence that more were involved." But two weeks after Clark made that statement the Justice Department issued a warrant specifically mentioning a conspiracy with two men involved. This was, for a time, the latest word from the Department of Justice on the subject; it seemed for a while to supersede Ramsey Clark's earlier "no conspiracy" statements.

The many different aliases used by Ray—Galt, Lowmyer, Willard and Sneyd—hinted "conspiracy." Was it possible that one man would use all these names? Or was there more than one man, after all?

There was also conflict in what witnesses saw at the scene of the crime. Witnesses in the rooming house from which the shot was fired had seen Ray run from that building. But King's chauffeur, Solomon Jones, devoted to the minister, told police that he had seen a man wearing a white hood scamper from some bushes near the rooming house immediately after the shooting. Later, just before the case went to trial the Reverend James Bevel, one of the most devoted of all the disciples of Martin Luther King, himself an officer of the Southern Christian Leadership Conference, announced that he knew Ray was innocent and that he (Bevel) had evidence to free Ray. Bevel sent Ray a telegram offering to represent him as a lawyer in court and said in the wire: "Of course I know you are not guilty."

This was followed up by the comment of Beverly Sterner, administrative assistant to Bevel, who insisted his offer to defend Ray was not merely a symbolic move to switch blame for the King murder from an individual toward white racism.

"This is a serious offer," the assistant said.

Ultimately, the court was to deny Bevel the chance to help defend Ray because, said the late W. Preston Battle, the trial judge, Tennessee law prohibited a non-attorney from representing a defendant in a trial. But Bevel's statement, never fully explained to the public, added strength to the conspiracy theory.

Following Ray's capture in London, Attorney General Clark once again tried to quiet reports of a plot involving more than one man.

Appearing on "Issues and Answers" on ABC, Clark said all evidence pointed to a lone gunman. "We have no evidence of any other person or people," he said. When pressed on whether somebody had paid Ray's expenses to travel in Europe and Canada following the shooting, Clark said: "He (Ray) is a person . . . who lived a life of crime, who obtained money through crime, and I think that there is a very plausible possibility as to the source of his funds."

With regard to the funds for paying for his defense, it was later to be found that Ray was selling his story to *Look* magazine and Dell Publishers for $150,000. The story was to be written by William Bradford Huie. Huie was in consultation with Hanes before the case came to trial. Huie initially convinced himself that Ray was a witless dupe in a conspiracy. He checked facts about Ray's travels: where he had been, what he did, people he met and talked with as he fled. Enough of these details checked out to make Huie believe Ray's entire story about being used by unknown conspirators. As Huie set about writing his story for *Look,* word leaked out about the articles, and what the writer would say: that Ray had said he was in the rooming house, following directions, but did not pull the trigger and was a decoy who got caught.

Subsequently, Huie would change his mind about Ray's story and disbelieve what the accused killer of Doctor King originally had led him to believe about the conspiracy theory in the assassination.

But Huie's early attitude in support of the defendant's story added to the body of thought that there was a conspiracy.

Today, in the minds of many people, the murder of Martin Luther King is unsolved—or at least only partially solved. There are so many unexplained factors: the short wave radio broadcast immediately after the slaying; Ray's clean getaway; his ability to finance his travels in at least five countries before his arrest; the statements of Dr. King's driver about a man in a hood dashing from the scene of the murder; the statement of Bevel that Ray was not guilty; the action of the federal government in swearing out a conspiracy warrant; the lack of any semblance of a motive attributable to Ray.

All of this made the murder of Martin Luther King a mystery even after Ray's "guilty" plea.

The questions which are raised by all of these factors and coincidences required newsmen to critically analyze what the government was contending in the case against Ray.

A criminal court jury in Shelby County, Tennessee, ultimately accepted a plea of guilt in the murder case against James Earl Ray. But there are millions of Americans who still do not believe the entire story has ever been told. The FBI says the case is closed. And Judge Battle devoted his last days as a judicial officer to trying to force the press not to write or report about this mysterious case.

The first episode in what was to become a bitter fight between the press and the law enforcement establishment occurred when Ray was brought to the jail in Memphis where he was to await trial. Ray had been flown from London to Memphis clad in bullet-proof overalls, his feet in chains. He was driven from the Memphis airport to the jail in an armored car borrowed from the city of Jackson, Mississippi. (This armored truck, a vehicle with a history, was called "Thompson's Tank" because it had been purchased by Jackson Mayor Allen C. Thompson in 1963 when racial troubles boiled over at the assassination of Medger Evers.)

As Thompson's tank drove Ray from the Memphis airport, photographers were herded by an army of sheriff's deputies to a position across the street from the Shelby County courthouse which houses the jail. Police seemed to be everywhere—in the street, in windows, on rooftops. Reporters who tried to get close to see Ray were not allowed to move nearer as the parade of police vehicles approached the courthouse building.

A dozen deputies, several carrying shotguns, lined the back entrance to the building. An unmarked car roared up. Five men armed with submachine guns leaped out of it and stationed themselves at the entrance to the building. The armored truck, carrying Ray, was close behind. A bus was driven in front of the courthouse entrance so that observers—including reporters—would not be able to see or photograph Ray. There were garbled shouts which echoed across the street and a flurry of activity as Ray was taken from the truck.

As he was being led to the jail, a CBS television crew stationed across Third Street, which adjoins the courthouse, turned on floodlights to film the historic moment of the return of the man accused of killing Dr. King. Sheriff's deputies and city policemen began yelling: "Turn off those lights, turn off those lights." As Ray was moving toward the door of the courthouse a lanky policeman dashed across the street, jammed his sawed off shotgun into the face of the startled television newsman holding a floodlight and shouted again to turn off the lights. The lights went off, but the cameraman shouted that he was permitted, under rules laid down by Judge Battle, to film Ray's arrival. "We make our own rules," the deputy shouted back. It was the first incident of conflict between the authorities and the press.

Very early it became obvious to reporters that Memphis authorities—including, and perhaps most of all, Judge Battle himself—felt that the press was a hindrance and could "get in the way and cause trouble."

Memphis is a community with a black population of about forty percent and to most, if not all, Martin Luther King had been a hero in life and was now a martyr. Many Memphis blacks sensed a recalcitrant, unfeeling white city government administration was at least partly responsible for the murder of Dr. King. This mood left Memphis public officials—indeed the state leaders—disturbed about what effect the return of the accused killer of the civil rights leader might have in the black community in Shelby County. There was reason for concern about an avid press. As the Warren Commission had pointed out, the press corps at Dallas had created a mob scene: there were too many reporters, most of them competing with each other. Their demands added to the havoc there and, subsequently, to the panic that prevailed during the hours of Oswald's capture and the moment of his death. Newsmen pressured politicians and police. The result was that the law enforcement authorities let down their protective guard making it possible for Jack Ruby to mingle with a group of reporters and murder Lee Harvey Oswald.

But no effort was made to seek press ideas in the beginning or throughout the Ray case about how to regulate news coverage. Many newsmen would have had constructive suggestions: after the chaos at Dallas the press establishment had developed an awareness that standards of self-restraint needed to be applied in certain situations where news of a sensational nature attracted large numbers of reporters and cameramen.

Speaking before the American Society of Newspaper Editors at their spring convention in 1964, Felix McKnight, editor of the Dallas *Morning News,* suggested that in critical situations which attracted large numbers of newsmen more "pooling" among reporters and cameramen would be necessary. "Pool" news coverage is an arrangement whereby a few newsmen—perhaps only one or two—cover an event firsthand, reporting personally back to large groups of reporters and photographers, giving them a firsthand account on which to base their story.

Such a sharing arrangement at Dallas would have solved many of the problems the press created with its shouting, shoving, clamoring for attention and recognition and, of course, for "the story." It would have taken an element of hysteria out of events which seemed to surround Oswald after he was taken into custody.

In its study of the assassination of President Kennedy the Warren Commission, recognizing the need for the press to be on hand when history is made, but recognizing also that too much press can create an impossible situation, recommended that representatives of the bar, law enforcement agencies and the news media work together to establish ethical standards concerning the gathering and presentation of information to the public.

But now in Memphis the authorities wanted no newsmen, pool or otherwise. They wanted to operate as much in secret as possible The concept that police could be trusted to conduct public business without outside observation was now taking control. The police wanted no publicity on how they brought Ray home to Memphis. "Trust us," the authorities seemed to be telling the American people; and a "trust the police" mood was on the country.

What would have happened if Ray had gone berserk, assaulted an officer and had been beaten into submission? Police credibility would have been irreparably damaged because it all would have happened in "secret." If Ray had slipped and fallen and injured himself, cut his face or wrenched his back and had claimed police brutality, a shadow would have been cast over law enforcement. If Ray had attempted suicide en route to the jail, or after arrival, the police would have been suspected. The press very well could have been a valuable ally in such situations, which fortunately did not arise.

Newsmen in Memphis were made to feel that they were "intruders" without rights. This callous attitude toward press freedom—which is, after all, a first amendment guaranty—was not limited to the police themselves, although they did "make their own rules." They knew that the judge who would try the case was behind them. It was the court, in fact, that took the most extreme, arbitrary position with regard to the press. W. Preston Battle, Criminal Court Judge in Shelby County, Tennessee, became, during this case, the embodiment of the worst the press feared in its conflict with the American Bar Association over the issue of "free press and fair trial." For members of the press, the attitude and actions of Judge Battle in the Ray case can only be described as a travesty of justice.

Of all the great American myths, perhaps the most unfounded and shopworn is the idea that American justice is even-handed and consistent. Nothing is more inconsistent than justice in its day-to-day operation. The foibles and idiosyncrasies of individual judges in the American system of justice contribute to this inconsistency.

In New Orleans, Judge Haggerty established guidelines governing how the press would perform in the coverage of the Clay Shaw trial. Having established rules limiting the contacts lawyers in the case might have with the press, Judge Haggerty proceeded to ignore his own rules. When District Attorney Garrison began his indiscriminate campaign to convince the world of a conspiracy in New Orleans, Haggerty took no reasonable precaution to control or discipline Garrison. The result was that Garrison had a media field day and, ultimately, newsmen had to take it upon themselves to try to show that what Garrison claimed was a conspiracy was, in fact, fiction.

In Memphis, Judge Battle, stern, autocratic, severe, went to extremes in the other direction in dealing with the mass media. He was, in many ways, the antithesis of Judge Haggerty. A reformed alcoholic, Battle seemed to enjoy very little in life or in court. He took himself seriously. Where Haggerty sometimes ruled with abandon, often reversing himself within minutes, Battle rarely drew an incautious breath. He always appeared to be dealing with every problem as if there were a great crisis awaiting his words.

Battle looked for support for his actions either in legal precedents or the Canons of Ethics, or even among lawyers. He seemed often to seek a sort of consensus in the law before ruling. When reversed by a higher bench, he bristled and sometimes complained in open court.

He frequently called recesses in court to research opinions of other courts and precedents, sometimes on very routine questions. He would often surprise members of the bar with whom he would come into contact socially in Memphis by asking directly what they thought or knew about a given legal proposition or case on which he might have to rule. Preston Battle, who candidly praised Alcoholics Anonymous for saving him from the gutter for the bench, was admired as a man who had saved himself and had become a good citizen and a good judge. But, he was not comfortable under pressure. Now, as he confronted the trial of James Earl Ray, he was under intense pressure.

He knew the world-wide implications that were tied to the Ray case, that his rulings and words would be transmitted all around the world. Unlike Judge Haggerty, he did not relish that spotlight of publicity.

He knew the implications at home, in Memphis, where there was a restless and angry black population of significant proportions. But he had made up his mind how he would act and was prepared to deal with the case in as heavy-handed a manner as he might deem necessary.

There were three documents to which Judge Battle seemed to attach great importance as he faced the Ray trial. The first of these was the U.S. Supreme Court decision in the Sam Sheppard case. The second was the finding of the Warren Commission as it related to the press. The third was the preliminary draft of the report by the committee of the American Bar Association headed by Justice Reardon of Massachusetts.

The Sheppard ruling castigated the news media, particularly the Cleveland Press, for its coverage of the Sam Sheppard case. But the decision warmly suggested that the trial judge could have cured the ills created by an irresponsible press by granting Sheppard a change of venue in the case, allowing the defendant to be tried in another Ohio district.

The thrust of what the Warren Commission had to say was to recommend that the press act in a more conscientious manner when crises attract large numbers of newsmen whose presence creates disorder and whose competitiveness stimulates chaos when calmness and reason are needed.

Finally, the early draft of the Reardon report, softened only slightly later on, urged courts to hold in contempt lawyers, police and officers of the court who spoke to elements of the news media about pre-trial matters—and further recommended that in some cases newsmen be cited for contempt.

It was the wholesale implementation of this final point—holding in contempt lawyers and newsmen involved in pre-trial publication of news about the Ray case—that put Judge Battle in

Memphis at the opposite extreme of Judge Haggerty in New Orleans. Haggerty did not seem to care what lawyers said through the media. Battle was often outraged when anyone close to the case said anything.

Most responsible segments of the press regretted the coverage in Cleveland which led to the Sheppard case ruling. At any rate, the finding of the Supreme Court in that case—that the trial judge could have cured the ill by changing the trial to another jurisdiction—was never considered seriously as applicable by Battle to the Ray case.

Most responsible segments of the press acknowledged, even embraced, the need to prevent another press mob scene such as the one at Dallas which culminated in Ruby's killing of Oswald. News executives and the Sigma Delta Chi honorary journalism fraternity would have welcomed a chance to cooperate on press coverage in Memphis.

But on the issue of the courts being vested with the right to hold the press in contempt, as recommended by the Reardon committee, and to thereby prevent publication of news about the courts, the responsible press balked and strongly protested. News executives felt that the power to punish by contempt was the power to jail reporter, cameraman, editor, news director, publisher, and that the very nature of the action was an intimidation of the press; it was to prevent such power from ever being imposed by any branch of government that Congress wrote into the Constitution that there would be no law abridging freedom of speech or of the press.

There are times in criminal cases when the press, if it is to meet its responsibility to the public, must write about incidents that may interfere with a given court's idea of a fair trial. For example, when President Johnson, his attorney general at his side, calls a press conference to announce that the perpetrators of the murders of three civil rights workers in Mississippi have been identified and are to be arrested and charged, that press conference may result in publicity which may be prejudicial to those men accused of the crime. Or, when President Nixon speaks of the guilt of the defendants in a California murder case during the trial of the case, his comments may result in prejudicial publicity. But the press does what it must do: it reports what the President says.

When a lawyer is disbarred for jury fixing in a criminal case while the trial is pending—as a lawyer for James R. Hoffa was disbarred in 1963—that action by the court may in theory damage Hoffa's right to a fair trial. Again, the press in such a case does what it must: it reports the action of the court.

When J. Edgar Hoover releases the list of the nation's "Ten Most Wanted Criminals," and identifies one of them as "public enemy number one" it may damage that "public enemy's" right to a fair trial when he is captured and charged and tried in a court of law. But again, the press does what it must do: it reports Mr. Hoover's list.

The press in Los Angeles faced the same dilemma after Senator Kennedy was shot, when Mayor Sam Yorty announced that sources close to the investigation had discovered that Sirhan had communistic ties. Newsmen in Los Angeles familiar with Yorty's frequent anti-Communist statements were skeptical. But the press was required to quote the mayor of a city. Fortunately, there were some reporters who called other sources to check on the Yorty claims. By nightfall there was widespread doubt cast by the media in California on the claims of the Los Angeles mayor.

The question is raised as to whether Lee Harvey Oswald could have received a fair trial after the assassination of President Kennedy. It is ludicrous to suggest that the press, following the murder of the President, should have withheld, during the hours Oswald lived following Kennedy's death, such facts as: Oswald's visit to the Soviet Union as a malcontent U.S. citizen; his marriage to a Russian communist; his purchase of a rifle by mail order (the rifle was found in the Texas Book Depository); his support of Fidel Castro and other pertinent facts of his life.

How all of this might have affected Oswald's right to a trial on a charge of murder is a question that cannot be answered, and might still be debated, had Oswald lived. Surely it must be said, if the Sheppard ruling—that jurors are influenced by the media even though they swear they are not—is taken seriously, then the "live" telecast of the death of Oswald, as Ruby gunned him down in the Dallas police station, must have affected Ruby's right to a fair trial.

There was no Warren Commission in Memphis to gather evidence, analyze it, study it and come up with findings that one man, acting alone, was guilty. A nationally known personality had been shot down in broad daylight. It was suspected that he was slain by highly skilled professional "contract" killers. The authorities—Mr. Hoover's FBI and Ramsey Clark, the U. S. Attorney General—were suggesting to the American people that this was the work of one man, not a conspiracy. And at the same time the government was swearing out a warrant charging Galt—and a man "whom he alleged to be his brother." Here was a case in which there were conflicting eye-witness accounts, not to mention a mysterious radio broadcast.

Journalists poured into Memphis from all over the world seeking answers to these contradictions. Responsible journalists made up their minds they would not be intimidated by Judge Preston Battle.

Questions needed to be answered in the public mind about the murder of Dr. King. The press was in business to try to answer such questions if agencies of government would not. More and more people doubted that Ray could have stumbled into Memphis, without any apparent or explained motive, planned and executed the killing, and then escaped without help or substantial financial resources.

The major reason the public interest in the possibility of a conspiracy bothered Judge Battle was his intense dislike for being reversed by higher courts. The area he was about to enter was lacking in clear legal precedents. He was not sure of his ability to punish newsmen, or even lawyers who talked to newsmen about the pros and cons of a conspiracy. And whatever action he took was certain to be appealed to higher courts—even to the U. S. Supreme Court, since federal constitutional questions relating to a free press were involved.

Every judge worries that his rulings may be reversed by higher judges.

Judge Battle took some of his reversals in stride, but there is no indication that he ever thought that he was wrong. Prior to being selected by his fellow judges to try the Ray case, Battle had suffered two major disappointments. In 1965 he had actively sought appointment to the Tennessee Supreme Court. He lost that appointment. At age sixty he knew that was his last chance. Then, in 1967, there was a second major blow: he was reversed by the Supreme Court to which he had been denied appointment in a case which, prior to the trial of James Earl Ray, was the most widely publicized over which he had presided. A well-known and wealthy Memphis grocer, Louis Montesi, had been found guilty of murdering his wife by a jury in Battle's court.

The Supreme Court reversed that conviction on the ground that Judge Battle had erred by admitting evidence to the jury that should have been withheld. Montesi was convicted a second time—and the case was reversed a second time—but Judge Battle bristled until his death under that Montesi ruling overturning his decision. Judge Battle said publicly and frankly that he disagreed with the Montesi case findings of the State Supreme Court. "I am still of the same opinion," he would say in open court.

Now he was fearful of being found in error in the Ray case. He often spoke in solemn tones about the possibility of reversible error creeping into the coming trial.

He worried about the tense racial situation that still prevailed in Memphis in October, 1968. He was aware that there was a hospital workers' strike going on at that time. He speculated that the strike by workers, most of whom were black, might still be going on when he tried the case. Then he hypothesized about what he might do if the strikers marched around the courthouse while the Ray case was going on.

"I have nothing against them marching," he said. "But if they come around this courthouse during the trial I'll just have to take some action to stop it. I can't have the jury that will decide this case seeing any demonstrations.

"I will try to work six days a week, if possible," he stated. "Of course I can't make the defense work that hard. If they claim the six day sessions prohibit them from providing an adequate defense I'll have to go along with them."

He went on: "Personally, I would like to work on Sundays but you can't do that, you know. I got reversed once for working a jury on Sunday."

Judge Battle, in the eyes of lawyers who practiced before him and knew him, and in the view of fellow judges who selected him to try the Ray case, was respected for his strong will. As a young district attorney, he had been suspended from his job and fined in court for driving while drunk. From that point he had come back, a teetotaler, to sit and rule on important criminal matters.

A graying man with heavy jowls, Battle was considered industrious, careful, even studious when it was necessary to research precedents. He enjoyed reading the Greek Classics. Some lawyers called him "old unflappable." But he had a tendency to be an absolutist: to make up his mind that he was right on a narrow legal question and then proceed, looking neither left nor right. In the Ray case there were times when he seemed to be looking through the wrong end of the telescope, focusing his complete attention on getting the case disposed of without acknowledging that a great deal of public concern, not to mention human emotion, was attending the unanswered questions about who killed Martin Luther King.

On July 19, 1968, Judge Battle issued his ten-point guidelines on press coverage of the case: a strict and far-reaching set of rules for coverage of the arraignment and trial of Ray.

Entitled "On Courthouse and Courtroom Procedure and Publicity," Battle's guidelines provided:

1. That the doors and corridors to courtrooms and offices in the Criminal Courts Building be kept clear to free access at all times;
2. That no cameras, photographic, television, radio or sound equipment, including tape recorders, be permitted in the courthouse and that no photographs of the jury be taken; in addition, no sketches in the courthouse;
3. That all persons entering the courtroom submit voluntarily to a search;
4. That no one enter or leave the courtroom while court was in session;
5. That no one except the defendant, counsel, members of the bar, court personnel and witnesses be permitted beyond the rail in the courtroom;
6. That no one except attorneys of record, and others qualified by virtue of their position be allowed to handle the trial's exhibits;
7. That all lawyers in the case, their assistants, and employees under their supervision be forbidden to take part in "interviews for publicity and from making extra-judicial statements" about the case until a verdict be returned;
8. That the county medical examiner, jury commissioners,

the criminal court clerk, county sheriff, police officials and other law enforcement officers, employees of the court and all other persons employed in the Criminal Courts Building be prohibited from making statements about the case;

9. That all witnesses, persons subpoenaed to grand jury or court, jurors and those summoned but excused from jury service be forbidden to make statements in interviews for "publicity";

10. That nothing in the guidelines be interpreted to prohibit "any witnesses from discussing any matter in connection with the case with any of the attorneys representing the defendant or the state.

It was remarkable that a man of Battle's experience felt he could control exploration of unanswered questions. He banned attorneys, their assistants and all court employees from making any "extra-judicial" or outside-the-courtroom comment to the press until after the jury returned a verdict. This order would apply to any witnesses in the case—anybody connected with it in any way, including police.

The judge wanted *no* statements made to the press by the principals, under these guidelines. Many members of the bar would read these guidelines and applaud them. Here the typical lawyer's theory of justice comes in conflict with reality. Judge Battle obviously felt that the system of justice was capable of producing something close to an absolute truth. He seemed to be saying that if operated in a total vacuum, justice could provide a satisfactory answer; that he could make it a search for truth. But unrelated to the publicity concerning a case, guilty men sometimes go free and innocent men sometimes go to prison. These miscarriages of justice on both sides occur in the most routine cases in which there is little or no press coverage. Years pass before truth comes to light—if it ever does—and as often as not it is the press, not the system of justice, which exposes the flaw that led to injustice.

In the Ray case the populace of a community, including a substantial black citizenry, was talking, thinking, examining every aspect of the case. The press would not stop trying to find out what was behind the murder of Dr. King simply because Preston Battle wanted to run his court in a vacuum.

Everything that happened to James Earl Ray now that he was incarcerated and awaiting trial would be of interest to the people. On one hand the press was interested in making certain that Ray, charged but by no means yet found guilty, was not mistreated and that his rights were not violated. On the other hand, the press was interested in determining, if it could, whether more than one man was involved in a murder.

In that situation Judge Battle's guidelines banning all "extra-judicial" statements were unrealistic.

The purpose of his guidelines was this: nobody would say anything to the press about the case. In a democratic society where the press is free, such a stringent rule is unreasonable. Shortly after his guidelines were made public—by the press, incidentally—Judge Battle seemed to sense he had gone too far.

One of those who had bridled under Battle's initial rule barring any "extrajudicial" statement was Arthur Hanes. He had talked at will in London—where press codes presumably bar newsmen from writing about pending court matters.

Hanes read Judge Battle's guidelines and privately let newsmen know he thought the "no talk" rule damaged his ability to help his client. He contended that it inhibited him from putting pressure on the police authorities to seek out conspirators he said were involved with Ray.

Hanes knew that the FBI had released to the press and public a flood of detailed background matter which tied Ray in with the killing. For instance, after Ray's arrest in London the FBI had released the following information: James Earl Ray had arrived in Birmingham in the summer of 1967 and had established an identity as Eric Starvo Galt. He purchased a white 1966 Mustang and obtained a driver's license in that name. During the fall and winter he made several trips to the West Coast where he took dancing lessons and a course in bartending. He left Los Angeles for New Orleans, December 15, 1967, and returned December 21. He was graduated from a bartending school in Hollywood, March 2, 1968.

On April 4, 1968, using the name John Willard, Ray checked into a rooming house facing the Lorraine Motel in Memphis, where Dr. King was staying. He refused a room on the north side of the house but took one near the back with a view of the balcony outside King's room. One roomer reported he saw Willard emerge from the bathroom with something wrapped in newspaper after the murder shot was fired. A Remington 30-06 pump rifle with a telescopic sight and a case containing binoculars were found lying on the sidewalk a few feet from the entrance of the rooming house. But the FBI went further: the agency announced that Ray had been arrested on five occasions between 1949 and 1959. Ray's long list of aliases was cited.

According to the FBI, Ray had purchased the gun in Birmingham under the name of Galt or Lowmyer. The Mustang had been impounded on April 11 in Atlanta where it had been parked in front of a housing project since April 5.

The FBI told the press that after the assassination Ray had gone to Canada where he had resided in a Toronto rooming house. He received a passport in the name Sneyd on April 24 and then flew from Toronto to London May 6 and then on to Lisbon May 7. Ray returned to London May 17 and apparently stayed there until his capture June 8. Ray was trying to board a plane to leave Britain when he was apprehended.

All of this was galling to Hanes. The FBI had released a list of charges against his client, detailing most of the evidence against Ray. The evidence to be presented by the state of Tennessee would, no doubt, follow closely that information which had been released in the name of the FBI.

Hanes, as former mayor of a Southern city, knew the admiration with which J. Edgar Hoover was held in the minds of most citizens of the region. As a matter of fact, he himself was an admirer of Hoover.

But as lawyer for James Earl Ray, he was at odds with the FBI.

The evidence produced against his client in court would be, for the most part, FBI-developed evidence. Some of the witnesses would be people who had been interviewed and induced to tell their stories in the first place by the FBI. He suspected that FBI agents very well might be called upon to testify against his client, bringing with them to the witness chair in Memphis all the prestige and stature of their organization.

When Hanes came to Memphis, then, the FBI, through previously released statements, had effectively accused his client of killing Dr. King. That was the impact of the press releases the FBI had put out about Ray telling who he was, what his past was, what his movements had been, up to and including putting him at the scene of the crime with a gun, listing him as a desperate fugitive—even correcting an error it made in the release regarding Ray's capture.

From Hanes' point of view, that was what had been fed to the public.

Now he came to Memphis and discovered he would not be allowed to say a word to the press; not be permitted to make a single "extra-judicial" statement.

The prosecution, through the FBI, had put into the public domain what the theory of the case against Ray was to be. The defense, under the rules of Judge Battle, could not do so.

Hanes was a clever and outspoken man. In England, where the press is supposed to be under ironclad rules about publishing information concerning a pending court case, Hanes had talked freely to reporters. In Memphis he recognized his conflict: on one hand he had a duty to his client, whom he felt had been treated unfairly; on the other hand he had a duty to the court to keep his mouth shut.

Judge Battle no doubt thought his directive to be within the boundaries set by the Supreme Court in the Sam Sheppard case. But in fact the high court in that case acknowledged a legitimate interest of the press in the news about the Sheppard case.

The trial judge, said the court, might have cured the problem of publicity saturation in the Cleveland area by transferring the trial to another Ohio city.

But Battle was intent on stifling press criticism, not transferring the case. Once his order was handed down, the judge, in a rare moment of uncertainty, began to reconsider his position. Perhaps members of the Memphis Bar advised him he had gone too far in banning *any* statement.

On July 22, three days after Ray's incarceration in the Memphis jail, the accused prisoner was arraigned in Battle's heavily guarded courtroom. The proceeding ended in eleven minutes. Ray sat there silently and allowed Hanes to enter the not guilty plea for him in response to the two charges: murder and carrying a dangerous weapon.

The hearing was hurried. Battle seemed preoccupied with

getting it over and having the prisoner put back upstairs in the jail over his courtroom. The judge set trial for November 12.

Hanes promised that the defense would be ready. He had three and a half months to prepare to defend his client—and he went to work immediately.

The following day, July 23, Judge Battle relaxed his press guidelines, saying that he had not meant to ban all press comment. He had meant to ban any statement that might be "prejudicial."

Newsmen were already anxious for details about Ray's present condition, especially since he was a prisoner whose captivity was marked by unprecedented security precautions: a suite of air-conditioned jail cells had been prepared for Ray before his arrival in Memphis. Steel plates covered the cell windows. Closed circuit television cameras had been installed in Ray's cell so that his every move could be monitored. Brilliant fluorescent lights surrounded the cells and were never turned off. Two spotlights shone into the 18 x 22 foot "tank" that was Ray's home. High in the corner over the door to Ray's cell, one television camera was placed. Another watched him from the opposite corner, and a third was located in a corridor outside the cell. It focused on an uncurtained shower stall. The cell was on the third floor just above Judge Battle's courtroom, and Ray could be moved with dispatch from his cell-suite to the courtroom during trial. Ray's family and his lawyers, the only persons permitted near him while he awaited trial, had to pass through a guard post on the first floor of the courthouse. The visitors approached first a heavy, steel-plated door behind which was a bullet proof room called the "control center" where deputies sat eight-hour shifts around the clock. Those seeking admittance to the area of the jail where Ray was located had to be cleared through this control center, and the visitors communicated by a microphone with those deputies encased in the control room. This nerve center of the protective system was equipped with three red and three green lights, and those on guard knew that three red lights meant "red alert" and no doors would be unlocked. Once the visitors were cleared by control center they passed through a door into a small anteroom and under a sign reading "no guns allowed," they were searched by deputies. From that point an elevator took them up to the cell area, where they stepped into the brightly lighted arena which gave a sort of "celebrity presence" to the drab old jail. Outside the cell, five feet from the entrance, two unarmed guards were stationed behind a desk. On one end of the desk a television set provided community entertainment for Ray and his watchers. On the other end of the desk a monitor set kept Ray's image in constant view. A second monitor was located in an office on the second floor of the forty-year-old building near the remodeled courtroom where Battle presided. A third monitor was in a wooden cabinet on the desk of Sheriff William Morris. A red light on Morris' desk flashed on whenever Ray's cell door opened. Ray's meals were prepared by a prisoner who had trusty status, selected personally by Sheriff Morris for his trustworthiness. The food was placed in a steel lockbox and the key to that box was kept in the bulletproof control center. A guard on duty always carried the foodbox to Ray's cell. The other guard fetched the cell key from the control center.

Even the guards were required to have security clearance. Special numbered tokens were given to the guards and exchanged with each shift. Without the tokens the guards were not permitted to enter or leave.

Judge Battle's initial order that no extra-judicial statements be made to the press about the case was intended to cover the jail security. He wanted to keep these elaborate security plans secret. It was the judge's feeling that for the public to know what he knew about the details of Ray's incarceration would have been prejudicial in that it would make Ray appear to be some sort of "super criminal" who could not be trusted even to have a bowel movement in private. But this strict order put the court and particularly Sheriff Morris under intense pressure from the news media whose members felt the public was entitled to know whether Ray was safe, well-fed, not ill—and who his visitors were.

When, on the day after arraignment, Judge Battle relaxed his strict "no extra-judicial statement" and said he had really meant no prejudicial statement should be given to the press, Sheriff Morris agreed to meet with reporters and try to answer some of their questions. He told them the county had spent about $6,000 for special security precautions. This was needed, he felt, to avoid making Memphis another Dallas. He discussed why the television cameras and the stainless steel food box were considered necessary. He described Ray's movements about his cell, his eating and sleeping habits, his affinity for doing pushups, reading and watching television.

He also told newsmen that Ray had received approximately $1,000 in contributions from people who wanted to aid in his defense. He steered away from detailed questions about security, dealing only with the basic facts of such unusual expenditures as lighting and the television monitors. He was not anxious to advertise how to get to Ray or the security program he had developed to control access to Ray.

Morris' press conference was conducted with Judge Battle's knowledge. Unknown to Battle, another principal in the case spoke to the press that day. When Arthur Hanes arrived in town a few hours after the sheriff spoke with newsmen, he was confronted by reporters who wanted to know the lawyer's reaction to the security precautions. Hanes, having been to the jail cell, had experienced the bright lights that kept his client on camera around the clock.

"Neither my client nor I likes the idea of a camera being focused on him twenty-four hours a day. He has to hide his head under a pillow in order to get any sleep. He even has the evil eye of the camera on him when he uses the bathroom. This, in my opinion, is an invasion of privacy, and it is hurting his health because he can't sleep with cameras blazing lights on him in his every move. Gentlemen, this is cruel," said Arthur Hanes.

He conceded that he believed "the sheriff and his people are trying to protect my client's political rights." At the same time, he said, "they are trampling on his individual rights."

The conversation with the reporters then turned to the evidence against Ray. Here was an opportunity to give his theory of the case as the FBI had earlier given its theory in press releases.

"There is a great conspiracy here and my client is being used in that conspiracy," Hanes declared. "It is a left wing conspiracy to create chaos and confusion and to promote rioting in the streets."

Hanes went on to say that he, his wife and even their seventy-year-old maid, Lena, had been threatened.

"My wife answers the phone and a voice says, 'death, death, death' or 'you will die.' "

He continued: "We are playing in the major leagues on this

one. My son and I are the only people who have talked with this man. My neck is out on this one."

Indeed it was. Even as he was talking he was protruding it further under a contempt-of-court citation in the hands of Preston Battle.

When Hanes' words appeared in the Memphis press, the judge was shaken. It is impossible to suggest that Hanes' statement influenced anyone about the guilt or innocence of James Earl Ray. But apparently, that was not really the principal question in the view of Preston Battle. He saw it as his duty to shut off press commentary about the case. He did not want the public reading or hearing about how Ray was kept or about Hanes' thoughts on Ray's defense.

Judge Battle immediately appointed a committee of seven attorneys to investigate the possibility that his court order had been violated.[1] His decision was not a normal legal procedure. Although there is some precedent for advisory committees to recommend judicial procedural matters, and, in fact, to investigate disbarment charges against fellow lawyers, there is hardly a valid reason for a judge asking a commission to make a judicial decision for him, and contempt is a question for judicial determination.

In a sense, the judge was passing on to a committee his own judicial responsibility. Understanding Battle's hypersensitivity to reversal and his search for community approval, his decision was characteristic. It is probable that he anticipated the committee would recommend to him that he hold Hanes in contempt. It is highly unlikely that he expected what he got from his "watchdog" committee.

On July 30, the group reported that four persons should be cited for contempt: Hanes for his airport statement, Sheriff Morris for his interview with reporters about Ray's incarceration, and a Memphis attorney, Russell K. Thompson, who at one point had been approached by Hanes about joining the defense team in the case and who had been quoted as saying publicly he thought the defendant might be innocent. The fourth recommendation must have shaken Judge Battle more than the others. The committee wanted him to cite for contempt Ramsey Clark, the Attorney

1. The members of the committee were Lucius Burch, chairman, J. Alan Hanover, Cooper Turner, Jr., James D. Causey, Leo Bearman, Jr., Lee A. Hardison, and Don Owen.

General of the United States, chief of all federal prosecutors, lawyers and U.S. marshals, as well as the official boss of J. Edgar Hoover.

His watchdog committee seemed at this point more imbued with the spirit of the Reardon report than the judge himself. The last thing he wanted was a long drawn-out court fight with the U. S. Attorney General. Nor did he want to create conflict with his sheriff—the man in charge of the security of the prisoner. And so he put aside for the present the question of contempt citations. Instead he merely reinstated his original order against *any* principal in the case making *any* comment whatsoever about Ray.

Hanes continued to antagonize Judge Battle even after the threat of a contempt charge. Battle was later to say that Hanes "generally made a nuisance of himself." In late July, Hanes walked into jail to visit his client and the guard who searched him found he was carrying a .38 caliber pistol on his person. He surrendered it voluntarily to Sheriff Morris when it was discovered in his pocket. He produced an Alabama gun permit which authorized him to carry the weapon. His life was in danger, he had said.

"Hell," said Hanes to newsmen, "I wasn't going to smuggle the thing in. That's ludicrous."

It may have been ludicrous. But, to say the least, Hanes' entering the jail with a pistol on his person was a shock to lawyers. Tennessee law prohibits carrying a pistol for the purpose of being armed. Morris confirmed to newsmen that Hanes had been found carrying a gun into the jail. He would not comment further.

However, Robert K. Dwyer, an assistant district attorney, released a statement saying: "Neither Mr. Hanes nor any other citizen has the right to go armed in Tennessee. It is a violation of the law. We are going to look into the situation." Nothing was ever done about it. No action was taken against Hanes. Perhaps the reason was that Hanes had said publicly that he had been threatened and that he would have argued that he had carried the gun because he feared for his life. At any rate, Judge Battle must have looked with absolute disfavor on a member of the bar and an officer of his court carrying a pistol into the jail to see James Earl Ray, for whatever reason. And it must have horrified the judge to learn that the lawyer was entering the jail to visit his client—a man notorious for prison escape—carrying the pistol concealed on his person.

In mid-August, three weeks after Hanes' "gun-toting" encounter at the Shelby County jail, Judge Battle had a visitor at his office in Memphis. William Bradford Huie, the free lance writer and novelist, called on the judge to make a highly unsettling disclosure to him.

Huie said that through the good offices of Arthur Hanes he had gained exclusive rights from James Earl Ray to write Ray's "life story." *Look* magazine had agreed to publish the "life story" in a series of articles, the first of which would appear before the trial began.

The agreement with Ray had been negotiated with Hanes while the accused man had been held in England, weeks before his return to Memphis, Huie said. Already James Earl Ray was writing his notes and answering questions which Huie was sending to him through Hanes.

Huie, who had been known in the past to pay large sums of money to persons accused of sensational crimes for the rights to their stories, told Judge Battle he felt that he was entitled to personally visit James Earl Ray. He was, in effect, providing Ray money to pay for his legal defense and his investigation of what Ray had told him would aid Ray's lawyer in preparation of his case.

Judge Battle disagreed. The import of what Huie was telling him was clear. If Ray's life story was published in *Look,* that meant the segment of Ray's life before, during and after the assassination of Martin Luther King would be published as a vital part of the story.

Already Battle had made it clear he did not want local newspapers publishing articles quoting Hanes concerning the theory of the defense in the case. He just as clearly did not want a national magazine with heavy distribution in Memphis publishing the story.

But Huie was not asking the judge—he was stating the plan of *Look:* the story would be published.

The judge denied Huie's request to personally visit Ray. To allow Huie in the cell would probably speed the publication of the story, the judge knew. He wanted to slow it if he could.

During July and August of 1968, James Earl Ray wrote ten thousand words for Huie, and Arthur Hanes carried these portions of the manuscript to and from the jail cell. Months later the contract, which actually had been entered into on July 8, was made public and it answered what earlier had been some imponderables in the case, primarily who was paying Hanes to serve as Ray's attorney. Indirectly, *Look* Magazine was.

Under the terms of the contract Huie was to receive forty percent of all proceeds from the magazine articles and a subsequent book. The remaining sixty percent was to be equally divided between Hanes and Ray. Hanes, however, by virtue of the lien rights on all Ray's property, had control of the entire sixty percent. Estimates of the value of the proceeds ranged as high as $400,000.

The advantage to Arthur Hanes was obvious. Huie was to provide him with the resources to make it worthwhile to represent Ray. Beyond that, it made it possible for Huie to become, in effect, a member of the defense team. Huie, over the years, had earned a reputation as a highly effective investigative reporter. Since 1955, a good deal of his writing related to stories about the field of civil rights in the South. A native of Alabama, he was a man who had learned that with a national magazine providing the money, it was not difficult to get persons charged with crimes to talk. One of his better known journalistic achievements concerned the story of the murder of Emmett Till, the fourteen-year-old Mississippi Negro who had been slain in 1955 after he made a remark to a white woman at a country store near Greenville, Mississippi. Two men were charged with the murder and acquitted by a jury. After the trial Huie published in *Look* the "true story" of how Till was killed. The writer quoted the defendants and Till verbatim and detailed intricate facts about the murder, clearly implicating the two men who had been exonerated by the jury.

It was assumed by many that the two defendants, having been tried and acquitted, therefore not subject to being tried again, had accepted money from Huie to tell the full story. He wrote it without attributing it to them, simply spelling out the facts as they had been related to him and as he checked them out to confirm them to his own satisfaction.

Again, in 1965, Huie had used money to persuade some Ku Klux Klansmen that they should tell the facts about the murders of three civil rights workers in Neshoba County, Mississippi. This story was published in the New York *Herald Tribune.*

Now he had signed a contract with Hanes and Ray. Huie had agreed to check out every fact that Ray gave him concerning his movements during that period when the FBI contended that Ray was involved in the murder of Dr. King. By this arrangement Arthur Hanes was certain of being paid for his representation of Ray, and he was also assured that Huie would serve as an investigator who might corroborate Ray's claim about his actions. Huie very well might be used as a witness for Hanes. In addition, a national magazine would publish the story and would make public Ray's side of the story. To Hanes the deal with Huie could only represent a valuable asset.

But for Judge Preston Battle, William Bradford Huie was a liability. Through his "press guidelines" Judge Battle had tried to intimidate the local press into near-silence about the case. The mere naming of a committee to advise him on contempt citations had the effect of warning lawyers and the press against a penetrating public discussion of the case.

And now Huie had acquired what other journalists could not get: the details of Ray's defense.

The day after it became known that Huie was writing the Ray story with the help of Arthur Hanes, Ray filed in Judge Battle's court a motion to quash the murder charges. The motion was entered into the record of the case by Hanes' son, Art Hanes, Jr. In the light of Hanes' deal with Huie to give national publicity to the case, the grounds cited were ironic.

"Pervasive and widespread publicity" had ruined Ray's chance for a fair trial anywhere in the United States, Hanes contended in this petition. Simultaneously Hanes declared that he was strictly observing Judge Battle's admonition to lawyers not to discuss the case. "From now on I'm giving only my name, rank and serial number," he told reporters.

On September 5, Hanes came to court to argue the motion his son had filed before Judge Battle. It was a brief hearing, during which he won a minor concession from the judge: the right to inspect some prosecution files. But when the "pervasive and widespread publicity" matter came up there was a testiness in the exchange between the lawyer and the judge.

Standing before the bench Hanes acknowledged that under ordinary circumstances "the proper motion at this time" would be for a change of venue to remove the case from the jurisdiction of the crime where news coverage would have been heaviest.

"But," argued Hanes, "I contend that publicity in this case has been so widespread that there is no jurisdiction in the land, not the smallest hamlet, that has not been permeated by a torrent of words.

"Somewhere, sometime some judge is going to have to take a stand. Some court must take unusual action to stop this vicious pre-trial adjudication."

Judge Battle answered: "I think it is ironical that you are here saying you can't get a fair trial when the press has castigated the court for an order restricting pre-trial publicity." He added this self-serving declaration: "In some cases where all sides curse the judge he has probably done what is right."

He turned down Hanes' motion to quash the indictment.

Obviously Preston Battle had read what the press in Memphis and across the nation had said about his strict guidelines and he disliked this disapproval. But in his own mind he was proceeding to do as he felt the Sheppard case directed and as the American Bar Association was suggesting in the Reardon report.

Still, Hanes was propounding an interesting theory and in a media-saturated society it is worth serious thought. Arthur Hanes was saying that there are some cases which develop where the public interest in the crime, and the press response to the public interest, are so great that the right of the defendant charged with the crime is inevitably damaged.

In such cases, he argued, it is a waste of time to try to get an impartial jury because jurors would be influenced by media coverage of the crime and events surrounding it.

It was "widespread and pervasive" publicity that led the Supreme Court to overturn the Sam Sheppard conviction, after twelve jurors had found him guilty. But if the media has the power to influence jurors, are there specific cases where a fair trial is impossible?

For example, was it possible for Jack Ruby to get a fair trial? While the nation watched the televised U. S. Senate memorial services for President Kennedy, the scene on the screen suddenly switched to Dallas where Lee Harvey Oswald was about to be transferred from the Dallas police station to the county jail. Oswald, handcuffed and surrounded by officers, walked toward a waiting police car. From the crowd of newsmen and spectators Jack Ruby suddenly emerged, pistol in hand, and pumped the fatal shots into Oswald's body. The nation watched, and then watched again the "instant replay" which the network offered minutes later.

Could anybody who saw that give Ruby a fair trial? Surely it must be said, if the Sheppard ruling that jurors are influenced by the media—even though they swear they are not—is taken seriously, then the "live" telecast of the death of Oswald, as Ruby gunned him down in the Dallas police station, must have affected Ruby's right to a fair trial. But can anyone argue seriously that the courts should have held in contempt the TV cameramen who photographed the scene of the killing, or the reporters who commented on it, or the networks which broadcast it?

The Sheppard case in Cleveland challenged press responsibility. But in the murder of Oswald, cameramen were filming a news event when a crime occurred. In such situations, the immediacy of electronic media poses some interesting problems for the administration of justice.

Another pertinent example involves the riots that occurred at the Democratic National Convention in Chicago in the summer of 1968. Television networks broadcast edited scenes of what later came to be called "a police riot"—law officers charging and attacking demonstrators.

Some of the film editing and commentary by newsmen brought criticism to commentators and the networks. Mayor Richard J. Daley attacked the media for biased reporting. It was charged that newsmen showed a one-sided picture of the clash; the harassment of police and "cop-baiting" techniques by the demonstrators were ignored by the journalists who concentrated their cameras and their attention on the violent police response.

Mayor Daley said the reporters were clearly prejudiced in their coverage. Reporters insisted they acted responsibly and in fact were themselves frequent victims of police brutality during the Chicago troubles. But this is of less interest here than the effect the news product might have had on prospective jurors.

Once the events were filmed and edited, the networks presented them as part of the news coverage of the convention. To the networks it was news, as the Oswald killing had been news. The effect the news product had on the public, as prospective jurors, in some future case against a policeman or demonstrator never was a consideration for the networks as they went about televising the story as they had it.

When the two-hundred-and-twelve-man Chicago study team called the "Walker Commission," which analyzed the disorders at the convention, released its findings, the press reported on these findings without regard to whether the contents of the Walker Report might influence the later trial of police officers and demonstrators. At one point the report called the police charge on demonstrators a "police riot." Elsewhere in the report, prepared under the direction of Chicago lawyer, Daniel Walker, the antics of the demonstrators were candidly detailed. The report included photographs of protesters carrying picket signs with obscene slogans. Methods of police harassment were outlined. The Walker report was news. Its effect on the ultimate trials that developed from the convention disorders was not the primary concern to the press.

It is infuriating to some lawyers, particularly those who must defend clients, to realize that freedom of the press imposes upon the news media the job of reporting to the people on matters which concern them. Everything that happened in Chicago concerned the public interest. A candidate for the highest office in the land was being nominated there. It is conceivable that the disorders there influenced the outcome of the election.

In such situations the first interest of the media is something editors and reporters call "the public's right to know," where the lawyer's ultimate concern is getting his client a fair trial by a jury uninfluenced by what the media has done.

But Hanes came to court on September 5 to argue more than the esoteric legal question of free press versus fair trial and to ask Battle for a landmark ruling on that subject. He lost that motion as he must have suspected he would. But he also wanted the lights out in Ray's cell. It wouldn't take "unusual action" to get that. When Battle killed his motion to quash the murder charges, Hanes turned at once to the matter of Ray's jail confinement. The flood lights in the jail cell were intolerable, said Hanes.

"This man cannot rest," he told Judge Battle.

"He hides under his cover or pillows to sleep," pleaded Hanes. "This constitutes cruel and inhuman treatment."

Battle directed Hanes to file this plea in writing.

Hanes resented the cavalier attitude of the judge. If his client was subjected to cruel and inhuman confinement, that condition would be extended by several days if he was required to file a written motion and then argue it before the judge. He would do that, he said. But his tone rang with displeasure.

On September 11—six days after the hearing—Hanes was interviewed by Roy Hamilton, veteran courthouse reporter for the Memphis *Press-Scimitar,* the afternoon newspaper.

James Earl Ray's health was declining as a result of the type of confinement he was forced to endure, Hanes told Hamilton.

"I don't think for a moment Sheriff Bill Morris is trying to drive this guy out of his mind," said Hanes. "But it's the effect of this type of surveillance that counts."

Reporter Hamilton wrote a story that quoted Hanes' comments. Hamilton reported that Renfro T. Hays, the Memphis private detective employed by Hanes, had made an investigation of the security conditions in the county jail. Hays' findings led Hanes to the view that the confinement was unhealthy for his client.

Hamilton's story of his interview with Hanes appeared in the *Press-Scimitar* that afternoon, September 11. The next morning a follow-up story was published by the *Commercial Appeal.* In this article by Charles Edmundson, who was covering the case for the morning paper, private detective Hays was interviewed and his findings on the security procedures were reported.

Edmundson, recognized as one of the most able reporters in the national chain of Scripps-Howard papers, quoted Hays as saying that many of the techniques used in the security for Ray resembled "devices used by Communist police agents to destroy the health and balance of their victims."

In retrospect the two articles by Edmundson and Hamilton seem less than sensational. The complaints by lawyer Hanes and his investigator, Hays, seem subjective but legitimate. After all, the arrangements made for keeping Ray in custody were extraordinary. What effect these arrangements had on Ray's health were matters of public interest—and legal interest.

If the peculiar conditions of incarceration were putting a physical or mental strain on the accused man then it was of concern to the press in its traditional role as a critic of the government. Hanes had already said to Judge Battle in court that his client was suffering and had to "hide" to sleep.

The publication of the two stories in which Ray's lawyer and his investigator were quoted as criticizing the jail security arrangements infuriated Judge Battle. He was outraged at both the lawyer and the investigator. He knew both reporters Hamilton and Edmundson. They were competent and highly regarded by lawyers and public officials in the courthouse.

But Judge Battle felt they had defied his guidelines by publishing the words of Hanes and Hays. And certainly, the judge felt, Hanes and Hays had violated his rules by talking to newsmen. He had directed that there would be no pre-trial statements about the case. It was a strange position for Battle. There was hardly a chance that the jail treatment handed to Ray could ever be introduced as evidence in the trial where the charge was murder, unless it was contended this treatment had caused the defendant to become incompetent. Judge Battle's point that he did not want to make Ray seem to be a "super criminal" ignores the fact that he was treated as a super criminal.

When the news stories were published in the Memphis papers, the judge called into session his watchdog committee of Memphis lawyers he had named to advise him on press guidelines. The committee immediately recommended that the judge hold Arthur Hanes, Renfro Hays, Charles Edmundson and Roy Hamilton in contempt of his court.

For several reasons there was some doubt in the mind of the judge about citing the two reporters. First of all, there was no precedent upon which to rely. A higher court might overturn his contempt finding against the reporters and this would open the door for more reporting on the Ray case before the trial. In addition, there was a natural reluctance to pick a more serious fight with the two Scripps-Howard newspapers. The *Commercial-Appeal* was edited by Frank H. Ahlgren, a tough-minded news executive who was not likely to take the contempt citation of his reporter without a major court battle. The afternoon paper was edited by Charles H. Schneider, a relative newcomer to Memphis, but a man whose entire life had been in the newspaper field. He, too, could be counted upon to back his reporter.

But Judge Battle had already let his watchdog committee down once when he refused to hold Hanes and Ramsey Clark in contempt several weeks back. He didn't want criticism from the bar because he asked for advice, then refused to take it.

If left unchecked, Hanes would continue to harp on issues and the press would continue to report what he said. He must act, Battle concluded. And since Hays had said much of the same thing as Hanes about the confinement of Ray, the private detective also had to be cited.

He ruled on September 17. In a dramatic, precedent-setting action he ordered the two newsmen, Hanes and Hays to show cause why they should not be held in contempt of court.

The hearing, at which the four appeared on September 27 was protocol, nothing more. The judge's action was a formality. But because of the seriousness of the event it was of history-making proportions.

Arthur Hanes made no attempt to deny the words Hamilton had attributed to him in the *Press-Scimitar*. Hays did deny that he had told Edmundson what the *Commercial Appeal* article quoted him as saying. Edmundson took the stand, testifying against his lawyer's advice, and effectively called Hays a liar.

Attorneys for the newspapermen built their defense around the constitutional guarantees of the first amendment: the right of free speech and a free press.

Representing the bar committee, Lucius Burch, the Memphis lawyer, contended that the newsmen were guilty of contempt because they had, in effect, aided and abetted Hanes and Hays in violating the court order.

Hanes' position was that he was doing his best to represent a client who was, even before trial, being subjected to cruel punishment in the manner in which he was incarcerated. Since the confinement had been at least informally approved by the court, he felt within his rights in speaking out in public against what he thought was an injustice done Ray.

Judge Battle held all four in contempt of court. Their actions constituted a "clear and present danger" to the administration of justice, he said, in that they had impaired the selection of an impartial jury and the opportunity for a fair trial.

It seemed to Judge Battle important that he not be overruled before he had a chance to try James Earl Ray for the murder of

Dr. King. To avoid an appeal by the men he had cited, the judge refused to pass any sentence on them. He could have given each of them ten days in jail, but the judge knew if he passed sentence there would be an immediate appeal.

And so he withheld any sentence. He told the four that their future conduct could possibly "mitigate or purge" their contemptuous actions.

In substance the judge was leveling a none too subtle threat: Hanes and Hays were to shut up. Edmundson and Hamilton were to stop writing controversial stories about Ray.

Refusing to pass sentence on them and thereby denying them a chance to appeal his punishment and perhaps have the contempt findings overturned was plowing new legal ground. There was every reason why he should have wanted to know very early whether his contempt actions would stand up on appeal. But Judge Battle was interested primarily in one thing: getting a verdict from a Memphis jury in a case which involved a crime done in Memphis. If he could cut off press coverage surrounding the case he would be in a better position to get a jury, he felt.

Lawyers for the newsmen wanted to appeal. They argued that the judge should pass sentence and let the reporters take it to higher courts.

Just how news stories about Ray's confinement and how his health was affected by it might influence prospective jurors in a murder case is unclear. Sheriff Morris had given his view of the jail situation some days before and had escaped a contempt citation. Now when the defense spoke out, Judge Battle held the lawyer, the investigator and the reporters who quoted them in contempt.

Judge Battle's action attracted national attention. Newsmen from all over the nation began their plans to come to Memphis for the trial. Preston Battle was roundly criticized in the press for seeking to muzzle newsmen and curtail the public's right to know about the courts, and about the jails.

The press argument was that if James Earl Ray was held in a custody that caused a decline in his health he should be removed from that environment. But whether or not he was removed, the public had a right to know about unusual confinement.

The *Commercial-Appeal,* in an editorial the day following the contempt actions by the judge, said: "Such handcuffing of the

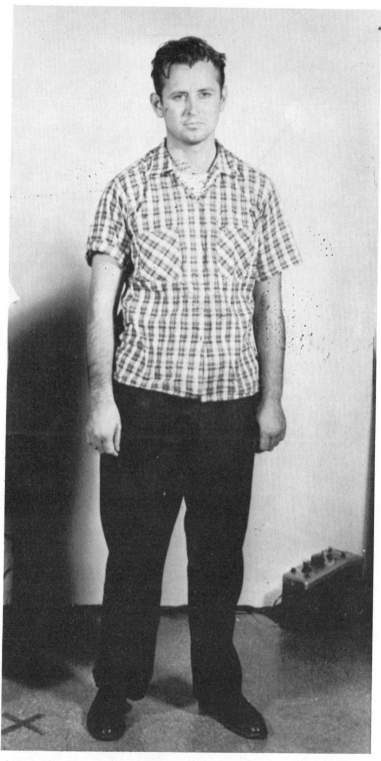

James Earl Ray in custody in St. Louis as a young man

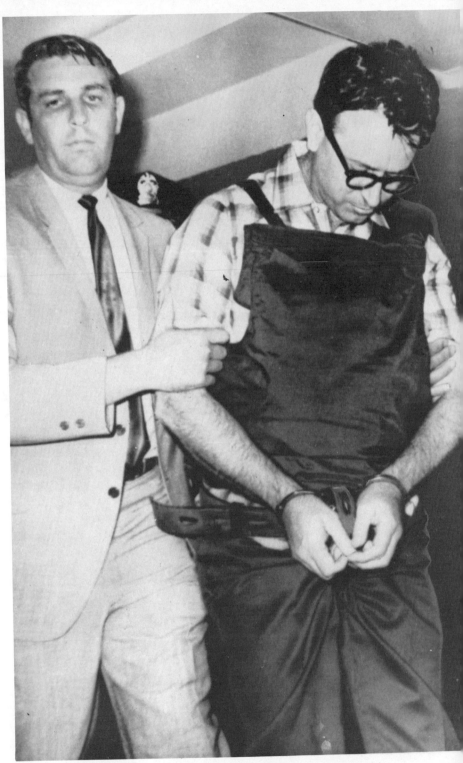

Ray wearing "custody coveralls" from London to Memphis

Ray entering Tennessee State Prison after the Memphis trial

Percy Foreman, the Texas
lawyer who represented
Ray in Memphis

Judge Preston Battle,
who presided in
the Memphis trial

Arthur Hanes and his son, Art Jr., who were fired by Ray

press and blindfolding of the citizens in a free country cannot be accepted by a responsible newspaper which must report all important happenings to the people."

The *Press-Scimitar*, in an editorial, said: ". . . As a newspaper, the *Press-Scimitar* has a responsibility to keep the community informed and, in our opinion, the responsibility is just as valid as the court's responsibility to the accused man. The court has in mind the rights of an individual, constitutionally guaranteed. The newspaper must add to the rights of the people, also constitutionally guaranteed, to know what is going on in their communities."

And *The Nashville Tennessean* commented on the editorial page that Judge Battle was "engaging in dangerous suppression of the freedom of speech," and added: "The judge's ruling is arbitrary and unrelated to the issue of a fair trial. It is difficult to see what a discussion of security precautions in the prisoner's cell has to do with selection of an impartial jury and the determination of the defendant's guilt or innocence."

And Hanes commented characteristically: "I think prejudice was shown like a grandmother's petticoat under a miniskirt."

There is not much doubt that with every new attack Preston Battle wanted to muzzle Hanes as much as he wanted to cut off the press. Actually, Judge Battle's contempt holding had less than the desired effect. In the first place, it did bring the wrath of the national press establishment down on Battle's judicial brow and more, rather than less, news exposure. Next, both Edmundson and Hamilton, the reporters, continued to cover the courthouse and the Ray case for their newspapers. Their stories seemed a bit more brief, and their editors now read with extreme care their articles on the Ray case. Lawyers for the Associated Press and United Press International now began to exercise caution in advising the Memphis bureaus of the wire services what not to send out of the city. But, with all this, the effort by Battle to subdue Hanes or to curtail the press interest failed.

Hanes had followed Battle's directive that he file a formal petition seeking to change the conditions in the jail. At a second hearing immediately following the contempt action, Hanes lost his effort to have the stringent security precautions in jail relaxed.

With Ray again in court, Hanes argued that the bright lights were keeping the defendant from sleeping. He said many of the same things in court that Judge Battle had found worthy of contempt when he read it in the press. Battle stared at the defendant, and to the judge, Ray appeared to be in good health.

"Ray has been sleeping more than I have lately," Battle said.

As the date of the trial approached, still more antagonism between Battle and the press erupted: a fight over who would see James Earl Ray tried for his life. Sheriff Morris had been flooded with requests to attend the trial from media all over the world. To handle the press arrangements, Morris hired Charles F. Holmes, a public relations man at Memphis State University.

In the second floor courtroom directly under Ray's cell, there were only seventy-six spectator seats. Of these, forty-two would be reserved for the press, the rest allotted to the public.

There were one hundred and forty-six applications for the forty-two press seats. Many major American newspapers were left off the list of papers finally accredited.

Only ten daily papers from out of town were granted seats. The Memphis press got nine; wire services three; radio and television networks, three; foreign press, five; national periodicals, four; miscellaneous, four; and four rotating seats were to be shared by all those not given a permanent seat. Battle had wanted no press controversy about the trial, but another storm of national press protest was now raised. Again, Battle was unyielding. He refused to switch the trial to a bigger courtroom. He rejected the idea of closed circuit television, an arrangement that was approved for the trial of Sirhan Sirhan in Los Angeles.

The Chicago *Tribune* lodged a formal protest at being excluded. So did the *New York Daily News,* the nation's largest paper with two million circulation. Some publications threatened legal action.

Throughout Battle's new conflict with the press, Hanes remained relatively quiet. On this issue he was satisfied. He had written a letter to Battle and won a press seat for WSGN radio, a small independent station in Birmingham.

On October 15, Hanes flew to Memphis for the stated purpose of going over some of the prosecution evidence. He verbally attacked the bar committee to Memphis reporters.

"They are a bunch of Harper Valley hypocrites," he said.

The remark was calculated to make news. At the time,

"Harper Valley PTA" was the title of a recording that was then the leading seller nationwide.

"I just cannot understand them, I've been in Memphis several times to prepare my case and that bar association hasn't even offered me the use of their library . . . . I'll tell you that would never happen to an out-of-town lawyer in Birmingham. My bar would at least be nice to them. I really like this town," he said, taking out a little insurance with the citizens, "but I just can't understand these lawyers."

At the same time, he used Judge Battle's guidelines to dig into the FBI.

The ban against press coverage "protects the prosecution and only muzzles the defense," he said to a *Commercial Appeal* reporter, adding that prosecution witnesses were making statements without fear of being cited by the committee. "Which witnesses?" asked the reporter.

"A fellow named Bonebrake," Hanes replied.

George Bonebrake, the FBI fingerprint expert who had testified at Ray's London hearing had, in a lecture to a police seminar in Wichita, Kansas, talked about the coming Ray trial and had been quoted in the Wichita *Beacon* as saying "that the latest fingerprints we found in Memphis matched those taken of the man arrested in London, and the same prints matched those taken of James Earl Ray when he was at the Missouri penitentiary."

Bonebrake had spoken a month earlier. The article had not been circulated in Memphis. But what Hanes had to say about it *was* circulated.

"I don't doubt they will cite me again, this time for something the prosecution said," Hanes complained. "That's just about like that committee."

Within a week the committee filed a contempt of court petition against Bonebrake. Battle ordered that he show cause why he should not be cited for contempt.

This time it should have been apparent to Battle that his extraordinary action against the press had only served to attract attention to the case he wanted "publicity free."

On his mind was still the nagging awareness that Ray's "story" was being written and prepared for publication by William Bradford Huie. He suspected some hint of the defense Hanes planned would be included in the first Huie article to be published in November. He knew other newsmen were developing stories about a conspiracy theory.

Some rumors about what Ray had told Huie were leaking out. Ray had told Huie that he was a "patsy"; that after his flight from prison, he had met in Canada a Latin known to him only by the name of "Raoul." Raoul, Ray contended, had paid him money to smuggle narcotics across the U. S. border and later came to Birmingham and gave him $3,000 to buy the Mustang that was the "get-away" car.[2]

The Associated Press, through the work of one of its investigative reporters, Bernard Gavzer, and others, had put together a story which detailed Ray's movements and hinted that Hanes might use conspiracy as a defense. However, Associated Press lawyers advised against using the story in view of Battle's sensitivity to publicity. The *Commercial Appeal* had also uncovered part of the story of the defense—Ray projected as a dupe in a plot devised by others—but had not published it. Hanes complained that the prosecution's side of the case had been published time and again but that national and local publications were afraid to print "Ray's story." In an interview with Jim Squires, Hanes outlined his conspiracy theory with the understanding that the details would not be attributed to him. Squires agreed that the *Tennessean* would publish the defense theory, if there was evidence to support it, and would not quote Hanes.

Hanes said he would seek to prove Ray had been hired to perform certain movements in the South that resulted in his being at the scene of King's murder when the bullet was fired. He then became the object of the police manhunt, according to Hanes. Ray was duped into being a "decoy" to lead police away from the real killers, the defense would theorize. Hanes said Ray did not fire the shot that killed King. The lawyer maintained that Ray dealt only with intermediates and did not know who was at the center of the conspiracy. Hanes said Ray had been paid money to be a decoy, but had not known he was in a murder plot.

---

2. Much later, after Ray switched lawyers, Huie was to write that "there were probably several Raouls" in Ray's life, but that he did not believe Raoul paid Ray to kill King. Huie wrote, "I believe that one or two men other than James Earl Ray may have had foreknowledge of this murder and that makes it a little conspiracy. But if there was a conspiracy I now believe James Earl Ray was probably its leader, not its tool or dupe." Huie never identified who might have had "foreknowledge" of the "little conspiracy" nor did he ever identify a "Raoul."

"If you speculate on this without quoting me, it's all right," Hanes said. "Ray has a right to have his story told."

The theory of the prosecution had been published through FBI reports and because hard-working newsmen developed facts. The *Tennessean* story by Squires, quoting sources close to the case, was published October 27 and sketched the defense theory of conspiracy the very day before the first Huie story in *Look* was to be released. The first Huie article did not take "The Ray Story" to the point of the King murder. That would come later. AP and UPI first declined to move the *Tennessean* story, acting on advice of lawyers, but finally did so on October 28. Most radio and television networks used it without hesitation. Battle ignored both Huie and the Nashville news story.

There was some talk in the now swollen press row that both articles would result in contempt citations. Neither did. Huie was to be cited later, following a second article which dealt with some points in Hanes' case for Ray. No action was ever taken against the *Tennessean*, which has no circulation in Memphis.

The AP story by Gavzer was released. UPI began moving numerous dispatches out of Birmingham and Memphis speculating on the prosecution and the defense. Most of them quoted "sources close to the case." Hanes was at work behind the scenes with other reporters. After Huie's second article in November the watchdog committee met and recommended that Huie be cited for contempt. Battle was slow to act. He took the recommendation under advisement but took no action. He also postponed FBI agent Bonebrake's "show-cause" hearing until after the trial.

The trial date was nearing. Newsmen came in large numbers to Memphis during the week of November 3-10 to undergo the elaborate accreditation process which included presenting their credentials of identification, being fingerprinted and photographed at the laboratory at Memphis State University and meeting Sheriff Morris and his press liaison officer, Charles Holmes. Most reporters came prepared for a two-month stay.

During that week before the scheduled trial most of the news stories in and out of Memphis centered on preparation of courthouse facilities. Workmen had installed ninety-six new cushioned, theater-type seats in Battle's courtroom, nineteen of them inside the railing for lawyers and court personnel. Jury quarters were refurbished and a pool table was added to the recreation area. Dormitory walls were paneled. Soft green carpets were installed in the jury's quarters and separate sleeping cubicles were constructed so that the jurors might have privacy and comfort for the long trial Judge Battle anticipated. It was wasted effort, as it turned out.

Arthur Hanes and his son came to town November 6, for a final pre-trial visit with James Earl Ray. Neither lawyer talked to newsmen. Ray, nearing trial, was getting nervous. He wanted a postponement of the case. He asked Hanes to go into court and seek a continuance. But Arthur Hanes had prepared the defense, based upon information Ray had given him, and was ready for trial. The *Look* magazine articles, published concurrent with the trial, could not hurt his case, he knew.

He was prepared to try to convince a Memphis jury that James Earl Ray was an innocent dupe in a remarkable conspiracy and that Ray did not know who the actual perpetrators of the crime were. He was prepared to take on the United States government and the state of Tennessee for failing to investigate a conspiracy theory. He believed he could create a reasonable doubt about his client's guilt or innocence.

Ray seemed disinterested. He was listless, nervous, ill-at-ease with his lawyer. He seemed almost suspicious of Hanes. The attorney left the jail cell unaware that Ray was making the decision to fire him.

Ray's brothers, John and Jerry, were urging him to push Hanes to ask for a continuance. From the outset the two brothers had created problems for Hanes as the lawyer sought to prepare his defense. In September the brothers, themselves both ex-convicts, tried to get a Savannah, Georgia, lawyer, J. B. Stoner, into the case as an associate to Hanes. It had been Stoner, an originator of the National States' Rights Party and a Klan attorney in Georgia, who had offered to set up a defense fund for James Earl Ray. Hanes threatened to remove himself from the defense if Stoner came into the case.

Initially Ray had been satisfied with Hanes. He hadn't wanted Stoner to represent him. But he disagreed with Hanes about his need to put off the case. And he also disagreed with his lawyer about whether he should take the witness stand during the trial and testify in his own behalf. He felt he should. Again, Hanes disagreed. The lawyer knew that a prosecutor would examine Ray about all his past crimes and would destroy the defense theory he had prepared to present to the jury. It was Hanes' plan to try to move carefully to create a reasonable doubt in the minds of the jury about whether James Earl Ray, alone, could have planned and pulled off the killing. He feared Ray's personal testimony would only hinder his attempt to create the reasonable doubt.

With these two points of disagreement existing between lawyer and client, Ray's brothers sought to tear down the confidence their brother had expressed in Hanes. Hanes, they said, was interested only in the *Look* money, and that was why he wanted to proceed at once with the trial. The brothers pointed out that Judge Battle had become increasingly hostile to Arthur Hanes because of the lawyer's words and antics both in and out of court. They also tried to convince Ray of the bizarre theory that George Wallace would be president by 1970, and that Wallace would not be likely to let the killer of Martin Luther King be executed. But the most compelling argument they made to James Earl in favor of getting rid of Hanes was that a new lawyer would probably mean a delay in the case. This, more than anything else, encouraged the defendant to dispose of Hanes.

And so, unknown to Arthur Hanes, Ray's brothers turned to Texas to talk with Percy Foreman, the widely publicized and eminently capable criminal attorney who had successfully defended Candace Mossler and her nephew, Melvin Powers, when they were charged in Miami with murdering Mrs. Mossler's millionaire husband, Jacques.

Ray's brothers told Foreman that James Earl was ending his relationship with Hanes and getting a new lawyer. Primarily because of his wish to delay the trial, on November 6, Ray broached with Hanes the subject of getting an attorney to replace him. Hanes knew he could not force himself on Ray. He had done his best to aggressively represent the man charged with King's killing. But he would not agree to ask for a postponement. He was ready for trial. He would not agree to let Ray take the witness stand, and he didn't really believe any other experienced attorney would do so. Ray did not make it clear to Hanes at the November 6 meeting that he was going to dismiss him. In the presence of Arthur Hanes, Jr., he simply opened the door on the possibility of another counsel. Hanes left Ray that day still prepared to come back on Sunday ready to go to trial the following Tuesday.

There are all sorts of theories as to why Percy Foreman agreed to take the case. Some say he wanted a part of the Huie-*Look* magazine money. Since he had never discussed the matter with Huie and was not likely to have relied on much the Ray brothers told him, this is doubtful. It is more likely that the defense of Ray was a challenge to a criminal lawyer in whom the competitive instinct was strong.

Percy Foreman is a giant of a man, standing six feet four inches, weighing approximately 240 pounds. His clothes are expensively well-tailored, but he is so big that his pants, with specially cut knee-length pockets, usually seem baggy and his coat constantly has a rumpled look. He came to Memphis wearing a little Alpine hat perched on his gray hair. This man, powerful but at ease, was to become James Earl Ray's lawyer. His competence, Ray knew, was unquestioned, and if Foreman took the case, it meant a strong likelihood of a continuance.

Foreman arrived in Memphis about 2 p.m. that Sunday before the trial was to begin. He and Ray's two brothers visited James Earl for four hours in his cell. Their visit went undetected by newsmen. What was said is protected by the lawyer-client relationship, but there can't be much doubt that Percy Foreman told James Earl Ray he would have to be clear about dismissing Hanes. Before Foreman could talk to him about representing him or legitimately become his counsel the dismissal of Hanes needed to be formal and in writing. Ray was now sure about making the change. At 6 p.m. Ray's brothers went to the office of Sheriff William Morris. They gave the Sheriff a handwritten note from James Earl Ray. It read:

Dear Mr. Hanes,

Due to some disagreement between me and you in regards to our handling of my case I have decided to engage a Tennessee attorney and perhaps someone else.

Therefore I would appreciate it if you would take no further action on my case in Memphis, Tenn. Also I appreciate what you have already did for me.

Sincerely, James E. Ray.

At 6:30 p.m. Sheriff Morris announced to newsmen that in four hours there would be a press conference to announce a new development in the case. Hanes at that minute was one hundred miles away, en route to Memphis by air. Sheriff Morris did not want Hanes to hear the news of his dismissal on the radio. He felt the attorney deserved to hear in person what had occurred.

Shortly after 8 p.m. Hanes arrived at the Memphis Holiday Inn Rivermont, then drove directly to Morris' office. He showed little surprise at the letter announcing that he was fired. He had thought about the possibility. He seemed resigned to it all when he talked with newsmen. He had thought Ray, when he had last seen him, appeared too relaxed to be "going on trial for his life within a week." Hanes told reporters, "Sometimes I think I was used, that it was never intended that I defend James Ray. It was all a part of the same conspiracy that killed Martin Luther King."

Percy Foreman's last-hour entrance into the case, and the postponement that resulted from that quick-change in attorneys, raises still another weakness in the national administration of justice: the ability of the criminal to use the machinery of the courts for his own purposes.

Hanes had worked out intricate financial arrangements to pay for Ray's defense. He had worked with his son to prepare the evidence. He had tested the ire of Judge Battle by challenging the jurist both in and out of court. He had been held in contempt because he spoke out in behalf of his client.

And now, with a three paragraph note, James Earl Ray fired Hanes; and by hiring a new lawyer, unfamiliar with the case, he was to try to force the court to grant him a continuance. If Judge Battle allowed the delay, there would be the postponement in the case which Ray wanted.

The man most concerned by Foreman's entry in the case was District Attorney Phillip M. Canale. Like Hanes, he was ready for trial. Canale and his assistants had worked as hard preparing the prosecution case as Hanes had on the defense. The district attorney's office had called more than eighty witnesses to come from all over the nation to testify. Now Ray was about to interfere with his plans.

Ray, the hardened criminal, was making the system of justice work for him. It is interesting that his letter dismissing Hanes was vague and not at all clear as to what differences of opinion he had with his lawyer. More interesting, Judge Battle never tried to learn about the differences.

The letter said only "due to some disagreements between me and you" Hanes was being fired. Those "disagreements" were ultimately gleaned by reporters. But Judge Battle never sought to find out what they were. All he knew was that Ray did not want Hanes. The truth was, Battle did not want Hanes either. And so, despite the vagueness of the Ray letter dismissing Hanes, Battle allowed the change to take place, at the risk of James Earl Ray using the devices of the law to help delay the case against him.

The trial date came. But now with a lawyer change, nobody expected the trial to begin on schedule. Foreman's agreement to represent Ray changed the trial's timetable.

When Foreman entered the courtroom, a hush fell over the crowd. He, not James Earl Ray, was the center of attention. Clad in a bluish-gray suit and vest, Foreman walked directly to Hanes, who along with his son and Michael Eugene, the British solicitor, was already seated.

"I'm sorry about this," Foreman said to Hanes.

"Aw, that's all right," drawled Hanes.

Seconds later Ray, pale and thinner than when jailed, entered the courtroom, escorted by two deputies. He kept his eyes on the floor and walked directly to his seat, which was situated behind Foreman at the defense table.

Dressed in a dark jacket that accentuated his prison pallor, and wearing a narrow necktie, Ray rose to his feet when Judge Battle ordered him given a copy of the letter he had written Hanes.

"Did you send that letter?" Battle asked.

"Uh, yes sir."

"You said you wanted to terminate the services of Mr. Hanes?"

"Yes, sir."

"You said you wished to hire another counsel?"

"Yes, sir."

Ray, chewing gum, answered the questions in a low monotone barely audible in the spectator section. Then he slumped to his chair and watched, often resting his chin in his hands and looking bored with the entire proceeding.

Judge Battle never probed deeper into what motivated Ray to change lawyers. He never asked Hanes, who was seated before him, whether there were, as Ray claimed, disagreements. He did not seek to determine if Ray was "using" him. He merely allowed Foreman to take over the case.

Foreman now asked a delay of at least ninety days, preferably longer, to prepare for Ray's defense.

Assistant District Attorney Robert Dwyer, Canale's right hand, interjected.

"He (Ray) has been here four months or better and it appears to me he's trifling with the court. The state of Tennessee is ready for trial. We have something like ninety witnesses alerted nationally and in various parts of the world to come in here. What assurances are there that at the last moment the defendant might not come in and say 'I don't want this gentleman (he pointed to Foreman) here.'

"I don't know this gentleman from Texas," he said of Foreman. "I've heard something about him. This is an unusual, unique case in the eyes of the world, but it is just another piece of business in these courts." He concluded: "Let's try this case today. Let's move it."

Judge Battle was again worried about being reversed by a higher court. The safe way was to give Ray a delay. He ordered a recess, suggesting that Percy Foreman and District Attorney Canale try to get together and work something out on the length of a postponement.

"Of course, Judge Battle," Foreman remarked wryly, "I get along fine with Mr. Canale . . . . I think I can get along with that other fellow (Dwyer) before the day is over."

An hour's recess produced no compromise. Canale returned to argue that the state opposed postponement. Ray was not the only man who had equity in justice. A delay would mean an "inconvenience to the citizens of Tennessee," would cost the state taxpayers money, he said, and he could not compromise the public interest.

Foreman, courtly and craggy-faced, replied: "Justice doesn't have a pricetag on it . . . this time." The judge agreed. He welcomed Foreman. The Texas lawyer was so comfortable to get along with; so unlike Hanes.

Battle granted a 111-day delay and indicated he would grant another one if Foreman found he could not be ready by the new trial date, March 3. The judge claimed he had no other choice. He could not force Ray to go to trial with an attorney he did not want. He could not force Foreman to try a case he had only been associated with for a matter of hours.

"It's an awful thing to have to continue a case at this time," he commented. "But the defendant's right to counsel of his own choice is guaranteed by the constitution of the state of Tennessee. A defendant in a legal case has an absolute right to hire his lawyers. This is an eleventh hour motion, so to speak—the 59th minute and 59th second. As far as I know, as late as noon Sunday everything was green light in this case."

As delighted as he was to get rid of Hanes, Judge Battle did not feel he could simply release Hanes to go his way with no strings attached to the court. Foreman would need Hanes' cooperation to catch up on Ray's defense. At the same time, Battle wanted to be sure Hanes did not go about the country, or even at home in Birmingham, broadcasting his personal views about the case. Battle ordered Hanes and his son to remain along with Foreman as attorneys of record, even though they would take no active part in the defense. As insurance, Battle ordered Hanes to post a thousand-dollar bond before leaving Tennessee to assure his appearance for possible sentencing on the still unsettled contempt of court citation.

Foreman was to face many difficulties with Hanes as he tried to prepare Ray's defense. For the first time in his life, he was locked in with a defense prepared by another lawyer. He would not have the advantage of laying the initial groundwork and conducting the initial interviews with witnesses. That defense built by Arthur Hanes had been leaked in part by the lawyer to newsmen. Ray, himself, had already told much of his story to the public through Huie's *Look* articles. The second *Look* article was published November 11, only hours before the trial had been scheduled to open. The third *Look* installment and Huie's book, tentatively entitled "They Slew the Dreamer" were scheduled for release days after the trial was now re-scheduled to begin, March 3. Foreman could present the defense in his own classic style, but he could not depart dramatically from the story Ray had told Huie and Hanes.

Hanes initially defied an order by Battle to turn over all defense files to Foreman. Foreman succeeded in obtaining some case files from Renfro Hays, the private detective, but they consisted mainly of meaningless newspaper clippings and some largely illegible handwritten notes.

In December Foreman went back to Memphis to report his progress to Battle. He was agitated and angry. Speaking in open court, he called Hanes incompetent and told Battle that Hanes had been prepared to go to trial with nothing. No doubt he was telling Ray the same thing.

"Mr. Hanes was going to trial to meet a publisher's deadline," Foreman said, pointedly referring to Huie's work. Foreman said he had instructed Ray to give no further information to Huie or anyone else. If he was hostile to Hanes, he was equally irate toward *Look* and Huie. "I'm too old and have been practicing law too long to prostitute my principles for a pandering press." He said he had turned down several offers by magazines and book publishers to finance the defense in exchange for "inside" informatio ..

Foreman said he had been unable to obtain the services of a Memphis lawyer because there were no funds to pay one and asked that Judge Battle declare Ray indigent. Battle obliged and instructed Hugh Stanton, the Memphis public defender, to make the resources of his office available to Foreman.

Now, Foreman raised for the first time questions about the mysterious FBI file on Martin Luther King. The file, he said, showed that J. Edgar Hoover, acting under orders of then Attorney General Robert Kennedy, had assigned a squad of agents to King several years before his death. Whether Foreman knew what he was talking about never developed in the brief "trial" ultimately held.

During his presidential campaign in 1968, the claim that Robert Kennedy had approved FBI wire taps on Martin Luther King became a national political issue. How much the FBI had allowed Foreman to know about their file is not clear. It is clear that the FBI knew there was nothing in the file relating to a conspiracy to kill King. The file could have shed no light on a conspiracy theory.

"I'm working on the presumption that someone other than

James Earl Ray was concerned with the murder of Martin Luther King," Foreman said. At this point he was working on a conspiracy theory—as Hanes had.

At what point Percy Foreman decided he would seek to plead Ray guilty is not clear. Surely followers of Dr. King wanted the FBI file kept secret. Now Foreman complained he had been trying to gain access to the file and that his failure to do so was slowing defense preparations to the extent that he might have to ask for another continuance.

Foreman later was to say he was unable to substantiate Ray's claims about a conspiracy. He was not prepared to take the remarkable set of coincidences that existed—the short wave radio broadcast, the statement of Dr. King's driver, the statement of Bevel, the government conspiracy warrant—to try to develop a conspiracy web. He was to contend that an "eyewitness" to the slaying, that Hanes had allegedly uncovered, was found to be of no consequence. With Public Defender Stanton's sixteen-man staff, Foreman was to say, he was unable to find a peg on which to hang a conspiracy defense.

On December 19, Canale discussed the possibility of Ray's pleading guilty with the civil rights division of the U. S. Justice Department, explaining that in turn the state would recommend a ninety-nine year prison term. Why this was necessary is not clear. The federal government had neither power nor jurisdiction over the case.

On December 31, Canale spoke with Harry Wachtel, a New York lawyer who acted as counsel for Mrs. Martin Luther King, in an effort to determine Mrs. King's reaction to such a plea. Canale then sought the approval of Tennessee's Governor Ellington for a settlement and got it.

Four days later on January 3, Canale again talked with the Justice Department and was informed that Attorney General Clark would approve of such a deal "informally," if it could be negotiated. That same day Canale was told by Wachtel that Mrs. King would approve of a ninety-nine year sentence. She was opposed to capital punishment, Wachtel said. But there was still no indication that Ray would agree to it.

In mid-January when the Reverend James Bevel, a director of Dr. King's Southern Christian Leadership Conference, rocked the nation by offering to defend Ray, prospects for a guilty plea further dimmed. He said he was convinced of Ray's innocence and indicated in a telegram to the defendant that he had evidence to prove it.

At first Foreman was skeptical. But on January 22, Foreman flew to Memphis and met with Bevel. Together they talked with Ray. It was decided to try and bring Bevel into the case. The conspiracy theory suddenly seemed likely. Judge Battle killed the idea, however, ruling that Tennessee law requires that counsel for any defendant be a licensed attorney. Bevel moved slightly away from his earlier statements that he had solid evidence to help Ray, but there were still indications he might be called as a defense witness. Meanwhile the bar association committee recommended that Bevel be cited for contempt. Battle postponed any action.

Bevel, criticized by other SCLC leaders, later said he would not be a witness. Instead, he threatened to be in Memphis and hold a "mock trial" in a building across the street from the courthouse.[3]

Foreman could see no help here for his case. He turned to what he had earlier called "a pandering press," and joined forces with the man many thought he had earlier regarded as the chief panderer, William Bradford Huie. On January 29, he entered into an agreement with Huie and Ray in which he was granted not only the financial rights formerly held by Hanes, but also a large share (sixty percent) of any photographic and movie rights to the Ray story by Huie. Together Foreman and Huie went before Judge Battle seeking permission to have Ray photographed in his cell by the national magazine. The money, they argued, would be used to finance Ray's defense efforts.

The Judge flatly refused the request for photographs. He ordered Huie arrested on the contempt citation which had been recommended by his watchdog committee. The writer made bond and seemed to be enjoying the entire proceeding. He had probably done more work than any other person on the actual con-

---

3. Bevel continued to maintain even after the Memphis case ended that Ray had not been the trigger man. In his book, **A Mind to Stay Here**, (Macmillan Co., 1970) John Egerton writes of an interview with Bevel after Ray had been sent to the penitentiary at Nashville. Bevel told Egerton: "Ray didn't do it. He may have been involved, but not at a conscious level, not with foreknowledge. He didn't pull the trigger—he couldn't, he wasn't capable of it. Someone else did it—a pro. Ray was the fall guy. He was used."

spiracy theory James Earl Ray claimed had brought him to Memphis. As remarkable as Foreman's change in attitude about *Look* and Huie seemed to be, the more marked change related to Huie's change in attitude about the case. No longer would he pursue the "conspiracy" theory.

On February 4, Foreman told Judge Battle he was not ready for trial. He would need more time to prepare for the defense. Judge Battle agreed to postpone the case again, this time until April 7.

Still later in the month, Foreman approached Battle informally about the possibility of Ray entering a guilty plea in exchange for a life sentence. In Tennessee such a sentence can be served in thirteen years and seven months. The judge told Foreman any "deal" would have to be made with the state, but he made it clear that in finally approving mutual agreement between prosecution and defense, he, as judicial officer, would not accept anything less than a ninety-nine year sentence—which would not allow Ray's release on parole for more than thirty years. He felt the crime charged and the international notoriety surrounding it required that he send Ray to prison for the rest of his days.

For the state, a guilty plea in exchange for a ninety-nine year sentence was a perfect settlement. It would avoid the expense of a lengthy trial, the appeals, and any mistrial, which because of Judge Battle's contempt actions was a possibility.

The racial situation was still tense in Memphis. It was possible that violence or demonstrations would occur while the trial was in progress. According to one official, the county had already spent close to $200,000 in preparing the prosecution and in keeping Ray secure. Every delay increased the cost to taxpayers.

The district attorney's staff was physically and mentally tired of the Ray case. Battle himself was feeling pressure. He said that he longed for the day when it would be over.

The bargaining that had gone on behind the scenes was secret. On March 7—a full month before the case was to come to trial—word leaked out that something was in the wind. The Huntsville *Times,* located near William Bradford Huie's home at Hartselle, Alabama, reported that Foreman had asked for a special hearing three days later, Monday, March 10. The Associated Press moved the story and speculation began to circulate that a deal had been made: that James Earl Ray was about to plead guilty.

Tennessee newspapermen and many lawyers doubted it. They could see no way that James Earl Ray could be persuaded to enter into such a deal. He was facing the electric chair sentence if convicted. But nobody had been executed in Tennessee for nine years. Was Ray ready to trade his spotlight, his Memphis jail—with all its discomfort from lights and television cameras—for a prison sentence where he no longer would be "on stage" but merely one of a prison population of over two thousand? It seemed doubtful.

Ray on March 9 signed an amended financial agreement with Foreman in which he said he had authorized the lawyer to negotiate a plea of guilty for him in exchange for a ninety-nine year sentence. In the agreement, Foreman said: "You have heretofore assigned to me all of your royalties from magazine articles, book, motion picture or other revenue to be derived from the writings of William Bradford Huie. These are my own property unconditionally.

"However, you have heretofore authorized and requested me to negotiate a plea of guilty if the State of Tennessee through its district attorney general and with the approval of the trial judge would waive the death penalty. You agreed to accept a sentence of ninety-nine years.

"It is contemplated that your case will be disposed of tomorrow, March 10, by the above plea and sentence. This will shorten the trial considerably. In consideration of the time it will save me, I am willing to make the following adjustment of my fee arrangement with you:

"If the plea is entered and the sentence accepted and no embarrassing circumstances take place in the courtroom, I am willing to assign to any bank, trust company, or individual selected by you all my receipts under the above assignment in excess of $165,000. These funds over and above the first $165,000 will be held by such bank, trust company or individual subject to your order.

"I have either spent or obligated myself to spend in excess of $14,000, and I think these expenses should be paid in addition to a $150,000 fee. I am sure the expenses will exceed $15,000 but I am willing to rest on that figure."

In a second letter on the same day, March 9, Foreman further detailed the financial arrangement and mentioned a $500 advance to Ray's brother, Jerry.

"You have asked that I advance to Jerry Ray five hundred ($500) of the $5,000, referring to the first five thousand dollars paid by William Bradford Huie. On January 29, Mr. Huie advanced an additional $5,000. At that time I had spent in excess of $9,500 on your case. Since then, I have spent in excess of $4,000 additional.

"But I am willing to advance Jerry $500 and add it to the $165,000 mentioned in my other letter to you today. In other words, I would receive the first $165,500. But I would not make any other advances—just this one $500.

"And this advance, also, is contingent upon the plea of guilty and sentence going through on March 10, 1969, without any unseemly conduct on your part in court."

Ray affixed his signature to both letters. He was hereby requesting the guilty plea. He also was paying Foreman the first $165,000 of any proceeds from Huie's writings for, to use Foreman's term, "saving a man's life."

It is interesting that there is no mention of a conspiracy in anything that was signed that day. But there was a clear inference that something was going on that disturbed some of the principals. This was indicated by the notation in the letter that "no embarrassing circumstance takes place in the courtroom." Perhaps the state wanted to get the case cleared up without the shadow of a conspiracy involving other people hanging on in the public mind. Perhaps Foreman feared that at the last minute Ray would renege and announce in court that he wanted to get rid of Foreman. After authorizing Foreman to approach the state formally with the guilty plea, Ray signed and initialed each page of a document prepared by the state in which he acknowledged as true fifty-six statements to be offered as evidence. Among them were statements that he was on the second floor of the rooming house and fired the fatal shot that killed Martin Luther King.

Foreman was convinced that Ray killed Martin Luther King acting alone. William Bradford Huie, the man who originally had checked out details in Ray's writing and had believed in the conspiracy now had changed the name of his book from "They Slew the Dreamer" to "He Slew the Dreamer." He was to say he had changed his mind about Ray's claim of a conspiracy. It is interesting to consider what would have happened to Huie's book had Ray not agreed to a guilty plea. But the deal was on, according to the agreement signed on the eve of the "trial," only if James Earl Ray didn't throw the entire case into confusion by making some "embarrassing" statement that there was a conspiracy.

Percy Foreman knew the mercurial personality of the defendant he was representing. The man who fired Arthur Hanes was capable of doing the same thing again. It might be touch-and-go in the courtroom to get Ray to accept his deal and stand behind the plea of guilty. The signed agreement assured Foreman $150,000 plus his expenses. It also seemed to assure that the case would come out with no "embarrassing" outbursts by Ray.

So it seemed.

2.

The "trial" of James Earl Ray lasted 144 minutes.

Under Tennessee law, even where there is a guilty plea a jury must be sworn, evidence must be presented, and the jury must nod assent to the agreement that has been reached between prosecution and defense and approved by the judge. In Tennessee, lawyers call this "the nodding jury" system.

James Earl Ray came down from his cell above the courtroom and was escorted in by deputies. As usual, he was looking down, never meeting any of the eyes of the hundred-odd spectators and newsmen who were staring at him. He wore a dark blue checked sports jacket, a white shirt and a bright blue tie, the knot slightly crooked. He stepped briskly to where Foreman was seated. Before taking his seat Ray glanced casually at two tables which had been placed in front of the jury box. Both were covered with white linens to hide mock-ups of the Lorraine Motel where King was slain, and Bessie Brewer's rooming house across the street.

When Foreman had noticed the tables and their coverings on entering court ahead of Ray he mused, smiling to himself, "It looks like the Last Supper."

Foreman, dressed nattily in grey, was affable to newsmen and to the prosecutors, Canale and Dwyer, as they waited for the case to begin.

District Attorney Phil Canale, a man who never demonstrates much emotion, chatted with his chief assistant, Robert K. Dwyer. Canale, a former traffic judge, is a man of few words. He had rigidly observed Judge Battle's order of silence about the case.

District attorney since 1955, his staff of twenty assistant attorneys general had built a reputation for being "tough."

Prior to the Ray Case, Canale had not been in court as a prosecutor since 1961, when he won the death penalty in a rape-murder trial. When Ray was arrested, Canale indicated he would again leave the courtroom work to his assistants.

He later changed his mind. The importance of the case, he said later, demanded that he take charge.

The dominant figure in the prosecution was his assistant, Bob Dwyer, forty-five, who was later to become a member of the State Court of Criminal Appeals. A silver-haired man with a movie-actor profile, Dwyer was relentless in cross-examination and·was at his best in a capital case.

"I believe in the Mosaic code," he would tell juries, "A welt for a welt, a hand for a hand, a limb for a limb, an eye for an eye—a life for a life."

The case Canale and Dwyer had to present was to be *prima facie:* evidence of good and sufficient quality to be accepted on its face. Foreman would stipulate that the evidence was true. Judge Battle would preside and advise the jury of the agreement that he had worked out. The jurors would listen and nod.

At 9:46 a.m. the bailiff, speaking through the public address system, called the court into session in the case of the state of Tennessee versus James Earl Ray.

Foreman began: "May it please the court, in this case we have prepared the defendant and I have signed and Mr. Hugh Stanton will now sign a petition for waiver of trial and request for acceptance of a plea of guilty. We have an order, I believe the clerk has this."

He looked at the court clerk, who nodded. Battle paused and asked: "This is a compromise and settlement on a plea of guilty to murder in the first degree and an agreed settlement of ninety-nine years in the penitentiary, is that true?"

"That's the agreement, your Honor," replied Foreman.

"Is that the agreement?" asked Battle again. "All right, I'll have to voir dire Mr. Ray. James Earl Ray, stand."

Ray stood, his lips trembling, his prison-white hands clenched tightly behind him. He stared through dark-rimmed glasses at the judge in the stuffed chair.

Judge Battle: "Have you a lawyer to explain all your rights to you and do you understand them?"

Ray: "Yes, Sir."

Battle: "Do you know that you have a right to a trial by jury on a charge of murder in the first degree against you, the punishment for murder in the first degree ranging from death by electrocution to any time over twenty years. The burden of proof is on the state of Tennessee to prove you guilty beyond a reasonable doubt and to a moral certainty and the decision of the jury must be unanimous, both as to guilt and punishment. In the event of a jury verdict against you, you would have the right to file a motion for a new trial addressed to the trial judge. In the event of an adverse ruling against you on your motion for a new trial, you would have the right to successive appeals to the Tennessee Court of Criminal Appeals and the Supreme Court of Tennessee or to file petition for review by the Supreme Court of the United States: Do you understand that you have all of these rights?"

Ray: "Yes, Sir."

Battle: "You are entering a plea of guilty to murder in the first degree as charged in the indictment and are compromising and settling your case on an agreed punishment of ninety-nine years in the state penitentiary. Is this what you want to do?"

Ray: "Yes, I do."

Battle: "Is this what you want to do?"

Ray: "Yes, Sir."

Battle: "Do you understand that you are waiving, which means giving up, a formal trial by your plea of guilty although the laws of this state require the prosecution to present certain evidence to a jury in all cases on pleas of guilty to murder in the first degree? By your plea of guilty, you are also waiving your right to *one,* your motion for a new trial; *two,* successive appeals to the Supreme Court, to the Tennessee Court of Criminal Appeals and the Supreme Court of Tennessee and *three,* petition to review by the Supreme Court of the United States. Has anything besides this sentence of ninety-nine years in the penitentiary been promised to you by anyone?"

Ray: "No, it has not."

Battle: "Has any pressure of any kind by anyone in any way been used on you to get you to plead guilty?"

Ray: "Now, what did you say?"

Battle: "Are you pleading guilty to murder in the first degree in this case because you killed Dr. Martin Luther King under such circumstances that it would make you legally guilty of murder in the first degree under the law as explained to you by your lawyers?

Ray: "Yes, legally, yes."

Battle: "Is this plea of guilty to murder in the first degree with an agreed punishment of ninety-nine years in the state penitentiary freely, voluntarily and understandingly made and entered by you?"

Ray: "Yes, Sir."

Battle: "Is this plea of guilty on your part the free act of your free will made with your full knowledge and understanding of its meaning and consequences?"

Ray: "Yes, Sir."

Battle: "You may be seated."

The plea had been officially entered. Now all that was needed was the approval of the jury. Twenty-six jurors had been summoned to court that morning. The first twelve on the list were marched in and seated. All were male. Two were Negroes.

Canale stood and explained the procedure under which the trial was to be conducted: in effect, that the jury was asked to approve the agreement.

"Now, gentlemen, can each of you sit here as jurors and accept that plea of guilty of the defendant and the recommended punishment which has been accepted, offered by the state and accepted by James Earl Ray, the punishment of ninety-nine years in the state penitentiary at Nashville? Can each of you do that?"

The jurors nodded as one.

Canale walked closer to the panel. He was about to make his best effort to kill the idea that Ray had been part of a conspiracy. He said: ". . . There have been rumors going all around, perhaps some of you have heard them, that Mr. James Earl Ray was a dupe in this thing or a fall guy or a member of a conspiracy to kill Dr. Martin Luther King, Jr. I want to state to you as your attorney general that we have no proof other than that Dr. Martin Luther King, Jr., was killed by James Earl Ray and James Earl Ray alone, not in concert with anyone else. Our office has examined over five thousand printed pages of investigation work done by local police, by national police organizations and by international law enforcement agencies. We have examined over three hundred physical bits of evidence, physical exhibits. Three men in my office, Mr. Dwyer, Mr. Beasley and Mr. John Carlisle, the chief investigator of the attorney general's office—you can see them over here—have traveled thousands of miles all over this country and to many cities in foreign countries on this investigation, our own independent investigation, and I just state

to you frankly that we have no evidence that there was any conspiracy involved in this.''

Canale hoped that through this speech and the "evidence"
that would follow, he could dispel the suspicions about a conspiracy in the King murder and thwart any criticism Memphis
might get for holding a trial that was nothing more than a formality.

Percy Foreman then rose to state his beliefs about a conspiracy: ''. . . . I never expected or had any idea when I entered
this case that I would be able to accomplish anything except
perhaps save the defendant's life . . . . it took me a month to
convince myself of the fact which the Attorney General of these
United States, and J. Edgar Hoover, of the Federal Bureau of
Investigation, announced last July: that is what Mr. Canale has
told you; that there was not a conspiracy. I talked with my client
more than fifty hours, I would estimate—and cross-examination
most of that time—checking each hour and minute, each expenditure of money down to seventy-five cents for a shave and a haircut, pursuing it. . . . If there is any one of you who feels for any
reason you would rather be excused, I am sure his Honor will
excuse you at this time before the jury is sworn and call someone
to take your place.''

One by one the court polled the jury: James W. Ballard, Gus
Cariota, Johnny Shaw, James N. Abraham, John W. Blackwell,
Amos G. Black, Jr., J. Paul Howard, Miller Williamson, Robert S.
St. Pierre, James R. Pate, Joe Stovall, Jr., Richard Lee Counsel-
lour.

Battle asked if both sides accepted the jury.

"We do, your Honor," answered Foreman.

"The state does, your Honor," said Canale.

But suddenly the rote performances were interrupted. James
Earl Ray was standing almost before anybody in court saw him,
so intent had the spectators been in following the formal repartee
between judge, lawyers and jurors.

When he began to speak, his voice seemed strained, almost
embarrassed, like a schoolboy asking the teacher to be excused.
Judge Battle leaned forward to try to hear him.

"Your Honor," he said, "I would like to say something. I
don't want to change anything that I have said, but just want to

enter one other thing. The only thing that I have to say is that I can't agree with Mr. Clark."

Foreman: "Ramsey Clark?"

Battle: "Mr. Who?"

Ray: "Mr. J. Edgar Hoover, I agree with all these stipulations, and I am not trying to change anything."

Battle: "You don't agree with whose theories?"

Ray: "Mr. Canale's, Mr. Clark's and Mr. J. Edgar Hoover's about the conspiracy. I don't want to add something on that I haven't agreed to in the past."

At this point, Foreman interjected:

"I think that what he said is that he doesn't agree that Ramsey Clark is right, or that J. Edgar Hoover is right. I didn't argue that as evidence in this case. I simply stated that underwriting the statement of General Canale that they had made the same statement."

Turning to Ray, he said. "You are not required to agree with it all."

Battle again addressed Ray: "You still—your answers to these questions that I asked you would still be the same? Is that correct?"

Ray: "Yes, Sir."

Battle: "There is nothing in these questions that I have asked you and your answers to them, you change none of them at all. In other words, you are pleading guilty to, and taking ninety-nine years. I think the main question that I want to ask you is this: Are you pleading guilty to murder in the first degree in this case because you killed Dr. Martin Luther King under such circumstances that it would make you legally guilty of murder in the first degree under the law, as explained to you by your lawyer?"

Ray nodded.

"Your answer is yes?" asked Battle. Again Ray nodded.

"All right, sir. That is all." He turned to the clerk.

"You may swear the jury."

Judge Battle probed no further, he searched no deeper. James Earl Ray tried to tell Battle in open court that while he was legally guilty of murder as Foreman had explained the charge to him he still had been involved in a conspiracy.

Here was a chance for the court to delve into Ray's claims of conspiracy, an opportunity to find out what, if anything, Ray was keeping secret. Here was a chance to move to put down all the rumors and reports and theories about a conspiracy—which J. Edgar Hoover, Ramsey Clark, Phillip Canale, and, most of all, Percy Foreman said never occurred.

But Judge Battle was interested in the narrow issue of legal guilt insofar as Ray was concerned. He could have then and there ordered Ray to take the stand and tell what he was talking about. He did not have the presence to suggest that the defendant, having waived his immunity by pleading guilty, might be called before a grand jury to see if others were in fact involved. The administration of justice succeeded in punishing a guilty man. But it made no pretense of initiating a search for truth or putting down what very well may have been a lie by Ray.

The jury was sworn and the "trial" continued. The state presented its case, consisting of five witnesses: The Reverend Samuel B. Kyles, minister of the Monumental Baptist Church, Memphis; Chauncey Eskridge, King's lawyer; N. E. Zachary, Memphis police inspector; Dr. Jerry Francisco, Shelby County medical examiner; and Robert Jensen, special agent in charge of the Memphis office of the FBI.

Kyles and Eskridge both said they were with King when he was shot.

Kyles described the murder in vivid detail. He said he was taking King to his home for "some soul food." He was walking just ahead of the civil rights leader on the motel balcony when the shot rang out.

"I looked at Dr. King and he was lying thusly," said Kyles, covering his head with his hands. "The shot had cut off his necktie, leaving a gaping wound."

Eskridge said he was standing on the ground looking up at King when the shot went by his ear, and the next instant King was dying.

Though both witnesses were put on the stand to prove a capital crime had been committed, Assistant Attorney General Dwyer, in questioning them, made a feeble effort to dispel some elements of the conspiracy theory. He asked both if they looked in the direction from which the shot came—the area around the rooming house—and if they had seen any "movement."

Both witnesses replied they had glanced at the rooming house area and had seen nothing.

Solomon Jones,[4] King's chauffeur, had told police he saw a man wearing a white hood scamper from some bushes near the rooming house. He was not called to testify. His statement conflicted directly with the state's theory that the only sniper's nest was in the bathroom of the rooming house and not the bushes two floors below.

Dr. Francisco, the state's third witness, testified that an autopsy on Dr. King had disclosed that the shot must have been fired from a point higher than the bushes. He said the angle of the wound in King's throat corresponded to the angle of a shot fired from the bathroom.

The fourth witness, Inspector Zachary, identified the material evidence brought into court earlier. Dwyer uncovered the evidence and held it up piece by piece; a green bedspread from the rooming house, which served as the outer covering of the bundle Ray had dumped as he fled the scene; the high-powered rifle, a .30 caliber hunter's weapon believed to be the gun that killed King; a blue zipper bag; a set of binoculars and a binocular case; two cans of Schlitz beer; a shaving kit; a T-shirt and undershorts; a pasteboard box; a hairbrush; a transistor radio; a pair of pliers and a hammer; a paper bag; a copy of the April 4, 1968, *Commercial Appeal;* and five rifle cartridges.

Jensen, the last witness, related how the items eventually led the FBI to identify their owner, first as Eric S. Galt, later as James Earl Ray.

"Did the investigation made by the FBI culminate in the arrest of James Earl Ray?" Dwyer asked.

"Yes," replied Jensen.

"That's all the state cares to offer at this time," said Dwyer.

After a brief recess, James Beasley, another assistant to Canale, outlined a list of stipulations about facts and evidence to which Foreman had agreed. The stipulations, he said, represented what government witnesses would have said had they been called.

The stipulations were designed to show that Ray was the "John Willard" who registered at the rooming house the day

4. On February 27, 1971, Solomon Jones was sentenced to eight years in federal prison after being found guilty of charges of conspiring to obstruct the mails and cashing government checks. The government charged that Jones intercepted Social Security and welfare checks and illegally cashed them. Jones told federal authorities that since Dr. King's death he felt police had tried to "frame" him. This was more than a year after Ray was sentenced.

King was killed; that he was the Eric S. Galt, who police chased across two continents; that he was the Harvey Lowmyer who purchased the rifle in Birmingham; and that he was the Ramon George Sneyd who was arrested in London. No effort was made to explain why the FBI had initially sworn out a warrant charging two men in a conspiracy.

The strongest stipulations in Beasley's narrative were:

Statements by Willie Anchues and Charles Q. Stephens, two roomers at the boarding house, that it was Ray who locked himself in the bathroom and was in there when the fatal shot was fired.

A statement by Ralph Carpenter that on the day of the murder he sold Ray the binoculars offered as evidence.

A statement by Donald F. Wood, an employee of a Birmingham sporting goods store, that Ray was the man who bought the rifle offered as evidence.

Statements by FBI experts that they found Ray's fingerprints on the binoculars, the rifle and several other articles discarded at the amusement store.

A ballistics report showing that the bullet that killed King was fired from a rifle of the type purchased by Ray, March 30, five days before the murder.

Statements by FBI experts that a microscopic groove made on the window sill of the bathroom corresponded to a microscopic groove on the barrel of the rifle.

There was little else in the way of evidence. There were no witnesses who saw Ray fire the shot. There was no conclusive proof that the rifle found on the street was the one that killed King. There was no cross-examination and no final argument. The most conclusive point was Ray's signed admission that he fired the shot. But why had he done it?

No motive was discussed by the prosecution. If James Earl Ray had a reason to murder Martin Luther King the jury never heard it. Did he hate Negroes? Did he have a secret hate for the civil rights leader? Was there anything in his past record which indicated he was a racist by nature? Had he ever raised his hand against a black man before?

There was no indication that James Earl Ray had ever tried to kill any man in his whole professional career as a criminal. He was a robber, a bandit, a fugitive, a convict. But he had never been charged with trying to murder anyone.

This was the never-proven and never-sought-for mystery in the trial. For without a motive to kill Dr. King there was always the question of whether the act was not induced by some monetary source. There would always be speculation that Ray was paid to kill King.

There were reports and rumors and hints that Ray had made racist statements while in prison; that he had fought with Negro inmates; that he had said he would kill King. Not a word of it was given to the jury. And Judge Battle never demanded a word of proof on what, if any, motive pushed James Earl Ray to participate in the murder to which he now pleaded guilty.

The jury members routinely raised their hands in an affirmative vote for the predetermined penalty. Judge Battle pronounced sentence: ninety-nine years. He then made a brief statement. He was nervous about what he had allowed to happen in court.

He knew the doubt and suspicion the aborted trial of James Earl Ray would arouse in the public mind. The case was closed insofar as Ray was concerned, he said.

"How about conspiracy and the punishment of any co-conspirators?" he asked. "It has been established that the prosecution at this time is not in possession of enough evidence to indict anyone as a co-conspirator in this case. Of course, this is not conclusive evidence that there was no conspiracy; it merely means that as of this time there is not sufficient evidence available to make out a case of probable cause. However, if this defendant was a member of a conspiracy to kill the decedent, no member of such conspiracy can ever live in peace or security or lie down to pleasant dreams, because in this state there is no statute of limitation in capital cases such as this. And while it is not always the case, my thirty-five years in these criminal courts have convinced me that in the great majority of cases, Hamlet was right when he said: 'For murder though it have no tongue, will speak with most miraculous organ.' "

Judge Battle was not through. He also took the opportunity to defend Memphis, his hometown, which had been condemned in dozens of publications for spawning the hate that killed Martin Luther King. One magazine had called it a "decadent river town."

"I submit that, up to now, we have not done too badly for a 'decadent river town.'" Battle said, "If I may be permitted to add a light touch to a solemn occasion, I would like to paraphrase the great and eloquent Winston Churchill, who in defiant reply to the Axis threat to wring England's neck like a chicken, said, 'Some chicken—some neck.' I would like to reply to our Memphis critic: Some River—Some Town."

3.

"Judges are apt to be naive,
simple-minded men."
Oliver Wendell Holmes

The reaction to the trial of James Earl Ray was less than positive.

"Why should this assassination case be tried by statements instead of formal legal procedures?" asked the *New York Times.* "In the ghetto and in the world outside the ghetto, the question still cries for an answer: Was there a conspiracy to kill Dr. King and who was in it?"

In Atlanta, Coretta King, who had approved the ninety-nine year sentence, urged the federal government and the state of Tennessee to continue to search "until all who are responsible for this crime have been apprehended."

Dr. Ralph Abernathy, who succeeded King as head of the SCLC, said his "belief in conspiracy has been strengthened by the courageous admission (in court) of James Earl Ray."

For the first time the Justice Department disclosed "the original allegations of a conspiracy are still open."

Canale later said that he would not rule out the possibility that a conspiracy existed in the King murder; but he had no evidence of one.

By February, 1970, officials of the FBI were declaring the case closed. The search for truth, such as it was, had concluded. But in the aftermath of "the search" there was still more litigation, controversy, and tragedy.

In the hours that passed immediately after the plea was entered, James Earl Ray faced the stark realization that he would spend the rest of his life in a Tennessee prison. He had remembered the words of Judge Battle explaining that he had also given up his right to appeal, and the statement by Percy Foreman to newsmen after the hearing, that he was through with the Ray case.

In shackles, sandwiched between two 250-pound policemen, he rode from Memphis to Nashville in a five-car motorcade carrying twenty armed state troopers. He wished now he had never seen Percy Foreman or Arthur Hanes; that he had gotten another lawyer and had taken his chances with a Memphis jury.

He talked to the officers in the car of getting a new lawyer, possibly one that would take his case to federal court, someone that would keep the James Earl Ray case alive.

"I couldn't say exactly what I wanted to in court," Ray told Patrol Captain Richard Dawson, seated beside him in the car, "but I wanted them to know that General Clark and some other people were wrong in their belief. . . . This had better be in the record."

Ray talked about his guilty plea. "When I went to court Monday I was convinced if I didn't plead guilty I was going to the chair. I wish the hell I hadn't now because with what they had on me I believe the worst I'd have gotten would have been life."

At 8 a.m., March 11, Ray arrived at the state penitentiary in Nashville. He was led through a horde of newsmen who had been waiting for him all night and was taken to a six-by-nine foot cell in the maximum security building, which was to be his home at least until completion of a six-week classification period.

Ray began immediately plotting a course which he hoped would lead to a new trial. On March 13, two days after his arrival at the prison, he composed and mailed to Judge Battle a brief letter:

> Dear sir:
> I wish to inform the honorable court that famous Houston attorney Percy Foreman . . . is no longer representing me in any capacity. My reason for writing this letter is that I intend to file for a post-conviction hearing in the near future and didn't want him making any legal moves unless their in Mr. Canale's behalf.

Ray said later he intended that the letter make clear to Battle that he thought Canale and Foreman had acted in concert to get him to plead guilty. Battle, tired from his work in the Ray case, took a vacation immediately after the hearing and did not receive Ray's letter for several days. He had only a few weeks to live. The letter, and a second one which followed, were not made public until after Battle's death.

Ray now wrote Arthur Hanes in Birmingham that Foreman was no longer his attorney and that he was trying to obtain the services of a new attorney, possibly one in Memphis. Hanes told several newsmen he was thinking about coming to Nashville to visit Ray but that he had no intentions of re-entering the case.

At this time there were at least two others as dissatisfied with Ray's decision to plead guilty as was Ray himself. They were his brother, Jerry Ray, and J. B. Stoner, the Georgia attorney with the Ku Klux Klan background.

Jerry, who was a prime mover in the decision to fire Hanes, had also become disenchanted with Foreman after he joined with Huie. It was the other Ray brother, John, who was closer to Foreman and had helped to convince James Earl Ray to plead guilty. So when James Earl decided that he wanted a new lawyer, he turned to Jerry for assistance. Jerry, in turn, sought Stoner's help.

Jerry had quit his job and was devoting full time to freeing his brother. As a member of the family, he was the first visitor allowed James Earl at the state prison. It was during one of these early visits that the decision was made to try to hire a new lawyer to take the case.

On March 22, Stoner arrived at the prison and requested permission to see Ray. Normally, because he had not been associated with Ray's criminal case, he would not have been allowed visiting privileges under prison regulations. But because Ray was then without an attorney and because Stoner was officially on record as Ray's attorney in civil matters, State Corrections Commissioner Harry Avery suspended the rules and allowed Stoner to visit.

Word of Stoner's visit leaked to Nashville newsmen and a large gathering was waiting for him when he came out of the prison, after a two-hour-and-twenty-minute meeting with Ray.

Stoner, a squatty, pale man who walks with a limp and chomps constantly on a black cigar, said that Ray maintained during the meeting that he was innocent of King's murder. He claimed Ray told of "new evidence" but he declined to discuss the nature of it, saying "I might need it later on for his trial."

The lawyer added, however, that he would not be working to help Ray gain a reversal of his conviction. Instead, he said, he would represent Ray in libel suits against *Life* Magazine and several other national publications "who interfered with Ray's right to a fair trial."

In the early sixties, Stoner toured Southern cities urging whites to arm themselves and to utilize dynamite and explosives to wipe out the threat posed by blacks to the white society. In 1964 he was a vice presidential candidate on the National States' Rights party ticket and since that time had continued as an organizer of Klan-type activities. He always spoke in a demeaning way of Dr. King and seemed to enjoy some private joke when he called him "Martin Lucifer King."

"The National States' Right party didn't like Martin Lucifer King and I didn't like Martin Lucifer King, and I've never shed any tears about what happened to him," he said.

As Stoner's party and the newsmen were leaving the prison, another visitor arrived: Jerry Ray, who told a reporter his brother would seek a new trial on grounds that Foreman had "pressured him into pleading guilty." A petition seeking to change the plea to not guilty would be filed with Battle. The petition, he said, would be filed either by Stoner or Memphis lawyer Richard J. Ryan with whom he and his brother were negotiating.

Jerry said the purpose of his visit to prison was to deliver to James Earl the "evidence" that would get him a new trial, copies of the financial contracts with Hanes and Huie and later contracts with Foreman. He publicly disclosed for the first time the amended contract under which Foreman's fee was reduced in exchange for the guilty plea.

"Foreman said he would take $150,000 if my brother pleaded guilty," Jerry said. "But he wanted everything he (Ray) would ever earn if he didn't."

Foreman, reached for comment later in Houston, denied Ray's allegations. However, he disclosed, also for the first time, the terms of the financial agreements in question. He estimated that the original contract under which he got sixty percent of all proceeds would have brought him about $400,000.

Three days after the meeting with his brother, James Earl Ray wrote a second letter to Judge Battle:

> I would respectfully request this court to treat this
> letter as a legal notice, of an intent to ask for a re-
> versal of the 99-year sentence petitioner received

in aforementioned court. I understand on one avenue of appeal, I have only 30 days in which to file review notice, to have previous sentence set aside. That is the appeal route to which I address the court.

I also would like to bring to the attention of the honorable court, that Mr. Percy Foreman, the attorney who was supposed to be representing me on this charge, stated in open court:

One, that since he "Mr. Foreman" was receiving no funds to help prepare case for trial, and he did not think he should be required to use his own funds, he requested the court to appoint consul to help defray cost, the court appointed public defender to investigate case and assist Mr. Foreman.

Two, Mr. Foreman said in open court he did not want, or expect to receive a cent for his efforts.

I think from Mr. Percy Foreman's statement to the press that he had a contract from me and Mr. William B. Huie "upon entering," the case for $400,000, and that he was now to receive $150,000 should lay to rest the above two lies Mr. Foreman told the court.

Three, I, James E. Ray, in turn, have not personally received a cent from Mr. William B. Huie.

My only reason for bringing the aforementioned facts to the attention of the court is that I would respectfully move that the court appoint an attorney, or the public defender to assist me in the proceeding. I have no stocks, bonds, nor have I received any funds from any source to engage consul.

Petitioner uses the word "assist" as I hereby request the court, that I be personally present at the hearing, and to assist court appointed consul so that their be no repetition of Mr. Percy Foreman actions.

The letter was mailed on March 26. Battle did not make its contents public. Memphis attorney Richard Ryan later came to prison to talk to Ray about representing him, but Corrections Commissioner Avery refused to admit him to see Ray.

Avery said prison regulations provide that during the first six weeks of a prisoner's incarceration, only his immediate family can visit him. After the six weeks is up, the prisoner can provide a list of persons he wishes to be allowed to see him. Avery subsequently used the regulations to bar Huie from the prison.

On the day of Ryan's futile effort to see Ray, the State Supreme Court handed down a decision which would adversely affect any effort to set aside the ninety-nine year sentence of Ray. The ruling, written by Justice Allison B. Humphreys, was unrelated to the Ray case but held that a convicted criminal cannot seek to invalidate a prison sentence on grounds he was misadvised by his attorney to plead guilty.

The court cited a standard applied by the "overwhelming majority of federal courts" in such cases. This federal standard holds that "incompetency of counsel . . . must be such as to make the trial a farce, sham or mockery of justice" in order for a prisoner to cite it as grounds in an appeal.

The decision was hailed by Assistant District Attorney General Dwyer in Memphis, as a ruling assuring that the conviction of James Earl Ray would stand. But the Ray case had not yet had its final tragic twist.

On the afternoon of Monday, March 31, James Beasley, the assistant district attorney who assisted in the prosecution of Ray, went to Judge Battle's chamber and found the veteran jurist slumped over his desk, dead from a heart attack.

The case again swirled in controversy. Opinions as to the legal effect Battle's death would have on any appeal by Ray were varied. Hamilton S. Burnett, chief justice of the State Supreme Court, and Judge Charles Galbreath of the State Court of Criminal Appeals gave separate statements to the press directly in conflict.

Judge Galbreath cited a state law which holds that any motion for a new trial pending before a judge at the time of his death is automatically granted. Chief Justice Burnett said the thirty days granted under Tennessee law during which convicted persons can file a motion for a new trial applies only to defendants who enter not guilty pleas and who are granted a full scale trial. By entering a guilty plea, Burnett said, Ray waived his right to appeal through normal channels. The conflicting opinions had no basis in law since they were "extra-judicial" statements.

On April 1, the day after Battle's death, four other Memphis judges disclosed they had found the two letters from Ray in Battle's possessions. They had not been filed with the clerk, nor had Battle disclosed that he had received them.

Judge Galbreath, in another statement to the press, said it would have to be determined if the letters constituted a legal notice of appeal through a motion for a new trial. Both had been received by Battle within the required thirty days. Burnett, asked about this, said the letters made no difference because Ray was not entitled to appeal through a new trial motion.

The out-of-court, in-the-press exchange by the chief justice and the lower court appeals judge would have shocked Judge Battle, no doubt, in view of his own stand against press statements about pending court matters.

Following Battle's funeral, Tennessee Governor Buford Ellington announced that another Shelby County criminal judge, Arthur Faquin, would assume jurisdiction over the Ray case. He had been designated earlier as a substitute in case Battle became ill during the progress of the trial. Faquin took no action on the letters, other than formally filing them with the clerk.

Meanwhile, Richard J. Ryan obtained an order from Faquin instructing Commissioner Avery that he had been hired by Ray and should be allowed to visit the prisoner. After a visit with Ray, Ryan formally filed with Faquin an "Amended Motion for a New Trial," which he said was intended as a followup to the letters already written by Ray.

Ray claimed in the amended motion that he was deprived of effective legal counsel because Hanes and Foreman had conflicting interests in contracting with Huie. He said he now wished to stand trial and that his March 10 hearing was a "farce, a sham and mockery of justice." The motion carefully used the exact language of the Supreme Court in its recent ruling on the incompetency of an attorney.

The state filed its own petition to dismiss the motion for a new trial by James Earl Ray. Faquin scheduled a hearing for May 26. The new judge thought this a good opportunity to dispose of other matters connected with the case pending in Battle's court, so he scheduled for May 23 a hearing on the seven contempt of court petitions. Four persons—Hanes, detective Hays, newspaper reporters Edmundson and Hamilton—had been cited but not sentenced. Huie and Bonebrake, the FBI man, had been ordered to show cause but not tried. The bar committee had recommended that Bevel be cited but no action had been taken on that recommendation.

When these matters were heard, the same watchdog committee which had so firmly recommended contempt citations, reversed itself and urged that the charges be dismissed. Judge Faquin was happy to agree. Thus died possible appeals which surely would have evolved from the attacks by Judge Battle on the traditional concept of freedom of the press.

When he heard the arguments of Ray's counsel on the contention that the trial had been a farce and that Ray had been poorly represented, the judge ruled that Preston Battle "had ample evidence in finding the guilty plea was properly and voluntarily entered."

The hearing may have settled the legal question about Ray's right to appeal. It resolved none of the nagging public speculation about a plot in which Ray was only a participant.

There were other suits filed by Ray. In Federal District Court at Nashville, Ray sued to void all financial contracts with Foreman and Huie.[5] Hanes was later made a party to this suit which claimed that he had given information to Huie for the final *Look* article in violation of the lawyer-client relationship.

The suit was later transferred to Memphis where it was dismissed by Federal Judge Robert M. McRae, Jr.

Still the case would not die. A guard at the prison was quoted in the press warning that if Martin Luther King's killer was treated as any other inmate and allowed to walk at large through the prison population, he would be killed by other inmates. The guard said most of the prisoners were armed with hand-fashioned daggers and dirks and he warned that many of them were psychotics bent on violence. Ray was assigned to a maximum security cell, in the same area where three men, all

---

5. Foreman employed the late John J. Hooker, Sr., as his counsel in the federal court suit. At one point Foreman had talked with James Earl Ray about getting Hooker to join in the defense of the Memphis case. William Bradford Huie, who described Hooker as "the most distinguished lawyer in Tennessee" reports in "He Slew the Dreamer" that Ray replied: "I won't have him. His son (John J. Hooker, Jr.) got ever' nigger vote in Tennessee when he ran for governor. I want you to get some Wallace lawyer for me."

black, serving ninety-nine years for killing a white policeman, were on death row. One of them said he was not interested in Ray. Society, not a man, had killed King, he said.

There was to be yet another quirk to the case. Tennessee Corrections Commissioner Harry Avery began to interview Ray in his office. It was presumably for a book Avery intended to write. Ray had been isolated from the press and from Huie but here was an official of government taking advantage of Ray's confinement in his charge. When Governor Buford Ellington heard of it he directed an investigation by the Tennessee Bureau of Identification. The commissioner denied any interest in selling a book. He was directed to turn over his notes to the TBI and on May 29 he was fired.

Before the year was out James Earl Ray was back in federal court in Nashville, this time protesting the restrictions imposed upon him in maximum security at the state prison. He was isolated, received not enough fresh air, inadequate exercise, and his health was suffering, he contended.

Judge William E. Miller directed the prison authorities to develop a plan which would give more freedom to Ray without exposing him to danger from other inmates. Prison authorities proposed a program which the judge approved.

James Earl Ray had finally won a point in a court of law.

Later he would be moved by state authorities to the maximum security section of the state's Brushy Mountain Prison in rural Petros. There he was working as a janitor when the second anniversary of Dr. King's death was commemorated.

Hopefully, future historians will record in greater detail what the full truth was regarding James Earl Ray and his claim that there was a conspiracy. Because of the outstanding record of the FBI, the integrity of Ramsey Clark (then the Attorney General of the United States), the self-esteem of Phil Canale, the state prosecutor, the moneyed investigative ability of William Bradford Huie, the author, and finally, because Ray himself entered a plea of guilty, there is a tendency to accept as fact the premise that Ray acted alone, in concert with no one, advised by no one, financed by no one. The memoirs of Ramsey Clark, J. Edgar Hoover, Percy Foreman, Arthur Hanes, Preston Battle, of James Earl Ray himself, may disclose bits and pieces of evidence which might make clearer the conspiracy picture puzzle.

Was James Earl Ray a racist? Did he despise Martin Luther King as some sort of black devil? Did he hate all Negroes? There are rumors and second-hand reports of statements attributed to Ray while in the Missouri prison and in casual conversation after his escape, in which he is said to have made anti-Negro declarations and even threatened King. Reports of these have been cited to indicate motive. These are legally unconfirmed. Canale offered none of them in court. Nothing in Ray's prison record documents a particular hatred for blacks, although like every other professional criminal, he had his in-prison conflicts with fellow inmates.

There was, in his selection of his first lawyer, Arthur Hanes, the indication that he wanted a counsel who had some identification with the deep South racial position in the civil rights turmoil. Since he was appearing before a Memphis jury, this was hardly earthshaking. His later association with J. B. Stoner who publicly referred to Dr. King as "Martin Lucifer" was a stronger hint that Ray might be hostile to blacks.

In the aftermath of the courtroom "search for justice" there are too many coincidences which contest the too-simple, prima facie case in which Phil Canale presented Ray as a lone gunman who killed without a motive.

The prosecutor offered no proof or even an out-of-court statement after the trial to indicate that Ray was a killer motivated by racial hatred. In the absence of solid evidence it strains credulity to suggest that Ray, the man who had always committed crime for proft, murdered King for nothing. Too many questions remain unanswered. And in Memphis the court did not seek the answers. It was no search for truth. It was no search at all.

Chapter 4

The State of California Versus Sirhan Bishara Sirhan:

Nothing But White Magic

1.

*"This even-handed justice
commends the ingredients
of our poisoned chalice
to our own lips."*
**William Shakespeare,
MACBETH**

He was a little man, standing less than five feet three, weighing 133 pounds. There wasn't much about his twenty-five years of life that he recalled with satisfaction. Yearning for success, he almost always failed: in school, with girls, at his work.

Sirhan Bishara Sirhan dreamed of being famous. It was not until fifteen minutes after midnight, June 5, 1968, when he took his cheap little .22 caliber pistol, loaded with mismatched ammunition, and succeeded in murdering a man who might have been President, that Sirhan finally won his longed-for notoriety.

He probably would have hoped for a more heroic setting than the dirty kitchen of a Los Angeles hotel. He was able only to manage a brief, twisted announcement—"Kennedy, you sonofabitch"—as he leveled his weapon at the senator. A split second later the little Arab immigrant fired and murdered Robert Francis Kennedy.

Witnesses saw it all. The senator's friends and followers disarmed Sirhan, subdued him, even protected him from violence. The police came and took him into custody.

Seven months after the assassination, Sirhan Sirhan was to stand trial. What was the trial all about? It would take fourteen weeks to hear the evidence and get a verdict; then most of another week to get a sentence. It would cost the taxpayers of California close to one million dollars. If Sirhan killed Kennedy,

205

why such an expenditure of time and talent and money and effort to prove him guilty?

The answer touches a basic imperfection in the administration of justice: how to cope with a defendant who contends he is mentally unstable and therefore should be held unaccountable for his acts. This was not to be a trial in the ordinary sense of the word. This was to be a prolonged legal psychoanalysis. Before it was over it would do little to enhance the image of the profession of law, nothing to credit the image of the administration of justice and would actually damage the image of the profession of psychiatry.

The trial made some procedural history: it was shown to newsmen on closed circuit television. The television camera was concealed in an air conditioning duct in the courtroom, making it possible for newsmen who could not find seats to view the proceedings on television in a courtroom annex on another floor. The court took careful measures to make sure that the availability of the closed circuit broadcast to newsmen was not violated by them. For example, guards kept a close watch to make certain that radio and television newsmen did not bring recording devices into the courtroom annex, to transcribe the voice broadcasts for later replay on radio or television. But still, the case was a landmark because it demonstrated that a trial can be televised without creating major interference in the administration of justice.

Judge Herbert V. Walker, sixty-nine, presided over the case. He was a man of good nature with a deep feeling for the public interest. The Sirhan trial was to be his last case. He said that although there had been a general outcry at the cost of the Sirhan case, he felt it had to be disposed of according to legal procedure, regardless of the expense and time. History, justice and the edification of people in doubt needed to be served, he said. Privately the judge said he wanted a full and satisfying public record to put down the sort of lurking suspicions which surround the Warren Commission findings on President Kennedy's assassination. And he said, too, that the knowledge which might be gained from this trial could serve to stop the actions of some other assassin.

The attorneys who sat before the judge were men of polished skill at the law: experienced, dedicated, aggressive men, each determined to win the case for his side.

First, there was the defense team of lawyers gathered to try to save Sirhan from the sentence of death. There was Grant B. Cooper, the chief defense counsel, who at sixty-five had had more than four decades of legal experience and an incisive knowledge of the California criminal code and procedures. Grant Cooper brought to the Sirhan case a "pre-trial publicity" problem of his own. He had been the lawyer who had represented defendants in a celebrated California gambling case involving the "Friar's Club." An investigation of Cooper was initiated in that case after he turned up with "secret" grand jury transcripts in his possession. There was some concern that his involvement in the Friar's case might affect Sirhan's right to a fair trial.

Russell Parsons, seventy-three, from Palm Springs, California, seemed to be tired and too old to be effective in the case. He was the first attorney Sirhan hired. He had the trust of Sirhan's family. He was to become a father figure to a belligerent young Sirhan during the course of an exasperating trial. He left to the other defenders the main burden of handling the courtroom maneuvering. Parsons devoted himself to handling Sirhan and in a sense became the young man's closest and only friend. At times during the trial Sirhan would impulsively reach out and hold Parson's hand.

The third member of the defense team was Emile Zola Berman, at sixty-seven one of New York City's most respected barristers, who came to California only to handle the psychiatric testimony. He was Jewish—one of those Sirhan hated. During the trial, he ignored the outbursts of his client against "the goddamn Zionists and Jews." Gradually he himself achieved a measure of rapport with Sirhan. Sometimes he gently put his arm around Sirhan's mother and comforted her affectionately. He took on the case only because he was a friend of Cooper, and Cooper asked him to come. Berman paid his own expenses and accepted no pay for his part in the defense.

Across the room were the three prosecutors. The chief among them was Lynn Compton, forty-seven, a gravelly voiced, former Rose Bowl hero (playing for U.C.L.A.) who had been in the district attorney's office seventeen years. Compton, his white hair cropped close in a GI crewcut, his manner sharp and curt, saw the death penalty as something he must work diligently to win from the jury.

David Fitts, also forty-seven, was a Stanford graduate with a mild speech impediment—but most articulate before a jury. Grant Cooper, the chief defense counsel, was to declare when Fitts completed his argument to the jury, "It was brilliant. One of the most brilliant I have heard in forty-one years at the bar." The soft-spoken Fitts complemented the demeanor and approach of his tougher associate prosecutor, Lynn Compton.

The third man at their table was John Howard, who at forty-four was the youngest of the lawyers to take part in the case on either side. He worked mostly at research and leg work and performed with a quickness that made it possible for the prosecution to keep abreast of the able team of defense attorneys.

Mary Sirhan, the short, rotund mother of Sirhan, was constantly in attendance at the trial. Dressed plainly, her hair combed back in a bun, she was seldom at ease in the strange courtroom. At times she wept. Her countenance reflected sadness and lost hope—although she was forever bubbling over with comments about how good this country had been to her. Usually at her side in the trial were her sons, Adel, thirty and Munir, twenty-one.

The Sirhans were torn in their view of the trial. They wanted Sirhan free but they were reluctant to admit he was mentally "sick."

Few Americans know what the McNaghton rule is or to whom it applies. But this rule was central to Sirhan's trial. It holds that a defendant may be convicted of a crime if he can distinguish right and wrong at the time the crime was committed. Psychiatrists often observe and interview those accused of crimes to seek to determine their mental state at the time they violated the law, attempting to establish whether the accused deserve exclusion from prosecution under the McNaghton rule.

The rule has come under attack in recent years as some psychiatrists have argued that a person can know the difference between right and wrong under the law and still be driven by a compulsion, or still commit a crime because of mental incapacity.

In some states and in federal jurisdictions the Durham rule has been considered a yardstick for legal mental incompetency. This rule, which postdates McNaghton, holds that the defendant is not responsible for a criminal act if that act is the result of a mental disease or defect. But legal and psychiatric thought has been moving away from the Durham rule because it seems to make a judge of the psychiatrist. In California the narrower McNaghton rule prevailed when Sirhan was tried. Legal precedent in California also provides that a man charged with the crime of homicide can be found guilty of an offense less than first degree murder if his mental state and condition was such as to affect his ability to "maturely and meaningfully premeditate and deliberate" upon the gravity of his act.

This California defense is called "diminished mental capacity" or "diminished responsibility." It meant, for example, that if it could be shown that Sirhan was not able to recognize the seriousness of his act because of a diminished mental capacity, he might be found guilty of second degree murder or manslaughter.

Thus, one who is mentally ill can be found partially responsible for murder and receive a second degree murder or manslaughter verdict from a jury, rather than having to prove complete insanity to win complete acquittal.

Until the formal trial opened Cooper simply pleaded his client "not guilty." And the thrust of Sirhan's defense was an effort to convince the jury that the young Arab was only partially responsible for the murder.

What is the appropriate penalty for political assassination in this country? One legally unrelated fact which could sway the jury's thinking was the technical possibility that Sirhan could be paroled if sentenced to life imprisonment. California law sets the "life" term at ten years to life. The state's Adult Authority is given custody of the criminal and the discretion to consider him for parole after seven years. Although it is difficult to imagine any prison review board ever turning Sirhan back into society, it was also unlikely that he would ever be put to death. No one had been executed in California since a man named Aaron Mitchell died in the gas chamber in 1967. Senator Edward Kennedy of Massachusetts was to ask later that Sirhan not be given the death penalty for killing his brother.

The Sirhan case conjured up memories of the Leopold-Loeb case in which Clarence Darrow argued that his two rich young clients should escape the death penalty not because they were insane, but because they were driven by psychological forces to commit a senseless slaughter of a young boy.

It was a novel theory then—that there was a valid test of

mental competence beyond a strict McNaghton interpretation of legal sanity. Darrow had been required to enter totally untested legal ground in the Chicago case of 1924. In Los Angeles the "diminished mental capacity" theory was a fact of the law. Thus the defense would be allowed to try to show that Sirhan, due to a series of events—an impoverished childhood in an environment of cruelty, rejection by his father, an exposure to violence and death, a fall from a horse—suffered diminished mental responsibility. His lawyers would seek to show that his hatred for Jews and those who defended Jews was a natural thing for Sirhan, as irrational as it might seem to other people. Robert Kennedy's friendly words for Israel triggered the hostility that had built up in Sirhan and caused him to do murder, Sirhan's lawyers would contend.

To the layman and to the jurors it would not be an easy position to make clear. When Darrow had argued for Nathan Leopold and Richard Loeb in the thrill killing of little Bobby Franks, the famed defense lawyer had to convince only Judge John Caverly. His clients were frightened, almost cringing young men. Cooper, Parsons and Berman, on the other hand, had to convince a jury of twelve that their client, who appeared arrogant and hostile in court, was not guilty because of "diminished responsibility." And failing that, they would then have to face the jury twice. For if the jurors rejected the theory of diminished capacity for Sirhan and found him guilty of first-degree murder, then it would be necessary to confront the jurors again to seek to argue them out of the death sentence.

In California—unlike the bobtailed jury system in Louisiana—all twelve jurors must agree on a verdict of guilty or not guilty. If they fail to agree there is a mistrial. When a California jury returns a verdict of first degree murder, the trial moves into a second phase in which the jurors take up the questions of punishment—with life imprisonment or death being the alternatives. If the jury fails to agree on the sentence after they decide on guilt, then a second jury of twelve is summoned to deliberate and decide on a sentence.

Thus Sirhan well might have had to rely on twenty-four jurors before his case would be disposed of by the courts in California. In California there was a heavy emphasis on trial by jury, even in dealing with and deciding close, complex, highly technical matters. The jury power is not the ultimate, however, since the judge has the power to reduce a death sentence to life imprisonment. But few judges exercise that power. Judge Walker had reduced only one death sentence of the twenty that had been handed out by juries in courts over which he presided.

In consideration of what was debated during the trial—a man's legal mental responsibility for his criminal acts—the trial produced neither a search for justice or for truth; it was a chase for unreality made spectacular only by the fame of the victim and the prominence of many witnesses and some of the lawyers involved in the case. The Sirhan case demonstrates the weakness of a system that relies on adversary proceedings to provide "perfect justice" particularly in exploring a man's mind.

In the end the jury found Sirhan guilty of premeditated murder and sentenced him to death in the gas chamber. But this was no surprise to anyone who followed day-to-day developments in the case. After all, midway through the trial Sirhan himself stood before the judge and declared himself guilty of premeditated murder; he declared himself deserving of the death penalty. Many weeks later the jury decided Sirhan was correct about himself and gave him just what he requested: the death sentence.

2.

*"There is pleasure, sure,
in being mad,
which none but madmen know."*
**John Dryden,
THE SPANISH FRIAR**

There is an old lawyer's story, often told by the prosecution to jurors when they argue cases after the panel has been sequestered for a long period, that a foreign visitor, in reviewing the system of justice in the U. S., commented: "How strange you do justice. You lock up the jurors and let the criminal make bond and go home."

Sirhan was not able to make bond. But the jurors were locked up for weeks on end. The business of acquiring the panel in the first place consumed sixteen difficult court days before twelve regular panel members and six alternates were accepted.

The business of security-checking the newsmen began each morning before court opened and continued through each recess until the close of court late in the afternoon. Every typewriter case, camera case, or pocketbook had to be searched. Credentials had to be shown. There had to be a personal "frisking" to make sure no reporter carried a concealed weapon.

The business of disposing of preliminary motions that had to be argued was often done behind the closed doors of Judge Walker's chambers. Often on these difficult questions he, the lawyers, the defendants and the court officers, would troop out of court into the judge's chambers to talk over a point of law, not considered proper for the press or jury to hear. In the selection of the jury these "chamber trips" were frequent because of the decision to ask the veniremen in private about whether Grant Cooper's involvement in the Friars' gambling case would affect the attitude of the potential juror because Cooper now represented Sirhan. One reason was to save Cooper the embarrassment of having the public constantly reminded that Cooper was in trouble in the courts himself because of the Friars' case.

The Sirhan trial was in its fourth day before a prospective juror was seated in the box. A widowed nurse with no "conscientious" objections to the death penalty was the first tentatively seated juror. Mrs. Rosa A. Molina, a middle-aged, soft-spoken woman from Los Angeles, was provisionally accepted by both the defense and the prosecution after more than two hours of intensive questioning. When an assistant district attorney asked Mrs. Molina if she would be prejudiced against the prosecution because it might have intent "to send this man to the gas chamber," she said no.

Mrs. Molina, who later would be excused from the jury by a peremptory challenge, was examined extensively by the judge, Cooper for the defense and Fitts for the prosecution. Her views on capital punishment, the credibility of experts in psychiatry, the Arab-Israeli "situation," publicity and a number of other subjects were probed with her in depth.

It was obvious from the painstaking examination that jury selection would be long and tiring. It took most of the day to seat Mrs. Molina. Both the prosecution and the defense got twenty peremptory challenges under California law whereby they might later strike any tentatively seated juror without giving a reason.

During the fourth day, the name Robert Kennedy came up in open court for the first time. In examining a prospective juror, Cooper explained that his client was charged with "murdering or allegedly murdering the late Senator Robert F. Kennedy during the time he was a candidate for the president of the United States." The defense and the prosecution seemed interested in the jurors' religious beliefs, racial prejudices and views on national and international politics. Conceding that any informed citizen would have read about or heard about the crime for which Sirhan was being tried, the attorneys questioned not whether jurors knew of the case, but whether, despite that knowledge, they could give a "fair and impartial" hearing to both sides.

The projected length of the trial, during which jurors must be sequestered, provided a major problem in jury selection. Three of the first seven panelists questioned said they could not serve on the jury without causing themselves severe hardship. Two others said they thought they might lose their jobs if they missed three months' work.

A prospective juror who said she was "unequivocally opposed" to capital punishment and branded Sirhan an executioner in open court was quickly excused from the jury.

"I am unequivocally opposed to capital punishment, whether it is inflicted by an individual or by the state," she told Judge Walker.

Mrs. Jeanette Hendler nodded toward Sirhan. "I would have difficulty finding this man innocent," she said. "He performed an execution."

Sirhan stared back unflinchingly.

"You mean before you have heard all the evidence, you would have your mind made up as to the guilt or innocence of this defendant?" Cooper asked.

"Yes," she answered.

Mrs. Hendler was "excused for cause" by Walker. She was only the second prospective juror among forty-four questioned who had said that she opposed capital punishment.

As the jury selection continued, Sirhan seemed to enjoy the proceedings. Neatly dressed in a charcoal-gray suit and a sky-blue tie, he waved to his mother and older brother, Adel, seated together in the courtroom. At times Sirhan would glare and again he would suddenly smile at the juror under examination. During examination of a prospective juror, Fitts asked: "Could you come back from the jury room and sentence Sirhan Sirhan, who is smiling at you there, to the gas chamber?"

Sirhan said quickly, "I was smiling at you, too, Mr. Fitts."

The questioning always came back to the death penalty: "Would you have the courage to look this young man in the eye and sentence him to the gas chamber?" Compton and Fitts and Howard asked for the state. This led the defense, when it was their time, to inquire: "Would you have the courage, no matter how heinous the crime, to come back into a courtroom, look the prosecution, the judge and your neighbors in the eye and sentence the defendant to life imprisonment, if you thought that was what the evidence warranted?"

Finally, on the eighth day, the defense and then the prosecution pronounced twelve people acceptable as a jury. Fifty-nine people had been questioned. Six alternates remained to be selected.

The jurors chosen were: Benjamin Glick, owner of a ready-to-wear shop on the city's West Side; Mrs. Irma O. Martinez, an employee of the Southern California Gas Co.; Alphonso Galindo, a civilian mechanic employed by the Navy; Gilbert F. Grace, a

Department of Water and Power employee; George Broomis, another DWP employee; Ronald G. Evans, a switchboard installer for Pacific Telephone Co.; Susan J. Brumm, a service supervisor for Pacific Telephone Co.; Albert N. Frederico, a plumber employed by the city of Los Angeles; Mrs. Mary Lou Busby, a mathematics teacher at Downey High School; Laurence K. Morgan, a systems analyst for International Business Machines; Bruce D. Elliott, a systems analyst for TRW Systems, Inc.; and Nell Bortells, a service representative for Pacific Telephone.

The eight men and four women of the jury represented a cross-section of the population.

They included city employees, a plumber, a high school teacher and a systems analyst who held a doctor of philosophy degree. Seven were Republicans; five were Democrats. Six of the jurors were members of minority groups—four were Mexican-Americans, one was an Italian-American and one was Jewish. The prosecution excused the only Negro prospect who had been tentatively seated.

Cooper told newsmen that he was disappointed that the black venireman, who had been tentatively seated for three days, had been dimissed by the state.

"I think he would have made a very fair juror," the defense attorney said.

Fitts, obviously irritated by reporters' questions about why the prosecution would excuse a Negro, said tersely that peremptory challenges are designed to allow attorneys to strike jurors without making public the reason. "I'm not going to say why we did it."

Mrs. Mary Sirhan, who attended every day during the jury selection, said of them: "They are nice people and they stand up and are sure of themselves. To consider taking a life, you have to be sure of yourself. It's up to their consciences."

When the trial resumed Wednesday Judge Walker heard arguments on a defense motion to quash the indictment against Sirhan on grounds that the grand jury which indicted him was "improperly constituted." These preliminary motions would be argued before the tedious business of picking six alternate jurors would get under way. These arguments, which lasted for three days, concerned the fact that the grand jury excluded poor people. This was relevant, the defense argued, because Sirhan was poor. The defense called Mrs. Sirhan and Sirhan himself to get testimony from them about their financial status to try to show that they are poor. Judge Walker, after hearing the testimony, denied the motion "because it is not relevant to these proceedings."

But the ruling of the judge aside, the world got its first close look at Sirhan. His raised right hand clenched into a fist, Sirhan nervously nodded assent to the oath of truth before the clerk finished administering it. He flashed a sudden broad grin to newsmen as he took the stand.

As Grant Cooper, his chief counsel, asked him questions about his income from 1964 through last year, Sirhan answered quickly, often before the question was completed. Sirhan's biggest income year was 1966, in which he earned $2,212 while working for a construction company in Corona, California, and the Yellow King Ranch in Chino, California.

Under cross-examination by Fitts and Compton, Sirhan was attentive and polite.

Q. "How old are you, Mr. Sirhan?"

A. (Big grin.) "I'll be twenty-five next month, sir."

Q. "Did you live at home during this time (1964 to 1968, when he held part-time jobs)?"

A. "Yes, sir, most of the time."

Q. "Were you in school these years?"

A. ". . . In 1964 and 1965."

Q. "This was at Pasadena City College?"

A. "Yes, sir."

Q. "Did you give any of this money you earned to your mother?"

A. "Part of it, yes, sir."

Q. "Did you get any of your withholding tax money back?"

A. "Some of it, yes, sir . . . almost all of it."

When Sirhan was through, newsmen asked Deputy District Attorney Fitts, who also questioned Sirhan, for his impression of the defendant on the stand. Fitts said: "Well, he's still enjoying it all, isn't he? He's a pretty sharp character." The defense attorneys, undecided whether to allow Sirhan to testify in his own defense before a trial jury were anxious to observe how he would react under questioning without a jury. Even had Sirhan lost control, a distinct possibility, the jury would not have seen it since members had been excused from the courtroom during the three days of arguments and testimony over the grand jury motion.

Sirhan was known to be a volatile character. Michael Mc-Cowan, a defense investigator, said that the pressure was strongly affecting Sirhan: "He's climbing the walls."

During these days, Sirhan began wearing a light blue sport shirt and slacks, rather than the suit and tie his mother had bought for him. Russell Parsons, one of his attorneys, said Sirhan wore the sports outfit "to break the monotony . . . he likes to do little things to interest him and break the monotony."

Sirhan's preliminary day in court was termed "satisfactory" by Cooper. It appeared to be marred only once when his mother was being questioned by Cooper about her contract to purchase their home:

Q. "Are you buying your own home?"
A. "Yes, sir."
Q. "When did you first start?"
A. "In 1962."
Q. "How much are you paying for it?"
A. "Around twelve thousand dollars . . . maybe a little more than that."
Q. "How much was the down payment?"
A. "Two thousand dollars."
Q. "How much did you put up on this two thousand dollars?"
A. "One thousand dollars."
Q. "Who put up the other one thousand dollars?"
A. "My daughter, Aida."
Q. "And where is your daughter now?"
A. "She passed away . . . in 1965."

At the mention of his sister, Sirhan became agitated, moving about in his chair and wincing.

Mrs. Sirhan disclosed that she had lost her job at the Westminster Nursery School, a Presbyterian facility in Pasadena, January 15. She told newsmen she had to quit the $195-a-month job as housekeeper and teachers' assistant "because they couldn't give me time to come here every day."

Afterward, outside court, she told reporters, "I'm just thankful this country gave me a place to raise my children."

The following day, after the judge ruled out the defense motion challenging the selection of grand jurors, the jury sat through a long day of legal droning as attorneys began the process of selecting six alternate jurors.

Sirhan, who had been showing increased activity in the courtroom, spent his day in court, reading mail, an Arabic newspaper story about the trial, and staring at reporters. He was obviously amused by some of his mail, which was censored by defense investigator McCowan and defense attorney Parsons. "I don't give him the threatening, hate-filled stuff," said McCowan.

The questioning of alternate jurors continued, with the prosecutor, David Fitts, asking each one: "Could you come down from the jury room and look this defendant, who by then you will have come to know much more than you do now, in the eye and say, 'For the murder of Senator Kennedy, I sentence you to death in the gas chamber?' " In almost every case the answer was in the affirmative.

A mental patient suddenly arose in the midst of the trial and announced, "This is duller than I expected—I want to leave."

Plainclothes deputies quickly led him from the courtroom and through the labyrinthine security area. The unidentified man, about thirty, told reporters he was "on leave" from a state mental hospital. He displayed a mental discharge from the service to Arthur W. Zuhlke, the sheriff's deputy manning the front security in the main corridor outside the courtroom.

"I had no legal right to keep him out, so I let him in," Zuhlke said.

Court was in session at the time of the outburst, but the attorneys and Sirhan were again closeted in chambers with Judge Walker, questioning a prospective alternate, and did not hear the disturbance. For some newsmen it was a chilling experience. It brought home to reporters the obvious fact that no security is foolproof.

Mrs. Sirhan remained calm during the disturbance. Earlier in the day, the mental patient had cornered her in a corridor just outside the courtroom and was in a heated discussion with her when she was escorted away by McCowan, the defense investigator.

The mother of Sirhan spent much of her time in court taking notes in Arabic in a small green spiral notebook. The notes were "my thoughts, my memories of the things that happened here.

They are just for myself," she told reporters. "Afterwards, I will keep it and read it. There are some things I see that I do not like . . . like the jurors—so many of them who don't want to be there (in the jury box)." She took notes in Arabic "because I can think English, I can write some English, but I cannot express my thought. That I do best in Arabic."

Once she was approached by a woman spectator who told Mrs. Sirhan that, as a Jordanian immigrant, she could not feel the death of Senator Kennedy as deeply as a native American. Mrs. Sirhan thought and replied cryptically: "Justice is more important than any country."

On the sixteenth day of the trial, after Sirhan complained to his lawyers that one woman on the panel "gave me a hard look," six alternate jurors were finally selected and agreed upon. They were sworn in at 11:35 a.m. But this long-awaited development was overshadowed by another event.

Los Angeles District Attorney Evelle J. Younger confirmed that he had asked the Nixon administration for an opinion on the "disposition of the Sirhan B. Sirhan assassination trial" because of its "international implications." This had been reported in the press. Younger said: "In the event the government wished to make any comment concerning the disposition of this case insofar as it may have international implications, and insofar as it may particularly relate to problems in the Middle East, I wanted them to be able to do so. I made it convenient for appropriate officials in the government—the present administration—to express an opinion to me. They declined and made no comment or recommendation." Younger refused to identify the "appropriate officials."

The admission by the attorney general that he had contacted officials of the federal government to make it "convenient for appropriate officials in government . . . to express an opinion to me," once again will cause some to wonder what the administration of justice is all about. Younger's discovery that "they"—the appropriate officials of government—declined to make a "recommendation" on the case only elevates the idea that somehow the U. S. State Department could have had an effect on the case.

What if the state department had decided it needed to make an impact on the Middle-East conflict and thought that the asking of the death penalty would salve the feelings of the Israeli gov-

ernment or that refusing to ask for the death penalty would serve
to ease Arab hostility to U. S. friendship for Israel? Of what use is
a jury verdict if the U. S. State Department has the opportunity to
exercise such power?

Now Younger closeted himself with Judge Walker and attorneys for both sides in a secret session in the jurist's chambers.
None of the parties present, including the usually talkative
Parsons, would comment on the session's subject matter. The
district attorney came out of that meeting and said his office
would accept a plea of "nothing less than first degree murder."
Then Younger gave his view of three avenues now open to the
defense:

1. The case could be tried to its conclusion.
2. "They would want to plead something that would get
some stipulation from us concerning life imprisonment."
3. "Or . . . he would plead guilty to first degree murder—
then we would try the penalty."

Should Sirhan plead guilty to first degree, the jury would
hear evidence as to his state of mind and then decide between
death and life imprisonment.

Younger refused to say whether the conferring lawyers had
discussions concerning the possibility of a defense plea of guilt
"because it might be prejudicial to the defendant and I couldn't
discuss it within the confines of the judge's gag order anyway—
which I fought vigorously."

The prosecutor was referring to still another of those "free
press versus fair trial" guidelines which Superior Judge Arthur
L. Alarcon issued the day Sirhan was charged with murder even
before the case was assigned to Judge Walker. This forbade any
comment by attorneys, police, grand jurors, subpoenaed witnesses and others officially connected with the case. Alarcon's
order directed those associated with the case not to release or
give opinions about evidence, documents, exhibits or similar
aspects of the case, on penalty of "swift action to punish for contempt."

Younger had appealed the order, charging it failed to balance the need for a fair trial with the right of free speech. But
attorneys for the Superior Court claimed that without some re-
striction, prejudicial publicity—in their view—was likely to oc-

cur. In any case, they pointed out, the order was not directed to news media—but only to those under the court's jurisdiction. Younger's challenge of the order was denied by the State Court of Appeals. The State Supreme Court refused to review it. When Judge Walker was assigned the Sirhan case, he also issued a set of guidelines. These were similar to Alarcon's, but Walker dealt more with the security of the defendant than anything else. Walker was interested in assuring that what happened to Lee Harvey Oswald would not happen to Sirhan. As a result, the judge's guidelines dealt in detail with how the press and public would be searched when they entered the courtroom, and with prohibitions against use of any electronic recording equipment in either the main courtroom or the auxiliary courtroom.

Under Walker's guidelines, authorities were not to discuss evidence in the case. But, unlike Judge Battle's guidelines in Memphis, Walker's did not prohibit all discussion of the case with newsmen. But Younger was making it clear that he felt bound by court guidelines not to discuss whether Sirhan was considering a plea of guilt.

Suddenly, on February 12, "free press versus fair trial" exploded as the overriding business of the court. The jurors were to report to be locked up for the duration of the trial at 8 o'clock in the evening on Lincoln's birthday. But that afternoon a news story appeared on the front page of the *Los Angeles Times* which was to shake the case to its foundation. The newspaper published a streamer headline which read: "Sirhan Guilty Plea Now Appears Likely."

This news story, purporting to quote sources close to the case, said that lawyers for Sirhan would enter a guilty plea, the state would not demand the death penalty and speculated that both sides agreed to a settlement. The Los Angeles paper qualified the prediction of a settlement with an indication that the only obstacle to the guilty plea was Sirhan's personal fear that he would not get a chance to tell the public why he murdered Kennedy. The article created a major stir, since the *Los Angeles Times* was the leading local paper with sources of great reliability in all areas of government and politics in the community.

The Associated Press and United Press International picked up the story, quoting the *Los Angeles Times* as saying the case would be settled, with the reservation the paper outlined. Radio and television stations picked up the news from AP and UPI. Lawyers for Sirhan recognized the damage this might do to their case. First of all, the jurors still at home might think that the defense was trying to work out a deal to save Sirhan's life. That could easily be interpreted by the jurors as meaning that he was guilty, contended his attorneys. These lawyers feared that if jurors read the story, heard it on the radio, or even heard second-hand of it, then Sirhan's defense would be damaged. The jury was locked up as scheduled that night.

When court convened the next morning—the day after the article appeared—Grant Cooper moved for a mistrial on the grounds that the publicity would be prejudicial to Sirhan.

"Whoever gave this information," he said, "is responsible for this article and is deserving of censure." This was an indication that he thought the prosecution had leaked the story to the *Los Angeles Times.*

"I realize, Your Honor, the pains you have gone to in order to see we get a fair trial, and that alone should impose some responsibility on the press," Cooper said. For the record, he denied on his own behalf and for his two associates, that the *Los Angeles Times* information came from any of them.

"The press," argued Cooper, "has an absolute right under the Constitution to print whatever happens in court and print whatever they can get from whatever sources they can get." He argued that it was the duty of the court "to see to it that these sorts of things don't happen."

It was an ironical statement. Judge Walker, it came to be known later, furnished information which led to the story in the *Los Angeles Times.*

Cooper insisted that Sirhan was entitled to a mistrial because these eighteen jurors and alternates, having been exposed to the publicity, could not be fair with the defendant.

The prosecution argued the other side. The story was speculation, Compton contended; "simply a surmise," he said. "I don't see how the state or Your Honor should be held accountable and should have to suffer a mistrial for it. I don't believe any reasonable, average, fair-minded citizen or juror could look upon the story as anything but speculation," he argued.

Each of the eighteen jurors and alternates was summoned

individually to the judge's chambers and questioned about whether he had read or heard of the story. Cooper was to point out in open court as he argued for a mistrial that ten of the eighteen had either heard about the story or read it themselves. One juror said he had heard on the radio that the defendant might change his plea from not guilty to guilty. That would make it difficult to find him guilty of a charge less than first degree, he told the judge and lawyers. This juror subsequently was excused for another reason—the death of his father—but he nonetheless was with the jurors during some of their considerations. If his mind was made up when he was locked up with the other jurors, how did that affect the total jury?

Judge Walker finally turned down the defense motion for a mistrial. He said the jury had told him and the attorneys when they were first selected that they would not be affected by earlier publicity about Sirhan or the Kennedy assassination. They had all heard or read of the case against Sirhan and had said it would not affect them. On that basis he refused the motion that this most recent publicity would affect them.

Speculation as to who had given the story to the *Los Angeles Times* ended during the session in the judge's chambers when he was discussing the mistrial motion with the lawyers. He himself had given the story to the *Los Angeles Times*, Walker confirmed. He had been having a conversation with *Times* reporter Ron Einstoss on the possibility of a guilty plea. He had told Einstoss of the discussions he knew were underway regarding a settlement and a guilty plea.

Einstoss was later to say that his paper already had "the story" from another source and that the judge merely confirmed what the paper knew. As it turned out, what the paper knew was in error. There was no plea. But the judge had told one of the reporters that the case would probably end in a settlement. The paper published it. If there was a reliable source surely it would be the presiding judge.

And so the *Los Angeles Times* editors, relying on the judge and other sources in the courthouse, reported that a deal was in the making. In retrospect, the story was vastly overplayed. There is always the possibility that a defendant will change his mind after he makes an agreement, before he goes before the bar of justice. In Memphis, Foreman knew that a highly volatile man like

Ray might turn around on his own lawyer and at the last minute rescind his pledge to plead guilty.

But if the *Los Angeles Times* erred in judgment by playing the story as it did, Judge Walker himself was the major offender. Defense attorneys assigned Judge Walker's actions as "misconduct" indicating that they would utilize this point as a basis for appeal. Whether it was judicial misconduct ultimately might be a matter for a higher court to decide legally.

For the present, the business of court continued. Judge Walker told the eleven men and seven women, who were regular jurors and alternates, that the officials at the Biltmore Hotel had pledged to make them comfortable. He promised the group one night out to dinner each week, with all other meals at the hotel. There would be private screenings of movies and bus trips on Sundays. "Because of the trips you will only get brunch and dinner on Sunday," the judge said. Also on Sunday there would be non-sermoned church services with only a liturgy.

"You're all grown up and entitled to have a cocktail or two before dinner just as I do," Judge Walker advised his panel. "But I'm sure you are conservative drinkers, especially because you'll have to pay for them yourselves."

The jurors would be able to keep up with their families by telephone, the judge promised. And he admonished them: "Take good care of your health."

This trial would be a strain on them, on the judge, on the lawyers, the witnesses and on Sirhan himself.

As the opening arguments began, the pressure started to build. Deputy District Attorney Fitts spoke for the state. He was thorough but unemotional in what he said. Fitts pictured Sirhan as an expert marksman, a careful assassin who scouted the scene of Senator Kennedy's murder two days before he fired the shots.

"On the second of June, 1968, there was a reception at the Ambassador Hotel in the Palm Court for Senator Kennedy. That was on a Sunday from about 8:30 until about 10 o'clock that night. Among those in attendance was the defendant, Sirhan Sirhan," Fitts told the jury.

The prosecutor said that Sirhan was seen by two persons, including Mrs. Miriam Davis, who "observed the defendant (in the kitchen area) lounging on a cabinet or bar . . . He was dressed in casual clothes. . . . She mistook him for an employee of the hotel."

Fitts told the jury that the prosecution would prove that Sirhan visited pistol ranges twice less than a week before he shot Kennedy.

"On the first of June, 1968 . . . his signature appears on the register at the pistol range in Corona," Fitts said, after saying that on the same day Sirhan bought several boxes of .22 caliber ammunition from the Lock, Stock & Barrel Gun Shop.

"On the 4th of June, the defendant went to the San Gabriel Valley Hunt Club, where he spent a number of hours and purchased a quantity of .22 caliber ammunition. The range master and five others will testify that he was there and spent hours there in rapid fire practice exclusively. They will testify as to his accuracy . . . it was impressive."

The gun itself, the prosecutor said, was bought August 10, 1965, "while the smoke still curled up from Watts." The original owner, Albert Leslie Hertz, passed the gun, a Cadet model Iver-Johnson .22 caliber, eight-shot pistol with a fixed cylinder, to his wife, who, two years later, gave it to her married daughter, Mrs. Dana Westlake.

Mrs. Westlake "delivered" the pistol to a George Earhart, a firearms collector in Pasadena, Fitts said. On February 2, 1968, Earhart sold the gun to Munir Sirhan, twenty-one, the assassin's brother.

"There was some haggling over the purchase price, mainly between Earhart and Munir Sirhan," Fitts said. When the sale price of $25 was finally agreed upon, he said, "Munir produced $19 and the $6 balance was paid by the defendant, Sirhan Sirhan."

A major defense contention was expected to be that Sirhan had several drinks just before the assassination, but Fitts said that "in the opinion of the police officers who were in charge of him, the defendant was not to any extent whatsoever under the influence of intoxicating drinks."

As Fitts quietly described the moments which led to the shooting, Sirhan sat in the courtroom expressionless. Occasionally, he would sip water from a glass, but he showed no emotion until the prosecution began to describe his own responses to those who asked him why he shot Kennedy.

Then, Sirhan broke into a wide grin, which he quickly covered with his hand, and looked to the audience of newsmen as though to make sure they were recording Fitts' remarks.

Moments after midnight, June 5, Fitts said, Sirhan stepped forward in the Ambassador's pantry and "at point-blank range, in rapid succession, fired eight shots. It is probable the first shot killed him; the shot which killed him was possibly fired from a distance of one inch."

Fitts said that in the pandemonium which followed, the assassin was asked again and again, "Why did you do it?"

Sirhan told athlete Rafer Johnson: "I will explain."

He told Jesse Unruh, former majority leader of the California Assembly: "I did it for my country."

" 'Why him? He was trying to help.' " Fitts said Unruh asked Sirhan in the bedlam.

" 'It's too late. It's too late,' " the prosecutor said Sirhan replied.

The prosecutor was about to discuss before the jury the subject of spiral notebooks taken from Sirhan's home by police officers shortly after the assassination, when he was interrupted by Grant Cooper for the defense, who asked for a conference between the attorneys and the judge. The notebooks were purported to be the personal diaries of Sirhan which contain, among other writings, statements that "Kennedy must die."

After a conference around the judge's desk, Fitts returned to his place before the jury and concluded: "The evidence will show that the defendant, Sirhan Sirhan, was alone responsible for the tragic incidents in the Ambassador Hotel the night of June 5. I thank you very much."

Compton, who was in charge of the Sirhan prosecution, said after court adjourned that the notebooks will be introduced into evidence, despite Cooper's objection.

Compton also said that it was not significant that Fitts did not mention whether the prosecution will press for the death penalty.

He said, "We can do that in closing arguments."

On the eighteenth day of trial, the opening defense argument was presented by Emile Zola Berman. Sirhan Bishara Sirhan was in an uncontrolled "trance" when he assassinated Senator Robert F. Kennedy, who was a man the tortured youth "admired and loved," Berman told the jury. Berman pictured Sirhan as a young immigrant plagued by failure and haunted by the traumatic scenes of violence he had witnessed as a small Arab boy.

"The evidence in this case will disclose that the defendant, Sirhan Sirhan, is an immature, emotionally disturbed and mentally ill youth," Berman said.

As the New York attorney vividly recalled the trying moments of Sirhan's life and suggested a disturbed mental condition, the assassin became agitated. Beating on the defense table with his hands, Sirhan repeated over and over, "no, no, no," shaking his head and attempting to rise from the chair. Judge Walker asked defense investigator Michael McCowan to "calm him down." McCowan finally was forced to physically restrain Sirhan.

Berman's opening statement described bloody, shocking scenes from the 1947 Arab-Israeli war in Palestine, when Sirhan was three years old. Those sights included "a little girl's leg blown off by a bomb," an explosion which ripped apart a man's body before the boy and an attack on Sirhan's own home in Jerusalem. He described a series of trances, or "spells", which Sirhan became a victim of during his childhood, and which plagued him up until and including the early morning of June 5 when he shot Kennedy "in a trance in which he had no voluntary control over his will, his judgment, his feelings or his actions." Berman told of failure after failure in everything Sirhan tried— flunking out of college, heavy losses as a racetrack bettor and an accident which cost him his job as a racehorse exercise boy.

He developed an obsession with mysticism, said Berman. "He became concerned with mystical thoughts and searched for supernatural powers of the mind over matter. He started mystical experiments in his own room. For example, he would concentrate on a hanging lead sinker to make it swing back and forth by the power of his mind and concentration. He would concentrate on a candle flame and make it dance, first to the right and then to the left," Berman said.

"He concentrated in front of the mirror in his own room and thought and thought about Senator Kennedy until at last, he saw his own face no longer, but that of Senator Kennedy himself in the mirror," Berman said.

"Sirhan will tell you himself from the witness stand that he never thought he ever would kill Kennedy, but through his mystic mind power, the doctors will tell you, he could fantasize about it and relieve that feeling of emptiness inside him."

Berman said psychiatrists and psychologists would testify that Sirhan was in a trance when he placed a blue steel revolver one inch from Kennedy's head and began firing.

"The killing was unplanned, deliberate, impulsive and without premeditation or malice, totally the product of a sick, obsessed mind and warped personality," the attorney argued.

Berman said that the 1967 six-day Arab-Israeli war, reminiscent to Sirhan of the horrors of his youth, "triggered his spells."

"In his fantasies, he was often a hero and the saviour of his people. In the realities of life, however, as our doctors will tell you, he was small, helpless, isolated, confused and bewildered by emotions over which he had absolutely no control."

When Berman was finished, the prosecution began presenting witnesses. There was testimony from nineteen-year-old Juan Romero, a busboy at the Ambassador Hotel who was at Kennedy's side when the senator fell, mortally wounded, and who administered to him in the first moments after the shooting.

"I see the guy put out his hand to the senator's head like that," Romero said in heavily accented English. "Then I see the guy put a bullet in the senator's head.

"I try to give whatever I could—some aid—it was all I could do."

"Is this a picture of Senator Kennedy with your hand under his head?" Prosecutor John Howard asked Romero.

"Yes, sir," the youth answered. "I see him try to move, and I told him the first thing that came to my mind.

" 'I hope you can make it.' The senator said, 'Is everybody all right? Is everybody okay?'

"Then he fell back. He had one eye open and one eye opening and closing."

Howard asked Romero if Kennedy was bleeding.

"Yes, I felt some blood on my fingers; my fingers were touching his ears."

"Was something said about Senator Kennedy's mouth?" Howard asked.

"Yes, it was kind of dry . . . he was chewing something and

somebody said 'Throw that gum away.' I was going to do it, then I changed my mind—I just couldn't do it."

Romero said he stayed at Kennedy's side until Mrs. Ethel Kennedy arrived and "pushed me aside."

Pictures of the dying senator have shown some object in his hand. Asked what it was, Romero said. "A priest or somebody handed me a rosary, and I put it in his hand."

Carl Uecker, assistant maitre d'hotel at the Ambassador and the man guiding Senator Kennedy through the hotel the night he was murdered, testified that Kennedy's appearance in the pantry was an unexplained one. It was there that Sirhan stepped around Uecker as Kennedy shook hands with Romero, and began firing the shots which mortally wounded the presidential candidate.

The original plan, Uecker testified, called for Kennedy to be escorted from the stage in the Embassy Ballroom, where he addressed his jubilant supporters, to the Ambassador Ballroom, where another party of supporters awaited him.

"I took the senator behind the stage (in the Embassy Ballroom)," Uecker said, "I was going to turn left to go to the Ambassador Ballroom and somebody said, 'No, we're not going that way. We're going to the press room (Colonial Room). I said, 'This way, Senator.'

"It was a last-minute decision. I don't know who made it."

As the party, led by Uecker and Edward Minasian, former caterer for the Ambassador, turned through the pantry doors to head for the press in the Colonial Room at the opposite entrance, Kennedy began stopping and shaking hands with hotel employees.

"The senator was really happy, and he stopped again and again to shake hands," Uecker said.

The assistant maitre d'hotel finally began to urge Kennedy, who was closely followed by a large group of supporters and members of his campaign staff, to move on toward the Colonial Room.

"I got his hand again, his right hand, and I said 'Senator, let's go now,'" Uecker recalled.

Then, a split second later, the hotel official "felt something, somebody, moving in . . . the next thing I heard was a shot. It sounded like a firecracker. Then I heard a second shot. Senator Kennedy's right arm flew up and he was turning."

Then Kennedy fell.

"It looked like the senator saw what had happened," Uecker said.

In the immediate chaos which broke out, Uecker and Minasian leaped on Sirhan, they testified, and drove his body into an adjacent steam table, where Uecker grabbed the assassin's wrist and began trying to force the gun from his hand.

"I hit him low and he (Uecker) hit him high," Minasian testified.

As Uecker fought with Sirhan for the gun, pounding the gunman's hand several times on the steam table, the weapon continued to fire until all eight shots in its chamber was expended and five other persons were wounded.

"He was very strong in his right hand," Uecker said. "I was trying very hard to keep the gun away from the crowds." In the confusion, Sirhan lost control of the gun, then got it back.

Vincent di Pierro, a part-time waiter whose father is maitre d'hotel and who had come to the hotel on his off-time to see Kennedy, told the court he saw the first shot fired but not the second: "I had blood all over my glasses. After the first shot, I had blood all over my face."

After the shooting stopped, Uecker and Minasian were joined in restraining Sirhan by athletes Roosevelt Greer and Rafer Johnson. Di Pierro recalled that the almost hysterical crowd which had pushed into the pantry area then began trying to get at the assassin.

"People started trying to beat him up, to grab him or hit him," he said. "They were really trying to kill him."

It was not until mammoth Roosevelt Greer, retired professional football lineman and friend of Kennedy, descended upon Sirhan that he was finally restrained and his gun wrestled from his hand—empty.

By then five other persons lay wounded.

Roosevelt Greer, speaking in a soft voice, told a hushed courtroom and a note-taking jury of his experiences that early morning of June 5, 1968, when standing just outside the pantry doors with the senator's wife, Ethel, he heard what sounded like a string of firecrackers going off inside.

Shoving Mrs. Kennedy to the floor and pushing Ambassador maitre d'hotel Angelo di Pierro on top of her for protection, Greer rushed into the pantry where he saw a "gun going off." Greer said he saw a large group of people fighting with Sirhan for the gun, which was taken from him and put on a table, "then I looked around again and it was in his hand."

Under questioning by prosecutor John Howard, Greer told of the next few moments when he rushed to the struggle:

Q. "Then there were a number of individuals disputing possession of the gun?"

A. "Well, he had control of it at that time."

Q. "What did you then do?"

A. ". . . I put his leg around my arm."

Q. "You mean you got his leg in an armlock?"

A. "Yes . . . I pulled him up on the table and I just got his hand and took the gun out of it."

Q. "Did you have any trouble taking the gun?"

A. "No, sir."

Q. "What did you do then?"

A. "I held on to it . . . it seemed as though people were trying to hurt him (Sirhan) . . . so I hit them . . . (gesturing slightly with his fists) I hit the guy on my right and then I kicked the guy on my left . . . then they seemed to realize that we were trying to save the guy . . . and they quit."

Q. "What did you do with the gun?"

A. "People started asking me for it, but I didn't turn loose of it until Rafer Johnson got there. I didn't know any of the other people. I gave it to him to keep."

Q. "How long did you stay with Mr. Sirhan?"

A. "I stayed with him until the police came."

Q. "How long was it until the police got there?"

A. "I just don't know, by that time I was a little unsettled—I was crying."

Q. "Did Sirhan say anything you heard?"

A. "No sir . . . except I heard him cry a little when his leg was twisted."

Asked afterward if he had any thoughts as he sat in the courtroom and saw Sirhan for the first time since the assassination, Greer, who was Kennedy's friend, quietly replied, "yes." He declined to say what his thoughts were.

Jesus Perez, a Mexican-American kitchen helper, who testified through an interpreter because of his broken English, was asked "to tell the jury what the defendant said and what you said" when Sirhan was in the pantry area shortly before midnight, June 4.

"He told me if Kennedy was coming through this place again," Perez said.

Judge Walker interrupted and informed the jury that "these people," apparently meaning Mexican-Americans, often "say 'told' when they mean 'asked.' "

"What did you say?" Howard asked.

"That I didn't know anything, whether he would come through there or not," he said.

"Did they say anything else to you?"

"There were some boys nearby who spoke in Spanish and he asked me what they were saying. I told him they weren't talking about him; they were talking about some pretty girls that were close by."

Martin Patrusky, a young bar waiter, said Sirhan asked him whether Kennedy would come through the kitchen area. He said he answered, "I don't know, I'm not the maitre d' here."

Jesse Unruh, the California Democratic leader, who had shouted out that Sirhan should not be harmed, took the stand and said on first glimpse in the kitchen he thought Sirhan was "either a Puerto Rican, Cuban, Mexican-American or some Latin American . . . . I asked him, 'Why him (Kennedy), why him?' and he said, 'It's too late,' and I said again, 'Why him, he was trying to help?' "

Still later Unruh testified, "It seemed to me like he said, 'I can explain.' " Again Unruh quoted Sirhan as saying, "I did it for my country."

In cross-examination, Unruh and Berman clashed over whether Unruh knew in advance that Kennedy had changed his route from the downstairs Embassy Room to the Colonial Room where the "pen and pencil press" awaited an interview.

Q. "You mean you were not privy to the change in plans?"

A. "No."

Q. "You were a big man in the victory, a big man in the party in California, were you not, and you were not privy to his (Kennedy's) plans?"

A. "Politics change very rapidly, my friend, as we discovered June 4."

Q. "You mean to say you were not privy to the changes in his plans?"

A. "Yes, but I don't know what you're trying to imply."

Q. "You don't have to worry about what I'm trying to imply; I'm just trying to get at the truth."

At this point, Judge Walker sustained a prosecution objection that Berman was being "argumentative."

The highly publicized "woman in the polka dot dress" found her way into the testimony when Vincent di Pierro, the son of the Ambassador's maitre d'hotel, said he did indeed see a "pretty girl" standing next to Sirhan seconds before the assassination.

Under cross-examination by Cooper, di Pierro said:

Q. "What caused you to notice him (Sirhan)?"

A. "There was a girl standing in the area."

Q. "Was it the girl who caused you to notice him?"

A. "Yes, sir."

Q. "Did you observe the girl first?"

A. "Yes."

Q. "Was it because she was a pretty girl?"

A. "Yes."

Q. "How was the girl dressed?"

A. "She was wearing a polka dot dress."

Then he identified a photograph of a Miss Valerie Schulte of Santa Barbara, California, as appearing to be the girl he saw standing next to Sirhan just before the shooting.

Prosecution lawyers said that Miss Schulte would testify.

On the twentieth day of trial William Barry, the security chief in the Kennedy campaign, testified that he was fighting through a crowd in the Ambassador pantry, trying to get to Kennedy's side, when a gun began to go off.

Unable to see Kennedy, Barry suddenly spotted the assassin and "spun and dove for him."

He told of seeing the senator, at whose side he had served throughout Kennedy's campaign, moments after the shooting: "My main concern was to get to the senator . . . . I found him on the floor. . . . I put my coat under his head."

As Fitts quietly asked how Kennedy looked at that moment, Barry ducked his head and paused for a long moment before answering: "I, of course, wasn't sure what damage had been done." Then he paused again, looked up and added: "But, I saw the head wound."

Barry, vice president of Bankers Trust Company in New York and a former FBI man, had the campaign job of keeping Kennedy safe while getting him through thick crowds . . . "I was running interference for him," he said. The night of the assassination he had already cleared a path through the celebrating crowd Kennedy addressed from a stage in the Embassy Room when the senator inexplicably turned and left the stage in another direction.

"He was called by someone at the mid-rear of the stage, and he turned and went out," Barry said. "The curtains were parted."

Asked who beckoned Kennedy, Barry said, "I couldn't see them, because I was committed on the other part of the stage. . . . I believe it was one of the staff of the hotel. . . .

"At the curtain, I met Mrs. Kennedy—she needed help negotiating the steps down from the stage—but this heavy crowd by now was completely between me and the senator."

The plan had been to go directly to the Colonial Room, where newspapermen were awaiting a late night interview, Barry said. But, contrary to that plan, the senator struck out on his own, following two hotel officials.

"When you entered the pantry, did you see the senator?" Fitts asked.

"No, I skirted the crowd and, at this point . . . I heard something that sounded like firecrackers," Barry said.

Continuing to rush toward where he thought Kennedy was, Barry "saw an individual standing . . . with a gun. He was pointing it—I spun and dove for him."

As Barry smashed into Sirhan, "The gun fell on the table," he said.

"Where did you hit him?"

"In the face . . . he was sinking . . . then I put what we called in the FBI a 'come-along' (headlock) on him," said Barry, a federal agent for seventeen years.

"People started to hit him. To protect him, I spun away from them . . . . Then I saw Rosey Greer, and I called for assistance. . . . I asked Rosey to take him away from the people; they were trying to do him some damage."

Miss Valerie Schulte, the mysterious "girl in the polka dot dress," turned out to be not so mysterious when she testified. Miss Schulte said she was headquarters manager for Kennedy in Golita, California, near the location of the University of California at Santa Barbara, which she attended.

The night of June 4 she came to the Ambassador to join in the celebration of Kennedy's primary victory and was in the pantry at the moment of the assassination. Her right leg had been injured in a skiing accident, and she was leaning on a crutch when Sirhan fired and pandemonium broke loose, she said. "I saw an arm extended with a gun, and I heard shots. At that time, I either fell or was pushed to the floor."

For the next several minutes, Miss Schulte said, she crawled about on the floor until she found a secure position behind a partition.

At the close of her testimony, she opened a shopping sack and displayed the dress she was wearing that night. It was a miniskirt with yellow polka dots on a green background.

She was followed on the stand by Los Angeles Police Officer Arthur Placencia, who had graduated from the police academy only three weeks before the assassination. He and his partner, Travis White, were in the first police car to answer the shooting call at the Ambassador.

Placencia told the jury of being directed to the kitchen scene of the shooting, handcuffing Sirhan, and rushing him from the hotel. He and his partner were accompanied, he said, by a man in civilian clothes who hopped into the front seat of the police car with White, while Sirhan was joined in the back by Placencia.

On the way to the police station, the two officers learned that the man was Jesse Unruh, then speaker of the California assembly and one of the state's most powerful Democrats.

Placencia said the crowd had followed them from the hotel and was trying to get to Sirhan.

"We had to roll up all the windows, people were trying to get in and get at the suspect . . . . There were people all around. . . . My partner had to turn on the red light and hit the siren one time . . . . That got rid of the people," Placencia said.

Under cross-examination, Placencia was asked by Cooper if he had not told the grand jury that he "heard someone say, 'Kill the bastard, kill him!' "

"I don't recall, sir," he answered.

Cooper probed at length on the condition of Sirhan's eyes. Placencia admitted the pupils were dilated and did not react when he shone a light on them.

Q. "What does that mean to you as an officer? Does that mean to you he was under the influence of a drug or alcohol?"

A. "Yes, sir."

Cooper then wanted to know why further tests were not run on Sirhan to determine whether or how much he had been drinking. The policeman said he did not recall.

Placencia told Prosecutor Howard, on redirect examination, that he did not smell alcohol on Sirhan's breath. Howard: "Were you shortly joined (at police headquarters) by a number of ranking police officers—a lot of captains and lieutenants and inspectors?"

A. "Yes, sir."

Q. "Did you feel it was your duty at that point to tell them how to conduct the investigation?" asked Howard.

A. "No, sir."

When Cooper asked Placencia why he checked Sirhan's eyes in the first place, the young policeman answered: "The reason I did it was because the older officers always do it, and I was eager for the experience."

Everett C. Buckner, Sr., range master of the San Gabriel Gun Club, followed the policeman to the stand in the long line of state witnesses. He testified that on June 4 Sirhan practiced "rapid fire" pistol shooting at the club range. After Sirhan had fired for about fifteen minutes, he came to Buckner and said: "I want the best box of shells you have, and I want some that won't misfire. I've got to have some that won't misfire."

Buckner said he gave them to Sirhan who went back to the range.

On cross-examination by Cooper, Buckner conceded that he had failed a police department lie detector test on certain questions. "Didn't you tell the police at one time that a lady out here said to Sirhan, 'Get out of here, goddamn you, somebody will recognize us,'?" asked Cooper.

Buckner answered the question, put to him by Cooper three separate times, three different ways. First he said, "I didn't quite understand what they said." Then, said Buckner, "I said it sounded like that."

Appearing exasperated, Cooper pressed Buckner one more time. "I told the police it sounded that way—I told the police I didn't know what was said, I couldn't hear well enough," Buckner replied.

Later, the author George Plimpton was called to testify. In the hours after Robert Kennedy was assassinated, Plimpton had told the Los Angeles police department that he had been drawn to the eyes of Sirhan Sirhan in the moments after the murder.

"I could tell you all about his eyes," Plimpton told the police at that time. "They were dark brown and enormously peaceful eyes."

Now, at Sirhan's trial, Emile Zola Berman, Sirhan's lawyer, wanted to know what Plimpton had meant by his statement.

The writer, who was traveling in the Kennedy entourage at the moment of death and had struggled with Sirhan for possession of the pistol, answered Berman carefully: "It is difficult for me to say . . . He struck me, compared to the rest of us, as enormously composed. The rest of us, given this sudden tragedy, were not composed . . . . Right in the middle of this hurricane of sound and feeling he seemed almost in the eye, in the midst of a hurricane. He seemed purged."

On direct examination, the author, who had worked for Kennedy during the senator's campaign, told of being only a few feet from Kennedy when the shots rang out. Plimpton did not immediately recognize the reports from the .22 caliber revolver as gun shots, "but I had a sense they were revolver shots."

The New York writer said he saw a struggle for the gun going on between Sirhan and Jack Gallivan, the broad-shouldered Kennedy staff member, and he went immediately to assist Gallivan.

"Did you see the senator at this time?" asked John Howard, the assistant district attorney.

"No, I did not have enough courage to look back in that direction," Plimpton said.

Paul Schrade, the United Auto Workers official, who was gravely wounded in the flurry of shots, took the stand after

Plimpton and told of his sensations at the moment of the shooting.

"I turned around . . . and all hell broke loose, and I heard some crackling like electricity and saw some flashes," Schrade said. "I remember thinking we were all being electrocuted, that there was some kind of electrical thing going off in the immediate area."

Schrade, who was struck just above the forehead by a bullet fragment, fell within a few feet of where Kennedy lay.

"I knew I was behind him (Kennedy), maybe a few feet," Schrade said, "I was shaking violently . . . . I began shaking and falling."

The union official lost consciousness as he fell, then awakened on the floor.

"The first thing I remember was a great pain and burning sensation in my head . . . and people walking all over me."

Schrade said he was on the floor for fifteen to twenty minutes before being lifted to an ambulance stretcher.

"Were you in pain the entire time?" Fitts asked.

"There was pain originally, then I was quite numb . . . . I felt blood running down my face and head," he answered.

There was conflicting prosecution testimony during the day about Sirhan's accuracy with a pistol. David Montellano, a Los Angeles youth who testified he saw Sirhan firing on a gun range the date of the assassination, said he had formed the opinion that the defendant was "not a very good shot."

"He was not hitting the targets very well, was he?" Russell Parsons asked for the defense cross-examination.

"No, sir," said Montellano, who admitted he had little experience with hand guns.

Then Michael Anthony Saccoman, who also had been at the range, testified that from his observation "judging from his gun and the targets I would say he was a good shot." Saccoman described Sirhan's Iver-Johnson revolver as a "piece of junk." Saccoman said Sirhan's target had a heavy concentration of bullet holes in the circle around the bull's eye.

"Did you ever discuss anything about hunting?" prosecutor Howard asked Saccoman.

"Yes," Saccoman answered. "I told him you could not use a .22 pistol for hunting. I told him it was illegal to hunt with a .22 because of its accuracy.

"He said, 'I don't know about that; it could kill a dog.' "

Testimony disclosed that Sirhan spent part of that death day, June 4, teaching a tavern waitress, Mrs. Claudia Williams, how to fire her pistol on the range.

Mrs. Williams, a shapely young blonde, testified that she went to the San Gabriel club about 4:00 p.m. for her first firing of a pistol she had received as a gift the previous Christmas. She found Sirhan engaged in rapid fire practice. Mrs. Williams said Sirhan taught her to fire the gun without cocking it, simply by pulling the trigger, and told her that his hollow point mini-mag bullets "were better than the ones I was using." She and her husband, Ronald, who had been firing a .30-30 rifle on a different part of the range, both testified Sirhan was still at the club when it closed at 5:00 p.m.

The next day brought a surprise witness. He was a black man, with a goatee, in his mid-thirties. In the first moments of his examination he said that he was a trash collector, and some reporters surmised that his would be routine testimony. But Alvin Clark, of Pasadena, unleashed an evidentiary bomb.

Sirhan told him more than a month before the assassination that he was "planning on shooting the senator."

"He asked me how I felt about the upcoming election, and I said I was going to vote for Senator Kennedy," Clark said. "And Sirhan said, 'Whatever do you want to vote for the son-of-a-b for, because I'm planning on shooting him.' "

As Clark spoke these words from the stand, Sirhan grinned, then quickly covered his mouth and began whispering with his lawyer, elderly Russell Parsons.

Clark said he then told Sirhan: "You would be killing one of the best men in the country."

The conversation between the trash collector and the assassin took place a few days after the April 4 assassination of Dr. Martin Luther King, Jr., Clark said.

"He was upset somewhat about the death of Luther King," said Clark. "He asked how the Negro people were going to react. I told him I didn't know—there wasn't but one person responsible for his death. He asked me what did I think the Negro people were going to do about it. I said, 'I mean what can they do about it?' "

Berman asked whether Clark and Sirhan got along well together.

Clark: "Yeah, well, Sirhan at this time, I thought very much of him."

Q. "Did you tell the FBI you would not want to take the oath (testify) because you hated Sirhan so much you would do anything to see him convicted?"

A. "Yes, I did."

Berman sat down.

Fitts, on redirect, asked the witness, "Have you told the truth here today?"

"Yes, I have," Clark answered.

It was telling testimony for the prosecution.

Two others wounded by the shots Sirhan fired also testified. Irwin Stroll, a young Kennedy volunteer, said he was hit in the leg by a .22 shell which "felt like someone kicked me."

"After I saw I had gotten shot, I pushed toward the dish racks and collapsed," Stroll said.

Stroll sued Sirhan for one and a half million dollars for his injury and is represented by famed San Francisco attorney, Melvin Belli. William Weisel, an associate director for ABC television in Washington was shot in the side. The impact of the bullet "felt like something falling out of my inside coat pocket and hitting my side," he said. He felt no pain, but when he looked to see what had fallen from his pocket, "the whole area was red."

The bullet lodged in his spine, and was removed by surgery, Weisel said.

On the twenty-third day of trial interest suddenly quickened in the real point of the defense case—the matter of Sirhan Bishara Sirhan's mental capacity, which the defense said was diminished when he shot Robert Kennedy.

For the first time newsmen learned that two weeks earlier psychiatrists for opposing sides, the state and the defense, had gotten together for a meeting in the office of defense attorney Grant Cooper. They met all day and tried to pool psychiatric data they had compiled on Sirhan.

This came to light after the lawyers and Sirhan met in Judge Walker's chambers. When the lawyers and Sirhan came from that meeting it was not known what they discussed, but when the transcript of their session was handed to newsmen, they found that it contained a discussion concerning the session among the psychiatrists two weeks before.

Now Chief Prosecutor Lynn Compton complained that he had not received copies of the defense psychiatric testimony. Compton was particularly interested in the report of a widely known psychiatrist, Dr. Bernard L. Diamond. Grant Cooper said he himself had not received all of Diamond's reports but that when he did they would be made available to the prosecution. "I don't see how anything could be fairer than that," he said.

The discussion with Judge Walker about the meeting of mental experts two weeks earlier did not include the psychiatrists' findings nor did it tell whether they succeeded in reaching compatible conclusions about Sirhan's state of mind. It did come out that the entire eight-hour session of the psychiatrists had been tape-recorded, that Cooper himself sat in on the last hour of the meeting and that Berman was there during the last two hours.

The criminal case was in its twenty-third day; a case in which the defendant's mental state was the only issue to be tried. But two weeks before, days after the case opened and the opposing sides declared they were ready for trial, vital information regarding the mental condition of Sirhan had not been made available to the lawyers for either side. This raises another point about the adequacy of the system of justice.

District Attorney Evelle Younger had at one point told a group of reporters out of court that the defense "might be surprised if they could see our psychiatrists' reports." The inference was clear: "We know something they don't know." Whether it helped the prosecution or the defense, if it related to Sirhan's sanity, which was on trial, why was the district attorney keeping it secret from the other side? On the other hand, why was Cooper not himself informed about what his own psychiatrists' reports said about Sirhan? And why was he not pressing to make his own expert witness findings available to the prosecution?

With the passage of time it was becoming more and more obvious that Sirhan's behavior was going to be a problem for the court. When the diaries he had written appeared in court in the hands of the prosecution, Sirhan Sirhan became visibly agitated and angry and demanded to see the judge in chambers. He did not want these diaries read in public, and the prosecution was obviously going to read them.

Police detective William E. Brandt, the diaries lying open before him on the witness stand, was testifying about finding the handwritten notebooks in Sirhan's home. Grant Cooper jumped to his feet and said: "Your Honor, can we have a recess? Our client requests it."

At this point, Sirhan was jabbing his fatherly defense lawyer Russell Parsons and whispering hoarsely to his investigator Michael McCowan. Sirhan began gesturing wildly.

It was forty minutes before the normal adjournment time of 4:00 p.m. Judge Walker surveyed the scene and announced the proceedings would end for the day at that point.

Sirhan had whispered to Parsons and McCowan, "No, I don't want anybody to read those . . . . I want you to object."

Parsons said, "We will object when the time comes."

Sirhan became emotional and said, "I want you to object now . . . . I want a conference with the judge right now."

Walker overruled a defense objection to the diaries being read. Cooper contended that Los Angeles police detectives and an FBI agent got the diaries illegally when they searched the Sirhan home without a warrant the night after the shooting.

Adel Sirhan, the assassin's thirty-year-old brother, admitted the officers to the home, according to police testimony.

Now the jury had viewed color pictures of Kennedy's head taken after an autopsy was performed on the senator. Two of the four women on the jury studied the photographs at some length. One juror, Mrs. Nell Bortells, refused to look at the photos.

The pictures accompanied the testimony of police crime laboratory specialist, Dewayne A. Wolfer, who testified that in his opinion the shot which killed Kennedy was fired from a range of one inch or less.

Prosecution exhibits in addition to the photographs included a bullet removed from the senator's back and bullet fragments removed from his head "both in surgery and in the autopsy." There were also fragments of bullets introduced which had been removed from the bodies of five other persons wounded during the assassination.

Kennedy's coat, which was cut from him as doctors fought

to save his life in the early hours of June 5, was also put into evidence. It had been raggedly sewn together by Wolfer.

Dr. Henry M. Cuneo, chief neurological surgeon at Los Angeles' Good Samaritan Hospital, told of the medical efforts to save the senator's life.

Emergency brain surgery began at 3:10 a.m., he said, and was over at 6:20 a.m. The devastation of the .22 caliber bullet which entered the senator's brain and the other two which caused body wounds was explained by crime lab specialist, Wolfer, who said the hollow point ammunition Sirhan was using "expands or blows up on contact with an object."

About 5:30 p.m., June 5, Cuneo and his assistants realized that "things weren't going well."

"Around 12 (noon) or 12:30 the brain waves (on an electro-encephalograph) didn't look bad," the doctor said. "They were only slightly less than normal."

"Then at 7:00 p.m.," he said, "there were no waves."

Thus, the state finally proved that Kennedy was dead and that Sirhan had killed him. It took twenty-four trial days.

On the twenty-fifth day of trial, when it became certain that Judge Walker would not exclude the diary in open court, Sirhan tried to plead guilty to first-degree murder. Twice he interrupted his trial. Once he leaped to his feet to address the judge and became so upset his attorneys asked for another early adjournment so they could closet themselves with him. Judge Walker again agreed.

"He's just blown his top and we're trying to control him," Cooper told newsmen. "He just feels his constitutional rights have been violated in taking his personal documents and putting them into evidence."

Cooper confirmed that Sirhan had wanted to plead guilty, that he expressed that wish in a meeting in Judge Walker's chambers that morning, "and we are not going to let him do it."

The young Arab reportedly told the judge, "I would rather plead guilty and die in the gas chamber than have people think I am getting a fair trial."

"We're running this case as his lawyers and we're not going to let him, as a client, run the case," Cooper said. "He doesn't know what the hell he's doing."

To change his plea, Sirhan "is going to have to fire his lawyers," Cooper said.

The diary, parts of which were made available to the press by the prosecution, included written threats against Robert Kennedy, former United Nations Ambassador Arthur Goldberg and Bert C. Allfillisch, a former employer of Sirhan:

"Robert Kennedy must be assassinated."

"Ambassador Goldberg must die, Ambassador Goldberg must be eliminated . . . ."

"I believe that I can effect the death of Bert C. Allfillisch."

After heated debate between prosecution and defense attorneys, Judge Walker ruled that portions of the diary were admissible as evidence.

While Compton argued for admission of the writings, Sirhan suddenly leaped to his feet, his face angry and contorted, and spoke loudly to the judge: "Wait a minute, that hasn't been admitted into evidence yet!"

Inspector William Conroy immediately grabbed Sirhan by both shoulders from behind and slammed him back into his chair. His attorneys were then able to quiet him, and the debate continued.

However, shortly after court resumed in the afternoon, Sirhan heard Walker rule that not only would much of his diary be shown to the jury but that all of it would be made available to the press.

He suddenly spoke: "Your Honor, I must apologize for interrupting . . . ." he blurted out, and was immediately surrounded again by his attorneys who jumped up and huddled about him.

Cooper asked for another recess, which was granted, then returned after a forty-minute break to request an adjournment for the rest of the day. Walker granted it.

After the outburst, Mary Sirhan and Sirhan's younger brother Munir went into Sirhan's cell area to talk with him and try to calm him. Mrs. Sirhan emerged weeping and told reporters: "They're taking all the trash and using it against him."

Walker upheld a defense objection to two pages on grounds they were "inflammatory."

"The court feels that the inflammatory nature of these pages far outweighs the probative value," Walker said.

On these two pages, Sirhan had used four-letter language

to describe the United States and had said, "I firmly support the Communist cause and its people."

After Walker ruled against showing those pages to the jury, Compton rose to say: "I strongly believe it is in the interest of the nation and of the public. . . . I feel they want to know . . . this defendant's attitude and feelings about this country."

"The court realizes that it is impossible to keep anything from the press if they really want to get it," Walker said.

Cooper strongly urged that the judge "admonish the press not to publish any material not shown to the jury."

"It could be highly prejudicial," Cooper said.

"Under Supreme Court ruling, Your Honor would have that right, and I think a responsible press would respect that."

However, Walker ruled against Cooper, emphasizing that the jury was carefully protected from seeing any publicity on the case and added, "I don't like putting my staff under any unusual strain. These things have a way of leaking out." Six pages of the diary, including that portion which said "Kennedy must die," would go to the jury, he said. The rest would be in the public domain.

As the argument on the diary raged back and forth with the jury absent, Sirhan became more and more nervous. He drank several cups of water, at one point pushed his chair far back from the counsel table, shrugged and raised his arm in a gesture of futility. He chewed on his fingernails, and finally, just before leaping to his feet, began to bounce up and down in his chair.

On the twenty-seventh day of trial, Sirhan became so overwrought that he could not be controlled by his lawyers and his outbursts threatened to disrupt his trial. While the state's case in chief drew near a close with the testimony from the final witnesses, Sirhan became more and more contentious at the defense table, at times causing his own attorneys to rebuke him before the jury. It was obvious throughout the morning session that the defense team of Cooper, Parsons and Berman were unsettled as Sirhan whispered gruffly to them, talked out loud and gesticulated wildly.

Shortly after noon the three defense lawyers, leaving Sirhan calmly smoking a cigarette in the courtroom, closeted themselves with Judge Walker in his office to "talk about our problem." They told Judge Walker they could not guarantee that Kennedy's killer would sit quietly in the courtroom. They explained how twice

Tuesday he had interrupted the proceedings with outbursts, ignoring their pleas to behave.

Judge Walker told the defense team to tell Sirhan that if he did not remain quiet, "he will be physically restrained in his chair."

At the afternoon meeting, the judge told the attorneys he would try to assist them in controlling the defendant.

In further testimony, defense lawyer Cooper questioned police lieutenant William C. Jordan, who participated in three interrogations of Sirhan in the early morning hours of June 5 just after the shooting. "The defendant is extremely intelligent," Jordan said. "He speaks very well. He was denied formal education, but he speaks like a person well educated.

"He was one of the most alert and intelligent people I have ever interrogated, or attempted to interrogate."

Jordan testified that when he first spoke with Sirhan at the Rampart Street Substation, he brought the defendant a cup of coffee.

"He asked me to drink out of the cup first," Jordan said. "I asked why and he gave no answer. The same thing happened on two other occasions after Sirhan was removed to the main police station."

On cross-examination Cooper, for the defense, led Jordan through a repeat recitation of his testimony about what happened at Rampart and then asked:

Q. "Wasn't the defendant handcuffed at all times?"

A. "They were loosened one time, I think . . . ."

Q. "Were his hands handcuffed in front of him or behind his back?"

A. "They were behind his back."

Q. "How did he drink the coffee?"

A. "How do you mean?"

Q. "How did he drink the coffee if his hands were handcuffed behind him?"

A. "I don't remember, Mr. Cooper. As I say, there was a period when he was uncuffed . . . . I don't remember exactly when . . . ."

Q. "As a matter of fact, didn't you know that he asked for something to drink and was refused?"

A. "No."

Q. "Do you recall a single occasion when the handcuffs were removed?"

A. "Yes, they were off . . . . they were removed for the medical examination and they were removed when he was booked."

Another witness that day, Dr. Faustem Bazilauskas, said that Kennedy "was not breathing" when he was brought to the receiving room of Central Receiving Hospital. The doctor said his firm impulse had been "to inject adrenalin directly into his heart . . . but Mrs. Kennedy . . . I don't think she could have taken it.

"Then we gave the adrenalin intramuscularly, which was effective . . . . Soon after the adrenalin he developed a good solid pulse and somebody screamed 'I've got a pulse!' "

Minutes later the senator was rushed to Good Samaritan Hospital where the emergency neurosurgery was performed and he lived for several hours. Great crowds of people descended on the hospital, Bazilauskas said, moments after Kennedy was brought in.

"There was a mob of people outside, and the ambulance driver (leaving for Good Samaritan) said he didn't know whether he could get through the crush or not."

Q. "Weren't there Los Angeles police officers?"

A. "Yes, but not enough. There were too many people outside."

Coroner Carlos Noguchi testified for the record that Kennedy's head wound was the fatal one. He was shot also twice in the side. Noguchi was the state's fifty-sixth witness. He was the last. The State closed its case.

After twenty-seven days, the state of Sirhan's mental health had hardly been discussed. This, under the law, is the manner of the adversary criminal proceeding. The state, which puts on evidence against Sirhan, is not interested in the defense theory that he is mentally ill. The psychiatrists who examined Sirhan for the prosecution had told the district attorney's office that while he has shown some emotional disorder, they were convinced that he was legally sane in that he knew right from wrong and was not suffering from a discernible diminished mental capacity.

It is the prosecution's job to put on evidence against Sirhan,

not for him. Thus, nothing had been said yet about the prosecution's positive findings about the defendant's sanity.

Evidence about his diminished mental capacity would come
when the defense lawyers began putting on their case for the
other side. Their psychiatrists had told them that there was clear
evidence of diminished mental capacity. After that defense evidence was in the record, then and only then would the state be
allowed to counter with the prosecution's psychiatrists. The
psychiatrists were employed by the side for which they testified.
While none of the state's case had included testimony from psychologists or psychiatrists, most of the defense evidence would
be on that subject. Little of it would touch on anything else.

The defense lawyers pondered again whether to risk putting
Sirhan Bishara Sirhan on the witness stand in his present frame
of mind.

They wanted to paint this jury a portrait with evidence designed to depict Sirhan as a pathetic immigrant, a mentally unstable assassin. But they were afraid that Sirhan himself would
interfere.

Under ideal circumstances they would have used Sirhan as
the first witness. But his antics in the courtroom had shaken the
confidence of his attorneys in his ability to function on the witness
stand. His lawyers themselves had had to admonish him severely
in front of the jury for whispering loudly and speaking out while
testimony was going on. He was becoming more and more hostile.

When, or if, Sirhan should take the stand consumed most of
the thoughts of the defense team. "We'll have to play it by ear,"
said Emile Zola Berman. "Some days he's calm. Some days he's
not. We just come and talk to him in the mornings to see how he
is."

All the hostility that drove Sirhan Sirhan to kill Robert
Kennedy boiled over in open court on the twenty-eighth day as
he stood suddenly and emphatically declared that he wanted to
plead guilty, wanted his lawyers fired, wanted to have his life
taken for his crime. The jury was out at the time.

Judge Walker turned down all three demands.

"I know of nothing in the law that permits a defendant under
any circumstances to plead guilty to first-degree murder and ask
for the death penalty," Judge Walker said.

His voice shrill, Sirhan declared: "I believe, sir, it is in my interests. It is my prerogative."

"Well, why is it in your best interest?" Walker asked.

"I killed Robert Kennedy willfully, premeditatedly and with twenty years of malice aforethought," Sirhan said.

Walker listened with impatience to Sirhan for a few moments, then told the emotional young Arab he was "incompetent" to defend himself. The judge warned Sirhan "any further interruptions will result in your being restrained.

"This means we will put a face mask on you and you won't be able to talk. Your arms will be strapped in the chair," the judge said.

The unexpected admission of murder and request for death came as Sirhan listened with obvious anger to a recitation of his school record, his grades, a school rating that his I.Q. was eighty-nine, and his performance on aptitude tests. His own lawyers were putting on the evidence.

After the judge denied the assassin's strange demands there was another unexpected development.

Sirhan's lawyers, after a brief out-of-court conference, asked to be relieved of the case. Cooper told Judge Walker he and his colleagues wished to quit.

"We have conferred with our client in his holding cell, and he has advised us definitely . . . he does not wish us to continue as his attorneys. I have conferred with my brethren of the defense and none of us has any desire to continue to represent this client."

Walker turned down this motion too. "I know of no law which permits counsel to withdraw in the middle of a case except for a good cause," he said. "You have presented a good defense, if not the only logical defense."

The twenty-eighth day produced other emotional moments. Sirhan's mother was called by his lawyers as a witness and became so shaken on the stand the trial had to be recessed.

She told of Sirhan's birth in Jerusalem in 1944. Mrs. Sirhan was asked how long her family had lived in the ancient city.

"Jerusalem," she said softly, "has been my family's home for generations and generations and generations . . . ."

"They called it the city of peace," she whispered so quietly that Cooper asked her to repeat it.

"They called it the city of peace . . . . (then her voice broke) I am sorry, I can't help it . . . that I feel this way."

Her youngest son, Munir, twenty-one, walked quickly from his seat in the audience to slip a note to the defense table, asking that his mother's ordeal be postponed.

"I can't imagine any worse circumstances for a mother to be called to the stand," Judge Walker said after the jury retired from the courtroom.

Then Los Angeles city schools official John T. Harris was called by Cooper to recite Sirhan's sub-par performance on mental and aptitude tests as a student. Again Sirhan began to berate his lawyers. Parsons interrupted the testimony of the school official to ask for a bench conference with the judge. The jury was sent from the courtroom. Cooper said: "Mr. Parsons just interrupted this witness and has expressed a desire to say something to Your Honor." He looked severely at his client. "Now, I want the defendant to listen to this . . . last week he was shown a list of witnesses whom we intended to call in his behalf, and he objected to approximately twelve of them (out of thirty). Whereas we, as lawyers, with years of experience at the bar, agree they are in his best interest, he has indicated he would forbid their calling." That very morning, he said, Sirhan indicated he would allow the testimony.

"I just talked with him (Sirhan) and now he informs me that he again forbade us from presenting these witnesses."

Cooper asked Sirhan to tell Judge Walker if that was a "fair representation of the general background."

"Yes, sir . . . ." Sirhan said.

"The defendant now desires to address the court," Cooper said.

"I request to go to chambers," Sirhan said from his seat.

"Request denied," Walker said flatly.

"Then I want to withdraw my original plea of not guilty and plead guilty to all counts and I request that my counsel be disassociated from the case," Sirhan said.

"Do I understand that you want to plead guilty to murder in the first degree?" Walker asked.

"Yes, sir," Sirhan said.

"What do you want to do about the penalty?" the judge asked.

Sirhan rose, placed his hands on the counsel table before him, and answered firmly: "I will ask to be executed."

Judge Walker pondered momentarily. Whether Sirhan killed Kennedy with premeditation would have to be a matter of evidence, he said.

"I withdraw such evidence," Sirhan said.

"There is no such procedure . . . the court will not accept your plea. And let me tell you here and now, this court will not put up with any more interruptions," Walker said. "Sit down, now. Any further interruptions will result in your being restrained."

Sirhan answered, "However, sir, I will defend myself."

Sirhan had retained competent counsel to defend him, the judge said. He pointedly asked the defendant if he knew the legal elements of first-degree murder and the defenses for a charge of murder in the first degree.

"No," Sirhan said.

"I find you incapable of defending yourself," Walker said.

"I will not have this shoved down my throat," Sirhan retorted.

The judge's bass voice rose and he said, "I will not accept the plea . . . the law tells me what I can do and what I can't do."

One of Sirhan's childhood friends from Old Jerusalem was called to testify how Sirhan grew up in the midst of murder, filth and terror, beaten constantly by his father and affected by the scenes of warfare on his doorstep.

Ziad Hashimeh, who is one month older than the twenty-four-year-old Sirhan, lived right across the hall from the Sirhan family and played every day with young Sirhan. As a boy, he said, Sirhan was "very sensitive" and urged him not to steal or lie.

Grant Cooper asked if Sirhan and Hashimeh ever saw "people die of starvation?"

"Oh, yes, sir, quite a few," Hashimeh said quickly. "Across the street there lived these villagers and every morning I see their faces. They were very thin, very pale. When we would have an extra piece of bread or the Sirhan's would have some extra, we would give it to them because they have no food, you see."

"How did you know they died of starvation?" Cooper asked.

"Well, when we hear a child dies—he does because he is sick because he has no food, you see," Hashimeh said simply.

Q. "Now, Sirhan's father . . . did you ever see him strike his wife?"

A. "Yes, sir."

Q. "Was Sirhan present?"

A. "Yes, sir."

Q. "How did he strike her?"

A. "By hand, sometimes, pushing her."

Q. "Did you ever see him strike Sirhan?"

A. "Oh, yes, quite a few times—the man, Mr. Sirhan, was too emotional."

Q. "How often did he strike Sirhan?"

A. "Well, I didn't count—many times . . . quite a number of times."

Q. "And did Sirhan cry?"

A. "Oh, yes."

Q. "With what did he strike him, a stick, his hands, what?"

A. "Well with a stick, yes, anything he could lay his hands on."

Q. "Where did he strike him?"

A. "On the bottom, the back, everywhere . . ."

Later, on the thirtieth day, the defense decided to risk putting on the defendant to testify in his own behalf. Sirhan took the stand. Gripping the rail of the witness box, Sirhan said he killed Robert Kennedy and had no doubt that he also wounded five other persons the night Kennedy fell in the Ambassador Hotel. The question came from his lawyer in a measured tone: "Did you on or about the 5th of June, 1968, shoot Senator Robert F. Kennedy?" asked Grant Cooper as he began his examination of the young Jordanian Arab.

"Yes, sir," replied Sirhan in an even tone. Later he added: "I wasn't aware of any of it."

Relaxing a bit, Sirhan smiled as Cooper read into the record a page from Sirhan's diary in which he wrote again and again that "Robert F. Kennedy must be assassinated."

"Is all of that in your handwriting?" Cooper asked.

"Yes, it is," Sirhan said.

Smiling at the judge and jury, occasionally looking down to examine the microphone around his neck, Sirhan said he did not know any of the five he wounded when he fired at Kennedy. He said he bore them "no ill will."

Under questioning by Cooper, Sirhan spent forty-five minutes on the stand. He said he remembered as a child seeing dismembered bodies of Arabs, victims of Israeli attacks and recalled his family fleeing Old Jerusalem when he was four.

Questioned by Cooper, Sirhan testified:

Q. "Do you yourself have any recollections (when you lived in New Jerusalem) in your childhood of . . . war casualties?"

A. "I recollect some quite vividly, I remember the soldier with his body exploded . . . . I remember seeing the soldier's leg with the boot on it."

Q. "Do you remember the death of your older brother, Munir?" (Sirhan's younger brother, Munir, twenty-one, was named for him.)

A. "I have a light recollection of that . . . . I used to walk around his casket."

Q. "Do you have any recollection of moving from New Jerusalem to Old Jerusalem?"

A. "I don't remember exactly that we were moving or not . . . but I remember we were in a panic when we left . . . . I was naked."

After moving to a crowded, filthy, semi-destroyed building where his family of eight lived in one room, Sirhan said the facts of life became bombings, shootings and death.

"I can tell you of incidents," he said. "We always had to go down to the basement and our mother stuffed our ears with cotton and we knew the bombings were coming."

Cooper asked Sirhan if he knew why his family left their home in New Jerusalem and moved into the Arab refugee section of Old Jerusalem.

"I have learned from history books and reading that the main cause was that the West wanted to bring in persecuted Jews from Europe and expel the indigenous Arabs to accommodate the Jews."

As Sirhan testified, his voice rose and he glanced excitedly about the courtroom.

He told of going to the wall which separated Old Jerusalem— where most of the displaced Arabs lived during the first Arab-Israeli hostilities—from the militant Jewish forces.

"We were on the ground, and we saw some policeman or soldier on the wall, and we hollered up to see if we could come up there," he said. "He invited us up . . . he had a telescope . . . a pair of binoculars around his neck, and he was looking at the Jewish part, at a big building that had been bombed.

"We looked and saw where the Zionists were rehabilitating the building, and I could see the emotions of the soldier as he looked, and he said, 'That's our land out there, our country, our property.' "

"Did you understand what he meant?" Cooper asked.

"I didn't understand then; now I do," Sirhan said.

As he told this story, the assassin clenched his fists and riveted his eyes on Cooper.

Earlier in the day Mary Sirhan had also recited childhood tales of Sirhan's life. At one point she had to be warned by Walker to restrict her answers to the subject matter of the questions. The tiny Arab mother, who has borne ten children and has seen five of them die, took every opportunity to emphasize the family's destitution in Jerusalem and its good fortune in America.

"We are lucky in this country . . . . I want to say . . ."

At this point the prosecution objected strenuously and Mrs. Sirhan was instructed to answer the questions without comment. Outside the presence of the jury she had made a loving statement about America.

Adel, Sirhan's brother, testified that he often went by his younger brother's room in their Pasadena home and heard him "talking to himself." He said Sirhan would sit before a mirror by his desk, light a candle and attempt to control the flame with his mind.

Adel said Sirhan became angry with television reports of Arab-Israeli conflicts and would "walk across the room with a sour face very fast and get away."

Adel was asked by the state if Arab-Israeli hostilities had not lessened by the time the family left for America in 1956. Sirhan became agitated, half rose from his chair and said "No." He was quickly slammed back into his seat by security chief Conroy.

When Sirhan appeared himself on the stand he seemed eager to answer all questions. At one point when Cooper asked if the winters were severe in Jerusalem, Sirhan said, "It gets pretty damn cold."

"You watch your language, Sirhan," Cooper said quickly.

At one point in the afternoon, defense lawyer Cooper told

Judge Walker that Sirhan "has asked me to apologize to you for his emotional conduct of last Friday."

"He said it is his desire to retain his counsel," Cooper said. "I don't feel that any great apology is due," Walker said. "I can appreciate his feelings to some extent."

The judge then looked at Sirhan and said, "Are you completely satisfied . . . with your counsel? . . . Are you going to follow their advice from here on out?"

"Yes, sir," Sirhan said, nodding and grinning. The lawyers wondered with newsmen how long his jolly mood would last.

On the thirty-first day Sirhan testified that he "loved" Robert Kennedy and "wanted him to be President," but that love turned to hate when he saw films of the New York senator participating in an Israeli independence celebration.

"At that time, the way I felt about it, if he were in front of me, so help me God, he would have died," Sirhan said with intensity, holding the rail of the witness stand. "I was watching television. That evening I brewed myself some tea—I went into the living room to watch television. As I was flipping the dial, a program on Robert Kennedy came on, a biography, that told of his career as a politician.

"And I sat down to watch it. It told of his achievements . . . as attorney general and a close associate of his brother, the President, and how he became senator from New York.

"At the last part of the program, sir, they were talking about Robert Kennedy always being for the underdog, for the poor, the scum of society . . .

"And there he was, sir, in a film from 1948 in Israel helping the Jews, as I thought, celebrating . . . the declaration of their new nation.[1]

"And the emotion with which the narrator spoke . . . that burned me up. Up to that point I liked Robert Kennedy. I hoped he would' win the presidency. But he was doing a lot of things behind my back that I didn't know about."

Questioned further by Cooper, Sirhan said when he wrote in his notebook May 18, 1968, that "Robert F. Kennedy must be assassinated before 5 June 68," he did not mean it to be a goal. He wrote it over and over.

---

1. Robert Kennedy made a trip to Israel in 1948.

"It was good only for the time it was written there," he said. "I was provoked."

In a full day on the witness stand; the emotional young assassin covered a wide range of subjects, including his hatred for Zionists and any and all politicians who supported them.

Cooper took Sirhan's two spiral notebooks and began providing page after page for Sirhan's evaluation and explanation. Meaningless phrases and doodlings were scrawled across most of the pages, interspersed with Russian and Arabic writings and a few names and rambling comments.

Late in the day Sirhan grinned self-consciously and commented, "Sounds like a crazy man writing." Cooper quickly asked, "Do you think you're crazy? You think you're normal, don't you?"

"No, I don't think I'm crazy," Sirhan said quietly. He said he did not remember writing the page in his notebook on which he wrote time and again that Kennedy must die. "That could have been the time he (Kennedy) was campaigning and he came out and said he's sending fifty jet bombers to Israel if he was elected President."

A few weeks later, Sirhan said, he heard a radio broadcast in which the "hot news was when the announcer said Robert Kennedy was at some Jewish club or Zionist club in Beverly Hills." He said when he heard the announcement about the jet bombers "I received the impression that Robert Kennedy was not all the good guy he claimed to be," Sirhan said.

Q. "And it made you mad?"

A. "Yes, sir, it boiled me up again. I was studying Rosicrucian philosophy at the time and I started blasting him mentally. Again, this is an illusion, but when I looked in the mirror I saw his (Kennedy's) face in the mirror, I was that burned up about it."

On a number of the diary pages "long live Nasser" is written and the name, "Howard Hughes."

"Is that the one with $5 billion?" Cooper asked.

"Most likely, sir," Sirhan said, grinning.

On one diary page is written "Sirhan Sirhan must begin to work on upholding solving the problems and difficulties of assassinating the 36th President of the United States."

"Were you thinking of assassinating President Johnson?" Cooper asked.

"No, but I hated his guts at one point when he said the United States upholds the territorial integrity of all the nations in the (Mideast) area. That's why I hated him."

On another page Sirhan had written: "Long live Communism."

Following his long, often angry recital of his version of the history of the Palestinian struggle, Sirhan was asked, "What is the impact this has had on your life?"

"I always felt that I had no country," Sirhan said, ". . . no place to really call my own. I was sick and tired of being a foreigner. I wanted a place of my own where the people would be speaking my own language, eat my own food, share my own politics and my own . . . something I could identify with as a Palestinian Arab."

He began to pound his fist on the witness stand rail and his voice grew harsh and loud as he concluded, ". . . my own country, my own city, my own land, my own business, my own everything."

His testimony often was punctuated with profanity.

After one of Sirhan's more colorful oaths Cooper smiled and asked, "I take it, you learned these words after you came to the United States?"

"Yes," Sirhan said and grinned.

Sirhan said he saw a magazine cover photograph of Israeli soldiers standing on the banks of the Suez Canal after the six-day war.

"How did you feel when you saw that?" Cooper asked.

"If I saw these guys in person, I would have blasted them. I would have killed them," he said angrily.

He spoke bitterly of the millions of dollars raised in America to send to the state of Israel. "President Johnson was trying to bring the military groups back from Europe to keep the dollars at home . . . these goddamned Zionists . . . pardon me . . . they pick up $370 million cold cash and give it to the Jews in Jerusalem.

"What gives?" he almost shouted. "The riots that were going on then in Newark, sir, they were economically inspired and they were taking money out of the country by the truckload . . . and I

didn't even have a damn job, sir, and here all this money is going
out of the country."

Cooper asked Sirhan if he remembered the 1963 assassination of President John F. Kennedy and he said, "Yes, sir."

"What did you think of that?" his counsel asked.

"I loved him more than any American could. Just a few weeks
before his assassination he was working very hard with the Arab
leaders (to try and bring peace to Palestine and return homes
and property to displaced Palestinians) . . . .

"He was going to put pressure on Israel . . . to help the
refugees . . . he was killed and it never happened," he added in
a quiet voice.

Sirhan's version of the establishment of a Jewish state in
Palestine included bitter denunciations of "Western Imperialism."
The French, English and Americans were responsible, he said.

"When you move a whole body of people from their lands,
their homes, their businesses and bring in an alien people, that
is wrong, sir," he said.

"Did it ever enter your mind that Jews and Arabs might be
able to live side by side peacefully?" Cooper asked.

He became angry and the words tumbled out.

"Well, now let me explain, sir, let me make this very clear
that the Arabs and the Jews, prior to 1948 and the entrance of the
Zionists into Palestine, were living very amicably together.

"The Zionists in this country brainwashed the American
public . . .

"Where is the justice involved, sir? Where is the American
public . . . their love for fighting for the underdog. The Jews
weren't the underdog. It's the refugees, the Palestinian refugees,
that were the underdogs.

"That burned the hell out of me."

Q. "Do you recall being angry at (Ambassador) Goldberg?"

A. "Yes, President Johnson called him 'The Able Ambassador' and to me he was only able, sir, in the respect that he was
on the side of Israel . . . he said the U.S. supports the territorial
integrity of all the nations in the (Mideast) area. He said all; all;
and he made it a hell of a long all."

Q. "Do you think he should die for that?"

A. "At the time I would have killed him if I had a gun. I
would have broken the television set. Period."

From November 1966 until November 1967 Sirhan was unemployed, he said, having left his job as an exercise boy at a Corona, California, ranch following an accident in which he was thrown from a horse.

In the ensuing year Sirhan began to read books and magazines on occult sciences and mind control.

With Cooper doing the questioning, Sirhan testified:

Q. "Do you recall a book on cyclomancy?"

A. "Yes, sir, I do . . . ."

Q. "What is cyclomancy?"

A. "Well, as a man in the book explained it, it is nothing but white magic. It said that you can do anything with your mind if you know how . . . the mind works."

Q. "And did you practice some exercises in mind control?"

A. "The book gave some elementary exercises, yes sir."

Q. "Can you describe some of them that you practiced?"

A. "Well, I know this sounds queer and unbelievable, but you can take a pan of hot boiling water and put your hands in it and think cool and it was cool . . . and I did it the other way around, I took ice water and put my hand in it and thought hot and it was hot."

Q. "Did you ever try any experiments with levitation (releasing the body from the laws of gravity)?"

A. "No, sir. That is too far (advanced) for me."

Sirhan said he had "visual delusions" while experimenting with cyclomancy and he could look at two dots inside separate circles and, after several minutes of concentration, make the dots come together in his mind so that he saw only one dot.

Cooper read off a list of books on mind control that Sirhan said he owned and studied. He said from studies in Rosicrucianism he could look at a candle flame in a dark room and see it in any color he chose.

"Did you ever experiment in thought transference?" Cooper asked.

"Yes, I played with that a little bit," he said.

He grinned and recalled: "I was in my room late at night once and my mother was in bed . . . and I thought just for the hell of it, I would try it.

"I thought hard to her, Mother, get up and go to the bath."

"I waited about ten minutes and it didn't work. But the minute

I got in bed I heard the radio go on and all the lights and heard the toilet flush."

"And your mother got up?" Cooper asked.

"Yes, and she never does that," he said.

Sirhan also told of trying to influence the thinking of a race horse he did not want to win in the first race at Santa Anita on March 19, 1968—his birthday. It was the first horse on the program and was owned by a former employer of his.

"I didn't want that horse to win and I thought and thought 'You s.o.b., you're not going to win' . . . .

"Three or four strides out of the gate and he wheels and he jumped the rail and he was disqualified."

The following day, Sirhan again took the stand to testify that he drove to downtown Los Angeles not to shoot Senator Kennedy but to view a Jewish parade. But the emotional young immigrant, blinded by his hatred of "Zionists," said he did not know that the parade to celebrate the six-day Arab-Israeli war was to be held the next day. Walking down Wilshire Boulevard in the early evening, he saw a "big Jewish sign, for some kind of fund, or something" and anger boiled up inside him. "A fire started burning in me . . . . I thought the Zionists or Jews or whoever it was were trying to rub it in that they had beat hell out of the Arabs."

"When you drove to Wilshire the night of June 4, were you planning to shoot Senator Kennedy?" Cooper asked.

"No, sir . . . I was looking for the parade . . . the way the Zionists go at it, I thought it was going to be a really big one."

"Did you have in mind shooting up the Zionist parade?" Cooper asked.

"No, the gun was completely out of my mind at that point . . . if you want to know what those goddamn sons-of-bitches are up to, you have to watch them."

"Driving like a maniac" toward downtown, Sirhan said he drove up and down Wilshire looking for the parade.

"I couldn't find them, and I was going to give up and go home," he said.

"Then, as I was driving down Wilshire, I stopped by a store, or building with a highly illuminated interior."

Q. "What did you learn the building was?"

A. "The Kuchel headquarters."

Q. "You mean former Senator Thomas Kuchel?"

Sirhan Sirhan on the night of his arrest

Sirhan during his trial

May 18 9.45 AM-68

my determination to ~~eliminate~~ eliminate R.F.K. is becoming

+ please pay to the order more the more of an unshakable obsession

pleo

port wine   port wine   port wine

R.F.K. must die - RFK must be killed Robert
F. Kennedy must be assassinated R.F.K
must be assassinated R.F.K. must be
assassinated R.F.K must be assassinated
RFK, must be assassinated RFK must
be assassinated RFK, must be
assassinated assassinated ~~as~~ Robert F.
Kennedy Robert F. pennedy Robert
F. Kennedy must be assassinated
assassinated Robert F. Kennedy
must be assassinated assassinated
assassinated assassinated
Robert F. Kennedy must be assassinated
Robert F, Kennedy must be
assassinated before 5 June 68
~~Robert~~ F. Kennedy must be
assassinated I have never heard
please pay to the order of of of of of
of of of of of of this or that   HL

8   0 0 0 0 0 - ▯
please pay to the order

A page from Sirhan's diary, introduced at his trial

Judge Herbert Walker, who presided at the Los Angeles Trial

Dr. Martin Schorr, one of the psychologists who testified for the defense

Mary Sirhan, mother of the assassin, and her son Munir during a visit to the offices of the authors of this book

A. "Yes, sir."

Q. "What did you do then?"

A. "Having seen that, sir, not having been able to find the parade, I decided to go in and see what was going on in the Kuchel store there."

He said he had four hundred dollars he had taken from his mother and maybe fifty dollars or fifty-five dollars more on his person.

"I heard two boys talking, saying there was a bigger party at the Ambassador Hotel, and I thought, 'What the hell, I'm on Wilshire Boulevard anyway,' and I couldn't see the parade—that was aborted—so I thought I would go down there and see what's going on."

Q. "What made you believe the party at the Ambassador was a public party?"

A. "Curiosity, sir, forced me to go down there."

Q. "I mean, what made you think you could get in . . .?"

A. "They, the two boys, started to go down there."

Sirhan testified that he had gone to the Ambassador June 2, two days before the assassination, to hear Kennedy speak. At that time, after wandering about the Ambassador lobby, eating Chinese fortune cookies and drinking coffee, Sirhan said, he finally heard Kennedy speak.

"Was that the first time you had seen Senator Kennedy?" Cooper asked.

"Yes, and my whole attitude changed," Sirhan said. "Before, I had associated him with the fifty jet bombers he said he would send to Israel . . . I pictured him as a villain, along with the Zionists.

"But when I saw him that day, he looked like a saint to me."

At another point Cooper again called attention to scribblings in Sirhan's diary. "RFK must die . . . Robert F. Kennedy must be assassinated."

Q. "It appears in your notebook what might appear to be goals, did you have them in mind as goals when you wrote them down?"

A. "Yes, sir, I did in reference to the assassination of Robert Kennedy." It was intended only "for the time it was written . . ." he said.

But Sirhan said he remembered little of what he had written

in his diary and that he wrote in frustration, and that the writings meant nothing to him the next day.

Sirhan swore he was alone in the assassination, not a Communist, nor an agent of any foreign government, nor in a conspiracy.

"You keep speaking in here (diary) of 'we' are going to do this and that," Cooper said. "Did you have anyone with you as an accomplice when you shot Senator Kennedy? . . . Did anyone hire you? . . . Were you paid by any foreign government?"

"No, sir," he said.

"Who is the 'we'?" Cooper asked.

"I don't know."

"Possibly the editorial 'we'?"

"Yes, sir."

At one point Sirhan had written, "We believe we can effect this action and produce this result. The hard fact is that this writing is going to effect the death of the above mentioned victim. One wonders what it feels like to do any assassination that might be some illegal work."

He was asked why he had written that he would kill a former employer, Bert C. Allfillisch.

"I don't understand that," Sirhan said, "I like him very much. I cannot explain that."

Again he was questioned about a second book of his diary which uses an obscenity to describe the U. S. and says the writer supports the Communists and looks for democracy to fall.

"When did you write that?" Cooper asked.

"I don't remember," Sirhan said.

"What were your feelings about the United States at that time?"

"Exactly what it says."

However, Sirhan said, "I don't feel that way . . . . I know it sounds queer, but that was just good for the period when I wrote it."

"What caused you to feel that way?" Cooper asked.

"I don't know," he said.

"Hasn't the United States been good to you?" Cooper asked.

"It wasn't good to the rest of my people, sir," he answered.

"To you?" Cooper insisted.

"It has been very good, sir."

Sirhan testified that earlier on the day of the assassination he had practiced with his .22 pistol on a firing range at San Gabriel. It was only by accident the gun was loaded when he left the range, he swore.

He said he tossed the loaded revolver on his car's back seat, "Because I had no reason to hide it."

Judge Walker cut off the examination for the day just after Sirhan said he walked into the lobby of the Ambassador. "The whole place was milling with people . . . there were a lot of television cameras and bright lights," he testified as the day ended.

The next day Sirhan resumed the stand and testified that he did not remember shooting Senator Kennedy. He swore he was drunk the night the senator was assassinated.

He remembered drinking coffee with a "beautiful girl" in the Ambassador, Sirhan said, "and the next thing I remember I was being choked." Sirhan stuck to this story—he did not know what he had done until he was arraigned the next day.

He had consumed several drinks at political gatherings in the Ambassador and was "too drunk to drive home," he said. He claimed a total blackout.

"The next thing I remember I was being choked . . . . I don't know who was doing the choking, but he was doing a good job." He had never had a blackout before, he said.

Sirhan testified that when he wandered into the hotel, he first found a party for Republican senatorial candidate Max Rafferty. There he bought a gin drink and wandered about, hoping but failing to see Rafferty's daughter, Kathleen, with whom he had gone to high school. After an hour or so he walked away from the Rafferty party and found another for Democratic senatorial candidate Alan Cranston.

In the meantime, he "bought a second drink" somewhere in the hotel. Not accustomed to alcohol, Sirhan said, he became intoxicated and does not remember how many drinks he purchased.

"Do you remember asking anyone where Senator Kennedy's reception was?" Cooper asked.

"No, sir, I don't know . . . to tell the truth, I didn't know myself . . . I felt that I was quite high in my own self, and if I got more drunk, there was nobody to take care of me. So I decided to go home. So I walked out."

Sirhan said he walked back to his car, parked about three blocks away, got in and then decided that he was too drunk to drive.

"Did you turn the motor on?" Cooper asked.

"I almost did, but I was too afraid . . . . I was afraid I would have an accident or get a ticket," Sirhan said.

"What did you do then?"

"I decided to go back to the party and get some coffee."

Sirhan's .22 caliber revolver, which he said was lying on the back seat of his car somehow found its way into the waistband of his trousers; he swore he did not remember how. He then walked back to the hotel and, in some room, which he could not describe, found the coffee and a girl, whom he did not know. She drank coffee with him, he said.

He didn't recall how many cups of coffee he had. Next thing he remembered, the act of murder was done, and he was being choked. That was his story and Sirhan told it easily and even seemed relaxed under questioning by his lawyer. With Cooper gently probing, Sirhan's answers were measured and matter of fact.

Then came cross-examination by the state. Compton was tough and thorough and while there was no hostility about him, there was a tone of cynicism in his voice. The prosecutor's questions raised doubts about Sirhan's tale of what he had done. The young Arab became angry.

"Were you there with me?" Sirhan asked Compton at one point. "How the hell do you know what went on? . . . Don't tell me, ask me; that's all right, just don't put words in my mouth."

At another point, Sirhan glared at Compton and told him he asked "stupid" questions.

"Well, I confess that sometimes I ask dumb questions," Compton said genially.

"Yes, sir, you do," Sirhan said and sat back in his chair with obvious satisfaction.

The defendant's temper flared again in his testimony when he said he remembered becoming angry at a police officer when he was taken to a substation shortly after the assassination. Sirhan said he asked the officer, who was drinking a cup of hot chocolate, if he could have a taste of the liquid.

"He said 'No,' and I kicked the cup right out of his hand," Sirhan said.

Compton began to bear down as he neared the end of his cross-examination.

Q. "You said the other day you were willing to fight for the Arab cause."

A. "The Palestinian Arab cause."

Q. "Do you think when you assassinated Senator Kennedy you helped the Arab cause?"

A. "I was never even aware that I killed this man."

Q. "Well, you know he's dead . . . ."

A. "I've read about it and been told about it . . . ."

Q. "And you have no doubt you killed him?"

A. "Well, all this evidence . . . no, I have no doubt . . . ."

Q. "Well, do you think the killing of Senator Kennedy by anybody helped the Arab cause?"

A. "I'm in no position to explain that; I'm no political observer."

Q. "Are you glad he's dead?"

A. "No."

Q. "Are you sorry he's dead?"

A. "No, sir, I'm not sorry . . . because I have no exact knowledge that I killed him."

Q. "Well, didn't you say the other day in the court, 'I killed Robert Kennedy willfully, premeditatively and with twenty years of malice aforethought?' "

This was an outburst Sirhan had made outside the jury's hearing—but the jury had heard it now. Cooper leaped to his feet and asked for a bench conference with Walker. It was granted, there was whispered conversation, then the attorneys returned to their seats. Compton resumed: "I have just one more question: are you willing to die for it (the Arab cause)?"

"Yes, I'm willing to die for it." Compton sat down. He seemed satisfied that his contempt for Sirhan's story had showed through.

He had managed to convey intense skepticism for what Sirhan claimed was his state of mind. And obviously Compton felt the jury had been with him.

Now Cooper had to try to repair, on redirect examination, the damage Compton's studied cross-questioning had done.

Obviously he was worried that the question Compton had put to Sirhan about the defendant's statement that he had killed Kennedy with premeditation and malice would influence the jury. In the presence of the jury the defense lawyer now read the entire court transcript of the wild session which the jurors had not heard. Obviously he was hoping to put the outburst in some perspective.

Q. "Twenty years ago how old were you?"

A. "Four years old . . . I didn't even know what malice was," Sirhan said.

Q. "Now, last Friday when you made that statement Mr. Compton asked you about, you were mad weren't you?"

A. "I was boiling . . . ."

Q. "You were mad at your lawyers, weren't you, at me . . ."

A. "At you, Mr. Berman, Mike McCowan, Mr. Parsons—at the whole defense table." Sirhan suddenly grinned at Cooper.

Q. "Did you have your lawyers' permission to make that statement?" Cooper asked.

A. "You were fired as far as I was concerned at that time." Now he was grinning at the jurors. They didn't return the smile.

On the thirty-fourth day, the defense called thirteen witnesses and heard several of them give damaging testimony on cross-examination. One witness, Howard Bidstrup, an electrician at the Ambassador Hotel, came to the stand to tell that he saw Sirhan with a drink in his hand. On cross-examination he went on to say that Sirhan spoke to him and then asked questions about Kennedy: how long the Senator had been at the hotel and what his security arrangements were.

Enrique Rabago and Humphrey R. Cordero, a pair of Kennedy supporters, were called to testify about a conversation they had with Sirhan between 10:30 and 11:00 p.m.—just before the assassination—to say he was holding a drink at the time. On cross-examination, they added that he seemed "sober" to them. The defense claimed Sirhan was drunk.

In addition, Rabago, under cross-examination, quoted Sirhan as saying: "Don't worry if Senator Kennedy doesn't win, that son-of-a-bitch is a millionaire. And if he wins he's not going to do anything for you or me or any of the poor people."

During the morning, the defense produced a series of witnesses designed to show that Sirhan's personality changed after an accident in 1967. The young Arab had ambitions to become a jockey, and was thrown from a racehorse during a workout at a ranch in Norco, California, where he was working during the latter months of 1967 and early 1968.

Millard Sheets, owner of horses stabled at the Grand Ja Vista del Rio Rancho at Norco, said he was present when Sirhan was thrown in December 1967, and he thought he was "very seriously injured or even dead."

"His face was very badly messed up with blood and mud . . . . It was frightening."

In a few moments, Sheets said, Sirhan began to moan and claw at his eyes.

"As he began to moan, he began to move . . . and dig deeply into his face with his hands . . . . I learned later that he thought he had gone blind in the accident," Sheets said. "But it was just the mud or the blood covering his eyes . . . . He said what sounded to me like several quiet prayers . . . . I sat down, because he was clawing at his face, and I held his hand out so he couldn't hurt himself . . . . I admired his courage, because I thought he was somewhat afraid of horses."

An ambulance came and, Sheets said, he later learned Sirhan was not seriously injured.

John Strathmann and his wife, Alice, who were "friends" of Sirhan, testified that his personality changed after the accident.

"Prior to the accident, what was his temperament, what was his personality?" Cooper asked Strathmann.

"He was a very intense person," said Strathmann, who had asked Sirhan to help him learn the Arabic tongue. "Whatever he was considering at the moment was the most crucial thing happening . . . . He was open-minded and very eager to learn . . . . He was very considerate."

After the accident, Strathmann said Sirhan was "considerably depressed, he was lonely and it gradually became worse, it appeared to me."

Mrs. Strathmann testified that Sirhan became very interested in the "occult" sciences after the accident.

"He would tell me there are bodies in the universe that we see out of the corners of our eyes, but never bring into focus, and he was trying to focus on them," she said.

"Do you mean astral bodies?" Cooper asked.

"I guess," she answered.

John Henry Weidner, owner of a chain of Los Angeles health food stores and Sirhan's last employer, testified that Sirhan was a neat, punctual, and satisfactory employee until shortly after the first of January, 1968, when he began to rebel against Weidner's authority.

"I soon discovered he had a dislike for the Jewish people as a nation . . . . He said that in America, the Jewish people were on the top and directed things . . . . He said they had taken his home."

On cross-examination, Fitts brought out that Sirhan told Weidner "there was more freedom in Russia and China than the U. S."

Gonzalo Catina, an Ambassador waiter, said he saw Sirhan about 10:00 p.m. June 4, in the Venetian Room, carrying a "Tom Collins glass," and Sirhan asked him to hold his drink while he set up a folding chair to sit in because "he was tired." Catina said he later saw Sirhan in the pantry.

Robert E. Austin, a Los Angeles police officer, said Sirhan appeared "very sullen or hostile" when he was brought in for questioning the night of the assassination. He confirmed that Sirhan kicked a cup of hot chocolate from the hand of another officer who refused to give the assassin a sip of the liquid. Sirhan later apologized for the incident, Austin said.

The long day of testimony was presented by the defense—but it was difficult to see that either side made real points with the jurors.

Finally, on the thirty-fifth day, the first of the psychiatrists and psychologists appeared. Dr. Martin M. Schorr, psychologist, was called to lead the defense's parade of mental experts.

Sirhan suffers from extreme paranoia, said Schorr, who spent nearly two days giving the assassin a battery of psychological tests. Schorr said Sirhan is unable to control his inner self and thinks the entire world is against him. "It came as no surprise to me that he made the statement the other day that he wanted to die," Schorr said. "We find not only impulses toward homicide, but impulses toward suicide."

Schorr, a highly experienced clinical psychologist from San Diego, said, however, that Sirhan is "not a raving maniac . . . .

He's not wild . . . . He's got a keen sense of justice, which comes from his private (mental) world."

While Schorr testified, Sirhan sat quietly, occasionally biting his nails and frowning. The doctor spent the entire day on the witness stand, talking about Sirhan's performance on three tests:

1. The Wechsler intelligence testing system, from which he learned that Sirhan has an above-average "verbal I. Q." and a near-moronic "performance I. Q." which projected "a psychotic picture, with patterning typically consistent with schizophrenia."

2. The Rorschach ink blot test, from which the doctor deduced that Sirhan is deeply paranoid and "listens to voices inside his own head . . . has no involvement with people . . . and shows highly unchecked emotions, in fact, dangerously high."

3. An extensive psychological questionnaire, on which Sirhan was abnormally honest, Schorr said, appearing to be dishonest on only two responses in the 566-question exam.

As for Sirhan's reactions to the test, Schorr said: "He was most anxious to convince me how normal and sane he is. This is an aberrant reaction . . . . In paranoia, this is a most typical reaction.

"The paranoid is most anxious to convince you how right he is and how wrong everyone else is."

Schorr explained Sirhan's ratings as:

Verbally—"What you would expect of a college student . . . in fact, of a good college student."

Performance—"Something you would expect of a child of five."

This discrepancy gave impetus to Schorr's first suspicion that Sirhan was paranoid, he said, because a paranoid individual "shows a markedly reduced capacity under stress." The pressure of having to relate to reality in a test situation was too much for Sirhan, the psychologist said.

The Wechsler result left him with two automatic conclusions, Schorr said—"Not to rule out psychosis or mental illness and . . . to rule out brain damage."

The doctor said he was "left with a psychotic picture" typical of the schizophrenic, "which essentially means a state where the individual no longer responds to the world of reality."

"The paranoia developed over a long period of years," he

said. "It is a hideous, insidious process, beginning with the early formative years . . . in the parent-child relationship."

Such a development has an almost predictable end years later, he said, when "the hate irradiates away from the parent or sibling to persons at large, the world around him, to groups."

There were a number of questions on the psychological test forms which Sirhan either refused to or declined to answer, Schorr said, including the following true-or-false questions:

"There is something wrong with my mind."

"Someone has control over my mind."

"People say insulting, vulgar things about me."

"I could be happy living in isolation."

Sirhan is so paranoid that "it only makes you wonder" why he did not shoot Senator Kennedy before he did, Schorr testified in his second day on the stand.

He said it was his opinion, based on the battery of psychological tests, that Sirhan was too mentally unbalanced to commit first-degree murder.

Describing the young Arab as a Dr. Jekyll-Mr. Hyde character who feels like "a puppet on a string," Schorr said, "it was simply a blessing" Sirhan did not try to assassinate Kennedy earlier than June 5, 1968.

After some haggling between the prosecution and the defense over phrasing, Schorr was finally asked by Berman: "In your opinion, could any such individual as described by you have the mental capacity to comprehend his duty to govern his actions in accord with the duty imposed by law and thus have the mental capacity to act with malice aforethought?"

"The answer is . . . no," Schorr said.

The psychologist, himself admittedly nervous on the stand, specializes in examining criminals. He told of showing Sirhan a blank piece of paper, asking him to visualize a picture on it and hearing him say: "This is a figure of that arrogant, self-assured bastard with the victorious smirk on his face. This is the true picture of the conqueror.

"It's that minister in Israel, Moshe Dayan, and he's looking down at people, but there's a bullet that's crashing through his brain at the height of his glory."

"I asked him, 'Where in relation to this picture would you be standing if you were part of this scene?'" Schorr said, and he added that the answer was: "Part of the scene? I am the scene! I'm the one killing him."

The blank card was part of a test in which Sirhan was asked to look at "ambiguous pictures" and visualize a story, Schorr said.

On another card, Sirhan saw "someone under a street light; he's lonely, has no home, no family, no country. He reminds me of myself; he's thinking of killing himself."

The suicidal strain runs strong in Sirhan, the psychologist testified, along with basic insecurity which makes him want to strike out at any and all he thinks are his enemies.

In a word association test, Schorr said, he got the following response: "I said, 'hate,' and he said, 'Jews,' I said, 'Jews,' and he said, 'Nazis.' Then he said, 'As I see it, there's no difference between the Nazis and the Jews in Israel . . . . They are the same for me. Injustice is injustice, and persecution is persecution.' "

Dr. Schorr's defense testimony left no doubt that the psychologist felt Sirhan was so sick mentally he could not have killed Kennedy out of any rational motive.

Now the prosecution got to attack Schorr's theories. Assistant District Attorney Howard began an extensive, meticulous cross-examination of Schorr in the afternoon. The psychologist continued to insist that Sirhan was a "psychopath with paranoic fragmentations." The Rorschach test indicated "he was moving toward paranoid schizophrenia," said Dr. Schorr.

The psychologist said that Sirhan's struggle within himself is such that neither side of his personality knows that the other side exists.

It is the schizophrenic tendency, Schorr said, which led him to say Sirhan has a Jekell-Hyde personality structure. At times the exchanges between prosecutor and psychologist approached "cuteness."

"When Mr. Sirhan told Mr. Compton in court, 'if it was you or me, I'd kill you first,' was that Sirhan Jekyll or Sirhan Hyde?" Howard asked.

"That was Mr. Sirhan Jekyll-Hyde," Schorr answered.

Schorr said the controversial Sirhan diary, in which the assassin wrote time and again that Kennedy must die, was a "sort of escape valve that discharges his hostility and tends to lessen the probability that he will act . . . . But he has to write constantly."

The doctor said he did not believe that Sirhan was "at all aware of that part of his personality that was the killer, the assaulter."

When Howard asked Schorr to describe how a "sane political assassin" would go about killing, the doctor said: "That would be the sort of man who certainly wouldn't write it down, leave it where it could be found, advertise it, predict the date . . . go into a crowded room in hopes of being caught . . . .

"It would be like another case when the man hides in an armory and shoots and tries to get away." He was obviously referring to Lee Harvey Oswald, the assassin of President John F. Kennedy, the senator's brother. He seemed to think Oswald was "sane." The mind of a man such as Sirhan can crack under the slightest pressure, Schorr said. He was clearly saying that he thought Sirhan had cracked at the time of the killing.

When Sirhan shot down Senator Kennedy he was killing his father whom he "hated and feared," Dr. Schorr testified as his cross-examination continued into the following day.

Asked by Prosecutor Howard to recite a selected portion from a summary written after extensive psychological tests, Schorr read: "By killing Kennedy, Sirhan kills his father, takes his father's place as the heir to his mother. The process of acting out this problem can only be achieved in a psychotic, insane state of mind. Essentially, the more he (the father) railed and stormed, the more the mother protected Sirhan from his father and the more he withdrew into her protection. He hated his father and feared him. He would never consciously entertain the idea of doing away with him, but somewhere along the line, the protecting mother fails her son. The mother finally lets down the son.

"She whom he loved never kept her pledge and now his pain had to be repaid with pain. Since the unconscious always demands maximum penalties, the pain has to be death.

"Sirhan's prime problem becomes a conflict between instinctual demands for his father's death and the realization, through his conscious, that killing his father is not socially acceptable. The only real solution is to look for a compromise. He does.

"He finds a symbolic replica of his father in the form of

Kennedy, kills him and also removes the relationship that stands between him and his most precious possession—his mother's love."

Schorr read these words to a hushed courtroom and a jury which took notes throughout. Sirhan displayed no emotion, staring from his seat directly at the psychologist during the reading.

His mother heard the testimony and asked at the morning recess for a private conference with her son. It was denied. She listened to Schorr's words being read and her chin trembling, she walked away muttering, "I don't like this. I don't like this."

A bitter battle developed during the afternoon between the prosecutor and the psychologist, as Howard pounded away at Schorr's testing methods and conclusions.

Failing to budge Schorr's analysis that Sirhan was severely disturbed and incapable of first-degree murder and the psychologist's reliance on the Rorschach test, Howard suddenly shifted his attack and introduced a letter written by Schorr July 10, 1968, to defense attorney Russell Parsons.

"You examined the defendant in November, is that right?" Howard asked.

"Yes, sir," Schorr said.

"Would you please read the last paragraph of this letter," Howard said.

"I would like very much to help you in the matter of preplanning jury selection," Schorr read, ". . . since so many headaches can be avoided by selecting a jury properly attuned to the personality structure of Sirhan."

The letter, regardless of its intent, was a mistake by Schorr. No doubt the jurors hearing the trial were asking themselves whether, in Dr. Schorr's view, they were "properly attuned to the personality structure of Sirhan." Few jurors understood what Schorr meant. Some of them probably felt it was uncomplimentary.

Late in the afternoon the prosecution, as part of its lengthy cross-examination of Schorr, began playing tape recordings of police interrogations of Sirhan the night of the assassination. When court adjourned, the jury had heard a recording of officers' attempts to get the young Jordanian to speak to them at the first precinct station (Rampart Street) to which he was rushed from the Ambassador.

Sirhan refused for hours to tell police his name, or to answer any questions.

When he was first taken to an interrogation room at the Rampart Street station at 12:45 a.m. June 5, 1968, he mumbled to police detective lieutenant William Jordan that he preferred to "remain silent."

The tape recording of Sirhan's first interrogation session contained a completely one-sided conversation between the young assassin and Los Angeles Patrolman Gene Austin.

Austin: "I hate to sit here and say nothing. Are you married? You start a conversation.

"You say something, then, anything.

"I'm sure you have already been told about your rights, is that right?

"Well, you can say yes or no. You got a girlfriend? Boyfriend? (pause) A friend?

"Did the detective tell you you have the right to remain silent? Did he tell you you have the right to the services of an attorney before making a statement . . .?

"Just nod if you don't want to answer. If he didn't tell you your rights, I will tell you.

"Do you understand that? Do you understand? Shake your head no if not, yes if you do. Neither one? Do you understand all I'm trying to do is to point it out to you what your rights are?

"Do you understand English? Do you understand English, or would you rather have somebody in here to speak in Spanish?

"The only things I'm asking are things we're going to find out anyhow. You know that.

"Do you speak English?

"Silent Sam.

"Well, do you speak English? What happened to your leg?

"You won't even tell me that?

"Why? What happened to your leg?

(The voice of another officer breaks in.) "He's just trying to be sociable with you. Can't you talk? Huh? We're going to be here a long time. Hell, we're just trying to get along with you."

(Austin breaks back in.) "We're not recipients of voodoo. We can't stare each other down."

Schorr had testified that he believed Sirhan was "dissociated" mentally at the time of the shooting and for several hours thereafter. He said Sirhan's "paranoia" is so severe his mind becomes fragmented easily and "probably will continue to do so."

"So, he's no better, you think, sitting here today than he was then?" Howard asked.

"I think he's worse," Schorr answered.

Schorr also said that he does not believe Sirhan, as he sits in the courtroom, really knows what is going on around him.

"His mind is so clouded, I don't think he's totally aware . . . but I don't know for sure," the witness said.

On the following day Dr. Schorr again heard the prosecution play recordings of Sirhan after his arrest.

In the early hours of June 5, with Los Angeles in an uproar over the shooting of Senator Kennedy, Sirhan lowered his guard of silence and fenced verbally with detectives and district attorney's investigators on a wide range of subjects. Still he refused to disclose his name, address or place of birth. Sirhan seemed happy to talk through the night about everything from literature to the cost of having babies—everything but the crime he had just committed.

Questioned shortly after 4 a.m., Sirhan and police lieutenant W. C. Jordan discussed justice and equality under the law.

Jordan: "Well, if you were in our shoes, and—well, I can't say that, because I'm putting you back in—you wouldn't try to convict an innocent person, you, yourself? You wouldn't—would you work hard to convict a person that you really, sincerely believed was innocent?"

Sirhan: "I don't really know. You're asking me this question as if you're putting me—you're giving me the responsibility of something so fantastic that it's beyond my mental and physical ability to-to-to cope with really."

Jordan: "I don't think it's beyond your mental ability. I think you've got a lot of mental ability. I think you have been putting us on a little bit here."

Sirhan: "What's he talking about . . .?"

Jordan: "See, right now—right now you're doing it. You're— very sharp. You're very sharp."

Sirhan: "Well, if you mean that as a compliment or a—"

Jordan: "I mean that as a compliment. I-I've got no reason to say otherwise."

Sirhan: "Well, I should thank you, sir."

Talking with policeman Frank Foster in a session at the jail which he did not know was being taped, Sirhan talked about Albert di Salvo, the "Boston Strangler." Sirhan said the sex killer's method of operation was "really cool." He expressed surprise that most of Di Salvo's victims were old women.

"Gee, man, that's something," Sirhan said. "I wonder often what provokes or causes such a man to do that."

Foster said, "The way they feel . . . is that it's a younger person and that he has a psychological factor that he should kill his mother."

"Oh," Sirhan said.

"Because he apparently had a bad childhood," Foster continued. "This is the way the psychologists have been setting up the pattern."

As early morning wore on, the patience of DA's investigator George Murphy was stretched a little thin because Sirhan still kept his identity secret.

"All this time, we've been trying to find out who the hell you are," Murphy grumbled.

"Who the hell am I?" Sirhan shot back.

Jordan, who was polite and solicitious to Sirhan throughout the interrogation, suggested lightly at one point that he might have to adopt the young suspect "to get your name."

Whenever the conversation got around to the Ambassador Hotel, the assassin either would not respond or said he did not know.

"Do you want to answer, or do you want to play twenty questions?" Jordan asked once.

"What's that, a new game?" Sirhan said lightly.

At times, Sirhan became pensive, at times bitter. When Foster asked him, "What do you hope to get out of life?" Sirhan responded: "Why don't you ask me what I had gotten out of life?"

"Well, what had you?" Foster asked.

"Nothing."

"Why?"

"They won't give me it. They won't give me it."

"Well, was it a mistake on your part or their part?"

"Oh, I don't know."

In the last portion of the recordings, Sirhan and police officer Frank Foster talked about life, the image of the police and the outdoors.

Foster: (talking about the police) . . . "It's like any profession, there are cases where there's misuse and misjustice and everything else connected with all professions."

Sirhan: "I agree."

Foster: ". . . Maybe he's just a common laborer . . . . Maybe he washes out toilet bowls, I don't know, or the highest person that can gain a position in the world, there's still injustice and maybe misuse of his powers even though it's his powers."

Sirhan: "Let me shake your hand. You're the first man—please, please, you're the first man that ever said that and expressed it, you know, in the same way as I feel it."

Foster: "How's that?"

Sirhan: "Feeling that I—I couldn't put these feelings, you know, the feeling that I have in more exact and proper words, you know, the way you've expressed it."

Foster: "How do you mean?"

Sirhan: "You know, misuse of authority."

At another point, when the two were discussing what it would be like if all people were exactly alike, Foster said, "It would get pretty tiresome after awhile for me."

"Well, if you were biased of mind in thinking, like me," Sirhan said, ". . . you know there would be no conflict on things. It would be beautiful."

At another point Sirhan tells Foster, "You should have been a nurse or social worker."

Sirhan: "Man, you should have been a minister or something."

Foster: "Why?"

Sirhan: "No, I—I don't stereotype policemen."

Foster: "Pardon me?"

Sirhan: "I don't—I can't—I can't conceive of you as a policeman." (Laughter)

Sirhan: ". . . Let's face it, the average citizen always tried—they kind of stereotype a policeman, you know."

Foster: "Yeah, well, sure . . ."

Sirhan: "Can you deny that and say you agree with me?"

Foster: "No, this is true."

On the fortieth day of trial, under intense cross-examination, Dr. Schorr breathed deeply and admitted he read news reports about Sirhan months before examining him and formed "an undifferentiated" opinion that the assassin might be psychotic. It was a stormy session for the doctor. His professional competence was being challenged. He didn't like it.

The psychologist confirmed that he wrote defense attorney Parsons July 10, 1968, four months before testing the killer of Senator Kennedy to suggest Sirhan sounded schizophrenic.

Under questioning by Howard, Schorr admitted that when he wrote Parsons July 10, he based his conclusions on news stories and "the *Life* magazine articles" on Sirhan.

"Don't tell me, doctor, that you diagnose patients on the basis of articles in *Life* magazine?" said Howard.

"Oh, no, sir," Schorr said quickly.

"When you wrote that letter, had you already made up your mind you were going to be a defense witness?" the prosecutor asked.

"Well . . . no, I had not," Schorr said.

"Did you have an opinion then . . . as to Sirhan's mental state," Howard wanted to know.

"I had all kinds of vague, undifferentiated ideas," the psychologist answered.

Schorr signed the letter, "with wishes for a hopeful outcome, Martin M. Schorr," and he was asked by Howard: "What was that 'hopeful outcome' you had in mind?"

"Well, uh, well, that justice would be served," Schorr said.

He backtracked on his earlier opinion that Sirhan was in a totally "dissociated" mental condition for hours after the June 5 shooting of Kennedy. His new opinion was formed after he spent nearly two courtroom days listening, along with the judge and jury, to the tape recordings.

The psychologist, on the stand now for five days, had first said he believed Sirhan was mentally disturbed from some point in time before the shooting of Senator Kennedy until "probably the time of his arraignment" eight hours later.

However, after listening to the police recordings, Schorr admitted Sirhan sounded "capable."

He said he did not believe Sirhan was under the typical paranoid delusion that "he was being pursued by real or imaginary people" or that he was responding to "voices . . . or influences from some entity somewhere out there."

The prosecution began an all-out attack on Schorr's professional integrity, charging that one of his summary reports on Sirhan was "cribbed or copied" from a book written by a New York psychiatrist.

Schorr was accused of copying six or eight paragraphs of his official summary of the Sirhan case from *Case Book of a Crime Psychiatrist,* by the New York expert, Dr. James Arnold Brussell, a psychiatrist who helped police capture the "mad bomber" of New York.

Schorr admitted lifting portions of Brussell's analyses for his own report. He denied it was improper procedure. His testimony seemed badly damaged by the disclosure that he copied from the Brussell book without giving the author credit.

The state sought to have segments of Dr. Brussell's book put in evidence. "A lot of this material (in Schorr's report) is cribbed or copied," deputy prosecutor Fitts argued.

"The jury is entitled to know the flavor of this book, whether it is a learned work of psychiatry . . . or the popular fiction which it appears to be."

Berman argued that the narrative of the mad bomber and other police cases were irrelevant to the Sirhan trial and Judge Walker agreed with him. Still, it was that book which Schorr had used to rely on in drafting his report on Sirhan.

"I used only language descriptive of Sirhan," Schorr said. "I copied almost exactly . . . I go to many books, because I'm not the best writer in the world."

The witness admitted he did not "use quotation marks or any footnotes . . . . I redesigned it to fit in with what I had already written in my earlier reports."

"So you went through the book, looking for exciting language, so you could make an exciting report. Is that right?" prosecutor Howard asked.

Schorr's effectiveness as a witness before this jury had been substantially damaged, the prosecution lawyers felt.

But the defense had a long list of psychological experts to present. Others now were called. Not all of them copied from books.

Dr. Orville Roderick Richardson said that Sirhan was mentally ill, and his illness affected his "judgment and perception." Sirhan did not know right from wrong, for example. He said Sirhan was suffering "paranoia to a psychotic degree with a schizophrenic process." The illness was "chronic and acute."

Richardson said there was no tangible evidence of brain damage in Sirhan's case, but did not rule out the possibility, as Schorr had done. Both psychologists noted that their tests showed Sirhan to be above average in vocabulary and verbal intelligence, but well below average in his ability to correlate thoughts and to evaluate situations.

Based on a battery of tests, Richardson described Sirhan as a person with "a deep distrust of others, accentuated at this time and amplified by a poignant sense of alienation and isolation. He feels profoundly alone, abandoned and on the edge of things."

While Schorr leaned heavily on what he called Sirhan's "hate and fear of his father," Richardson said the assassin "remains in a position of angry, demanding dependency on his mother."

Glancing occasionally at the pensive Sirhan, Richardson described him as follows: "Paranoid. Blaming. Suspicious. Critical. Helpless. Cautious. Vulnerable. Confused. Lacks stamina. Unpredictable. Scattered. Obsessive. Compulsive. Suicidal. Homicidal. Has a weak ego. Erratic. Socially inadequate. Anxious. A very ill person, descending into mental illness."

Although Dr. Richardson declined to speculate on Sirhan's mental state the night of the shooting, he said the young Arab was probably more normal right after the assassination than when he examined him still later on July 10.

"Prior to the assassination, he would be gathering into a psychotic rage," Richardson said. "The assassination served as a release."

However, Richardson genially admitted under cross-examination, Sirhan's strict confinement, in which he was not allowed out of the sight of security personnel, would serve to strengthen his paranoia.

Unlike that of Dr. Schorr, Richardson's testimony was gently dealt with by the prosecution. The tall, smiling psychologist admitted that his testing of Sirhan might have been influenced a bit by the defendant's Arab cultural background. He described Sirhan as being "like a good engine that's out of tune and needs a lot of work."

He said that during one test he discovered that Sirhan apparently had deep "sexual problems." Sirhan blocked his attorneys' attempts to call as witnesses two girls he allegedly had had fantasies about but never dated. There was no evidence he had dated any girl on a regular basis.

Under cross-examination by Fitts, Dr. Richardson was asked how he was received by Sirhan when he went to the assassin's cell to test him.

"He ushered me into his cell like it was his place and he made polite apologies for the fact that we would have to be observed," the psychologist said, "and that he couldn't offer me hospitality."

"Isn't that a little bit unusual for a paranoiac?" Fitts asked.

"No, that would depend on how he sees me," Richardson answered. "The paranoid sort of divides the world into the good guys and the bad guys."

At one point Richardson admitted that he felt "general anger at Mr. Sirhan and wanted to punish him" after learning of Kennedy's assassination.

Fitts said for the prosecution: "You as a psychologist are still a human being, with biases and prejudices, aren't you?"

Richardson said, "Yes." He added that psychologists pride themselves in "seeing ourselves as fallible tools. That's why we're always running off to Beverly Hills to have ourselves probed."

"Is that because they (psychiatrists) can charge $40 an hour in Beverly Hills?"

Richardson grinned and answered, "I've heard that's so."

As the trial moved into its forty-third day, the defense continued to compile psychiatric testimony to prove that Sirhan Sirhan was mentally ill.

Four separate expert witnesses, psychiatrists and psychologists, said so in testimony during the day—although there was some difference of opinion among them as to the degree that Sirhan was mentally disturbed.

Whether any of the evidence was making an impact on a jury of laymen, particularly after the prosecution cross-examined the mental experts, was not discernible. After all, the jurors had been looking at Sirhan in court; they had seen him on the witness stand, at the defense table, in varying moods and poses. To these men and women from diverse walks of life, psychiatric terms may have been quite mysterious. Or, there may have been some jurors who had experienced, in their own families, direct contact with psychiatrists. For them, what was said may have had clear meaning. One thing seemed sure: the defense was relying heavily on the weight of a large volume of testimony about Sirhan's mental condition to try to save him from a death sentence.

Dr. Orville Roderick Richardson completed his testimony for the defense. The psychologist said there were times when Sirhan—earlier described as suffering from paranoia to a psychotic degree—would see himself as assuming "a high-minded, very idealistic, even sternly ethical" position.

It was in Sirhan's inability to judge right from wrong as "the normal individual in this culture understands it" that his "illness" was most noticeable, Richardson said. He theorized that if Sirhan had been "lucky," nobody would have known he had a serious problem. If Sirhan had received psychotherapy Senator Kennedy would not have died, said Richardson.

Another defense psychologist, Dr. Stephen J. Howard of the University of Southern California, took a lighter line on Sirhan's mental condition, but still described him as a "borderline psychotic." This means he is "an individual who can go in and out of a psychosis under the very minor stresses which he might encounter in daily life. Borderline does not mean he is normal, by any means; it just means he is not a hopeless psychotic."

Dr. William Crain, a psychologist for the Los Angeles Department of Mental Health who reviewed results of Sirhan's psychological examinations, diagnosed him as "a schizophrenic of the paranoiac type."

The most effective witness of the day was Dr. Eric Marcus, a member of a panel of consulting psychiatrists called by California's superior courts to make examinations in cases where the mental stability of a defendant is called into question.

Marcus, assigned by the court to make a study of Sirhan in this case, said he believed the assassin had been mentally ill for more than two years and that "he started showing signs of mental illness no later than the time when he fell from the horse." This had been in September, 1966.

"His adjustment and mental state have deteriorated since . . . it has not been a fluctuating thing but a slow, insidious process," said the witness.

Marcus said the prosecution's chief psychiatrist, Dr. Seymour Pollack, agreed that Sirhan was mentally ill but also believes: "His whole mental illness has nothing to do with the crime he committed. . . . . I fail to see the logic."

Marcus said he and Pollack were "rather consistent in the opinion that the defendant is mentally ill. Dr. Pollack recommended psychiatric treatment for him."

Marcus, whose consulting fee was paid by Los Angeles County, said Pollack, paid by the state, diagnosed Sirhan as a "paranoid schizophrenic."

"This I agree with," said Marcus, who also testified that he believed the killer of Senator Kennedy was unable to "maturely premeditate" the assassination.

Marcus, emphasizing that he did not believe the defendant suffered brain damage in the 1966 fall from the horse, said the accident and Sirhan's subsequent loss of his job represented "the last straw." Marcus said Sirhan viewed himself as a superior human being and could not psychologically withstand failure. The Palestinian immigrant had failed academically in college and had been unsuccessful as an employee and an apprentice jockey, Marcus said. As a result he began to move toward schizophrenia after the accident.

"He was mentally disturbed and became increasingly mentally disturbed during the spring of last year," the doctor said.

Marcus testified that he based his diagnosis on Sirhan's story, reports from investigators and the results of psychological tests, administered by psychologists for the prosecution and the defense. The diary, in which Sirhan had written time and again that Kennedy must be killed, was "typical of people who have threatened the President or are now in mental hospitals." Marcus said he had studied books and treatises on political assassinations as well as a "package of letters written by insane murderers." Sirhan's diary was "quite similar, particularly to the threatening letters written to the President."

For the first time in the three months of Sirhan's trial the name of Lee Harvey Oswald was introduced into the record. Under cross-examination by the prosecution, Marcus said Oswald, assassin of President John F. Kennedy, the senator's brother, was an example of the lone assassin. He contrasted "the act of political assassination" with "the man who assassinates politicians." Oswald is the latter, he contended. So is Sirhan.

The assassination attempt on then President Harry Truman by a group of Puerto Rican nationalists about twenty years ago was an example of assassination as a political mechanism, Marcus said. Oswald and Sirhan are examples of assassination by "isolated individuals who are almost always found to be seriously mentally ill individuals."

Marcus told about giving Sirhan Sirhan six ounces of alcohol to see how he reacted. Marcus, a Jew, found among other things that the young Arab became violently anti-Semitic, which was surely no surprise. With the alcohol Sirhan became "sort of a wild beast." Marcus conceded that the six ounces he gave Sirhan in his jail cell was probably more alcohol than the assassin had had the night he killed Senator Kennedy. But the results were interesting: Sirhan, having consumed the liquor, became "extremely irritated, agitated, restless. He was cursing. He had to be restrained physically."

Before drinking the liquor Sirhan had been extremely polite to him, the doctor said. But after the alcohol was given him, Sirhan turned on Marcus and said: "Get that bastard out of here." At another time he said: "I hate his guts."

Still again Sirhan shouted, "I'll get even with those Jews." And "twenty years in Palestine is long enough for the Jews."

The psychiatrist said Sirhan thought the uniformed deputy sheriffs around him "were Israeli soldiers." A` one point he seemed to believe that Marcus was his older brother, Adel. He asked Marcus to "take him home. . . . He kept asking me to speak Arabic."

Fitts, for the prosecution, led Marcus through a careful cross-examination in which the witness said, after reading transcripts of what Sirhan told police in the early hours of June 5, that he believed it was a "toss-up" whether the assassin was lying about not remembering what happened.

Fitts asked: "Well, if he was suffering from retrograde amnesia (a state induced by emotional shock), he would still be asking questions of the police, like why was he there and what had he done, as if he were suffering from real (organic) amnesia, wouldn't he?"

"Yes," Marcus said.

"That leaves me with the only working hypothesis—that he was malingering (lying), doesn't it?" Fitts asked.

"Yes, I guess it does," the doctor said.

On re-direct questioning, defense counsel Cooper asked: "Would it make any difference to you and your diagnosis if the defendant had been perfectly conscious (at the time of the shooting) or suffering from amnesia?"

"Not to my major conclusions, no," Marcus said.

He was asked about the diaries in which Sirhan wrote threats to many people. Marcus said when the defendant practiced firing his pistol, "he might have been thinking of . . . (Ambassador Arthur) Goldberg, whoever showed up first in Los Angeles, or even President Johnson." Kennedy may have been Sirhan's victim only because he was the first object of the assassin's hate "who showed up in Los Angeles."

Resisting all suggestions by the prosecution that Sirhan's diary-keeping was merely the product of "doodling," Marcus insisted that it was the product of a sick mind.

Markings in Sirhan's high school textbooks indicated he had been fascinated by the subject of political assassination for many years, Dr. Marcus testified.

The defense produced two high school history texts in which Sirhan had underlined passages about the assassination of President William McKinley and Austrian Archduke Francis Ferdinand, and Grant Cooper asked Marcus: "What does this mean?"

A. "It means he had been thinking about assassination of one kind or another for an awfully long time."

Q. "Does this have some significance to you as a psychiatrist?"

A. "Yes, there are some recent studies about the development of paranoid schizophrenics, particularly those who commit murders, showing that the schizophrenic process takes about ten years to develop."

Q. "Could he maturely premeditate and deliberate . . . with malice aforethought, a killing?"

A. "He could not if it involved an area he had a mental conflict about . . . otherwise, yes."

Before the day was out Dr. Marcus had completed his testimony and was followed by the star of the defense show of witnesses on mental disturbance, Dr. Bernard L. Diamond.

The graying, sober-faced psychiatrist-lawyer is one of the nation's foremost forensic psychiatrists and he was expected to be glued in the witness chair for most of a week. Defense attorneys said his testimony was expected to help Sirhan. This meant the prosecution could be expected to hammer away at his theories at length.

Dr. Diamond, full professor of law, criminology and psychiatry at the University of California, began his testimony by declaring that Sirhan was "schizophrenic."

He came to the witness stand late in the day and spent only a few minutes there before court adjourned. He was asked by the defense on direct examination whether he believed on the basis of his study of Sirhan, that the defendant remembered the writings in his diaries. "I would prefer to say that he had no recognition of them . . . they had no meaningful association in his mind . . . that applied not only to the Kennedy material but to all the material in the notebook."

The next morning he told of visiting with Sirhan in his cell and having the defendant turn to him and ask: "Do you think they had a handwriting expert forge this?"

Under hypnosis, Sirhan Sirhan yanked an imaginary pistol from his belt, fired it again and again, shouting obscenities, then fell back gasping, Dr. Diamond recalled from the witness chair as he told how he had tested the defendant.

Diamond testified that on another occasion Sirhan turned to him and said: "To Kennedy I was drawn like a magnet. I loved the man, I hated him."

"I kept prodding him . . . . I said, 'You're in the Ambassador Hotel pantry now . . . . There comes Senator Kennedy.'

"Then suddenly Sirhan simply pulled an imaginary gun out of his belt . . . . He fired it convulsively over and over again, shouting 'You sonofabitch!' "

Diamond said that he and Dr. Seymour Pollack, chief prosecution psychiatrist, who was with him at the time, both "jumped," startled.

"The expression on his face was of the most violent rage," the defense psychiatrist said. "There was a momentary pause and he started to choke . . . . He was gasping for breath. He then went into a deep sleep."

Diamond, who had hypnotized Sirhan six times since January 4, said, "In my opinion that was a reasonably authentic reenaction of the shooting of Senator Robert F. Kennedy."

On an earlier occasion, Diamond said, Sirhan told him while under hypnosis what he remembered of the June 5 assassination.

"He didn't know how long he had been standing there (in the pantry). He was just standing there when Senator Kennedy and a crowd of people rushed into the room from the other entrance. 'They just rushed at me,' Sirhan said. He said his first thought on seeing Kennedy was that he wanted to shake hands with him . . . then in a fraction of a second they (the Kennedy party) came right up to Sirhan so that they were almost in direct contact.

"And he shot . . . wildly."

Under hypnosis, in which state the patient may or may not be telling the truth, Sirhan told Diamond that shortly before the shooting he was drinking coffee with a "pretty blond girl."

"I asked him what his thoughts were at that time, whether he had any thought of doing anything with the gun," Diamond said.

"He said he was thinking about having sex with her, planning whether to ask her to leave the hotel with him."

In still another experiment, Diamond had the young assassin produce writings under hypnosis, which the doctor said were "similar" to much of the material in Sirhan's notebooks.

Diamond testified that with Sirhan under hypnosis he asked questions and got the following written responses from the assassin:

Q. "Sirhan, write about Kennedy."
A. "RFK, RFK."
Q. " . . . Tell us more than his name . . . ."
A. "Robert F. Kennedy. Robert F. Kennedy. RFK. RFK must die."
Q. "When must Kennedy die?"
A. "Robert Kennedy is going to die. Robert Kennedy is going to die."
Q. " . . . Sirhan, is Kennedy dead yet?"
A. "I don't know."
Q. "Is Kennedy dead?"
A. "No, no, no."
Q. "When is now? What is the date today?"
A. "Friday, 31 January."
Q. "Is Kennedy alive?"
A. "Yes, yes, yes."
Q. "Does Kennedy talk to you?"
A. "No, no, no."
Q. "Is this the way you wrote at home (in diaries)?"
A. "Yes, yes, yes, yes, yes."
Q. "Are you crazy?"
A. "No, no, no."
Q. "If you are not crazy, why are you writing crazy things?"
A. "Practice, practice, practice, practice."
Q. "Practice for what?"
A. "Mind control, mind control, mind control."
Q. " . . . Were you hypnotized when you wrote in your note-books?"
A. "Yes, yes, yes."
Q. "Who hypnotized you when you wrote in the notebooks?"
A. "Mirror, mirror, my mirror."

Diamond said Sirhan explained under hypnosis that he learned to put himself in a trance by staring into a mirror in his room from Rosicrucian literature in correspondence courses. The Rosicrucian order teaches that man can control matter with his mind, through concentration and practice.

Once again, the administration of justice had come the full circle from New Orleans and Clay Shaw. There the prosecution used hypnosis to help witness Perry Raymond Russo "recall events." Here the defense used the same technique to help Sirhan "recall events." In both cases the jury rejected the testimony with opposite results. In New Orleans Shaw was cleared. Here Sirhan was to get a death sentence.

The following day Dr. Bernard L. Diamond summarized his findings on Sirhan and the assassination in a report, which he conceded might sound "absurd and impossible . . . highly unlikely,—preposterous!" to the laymen. The report said: "The combination of events which led to the assassination of . . . Kennedy by Sirhan started, I think, with Sirhan's exposure to violence and death in Jerusalem in 1948 and it continues with his immigration to the United States, the development of his mental illness, in which his whole personality altered and he became preoccupied with revolution, violence, destruction, paranoid fantasies of glory, power and becoming the savior of his people.

"As his delusional fantasies grew bolder, and his fanatical hatred and fear of the Jews increased with each radio and television broadcast concerning the tension in the Middle East . . . . Sirhan was withdrawing into a ruminative, brooding, isolated sense of failure and insignificance.

"To improve his mind and to gain control, he hoped, over his personal destiny, he read mystical books and subscribed to and studied the Rosicrucian correspondence courses in self-hypnosis and mind power. He practiced his lessons diligently to the point where he became frightened by his own magical, supernatural powers of concentration.

"He actually believed that he could stop the bombers from reaching Israel and thereby save the Arabs, simply by willing the death of all who would help the Jews.

"His experiments in inducing the magical trances worked better than he realized—they worked so well that they frightened Sirhan and convinced him that he was losing his mind, that he was going insane. Repeatedly, he would practice his lessons . . . looking in the mirror, thinking thoughts of love and peace, only to emerge from his trance . . . to find his notebook filled with incoherent threats of violence and assassination.

" . . . Through chance, circumstances, and a succession of unrelated events, Sirhan found himself in the physical situation in which the assassination occurred. I am quite satisfied that he had not consciously planned to be in that situation . . . . If he had been fully conscious and in his usual mental state, he would have been quite harmless, despite his paranoid hatreds and despite his loaded gun.

"But he was confused, bewildered and partially intoxicated. The mirrors in the hotel lobby, the flashing lights, the general confusion—this was like pressing the button which starts the computer. He was back in his trances, his violent convulsive rages, the automatic writing (diary), the pouring out of incoherent hatred, violence and assassination.

"Only this time it was for real, and this time there was no pencil in his hand . . . only the loaded gun.

"Sirhan would rather believe that he is the fanatical martyr who by his noble act of self-sacrifice has saved his people and become a great hero. He claims to be ready to die in the gas chamber for the glory of the Arab people."

Dr. Diamond warned the court the report would sound "absurd" to the ears of a layman. Perhaps he was right.

On the forty-eighth day, there was another violent eruption of emotion from Sirhan. He pounded the counsel table angrily and cursed as Dr. Diamond was subjected to a bruising cross-examination from the prosecution. Assistant prosecutor David Fitts slashed away at Diamond's theories, at his manner of testing, at his conclusions.

The assassin had to be restrained in his chair when Fitts sought to delve into the relationship between Sirhan's mother and father. Fitts called the Arab family "liars" trying to protect Sirhan.

Senator Robert Kennedy's killer muttered as he glared at Fitts and tried to rise from the chair. He was held down by a security guard.

On the stand, Diamond, the key witness in Sirhan's defense of "diminished mental capacity," was challenged time and again by Fitts on his theory that Sirhan shot the senator in a "dissociated" mental state, disconnected from reality.

The two men—doctor and lawyer—snapped constantly at each other all day, with Judge Walker, prodded by defense attorneys, stepping in occasionally to calm them down.

Diamond resisted Fitts' efforts to portray Sirhan as a calculating killer, saying he refused to consider the defendant's mental symptoms one at a time, but would only talk about his illness as a "total picture."

"I cannot allow you to put words in my mouth," Diamond protested. "I'm not dodging your questions . . . Mr. Fitts, if you would allow me to explain . . ."

"Don't quibble with me," Fitts cut back.

At one point, Fitts suggested sarcastically, "Don't you really think Mr. Sirhan was playing fun and games with you (when Diamond had Sirhan under hypnosis)?"

"No, he wasn't playing fun and games," the psychiatrist shot back, his face flushed.

Diamond, who considers himself somewhat of an expert on guns, declared Sirhan's .22 caliber Iver-Johnson revolver was "a piece of junk" and added:

"No one who knew anything about target shooting . . . or assassinating, for that matter, would use such a gun . . . ."

"Could it kill a dog?" Fitts asked coldly.

"It could kill a man and it did . . . but that's not a gun you select to kill with . . . the reason he bought this gun was because it was cheap," Diamond said.

Fitts wanted to know if it "bothered" Diamond that Sirhan was riding around Los Angeles the night of June 4 with a loaded pistol.

"Yes, it bothers me a good deal," the witness said, ". . . It shows Sirhan was utterly irresponsible . . . and has no respect for firearms whatsoever."

Pointing out that several of the eight shells in the revolver were mini-mag, hollow point ammunition used primarily in hunting, Fitts got Diamond to admit mini-mags are "more lethal" than normal .22 caliber ammunition. However, the psychiatrist insisted that no one knowledgeable in weaponry would fire such ammunition from a pistol of poor quality, because it might damage the gun.

"Well, if it was the best kind of gun you had," Fitts said slowly, inspecting his fingernails, "and you wanted to kill a senator, you'd use mini-mag ammunition, wouldn't you?"

Diamond paused, then said, "In my opinion, anybody who

wanted to kill somebody and knew anything about what they were doing would not use less than a .38."

"Well, assume for the moment that this individual with the .22 shot a senator," Fitts said. "Would that indicate he was mentally ill?"

"It would indicate that he had a lack of knowledge, of how to go about killing people," Diamond said.

"Well, you can't quarrel with success," Fitts remarked.

"Yes, Mr. Fitts, I *can* quarrel with success," the psychiatrist said.

The attorney and the witness argued over almost every other piece of prosecution evidence touching on premeditation. One of these issues was the notebooks of Sirhan. The assassin's notebooks were written while Sirhan was in a self-induced trance, Diamond said. Fitts could not shake this opinion.

Diamond said that Sirhan feared someone would find the notebooks and believe him mentally ill.

"If that's the way he felt about these notebooks . . . why did he not destroy them?" Fitts asked.

"Because he's mentally ill," Diamond said and smiled. "It's so characteristic of a schizophrenic that every scrap of paper invested with words with meaning to them becomes very valuable."

Q. "Well, wouldn't the usual Sirhan see these figures and destroy them?"

A. "No, he would not because the usual Sirhan is a very sick man."

In summation of his diagnosis, Diamond had said he "agreed" that his picture of the assassin may sound "absurd and impossible . . . highly unlikely, preposterous."

Fitts asked him, "Who are you agreeing with?"

"I agree with the public and the world," the psychiatrist answered.

The witness also was asked if it is "possible to fake answers to the Rorschach test."

"I have never seen it done successfully," he said.

On the forty-ninth trial day, defense witness Dr. George DeVos, a psychologist and anthropologist, testified that Sirhan's Arab birth had no effect on his responsiveness to psychological testing. DeVos said, in answering Sirhan's attorney, that he reviewed all of Sirhan's tests and came to the conclusion he "was a paranoid schizophrenic."

Under cross-examination, DeVos resisted examining specific test questions, saying that a psychological diagnosis must be based on all the results.

"I am sorry, I just can't look at one segment," he said. "We're trained not to do that . . . it's just like trying to look at a mole on Sophia Loren."

Dr. Georgene Seward, a woman psychologist from the University of California, backed up earlier defense testimony that Sirhan was extremely paranoid, with "a schizophrenic reaction."

She acknowledged to the prosecution that the fact that he was tested while in jail, facing trial for his life, might have magnified his anxiety and affected his test results.

"A person under such a situation might possibly try and falsify the tests, if that's what you mean," Dr. Seward answered John Howard.

Before the defense rested at 3:50 p.m. Cooper read into the record the transcript of a scene February 25 in Judge Walker's office, in which the volatile assassin delivered an ultimatum to the court.

Upset over the prospect that his personal notebooks would be admitted into evidence, Sirhan told Judge Walker: "If these notebooks are allowed into evidence, sir, I will change my plea to guilty, not so much because I want to be railroaded into the gas chamber, but to deny you the pleasure. sir, of telling the world, 'I put this fellow in the gas chamber after giving him a fair trial,' which you have not done." As the jury heard of this scene for the first time, Cooper closed his reading of the transcript with Walker's admonition to Sirhan: "You have employed three counsel who are competent . . . . They are running the lawsuit . . . . Suppose you start thinking about that and what you said to me."

"With that, the defense rests," Cooper said.

Now the state would offer rebuttal testimony. The first piece of evidence prosecutors sought to introduce was a film of Senator Robert F. Kennedy's last speech. There was a strong protest from the defense. Judge Walker agreed with the defense. He said that to project the twelve-minute film in the courtroom would be "inflammatory." The judge explained: "The court realizes that here was a young man who had just made what he considered to be a major victory; that he was very happy and gay and congratulating everybody . . . . This contrasts between that (scene) and what has happened in this courtroom. It should not be shown to the jury."

The prosecution argued vigorously for the right to show the film.

"I submit that the jury is entitled to see this picture," prosecutor John Howard said, ". . . because the inference was whether there was or was not any triggering statement in that speech. The position of the prosecution is that there was nothing in that speech about Israel to cause Sirhan to kill Kennedy."

"I object on the grounds that the film is immaterial," Cooper argued. "The defendant did not testify that he heard the speech, there is no testimony that he did, and no testimony by any defense witness that this did trigger him. There is no testimony that the defendant was ever in that room when Kennedy made that speech." The film was ruled out. New Orleans would not be repeated.

The following day, Dr. Seymour Pollack testified as a rebuttal witness for the state. A "highly emotional" Sirhan Bishara Sirhan assassinated Senator Robert F. Kennedy "for political reasons," the prosecution's chief psychiatrist said in opening the state's rebuttal attack on defense mental experts.

Dr. Pollack, who agreed that Sirhan was paranoid, argued that "up until the time of the shooting there were no very significant signs of paranoiac symptoms.

"Any one of us could have met Sirhan and wouldn't have been able to detect any signs of psychopathy," the University of Southern California psychiatrist said. "Even if I had gotten to know him fairly well, I wouldn't have been able to forecast in any way that Sirhan would do what he did."

When court adjourned, Pollack had not yet explained what he believed Sirhan's political motives were. He had, however, begun to develop his thesis that the young immigrant's politics were shaped by his identification with the Arab cause.

Dr. Pollack conceded that, growing up in war-torn Jerusalem in the 1940's, Sirhan saw "bombings, witnessed death and dismemberment." The defense has said these experiences helped make the assassin a mental cripple, not responsible for his acts. But Dr. Pollack said that the incidents simply made him a frightened young boy.

"At no time is there any evidence he went into traumatic trances . . . . There was no change in his state of consciousness, only evidence he was very frightened."

He argued that Sirhan was fairly normal for years after he emigrated to America with his family in 1956, at the age of twelve.

In junior and senior high school "he continued to show no peculiarities," although he did "develop stronger feelings about social and racial discrimination," Pollack said.

"He became increasingly interested in the political structure of our country, but he continued to identify strongly with Palestinian Arabs," Pollack said.

Sirhan's mother, for whom he had deep feelings, "pictured America to Sirhan as the world of tomorrow, a world filled with promise . . . ."

"Underlying feelings of anger" began to develop against all those he felt were oppressing minorities, Pollack said. Sirhan became angry at "the British, the Jews and the world at large" because of what he felt were acts of oppression against Palestinian Arabs. "He didn't understand why God would allow this treatment to continue . . . although his thinking was not crystallized." In high school, "he identified largely with Mexican-Americans, Negroes and poor Americans, he identified with poverty and discrimination," offered Pollack.

"He believed our American ideals were becoming subverted by our political leaders . . . he became increasingly hostile toward what he believed was American hypocrisy."

Pollack said Sirhan described himself as a "displaced Arab living in America."

However, Pollack emphasized, he did not believe that Sirhan at any time "believed strongly in communism. He favored democracy rather than autocracy."

When court adjourned, the psychiatrist was explaining for the prosecution that "two events significantly affected Sirhan" in his late teens.

"The first was the death of his sister, Aida . . . which left him very disturbed," he said, "She was almost a second mother to him." Aida died of leukemia in 1964 and Sirhan, "a sensitive young man, reacted very strongly." Pollack was about to mention the second event, the arrest of one of Sirhan's brothers, when a legal squabble developed in the courtroom. "The second was the arrest of his brother," the witness began, only to be interrupted by the sound of Cooper's hand slamming on the counsel table. Cooper, apparently feeling testimony about his brother's arrest would hurt Sirhan, began to object, then settled for an attorney's conference at the judge's bench. Judge Walker temporarily solved the problem by adjourning the trial until Tuesday morning, April 1. Court would not be held Monday in deference to the memory of former President Eisenhower, who had just died. The courtroom was hushed for "a minute of silent prayer" after Walker learned of former President Eisenhower's death.

"I have the sad duty of telling you that President Eisenhower has died," the judge said to the courtroom. Later in the day, Walker decided to suspend the trial Monday to honor Eisenhower "because certainly this man was one of the greatest Americans of our generation."

Court resumed Tuesday and Sirhan once again exploded in a burst of rage. It came suddenly after the state sought to show Sirhan was trying "to focus attention on the plight of the Arab refugees" when he murdered Robert Kennedy. Dr. Seymour Pollack was in the witness chair.

"He saw Senator Kennedy as having sold out to American Jews . . . as an example of American political chicanery," Pollack said. He testified confidently that he saw Sirhan not as a hopeless mental cripple but a scheming political assassin—and a liar. Sirhan threw the trial into a brief, unscheduled morning recess by leaping to his feet and shouting: "I'm not going to sit here and let him call me a fucking liar, your honor sir . . ."

Three security guards surrounded Sirhan immediately and put him back into his chair. He continued muttering and pounding his fist savagely on the counsel table until Judge Walker glared down at him and said: "You settle down or I'll do what I told you I was going to do."

He had threatened to muzzle Sirhan and strap him to his chair. The jury was quickly ushered from the courtroom and, after a twenty-minute recess, the trial reconvened with Parsons apologizing to Walker for his client.

"I accept your apology, but I want it distinctly understood that if there are any more outbursts, I will do what I told him I would do," the judge said.

Back on the stand Pollack said: "I believe this blanket denial reflects his attempt to avoid the serious consequences of his act."

The witness also described much of the material in the Sirhan notebooks as "doodling" and said the pages where Sirhan had written over and over "RFK must die . . . . Kennedy must be assassinated" represented examples of "his intention to strengthen his courage to carry out his plan to kill Kennedy." Pollack said he does not believe Sirhan was suffering from amnesia. "And if this amnesia is present, it is retrograde amnesia . . . which developed at least a day or two after he was apprehended," Pollack said.

"However, if an individual can't deny his act, the next best thing is to say that he didn't remember it, couldn't remember it . . . and, if he thinks about this long enough, the individual can convince himself that he honestly doesn't remember what took place," the psychiatrist said.

Pollack admitted that he believes Sirhan to be paranoid, but not to the degree defense experts do. He said he hypnotized Sirhan three times while examining him, each time with remarkable ease. "It is very difficult to hypnotize an individual who is frankly psychotic. I don't believe he expected to be caught or wanted to be caught," he said. "I don't think he thought he would be punished . . . He saw these people (politicians) as murderers and felt . . . . if they were killed, the persons who did it should not be punished in the eyes of the world."

On the fifty-second day Dr. Pollack said Sirhan Sirhan was not psychotic—then under cross-examination he said that he was. The doctor became uncomfortable on the witness stand as some of the defense psychiatric witnesses had been on cross-examination. Dr. Pollack said Sirhan was an assassin who knew what he was doing. He later admitted from the stand his diagnosis might have been different had he spent more time with Sirhan.

His written report on the defendant created difficulty for him as he testified. Defense lawyer Grant Cooper showed the prosecution witness a copy of his confidential report to District Attorney Evelle Younger.

"Is Sirhan a psychotic person?" Cooper asked after reading portions of Pollack's report aloud in court.

"Yes," Pollack said.

"This morning you told us he was not psychotic," the attorney said.

"I said he was not clinically psychotic," the psychiatrist said.

"Well, you didn't put "clinically" in that report, did you?" Cooper asked.

"No." At another point he said Sirhan was "a borderline schizophrenic."

Pollack's cross-examination began in mid-afternoon with Cooper asking genial questions. By 4 p.m. Cooper was slashing away at the prosecution witness, and Pollack was nervously gulping cups of water he poured for himself.

He admitted he was "not that satisfied with the twenty-five hours" he spent with Sirhan. "Within the time I had, I had to arrive at this conclusion, that Sirhan was not psychotic, because it was the only reasonable medical conclusion."

Q. "So, if you had had more time, you would probably be able to demonstrate that he was psychotic, is that right?"

A. "It's possible I might have been able to find more evidence than what appeared had I spent, say, 250 hours."

Cooper picked up the report written February 5 by Pollack for the district attorney. "Didn't you write, 'I believe Sirhan provides evidence of a morbid personality . . . . With more intensive professional exploration of this defendant's thinking and personality characteristics, there would probably be revealed more definite signs and symptoms of psychosis . . .'? That was your opinion on February 5, was it not?"

A. "Yes."

Q. "And did you spend more time (after writing the report) with Mr. Sirhan?"

A. "No."

Q. "You realize, doctor, that this defendant is on trial for his life?"

A. "Yes."

Q. "Then, don't you feel you should have asked for more time with him?"

A. "If you're asking me why I didn't ask for more time . . . you may remember at the meeting in your office (February 2 with psychiatrists for both sides) Dr. Diamond showed a great deal of anger at my not committing myself and said he saw no point in my seeing Mr. Sirhan any longer . . . . I took this very seriously . . . . For a long time, I had asked the district attorney's office for a chance to examine him."

Q. "Doctor, did you ever think of calling me? . . . After all, we've been friends for a long time; we've talked about this case, why didn't you call me?"

A. (After a pause) "I didn't call, Mr. Cooper. I should have called."

From this point in testimony, Cooper began to strike harder and harder at the discrepancy between Pollack's verbal—'not psychotic'—and his written report to Younger—'psychotic'."

"You said he was a borderline schizophrenic with paranoid tendencies and hysterical features (in the report), didn't you?" Cooper asked.

"Yes," Pollack answered.

"What is that?" Cooper asked.

"Someone I suspect who may have minimal evidence of peculiarities, but who hasn't shown any clinical signs," Pollack replied.

Cooper read from the report: "I believe Sirhan's motivation was entirely political . . . . The killing of Senator Kennedy was a political assassination by a psychotically disturbed defendant."

The attorney wanted to know if that meant Pollack thought the assassin was a borderline schizophrenic.

His voice rising with emphasis, Pollack said, "I have said repeatedly that Sirhan is mentally sick, ill . . . that psychosis might be underneath. I detected none in later interviews, however. But the degree of paranoid thinking led me to suspect psychotic tendencies in his character."

At one point Pollack said: "I'm trying to explain the little subtleties in his thinking that led me to suspect he might be psychotic."

Cooper hit at the fact that test results by two anthropological psychologists—Dr. George DeVos and Dr. Georgene Seward—who were picked by Pollack to examine Sirhan—described him as "paranoid schizophrenic."

"If I only had what they had, I could, probably would, arrive at the same conclusion they did," Pollack said. "But it contrasted with what I saw clinically."

Defense experts had said Sirhan both loved and hated Robert Kennedy.

"It wasn't that he both loved and hated Senator Kennedy at the same time," Pollack said. "He had loved Senator Kennedy . . . had formed a strong attachment for him in a personal way, just as he had loved President Kennedy. But then (learning Kennedy's support for Israel) he hated Senator Kennedy . . . wanted him dead. His love actually turned to hate."

The harassed witness said two highly qualified psychiatrists "could look at the same set of symptoms and one doctor could say one thing and another doctor say another . . . ."

"But the inferences we draw are generally more alike than less alike," he added quickly.

Seymour Pollack had scarcely seated himself in the witness chair the following day when Grant Cooper began harassing him with what seemed to be contradictions in his views of Sirhan Sirhan. Dr. Pollack sent a report to the district attorney in early February which said Sirhan should receive mental treatment—and should not die for his crime. The report said Sirhan was mentally ill. "This mental illness should be considered substantial . . . and a mitigating circumstance in the question of penalty. Should a conviction of first-degree murder be obtained, Sirhan should avoid the death penalty and be sent (to a state hospital) . . . for treatment." The prosecution had not ruled out the possibility of asking for the death penalty.

Under cross-examination by Grant Cooper, Pollack explained that he was "very strongly opposed to capital punishment for moral—ethical reasons."

Despite that, Pollack's testimony that Sirhan killed Kennedy for political reasons with premeditation and malice could help put the Arab in the gas chamber.

"I felt that . . . as a psychiatrist . . . my strong convictions should not influence my findings," Pollack said.

"And it didn't?" Cooper asked.

"I hope it didn't," the witness said. "However, I was trying to point out in the report that in spite of all my searchings and probings, I couldn't find evidence of mental incapacity (at the time of the shooting). Yet I believe he is mentally ill and that a man who has committed such a crime shouldn't be given capital punishment."

After the trial adjourned for the day, it was learned the February 5 report was written at the request of both prosecution and defense attorneys. This apparently was a factor at the time a deal was being negotiated to settle the case without trial. The purpose of the request by the lawyers was to convince Judge Walker to accept a plea of guilty from Sirhan in return for a guarantee that he would not be sentenced to death. Walker declined. In this report Pollack called Sirhan "Psychotic . . . a borderline schizophrenic."

Several weeks later Pollack wrote another report in which he described Sirhan as paranoid but not psychotic.

Cooper, who questioned Pollack at length about this "discrepancy," confirmed after trial that the defense had asked for the first report.

On the stand Pollack said that he believed Sirhan, had he escaped, would have killed again.

"You have said if Sirhan had escaped he would have killed others," Cooper said.

"From what he said in conversations with me . . . yes," Pollack said.

"You said he would have killed Vice President Humphrey," Cooper said.

" . . . Yes, I would certainly agree . . . then, too, I was referring to the people he mentioned here (in his notebooks) like Ambassador Goldberg," the doctor said.

Pollack said Sirhan's main motive in shooting the New York senator was to "focus world attention on the plight of the Arab refugees," and on what Sirhan sees as the "hypocrisy" of American politics, which tends to support the Israeli cause against the Arabs, Sirhan's people.

Recalling at length the young immigrant's refusal to tell police his name or anything about himself in the hours after the assassination, Cooper asked Pollack: "During all this period of time was Sirhan trying to . . . bring the attention of the world to the Arab-Israeli situation?"

"What do you mean, Mr. Cooper?" Pollack said.

"After his arrest, aside from the first comments he made of 'I can explain, I did it for my country,' . . . aside from that when he wouldn't tell them which country he was from or anything else . . . is it your opinion this was the conduct of a man trying to bring the attention of the world to his cause?"

"He was not a martyr . . . he had mixed feelings . . . he was concerned and frightened about his own plight," said Pollack, who also said Sirhan had a deep respect for human life and was only driven to kill by the most obsessive motive.

The psychiatrist disclosed that Sirhan told him he expected to get "a couple of years" in prison for his deed. Pollack conceded that that was not "mature thinking in my opinion."

"Well, what kind of thinking was it . . . that he could assassinate a senator who was a presidential candidate and only get a couple of years?" Cooper said.

"It is the same kind of thinking that a black nationalist has who doesn't think he should get too much time in jail for killing somebody in a racially justified situation," Pollack answered.

Again, Pollack said, "He thought it was good to kill Senator Kennedy. He believed he was right . . . and that is not necessarily a delusion . . . he thought he would be looked up to and would be considered a hero . . . He believed he was doing what was not only right but should be done, a good thing."

Sirhan Sirhan told Seymour Pollack he believed that Senator Kennedy "told God what to do."

"Sirhan said that in anger," Dr. Pollack testified. "And he meant just that—that Bobby Kennedy was that strong, that he could tell God what to do."

This came at the close of Dr. Pollack's long cross-examination by chief defense counsel Grant Cooper, who continually asked pointed questions about the psychiatrist's conclusion: that Sirhan is mentally ill but his illness did not affect his assassination of Kennedy.

Pollack has said he spent some two hundred hours studying psychological reports, testimony of witnesses and other evidence in the case. He based his final decision, however, on the fact that during the twenty-five hours he spent examining the young Arab in his Hall of Justice cell, Sirhan, showed no "clinical" signs of psychosis.

On re-direct examination by prosecutor Howard, Pollack insisted he did not have his mind made up when he attended a meeting with defense psychiatrists and psychologists February 2, but made it up between then and February 5, when he wrote a letter to the district attorney containing his diagnosis.

It was at the February 2 meeting that, Pollack said, Dr. Diamond became angry with him. Diamond was upset because Pollack, the prosecution expert "would not give an opinion." Diamond accused him of not "playing fair," Pollack said. It was then, Pollack said, that Diamond let him know he didn't want him to see Sirhan again.

Under cross-questioning by Cooper, Pollack said he watched Sirhan's courtroom "temper tantrums," including the one in which he tried to fire his lawyers and sentence himself to the gas chamber. He had observed similar reactions while examining Sirhan in his cell.

"On more than one occasion he exploded and told me he was through with the whole damn thing, that he was tired of the psychiatrists bugging him . . . that he wanted out, that he wanted to plead guilty," Pollack said.

"Do you think he was faking any of this, putting on a show for the court or the jury?" Cooper asked.

"No, I do not," the doctor said.

"It was genuine, you think, doctor?" the attorney asked.

"Yes, I don't think he was dramatizing," he said.

" . . . . And do you think this conduct in the courtroom . . . was normal?" Cooper wanted to know.

"No."

Sirhan often sits in the courtroom and smiles "inappropriately," said Cooper, as though at some private joke while quite serious business is being conducted. Sometimes he laughs softly.

"You did observe inappropriate behavior, right?" Cooper asked.

"It is inappropriateness, Mr. Cooper, of the same kind that I myself might smile at in situations of embarrassment, like on cross-examination," Pollack smiled.

It was hard to imagine that the great mass of psychological testimony presented to the jury had not confused the men and women who would decide the life or death question for Sirhan Sirhan.

Now, a self-nominated prosecution psychologist took the stand and ripped into the test results and findings of psychologists on the other side, branding their work inaccurate and biased.

Dr. Leonard B. Olinger seemed shaken, however, to learn on cross-examination that two of his colleagues, both of whom outranked him academically, had also examined the defense work and concurred with it.

Olinger, a clinical psychologist and instructor at the University of Southern California, admitted on cross-examination that he called the district attorney's office and offered himself as a witness for the prosecution after reading news reports about defense psychological tests. He accused Dr. Martin M. Schorr and Dr. Orville Roderick Richardson of violating most of what he considered the "ten commandments of psychological testing."

According to Olinger's view, the defense experts did not observe strict adherence to prescribed procedures; did not use absolute integrity in scoring; overlooked much of the data and projected themselves into the data; looked for "more exotic explanations" when "more simple and obvious explanations" were available; made the facts fit their theories; were swayed by what they already knew about Sirhan; did not take into account the "global view of the subject," in that they did not consider fully Sirhan's cultural, social, economic, educational and sexual background.

These were examples of the failure of the defense psychologists, said Dr. Olinger. But when Grant Cooper, the chief defense counsel, began to cross-examine Olinger, the youthful psychologist seemed somewhat subdued when he was told that two of his senior associates saw the work of Dr. Schorr and Dr. Richardson differently.

Q. "Do you know Georgene Seward?"

A. "Yes, sir, I do."

Q. "Have you seen a review she did of the diagnostic evidence . . . ?"

A. "I have not."

Q. "How long have you known Dr. Seward?"

A. "Close to nineteen years."

Q. "Is she a professor at the University of Southern California?"

A. "Yes, sir."

Q. "How long has she been a professor?"

A. " . . . . I would guess she has been a professor most or all of the nineteen years I've been there."

Q. "Did you know that she found Dr. Schorr's material sufficent for a diagnosis?"

A. "No."

Q. "Do you know Dr. George DeVos at the University of California at Berkeley?"

A. "No . . . I have heard of him."

Q. "Did you know he found . . . Dr. Schorr's material sufficient?"

A. "I didn't know that."

Seward, Schorr, Richardson and DeVos all said they had considered Sirhan, on the basis of tests, psychotic—severely ill.

Just before his cross-examination, Olinger said Sirhan's mental label would more likely be "a pseudo-neurotic schizophrenic," admitting that this was a label not listed with the American Psychological Association.

He also said it was his opinion that Sirhan could form "the specific intent to commit murder . . . could premeditate murder . . . and do so with malice aforethought."

Olinger told the defense how he became associated with the case: "I spoke to Mr. Compton and Mr. Howard."

Cooper: "Who suggested your name to them?"

Olinger: "I suggested my name to them."

Later in the day, outside the courtroom, prosecution attorneys disclosed that they did not plan to demand Sirhan's life in return for that of Robert Kennedy. "We rarely ask for the death penalty in such cases," Lynn Compton, the chief prosecutor said. "We will ask the jury for an appropriate penalty. We will leave it up to them—life or death."

When, on the fifty-sixth day of trial, Olinger came down from the witness box, the state said there were no more witnesses. The jury left for a rest and lunch at the Biltmore Hotel, where the panel was quartered during trial. The lawyers for prosecution and defense closeted themselves with Judge Walker, and the rest of the afternoon was spent in his chambers discussing the instructions the court would ultimately deliver to the jury.

When each side finished arguing to the jurors, Judge Walker would give a "charge" to the group on how to apply the law to the facts they had heard. This, as a rule, is something close to a pro-forma recitation. But usually the jurist invites from the attorneys their suggestions as to special instructions that relate to the case at hand. Naturally, there is some disagreement by opposing sides, and ultimately the judge must decide what the jury is told.

Arguments would begin the following day.

The prosecution would argue first and last with the defense statements coming in a body between the prosecution arguments.

Deputy District Attorney David Fitts was expected to lead off for the state with a three-hour recapitulation of the state's evidence. The defense would then follow with Russell Parsons, the seventy-three-year-old courtroom veteran who had held Sirhan's hand often through the trial. He would be followed by Sirhan's counsel from New York, Emile Zola Berman, a Jew defending an Arab. Chief defender Grant Cooper, one of California's best-known criminal attorneys, would say the last word for Sirhan. It was not certain whether John Howard, the cigar-chewing young deputy prosecutor would argue briefly. But the final summing of the case would be done by Lynn Compton, the chief assistant to the district attorney, who had directed the main course of strategy for the state.

This trial had now produced more than eight thousand pages of trial transcript, bound in more than one hundred volumes. A total of ninety witnesses had appeared—sixty-one for the prosecution. The trial's cost was approaching one million dollars.

On the fifty-seventh day of trial, prosecutor David Fitts argued for four hours that the young Arab was guilty of first-degree murder. Sirhan was disturbed, Fitts conceded, but he knew what he was doing, he meant to do it, and he did it with malice.

Sirhan Sirhan made a "cold and calculating decision to take

the life of Robert F. Kennedy" long before he assassinated the senator, prosecutor David Fitts argued.

"This defendant did not act in a rash or impulsive manner . . . when he fired a bullet into the brain of the senator," Fitts said quietly in opening the prosecution's summary of the case against Sirhan.

"Put it all together," Fitts said, "the notebooks, the outspoken hatred of Kennedy, the clipping in his pocket, his visits to the pistol range, his rapid-fire shooting there, Sirhan's uncharacteristic interest in attending a public assembly, his inquiry in the pantry (whether Kennedy would pass there), his condition at the time of the shooting, the cute way he avoided identifying himself to the police, leaving his identification in the glove box of his vehicle." Fitts was bothering Sirhan.

"No, no . . . make him stop lying," Sirhan said to his attorneys, trying to stand up. Security chief Conroy held Sirhan in his chair and Judge Walker immediately interrupted Fitts to declare a quick recess.

The jury was hustled from the courtroom, as was Sirhan. After a twenty-minute cooling-off period, Fitts resumed his summation, observing: "To the police mind, to the prosecution mind, which might be somewhat limited, this suggests a deliberate premeditated murder committed with malice aforethought."

The young Arab cursed Fitts when the prosecutor touched on a sore point, saying, "I gather Sirhan has never been much of a hand with the ladies."

"Fucking bastard!" Sirhan muttered.

Fitts tried to personalize his argument, telling the jury time and again that the complexities of psychiatry were as puzzling to him as to them.

"Every person who commits a crime such as Mr. Sirhan has committed has suffered from a lack of mature reasoning," said Fitts. "Society is still grappling for a solution to the problem of crime . . . with poor tools.

"I've dealt with criminal responsibility for fifteen years, but I haven't seen any progress . . . . In terms of judging conduct, we seem to be back just where we were—twelve people in a box—twelve people representing society, judging standards and conduct.

"There is nothing better yet than the jury system. There is no computer . . . and nobody is working on one."

Fitts paused a moment, then addressed himself to what he believed was the responsibility of this jury: "We admit Sirhan is less than a full man, how much less I don't know. He is the man you see in the courtroom, the man who testified on the witness stand, eagerly and with a dramatic flair, with an intelligence somewhat unusual in our criminal courts—if you will take my word for it.

"He couldn't wait for the next question . . . . He was theatrical. He deliberately used four-letter words, then would look at the judge, smile and say 'I'm sorry.'

"Do you think that man didn't know what he was doing? I'm certain he did. Sirhan is 'not normal' but no man who commits murder is normal. . . . The question is whether or not, given his degree of mental impairment or, if you will, diminished capacity, Sirhan yet had the ability to harbor malice against a human being, to premediate murder . . . what it means to you, not to a doctor, but to you—that's your job."

The prosecutor spent a major portion of his summation attacking the testimony of the defense's eight psychologists and psychiatrists. Dr. Diamond, whom he cross-examined, Fitts called a "Johnny-come-lately."

"I agree his is an absurd and preposterous story, unlikely and unbelievable," Fitts said. (This is what Diamond had said of his own theory that Sirhan killed Kennedy in a state of self-hypnosis.)

"Well, I can't improve on Dr. Diamond," Fitts said. "You understand it was impossible to have the last word on Dr. Diamond, so we'll let him have the last word."

His lip curling in derision from time to time, Fitts dissected Dr. Schorr.

"I'm really sorry the defense started with Dr. Schorr, because he may have left a bad taste in your mouth for the whole profession of clinical psychology," he told the jury.

The prosecutor branded Schorr's work "disgraceful" and his conduct "peculiar."

Harking back to a July 10 letter the doctor wrote defense

attorney Parsons, Fitts said, "Now this was a most peculiar letter for someone who was supposed to be objective to write.

"In it he was soliciting to be permitted to assist in the selection of a jury in order to get a jury attuned to a sick defendant . . . . Can you imagine this clinical psychologist approaching his task in this fashion?

"And he closed with best wishes for a successful outcome," said Fitts.

During his more than a week on the stand, Schorr explained his "best wishes" salutation as a desire to see "justice done."

"That's not what you say to a defense lawyer," Fitts said wryly. "I think this indicates the state of mind of the objective Dr. Schorr when he administered the tests."

It was on the basis of results from Schorr's tests and those of Dr. Richardson that a number of other experts based their conclusions that Sirhan was sick.

"At least Dr. Richardson more closely adhered to the ten commandments of careful testing outlined by psychologist Olinger," Fitts said "At least he recorded all the responses, which Schorr did not do.

"Now look at Dr. Schorr's piece of work. . . . I think it's disgraceful . . . He said he was trying to make tapes of what Sirhan said, but somehow they kept sticking.

"You know that's bothered me . . . It's a simple thing—if the spool is going around, it's recording . . . And he destroyed all the tapes he did have."

Gesturing out at the small courtroom jammed with newsmen, Fitts said, "But in the Sirhan case, which hasn't attracted all these gentlemen for nothing, he destroyed all the tapes."

Fitts wondered, "What are we getting here, Dr. Schorr or Sirhan? In a case of this magnitude I find it inexplicable, I find it deplorable."

At another point, the prosecutor sarcastically referred to "Schorrism" when emphasizing that Richardson and Olinger had "never heard" of some of Schorr's methods.

Smiling innocently at the jury, Fitts recalled that Schorr compared Sirhan to "the man without a country—Nathan Hale." Of course, Nathan Hale was the man "who wanted to give more than one life for his country," Fitts pointed out, adding: "When some member of the press suggested to Dr. Schorr at a recess that he had the wrong Hale, he came back on the stand and said he meant Edward Everett Hale . . . . Philip Nolan was the man without a country.

"That may be illuminating with respect to the intellectual acumen Dr. Schorr brings to his interpretations," the prosecutor sighed.

"It has been suggested by the defense psychiatrists that this defendant exists in a delusional system . . . thinking he is something in the nature of a new messiah who should receive complete social acceptance by everybody in the world.

"That has never been the attitude of this defendant . . . . One would suppose the new messiah to be saying, 'I did it and I'm glad.' "

It was an effective performance by David Fitts. He argued to the strength of the prosecution and ignored the strength of the defense. He was caustic, needling, demeaning in his analysis of what was wrong with the defense testimony.

The eyes of the jurors focused on Fitts throughout the day—with only one abrupt interlude when Sirhan interrupted and sought to rise from his seat to protest Fitts' statements.

Even then, the outburst worked to add emphasis to what Fitts was saying about Sirhan: that he knew what he was doing; that his actions were calculated.

The defense took over the next morning.

Russell Parsons, Emile Zola Berman and Grant Cooper argued eloquently and intelligently for Sirhan Sirhan.

Parsons began, and his forty-five-minute speech was a plea for mercy for this young Arab immigrant whom the old lawyer had treated almost as a son.

"I've sat here and had him reach up and hold my hand like a baby," said Parsons to the jurors. "You've seen him. One minute he seems smart as a whip and the next he doesn't know right from wrong . . .

"I've come to kind of like this fellow . . . . Like the state's doctor (Seymour Pollack) said, 'you can't be around him very long and not feel sorry for him.' "

He dwelt for a time on Sirhan's early life in Jerusalem; the sorrow and tragedies and horrors he experienced as a child. He

was only four when warfare broke out and he and fifty other people were forced from their homes and required to take refuge in
a partially destroyed eight-hundred-year-old home.

"They hardly had enough to exist on," Parsons related.
"It is unbelievable that people have to exist under these
conditions in these modern times. But they did . . . . The
fighting and killing around him must have left a scar on him. How
could it do otherwise? They built a barbed wire fence around his
home. You know what that means . . . he saw part of a man hanging on a wire . . . and in the place where they lived they pulled an
arm out of the well."

He told how Sirhan's brother was killed as a child, pushed
over barbed wire by a truck. "Sirhan was young. It must have left
an impression on him."

Parsons recalled that when the Sirhans decided to move to
America, Sirhan did not want to come. "As bad as it was, it was
his home." Sirhan ran away from home because he didn't want to
leave Jerusalem. He returned to his parents and brothers and
sisters in time to come with them to this country. "But that boy
had scars on him then," Parsons said.

Toward the end the old lawyer began to exhort the jurors to
demonstrate courage in rendering a verdict.

"I would like for your verdict to spell in every hamlet, on
every desert in the Arab world and in Europe that you can get
justice in America . . . and that's neither life imprisonment nor
death, because this case doesn't warrant it . . . not for this poor
sick wretch who needs psychiatric treatment.

"It's going to take a little courage to return a proper verdict
in this case . . . but it must be done," said Parsons. He told the
jury he felt its members had the necessary courage and he sat
down.

It was an emotional moment for the aging advocate. This was
probably his last appearance in a major case. He felt close to his
client. He thought that Sirhan needed help, not punishment.

Parsons was followed by Berman. The New York lawyer
called Sirhan "a man, yes, in years. But a little boy, emotionally . . . . It would be easy for us all if he were just a kid. We could
spank him, teach him and forget it as the product of a temper tan-
trum. But this is the product of a sick mind."

He went over Sirhan's petulant temper outbreaks in court. "We are satisfied this is no act . . . except that of a little man with an immature mind." He told the jurors they were required to "make a distinction between a man with a clear mind and rational judgment . . . and a baby—or, if not a baby, a very small child in the body of a man."

Berman told the jury he wanted to talk with them "about a thing called trauma . . . a blow to what makes a person become what he is . . . I want to trace what it was, step by step, that put him in the posture that created the act that blighted our nation," he said.

Berman spoke specifically about the "trauma" he said Sirhan suffered after arriving in America. He recalled a conflict between Sirhan and his father—dear old loving dad, you might say.

"Sirhan interfered as a careless kid" with something his father was doing and "papa was about to strike him when Adel stepped between them and would not allow his father to beat Sirhan.

"Papa immediately confronted mama and laid down the gauntlet—she must choose between him and the children . . . . Can you imagine what such a scene would do in front of a child? Mama said something to the effect of 'you are my husband and he is my child.' So dear old ever-loving dad took all the family's money and went back to Jordan and has never been heard from since.

"That was trauma number one. Sirhan felt some guilt for his father's betrayal."

The second trauma, Berman said, was the death in 1964 of Sirhan's sister, Aida, whom he had nursed as she lay dying of leukemia.

Failing in college, being thwarted in his ambition to become a jockey and the crushing defeat of the Arab bloc by Israel in the six-day war of June, 1967, were other traumas.

Sirhan, said Berman, "is so unaware of his social obligations to our society that he must be under control and have psychiatric assistance."

Emile Zola Berman is a measured man, a phlegmatic intellectual, a deliberate lawyer.

Now suddenly he almost shouted: "I'm not a beggar. I don't

beg for people. But I ask you in the name of all I know about life . . . I ask you in the name of humanity, not to send up for first-degree murder, a mental cripple."

To those jurors who recognized the position of this slender, bespectacled little New York lawyer, his peroration was moving. He was pleading for Sirhan's life despite all the hatred his client felt for Berman as a Jew. For Berman, who by this time was making a major sacrifice in money and time, far removed from home and law practice, his role in the case represented the highest ideal for which the organized bar takes credit: every man is entitled to a lawyer. Even Sirhan, the Arab, was entitled to the services of Berman, the Jew.

Grant Cooper now rose to open the final summation for Sirhan Bishara Sirhan. He would not complete his argument that day.

He must have been aware that his would be the last word to be spoken for Sirhan before the jury deliberated. He took his time. He took into account the full weight of the crime.

"We are not overlooking the fact," he said peering intently at the jury, "and you wouldn't let me, that the man who was killed was Senator Robert F. Kennedy. He left a wife and, I think, eleven children, one of whom was born after his death."

Whether Sirhan "likes it or not he deserves to spend the rest of his life in the penitentiary" for killing Senator Kennedy, Cooper said.

"I, for one, am not going to ask you to bring in anything less than murder in the second degree," said Cooper. The assassin sat in rapt silence, occasionally biting his fingernails, as Cooper's voice boomed out: "We are not here to free a guilty man . . . . We tell you, as we always have, that he is guilty of killing Senator Kennedy. We are not asking for an acquittal."

The silver-haired attorney, slicing the air with his hands for emphasis, turned and faced Sirhan to say he believed the facts should put his client in prison.

"While you could, and very well under the evidence we could ask you to (bring in a lesser verdict) . . . because of the testimony of all the psychiatrists and because of this man's conduct, I wouldn't want Sirhan turned loose on society when the psychiatrists tell us he's getting worse." Cooper said he, too, had come to feel a personal affection for Sirhan.

"There are two sides to Sirhan Sirhan—the good Sirhan and the bad Sirhan; the bad Sirhan is a nasty Sirhan," Cooper said. "But I have learned to love the little good Sirhan. But, we also owe an obligation to society."

Cooper had only opened the door on his theory of defense in his closing argument when court adjourned for the day. The following day Cooper and chief prosecutor Lynn Compton were before the jury giving opposing points of view—first Cooper and then Compton, who would close for the State.

The final thrust of Cooper's argument for Sirhan Sirhan was that if Robert Kennedy had been just another "John Smith" the jury would have brought in a verdict of second-degree murder without hesitation.

Cooper "spoke the last words for Sirhan" in a closing argument that suggested the jurors would rush to bring in a second-degree murder verdict if the slain victim had been an average man on the street.

"Suppose," said the veteran of forty years in the courtroom, "that the deceased in this case had been a fellow named John Smith . . . a nonentity . . . a Jose Gonzales . . . a George Washington Brown . . . just one of the crowd . . . and you heard the same kind of testimony by court-appointed psychiatrists you had here. Would you hesitate two minutes to return a verdict of second-degree murder? You wouldn't hesitate one minute."

He asked that the jurors not allow the fact that Robert Kennedy was the man slain by Sirhan to color their decision or "sway you from your duty." He emphasized that the jury need not find that Sirhan suffered from diminished capacity to find him guilty of less than first-degree murder—they need only have a doubt. "If you have a reasonable doubt the defendant has a right to a verdict of second-degree."

Cooper built much of his defense argument around the premise that Sirhan may have premeditated the murder of Kennedy, killed the senator with "malice aforethought," but did not do so maturely and meaningfully.

The difference between first and second-degree murder in California lies in the phrase "mature and meaningful." In both cases the killing contains the elements of premeditation and deliberation but in second-degree, Cooper explained, "premeditation and deliberation is diminished by substantially reduced mental capacity caused by mental illness . . . intoxication . . . or any other cause.

"I don't care if he was in a hypnotic state at the time he fired the shot, or as Dr. Diamond said, in a trance," Cooper argued. "The question is whether he could maturely and meaningfully premeditate."

Cooper said he was "not suggesting Sirhan Sirhan should be given a medal. In a sense I've aligned myself with the prosecution only in order to find justice . . . . I think second-degree will take care of the situation."

Cooper alluded briefly to a disagreement between himself and co-defense counsel Parsons, who had said he believed Sirhan should be treated psychiatrically, and returned to society. Cooper was not asking for less than second-degree murder, which carries an imprisonment penalty of five years to life, saying he did not want Sirhan turned loose on society.

"Mr. Parsons may have slightly different feelings, as he has the right to," Cooper said. "But a lawyer has the right to exercise his discretion.

"Even though this case is susceptible to a plea for manslaughter—because of the testimony of the psychiatrists—we're not going to ask for it."

Arguing carefully and exhaustively, Cooper adopted the position that the prosecution is right in charging Sirhan with premeditated murder.

"Probably he had the intention to kill somebody . . . President Johnson or Vice President Humphrey or Ambassador Goldberg . . . because in one of his writings he said he planned to overthrow the entire government of the United States. He just hadn't formulated a plan yet, he said."

That sort of thinking, Cooper contends, is not mature.

"If you accept what Dr. Diamond says, he'd be not guilty by reason of insanity," the defense chief argued.

"Sirhan's motive, in his sick mind, was a good motive . . . he thought it was right to kill Senator Kennedy . . . he thought he shouldn't be punished for it . . . .

"He thought he would start a third world war . . . throw the whole country into anarchy.

"Ladies and gentlemen of the jury, in all honesty, is that the thinking of a mature mind?"

Recalling Dr. Pollack's testimony that Sirhan shot the presidential candidate in order to "draw the attention of the world to the plight of the Palestinian Arabs," Cooper mused: "If that were the motive, it is a little difficult to explain his behavior in jail (right after his arrest) . . . .

"He wouldn't give the police the time of day . . . his name, even that he was an Arab. If he wanted to proclaim it (the Arab cause) to the world, why didn't he proclaim it at that time?"

Then Cooper wanted to know "why, in God's name, did Sirhan Sirhan deny the writings" in his notebooks, the writings which, in a rambling fashion, threatened death for Kennedy and other political figures.

"I don't know unless, as the psychiatrist said . . . he did indeed have amnesia . . . .

"He sat on that witness stand and said he recognized the handwriting, he said 'these were my writings and these were my thoughts at that time.' Ladies and gentlemen, he wasn't trying to kid you . . . he just said, 'I don't remember writing them.' "

Cooper also reviewed the testimony of "the little man in the green suit, Dr. Schorr . . . Dr. Schorr who plagiarized a book."

"Frankly, I'll tell you I wasn't happy with Dr. Schorr," Cooper said. "I could have crawled under the table when I found out . . . that he could have been so stupid as to spoil his testimony by copying somebody else's work just because it sounded better."

But the defense attorney pointed out that Schorr did not copy any of the test results he obtained from Sirhan. And, he added, Schorr reached the same conclusions, independently, as three other psychologists in the case.

But, "the little man in the green suit made a terrible faux pas which I wish had never happened," Cooper said, shaking his head.

In closing Cooper paused at length, gave the jurors a searching look, then said softly, "I now pass from our shoulders to yours the responsibility and the proper and intelligent fate of Sirhan Sirhan."

Lynn Compton countered by slashing directly at the defense psychiatric testimony. He called seven of the eight psychiatrists and psychologists who said Sirhan was schizophrenic "the magnificent seven."

He said: "If you believe Dr. Diamond with his mirror act and all this testimony about him being in a trance, so confused the poor fellow didn't know whether he was afoot or on horseback . . . you have to turn him loose. But if you don't buy all those so-called experts there's nothing left but plain, old cold-blooded murder."

Compton spoke in a slow drawl, perched much of the time on the end of the counsel table a few feet from the jury. He blistered Dr. Diamond's theory that Sirhan killed Kennedy in a state of self-hypnosis induced by mirrors in the Ambassador Hotel.

Compton went on: "I can be frank to admit that right now I can't answer the simple fundamental question—did Robert Francis Kennedy, a young, highly successful man at the peak of his career, a former attorney general of the United States, a senator from New York and a candidate for president . . . did he breathe his last breath on that dirty floor of the pantry of the Ambassador Hotel with the mops and dirty dishes . . . did he leave a widow and eleven children and expire with a bullet in his brain because he favored U. S. support of the Israeli state or because he somehow became a father image, in some complicated Oedipus complex, for Sirhan?

"I've heard these psychiatrists and psychologists go round and round with their jargon . . . Was it because Sirhan hated Jews and Zionists or because somehow poor Kennedy unwittingly became a substitute for Sirhan's father?

"I submit that the answer to that question determines whether Sirhan is guilty of anything or guilty of first degree murder."

"Not one of the 30,000 to 35,000 felons (the DA's office handles yearly) demonstrated mature, meaningful judgment. That includes the college kid who gets caught with marijuana, the twenty-five year old who shoots heroin into his veins, the man who holds up a liquor store and runs a tremendous risk for fifteen dollars . . . .

"What about the guy who smashes a jewelry store . . . one does it because he's hungry . . . another is not hungry, just greedy, a third does it because he believes if he takes the diamond home and puts it in the head of an idol it will assuage the evil spirits. The last guy does it for crazy reasons."

Was the murder of Kennedy "for crazy reasons, or was it for reasons which you and I might not like but they aren't all that crazy?" Compton asked.

Compton pointed out to the jury that second-degree murder carries with it the element of malice, that all the psychologists and psychiatrists had said Sirhan was capable of malice.

The following day, the state in its final argument suggested that Sirhan Sirhan's jury disregard all the psychiatric and psychological evidence they had heard and decide the degree of guilt on the basis of common sense.

Compton struck out at psychiatry as an inexact profession, with no place in the courtroom.

"The whole reason for their discipline is finding something wrong with somebody, you know. What better way to foist their theories on the whole world than in the case of Sirhan Bishara Sirhan. They could take any one of you (jurors) and tomorrow you could go out and kill somebody and there will be something in your background they'll find to explain it."

The crew-cut, former football star reserved his harshest words for "the ubiquitous Dr. Diamond."

"A walking lie detector, handwriting expert, gun expert . . ." is Dr. Diamond, Compton said, and "anybody who didn't agree with him was a liar."

The psychiatrist's assured courtroom manner had seemed to anger Compton.

"Nobody knew what happened until . . . Dr. Diamond descended upon the scene and solved his whole case . . . . And he did it with mirrors . . . . I get this picture of Munir Sirhan standing, waiting to get in the bathroom for hours while Sirhan is in there practicing his mirror act," Compton said, and laughed wryly.

The prosecutor said the quality of the psychiatric testimony reminded him of a line from Charles Dickens, "The law is an ass."

"Well, the law became an ass the day it let psychiatrists get their hands on it."

"If you were in your living room and I came over and I said,

'Look, this guy goes out to the Ambassador June 5 and he parks his car three blocks away, puts his wallet in the glove compartment, sticks his gun in his pocket . . . goes into the hotel . . . into the kitchen' . . .

"Now that's something else—I suspect many of you have been in the Ambassador Hotel but I doubt if you have been in the kitchen . . . anyway this guy asks if Senator Kennedy is coming back this way . . . then Kennedy comes this way and he walks right up and puts a bullet in his brain . . . .

"I can't believe . . . anybody using good common sense, from that set of facts, could draw anything but one conclusion."

The conclusion, Compton and his office believed, is that Sirhan is guilty of "coldblooded murder." If, the attorney argued, Sirhan is quite sick mentally and is deteriorating rapidly, it does not show. "If he was a vegetable on June 5, he should have been a gibbering idiot here" on the stand. "We are not here to decide whether Sirhan is a clever assassin or even a smart one," he said. "Simply the question is, was his premeditation of a quality that you think he should be held responsible for killing Senator Kennedy?"

As Compton seemed to work from point to point on the complicated case, he kept throwing "common sense" in liberal doses at the jurors.

"And another thing, he's not delusional—he doesn't think he's Napoleon, he doesn't think he's Nasser, he thinks he's Sirhan." Compton jerked a finger over his shoulder in the direction of the frowning young Arab.

The whole problem with the psychiatrists and psychologists, Compton said, "is that they're doing nothing more than trying to give their own horseback analysis on the same evidence you've got. I say reject their tests. I think it would be a frightening thing for the administration of criminal justice in this state if a case of this magnitude turns on whether he saw clowns playing pattycake or saw them kicking each other on the shins in his inkblot tests. I say, throw them all out in one big bag."

Compton concluded: "This defendant has received justice to the nth degree under the system in this country. There was a tremendous effort on the part of the authorities in this city just to prevent him being lynched . . . he had three of the finest law-

yers . . . investigators at his disposal and psychiatrists to come
to his aid. We had a discovery procedure as broad as possible . . .
no secrets . . . a public trial so the world (could watch) through
the media . . . then finally, a jury trial . . . and an extremely fair
and open-minded judge . . . and the prosecution had the burden
of proof.

"This is justice. It has been served. The system has worked."

Judge Walker now gave his charge—his instructions—
to the jury. He spoke for fifty-five minutes, explaining that the
jurors could find the assassin guilty of less than first-degree
murder if they had "reasonable doubt whether he could maturely and meaningfully premeditate and deliberate" Kennedy's
death. This was after all the only point of this long trial.

The seven-man, five-woman panel walked from the courtroom with Sirhan's fate in their hands. Judge Walker instructed
the jury for fifty-five minutes, sending them out to begin deliber-
ations at 2:55 p.m.

The twelve included last minute addition, George A. Stitzel,
pressroom supervisor for the *Los Angeles Times,* who was added
to the panel in the morning, replacing Ronald Evans of Inglewood,
California, a telephone switchboard installer who was excused
because of the death of his father. Walker said the jury would
deliberate only during regular court sessions hours—9:30 a.m. to
4 p.m. with a one-hour-and-forty-five-minute lunch break. The
jurors deliberated for sixty-five minutes, then retired to their
hotel for the night.

The following day the jury began going through the mountain
of evidence piled up during the fourteen-week trial. During the
first hour, the jurors elected Bruce Elliott, youthful electronics
Ph.D. and bachelor, as foreman.

The beige walls of the jury room had but one adornment, a
calendar with a picture of the "Peanuts" comic strip character
Snoopy, wearing his famed World War I flying helmet and long
scarf.

As they deliberated, a few miles away in the modest Sirhan
home on East Howard Street in Pasadena, the assassin's mother
and brothers wait for a phone call. Mary Sirhan has been faithful
in her attendance throughout the exhaustive trial—until this week.
She chose to remain at home rather than hear the closing argu-

ment of chief prosecutor Compton, who called her son a "cunning, vicious" killer and asked for a verdict of first-degree murder. Today she preferred to wait to hear the outcome from television or from Sirhan's attorneys.

Four floors above the sparsely furnished room where the seven men and five women were debating the degree of his guilt, Sirhan dozed, read and talked briefly with Parsons.

Parsons, who visited Sirhan in mid-afternoon, said he found him "in pretty good shape. He doesn't seem worried."

The attorney said that Sirhan had two or three "Arab-Israeli" books and a Bible in his cell, which he had been reading between naps.

The jury returned to the courtroom during the afternoon to ask Judge Walker for clarification of his instructions on second-degree murder.

Walker told the panel members that if they find Sirhan's mental capacity was "substantially reduced," they must consider what effect that had on his ability to commit first-degree murder.

And if that capacity "was diminished to the extent that you have a reasonable doubt whether he did maturely and meaningfully premeditate, deliberate and reflect . . . or form an intent to kill," the judge said, "you cannot convict him of a willful, deliberate and premeditated murder in the first degree . . . you can find . . . second degree."

Parsons again visited Sirhan and said his client had told him of his belief that he might be on one end of a prisoner swap such as the Francis Gary Powers-Colonel Rudolf Abel exchange.[2] The conversation made it clear that Sirhan expects a life sentence—not death.

On the sixty-second day of the trial, the jury found Sirhan Bishara Sirhan guilty of first-degree murder.

It took the jury some seventeen hours of deliberation to reach the verdict read to a hushed courtroom at 11:15 a.m. The slight, hollow-eyed assassin took the words, "Guilty of murder in the first degree," calmly. When he walked into the courtroom he was smiling, and he nodded pleasantly to Parsons as he

---

2. In 1962, the United States obtained the release of Powers, a downed U-2 spy plane pilot, from Russia in return for Abel, a convicted Soviet espionage agent.

took his seat at the end of the counsel table. That smile faded as his eyes searched the audience for members of his family.

His mother, Mary, and brothers, Adel and Munir, were a twenty-minute drive away in their Pasadena home, listening on radio and television for the verdict.

Sirhan grinned again as jury foreman Bruce D. Elliott, who is only three years older than he, handed the written decision to the court bailiff, who passed it to Judge Walker. The jurist checked the results, then asked Mrs. Alice Nishikawa, court clerk, to announce the verdict. She read it in a clear voice: "guilty of first-degree murder." The jury also found him guilty of assault with intent to kill five victims, wounded when he shot Kennedy. Sirhan sat as though stricken as Walker polled each of the jurors, asking if they agreed with the decision.

Each juror in turn answered "yes" in a low voice. They did not look at Sirhan.

"Record the verdict," Walker ordered.

For the next few moments there was no sound in the armor-plated courtroom except for the thud of the clerk's stamp falling with finality on each of the six verdicts. Now the jury must go to work again to decide whether Sirhan's penalty would be death or life imprisonment.

Then Walker called the attorneys to his bench and for a moment Sirhan sat alone, twisting his hands before him and staring straight ahead.

Defense investigator Michael McCowan stepped to his side, then bent over to console him.

"He had begun to get angry," McCowan said later, declining to repeat what the young Arab said. Neither Parsons nor Cooper would disclose the nature of their conversations with Sirhan other than to say "he was disappointed."

The proceedings now moved into the "penalty phase." In repudiating the defense, which portrayed Sirhan as a mental cripple unable to control his emotions, the jury had saddled itself not only with deciding his fate but with another "trial": The defense would produce witnesses and argument in an effort to get a life sentence.

Sirhan spoke one word during the arguments on the penalty phase.

After Cooper explained he wanted to call Arab experts to testify that Sirhan spoke the truth when he described his terror-ridden childhood in Old Jerusalem, he turned to the defendant and said: "Is that about what you wanted?"

"Beautiful," Sirhan said.

Walker turned that request down.

Cooper, obviously unhappy, refused to say what else the defense would lean on. The state would not call any witnesses, Compton said, but would rely totally on argument.

"This is a unique case, without precedent," Compton told the news reporters. "I think the jury will express the conscience of the nation. What is an appropriate penalty for political assassination in this country? I don't know."

Compton admitted that the state's earlier willingness to accept a guilty plea and settle for life "imposes a certain responsibility on us," but he would not say what that was.

On the sixty-third trial day, it was learned that the brooding young Arab, angered at the verdict, had privately renewed his demand for a death sentence. Issa Nakhleh, chief of the Palestinian Arab delegation to the U.N. and a defense consultant, confirmed the report. Nakhleh was in New York when the verdict was announced and flew back to Los Angeles, apparently at the request of Cooper. Nakhleh, a British-educated attorney, had a calming influence on the volatile Sirhan.

By demanding a death sentence, Nakhleh said, Sirhan believed he was showing the trial up for what he thought it was—a travesty of justice. But Nakhleh had nothing but praise for the conduct of the trial.

"I think Judge Walker is an eminently fair man," he said. "The trial has been very fair."

The Arab diplomat was not so kind in his assessment of the jury.

"They just disregarded all the scientific evidence, which has been accepted by California law," Nakhleh said. "How can they do that?"

The only evidence presented before the attorneys began arguing on punishment was brief testimony from Mrs. Sirhan.

The assassin sat quietly as he heard Cooper ask his mother:

"In his entire life before this shooting, has Sirhan Sirhan at any time been in any trouble?"

"He has never been. That is not from me or him. It is because I raise him up on the law of God and his love."

John Howard, for the state, argued: "We think it important that Mr. Juan Romero, a busboy at the Ambassador Hotel, could shake the hand of a presidential candidate. Mr. Romero's privilege afforded this defendant the opportunity of firing a bullet into the brain of that same candidate. The question to be resolved is the proper penalty for political assassination in the United States of America."

The prosecutor hit hard at the scowling defendant in his brief, no-nonsense argument. "Perhaps you observed his reaction when Mr. Russell Parsons, in his address to you, urged in all sincerity that America pray for the . . . Kennedy family," Howard said. (Sirhan had grinned, then covered his face with his hand.) "You could not have failed to see the smirk on the defendant's face when he declared from the witness stand, 'I don't know who shot Senator Kennedy.' "

While Howard never used the words "death penalty" or "gas chamber," he left little doubt which punishment he preferred. "We have lavishly expended our resources for the sake of a cold-blooded political assassin while content to send patriotic Americans to Vietnam with a seventy-dollar rifle and our best wishes. Sirhan was entitled to the fair trial which he has received. He has no special claim to further preservation."

Then the normally harsh, clipped voice softened and Howard closed: "I urge you to apply the only proper penalty for political assassination in the United States."

Parsons delivered a fourteen-minute argument for Sirhan's life, asking the jury to "let the bells ring out throughout so the world can see justice in America . . . . But how easy will it be two weeks hence . . . how easy after he has been executed . . . when you are alone . . . and you stop and think, 'My God, could I have been wrong?' "

Grant B. Cooper said the last word for Sirhan. He said Sirhan was a victim of "hate generated in the bowels of war." He called to mind for the jurors a quotation which became part of Senator Kennedy's campaign dialogue as he ran for the presidency. If the senator could come into the courtroom, said Cooper, he would probably ask the jurors, "to tame the savageness of man . . . to make gentle the life of the world."

"You are gathered here to decide the ultimate issue," Cooper said, and his voice dropped. "And that issue should be God's alone to decide."

Cooper told them a sentence of life would be "a kind of posthumous tribute to Senator Kennedy," a man who abhorred violence.

"Let the circle of violence end right here in this courtroom," he pleaded.

Turning to the assassin, Cooper said: "Sirhan Sirhan, I've done all I can do for you and for the American system of justice, which I revere."

Then, the eloquent attorney looked out into the second row of the audience and addressed Sirhan's gray-haired, fifty-six-year-old mother.

"And to you, Mary Sirhan, his mother, I say there is nothing more I can do. I now entrust the life of your son to the hands of this American jury, confident justice will be done.

"And, Mary Sirhan, may your prayers be answered."

Judge Walker instructed the jurors briefly before sending them out for their final decision in the case. The jurist told the panel that they must not consider the possibility of Sirhan being paroled in reaching their verdict.

Under California law the state's Adult Authority may parole any criminal sentenced to life, if he is ruled "safe" to return to society.

On the sixty-sixth trial day, a buzzer rang three times in the courtroom, announcing that the jury had agreed, after twelve hours of deliberation, on a penalty for Sirhan. Moments later Sirhan was brought into the courtroom, smiling broadly and chewing vigorously on a wad of gum. He slipped into his seat next to defense attorney Russell Parsons and whispered, "Let's hope for the best."

At 11:38 a.m. the clerk informed a hushed, straining audience that the punishment had been "fixed" by the jury at death in San Quentin Prison's gas chamber.

As Clerk Alice Nishikawa asked each juror in turn if death was indeed his or her decision, Sirhan sat motionless and pale.

After the jury filed slowly from the courtroom he walked casually toward the door into his security area: "Don't be concerned. Even Jesus Christ couldn't have saved me," said Sirhan Bishara Sirhan. For once he was calm. Grant Cooper, his lawyer, wept.

"I hope this puts people on notice that we simply cannot tolerate this type of solution to political and social problems," chief prosecutor Lynn Compton said. "And that runs the gamut all the way from assassination down to occupying buildings . . . ."

Chief defense counsel Cooper said he believed the jury felt pressure from the underlying and overriding feelings of the community and the entire United States. "This is no criticism of the jury, I'm not saying he (Sirhan) didn't get a fair jury, but they are human beings, governed by the same emotions . . . as you and I. They can't help but be affected by the unrest in this nation. Now for the first time they were put in a position of upholding law and order."

Cooper seemed to have a premonition that the verdict would be death. As he waited for the jury to file into the courtroom, the veteran shook his head, frowned and said: "I don't like this. The weak ones crumpled just like they did on second degree."

While insisting he was not criticizing the jury, Cooper said: "If the victim had not been Robert Kennedy I think the district attorney would have taken a plea of second-degree murder. I believe this, I almost know it."

Compton, whose appeal to common sense had closed the state's case against Sirhan, was asked if the death penalty was what the American people wanted.

"Yes, I think so. Because I happen to believe that a great majority of the American public favors capital punishment. This is the kind of case that calls for it," he said.

Cooper retorted bitterly. "I heard Mr. Compton say this might act as a deterrent," he told a press conference.

"Do any of you, and any of you within hearing of my voice, think this will act as a deterrent to those with crazy minds who assassinate public figures . . . this is only done by people with warped and diseased minds. This verdict won't stop them."

Then, his voice sounding tired and his face reflecting defeat, the veteran defense lawyer said: "I had hoped the circle of violence would end here."

But the fight for Sirhan's life was just beginning.

On May 14 Cooper, who had hoped to leave the case if a life imprisonment verdict had been returned, would begin making motions for a new trial.

During the preparation of this book there came unannounced to the office of John Seigenthaler one morning in October, 1969, a gray-haired woman and young man whose faces were familiar to the reporters working in the newsroom.

It was Mary Sirhan and her son, Munir. Seigenthaler was out but Frank Ritter and other members of the staff took her to lunch. It was a strange visit. She was pleading for help for her son—but what help she thought she could get in Tennessee, from Nashville newsmen, was not clear. Still again, later in the development of the book, Mrs. Sirhan telephoned Seigenthaler from Los Angeles. Her conversation was vague, disorganized and pointless. She wanted to know if anything could be done to help her son. She had been told by some person she would not name that the editor might know how Sirhan could be helped. The incidents remain small imponderables in a ponderable case.

And so the third political assassination case of 1969 ended. Sirhan's attorneys felt that the jury was fair, under pressure, and mistaken. The prosecution felt that the conscience of America was purged. And outside the Hall of Justice a lone Arab picket, wearing a sport shirt and slacks, walked with a sign which read: "Save Sirhan from the bloodthirsty Zionists."

The savageness of man had hardly been tamed. And if this trial of Sirhan's mind, which took so many weeks, so much effort and so much money, is typical of the American system of justice, the nation's criminal courts are in serious trouble.

Chapter 5

It Won't Be Done

1.

*"The mood and temper of the public
in regard to the treatment
of crime and criminals
is one of the most unfailing tests
of the civilization of any country."*
Sir Winston Churchill

The criminal trials of Clay Shaw, James Earl Ray and Sirhan B. Sirhan cast long, threatening shadows over the administration of justice. The American system of justice is considered "different" because it has built-in procedures that emphasize that the rights of the accused be protected. But each of these cases demonstrates that the "difference" is a myth.

No interpretation of these three cases can be made to indicate that the trials were in the public interest. Often what occurred can be correctly described as running contrary to public interest. A critique of each of the three cases disturbs the conventional idea that the American system of justice is close to perfection. It is not. And unless it is soon reformed the symptoms of doubt now being expressed among many in society—particularly young citizens—can be expected to spread across the broad mid-section of the American body politic.

Shaw should never have been tried. As the ranking official of the American Bar Association, William T. Gossett, said immediately after the trial, he suffered the cost of legal counsel, two years of public exposure and great anxiety over the outcome on a matter that should never have been brought into the criminal courts.

Ray was charged a lawyer's fee of $150,000 to work out a deal the public defender could have handled for nothing.

Sirhan went through a prolonged sanity hearing and received a sentence more severe than one which could have been negotiated before a jury was seated to try the case.

*   *   *   *

A review of day-to-day developments in the conspiracy trial at New Orleans reveals many scars the case made on the face of justice. Some of these have healed because they were forgotten the moment the jury cleared Shaw. He was acquitted and so there was no appeal. Thus, many of the weaknesses shown to exist during the trial remain unchallenged as a part of the trial system.

In retrospect, the Shaw trial defined three glaring areas of needed court reform: *1. trial procedures; 2. the power and responsibility of the trial judge; 3. the power and responsibility of the prosecuting attorney.*

*   *   *   *

1. *Trial Procedures.* The method of trying criminal cases has evolved from laws governing the courts, rules adopted by the courts, legal precedents and trial tradition.

In the Shaw case some of the offenses committed in the name of trial procedure are indigenous to Louisiana and peculiar to a few other states. Some of the procedures are built into the administration of justice in its broadest national sense.

At that time Orleans Parish courts did not pay jurors for their services.[1] This meant that those called to jury service had to be able to forego their employment income for a period of jury service. It is unlikely, because of this, that the juries in New Orleans, particularly in cases that lasted for weeks, attracted representative cross-sections of community citizenry.

The Shaw trial lasted six weeks. Judge Haggerty was to comment at one point on the difficulty of getting a qualified jury to serve. Noting that more than 1,200 veniremen had been subpoenaed, he remarked that this set a record in Orleans parish. Never before had so many prospective jurors been excused. No doubt the free-wheeling manner in which Jim Garrison had spoken on the pending case had a great deal to do with the claim by many jurors that they had made up their minds about the

---

1. Shortly after the Shaw trial, legislation was passed to provide pay for jurors.

case. But neither can there be much doubt that few prospective jurors were anxious to be locked up for five weeks, away from work and home—even though the state of Louisiana provided comfortable motel accommodations. How many would-be jurors convinced themselves they had made up their minds because they felt they could not serve without pay is an unanswerable question. At one point, Judge Haggerty was quoted as saying the jurors were "living high on the hog" in their motel quarters. Comfortable accommodations would seem to be the least the state could provide for citizens who were making such a sacrifice of time and money to render a verdict in a criminal case that should never have been tried in the first place.

Throughout the history of American jurisprudence, a bedrock principle has been that the best safeguard against injustice was the knowledge that ultimately criminal charges would be decided by "twelve good men and true" who made up a jury of the defendant's peers. Louisiana law provides that in criminal cases, nine jurors can decide on the guilt or innocence of the defendant. This means nine of the twelve jurors could have convicted Shaw and he might have gone to prison for twenty years.

In order to expedite the trial of civil cases, the practice of using the so-called "bob-tailed juries" has gradually become accepted in many jurisdictions. The practice has not spread with regard to criminal cases, however. In fact, only three states other than Louisiana have "bob-tailed" juries in state criminal cases: Hawaii, Oregon and Florida.

Glenn R. Winters, executive director of the American Judicature Society, writing in the St. Louis University Law Journal in the fall, 1968 edition, reports: "The use of juries of less than twelve is a factor in reducing jury costs and making jury trial more available. The unanimous verdict quite generally prevails in criminal cases, but the use of less than unanimous verdicts in civil cases is on the increase."

In Clay Shaw's case, there was a jury of "twelve good men and true." But it could hardly have been comforting to Shaw to realize that Garrison had to influence only nine of those twelve to send him to the penitentiary.

Judge Haggerty said during the selection of jurors in the Shaw trial that some constitutional questions had been raised as to the validity of a nine-man verdict. But he left no doubt with newsmen who questioned him that he would accept a nine-man verdict. "That is the law in this state," he said. "Any vote such as nine to three, ten to two, eleven to one or twelve to zero would be acceptable. Any other verdict such as eight to four would result in a hung jury if the jurors persisted in voting that way."

Haggerty said he planned to abide by the nine-man verdict law "until the U. S. Supreme Court rules otherwise." There is no magic formula that argues for an even dozen jurors being required to decide criminal cases, but what sort of justice is it that would require Clay Shaw to go to prison for twenty years if convicted in New Orleans by nine jurors and at the same time require that he be tried all over again if only nine, ten, or eleven men voted for conviction in another state? Since Shaw was cleared, the matter of "bob-tailed" juries in criminal cases would have to await resolution by the U. S. Supreme Court for another appeal another day.[2]

There is still an additional point: Garrison had led the nation to believe Shaw was involved in President Kennedy's murder. But his assistant, James Alcock, said "in order to convict Clay Shaw, we aren't legally required to prove even that John F. Kennedy is dead." What Alcock apparently was saying was that had Shaw talked with anyone about assassinating the President, he could have been convicted even if President Kennedy had never been slain.

Periodically, federal authorities have charged various persons, some cranks, with plotting to harm a President, sometimes when the plots were not even seriously contemplated. But that point was not valid here. John Kennedy had been killed; everyone knew he was dead. Garrison said he had "solved" the murder.

Alcock's comment was so strange because of the long series of statements Garrison had made to the effect that he had uncovered "the" plot that killed Kennedy. He failed miserably to prove his conspiracy theory. He also failed to prove that Shaw was involved in a plot which never materialized. Still Shaw was under the shadow, and Alcock's statement did nothing to remove the shadow.

There is a conflict between the law which permits the state

---

2. The United States Supreme Court ruled in June 1970 that the twelve-man jury, traditional in criminal trials since the fourteenth century, is not required by the Constitution. Ruling in a Florida case where a six-man jury sentenced a Miami man to life in prison, the court overturned an 1898 decision that the twelve-man jury is required for Federal criminal trials.

to try to send a man to prison for a mere conversation, when no actual crime is committed, and the rule of the court which allows the prosecutor to show far more than a mere conversation—a violent film, for example—to try to convict a defendant. Judge Haggerty said more than once that he could not stop the state from "overproving" the case against Shaw. Thus he permitted all sorts of evidence to go to the jury about what happened in Dallas the day Kennedy was killed. It concerned Shaw in no way at all; but the law of the state and the rules of evidence made that unimportant in the wisdom of the judge.

There is an even larger question raised by the Shaw trial: the viability of the adversary trial procedure by which opposing lawyers take strong, at times violent, conflicting positions. Some legal scholars insist that the adversary system is the touchstone of American justice. Theoretically, opposing counsel going at the critical issues hammer and tongs supposedly forges a chain of truth inescapable to a jury.

It very well may be that the adversary procedure contributes considerably to the adequate resolution of legal issues tried in the courts of the land. When properly supervised it may even represent the best method of trying criminal cases. But in terms of finding truth for the purpose of administering justice, it can serve to confound the search. In New Orleans it can only be concluded that the adversary system, as joined by the prosecution side, at least, actually was seeking an untruth. Numerous trial incidents document this. The prosecution called as a witness Lyndal Shaneyfelt, an agent and photographic expert for the Federal Bureau of Investigation who had made an extensive study of the films taken by Abraham Zapruder of the death of the President.

The prosecution used Shaneyfelt's presence on the stand to show again to the jury the bloody scenes at Dallas through the Zapruder film. The prosecution asked Shaneyfelt many questions about the details of the FBI probe of the murder of President Kennedy. But the prosecutors never once asked him his expert opinion about whether the President was shot in a crossfire—as Garrison had repeatedly claimed in public and as he stated in his opening argument to the jury—or whether the shots had come from behind, as the Warren Commission contended.

The state called Shaneyfelt, a photographic expert, as a witness who could be believed. But on the crucial question of whether the Zapruder film he had studied showed him from which direction the bullets had come which killed John Kennedy, the state was silent. When the time came for the defense to cross-examine Shaneyfelt, Shaw's counsel elicited the expert testimony. The shots, Shaneyfelt said, with the state now objecting to testimony by a witness the prosecution had put on the stand, came from behind the President. But what if Shaw's lawyer had not risked the question fearing the FBI man's answer might have been less helpful to the defendant? And so Garrison sought to hide evidence that could have aided a true search for an answer.

Credit goes to Shaw's attorney-team for developing the facts. But an adversary system which allows—even encourages—a prosecutor to put on testimony and then try to withhold vital, valuable evidence by his witness can hardly be accurately described as the "touchstone of justice."

Again, Garrison had subpoenaed FBI ballistics expert Robert A. Frazier; but the prosecution never put Frazier on the witness stand. The reason, obviously, was that Frazier, like Shaneyfelt, disagreed with Garrison's conclusions; he felt the shots fired came from behind and above Kennedy. Here was another expert witness, who, when finally called by the defense, disagreed with Garrison's "cross-fire theory." Having felt the sting of Shaneyfelt's testimony, the prosecution lawyers now passed up the opportunity to call Frazier to testify. This left the obligation on the defense to put Frazier on the witness stand. When Dymond called the FBI expert, he testified there was no evidence at all to indicate the shots came from anywhere but above and behind. Frazier testified that the acoustical characteristics of the high speed bullets could have led witnesses on the scene to believe shots fired from the rear were being fired from the front.

Dymond: "Do the bullets used to shoot the President have any acoustical characteristics of high speed projectile that travels faster than sound?"

Frazier: "Yes. These bullets travel about 2,600 feet per second and sound travels about 1,000 feet per second. As a result, when a person stands in front of the gunfire he will hear a report—a sort of sonic boom—made by the bullet itself, before he hears the explosion of the gunpowder."

Dymond: "Would you say this sonic noise can be confused with the gunpowder explosion?"

Frazier: "Yes. It is easily confused unless you are listening particularly for it or unless you have been trained specially to hear it."

A few seconds later he said: "There was nothing inconsistent that I found to indicate the shots came from anywhere but above and behind."

Here was an expert from the FBI who had some light to shed on the case. Prosecutors who had first subpoenaed him did not want him, in an adversary proceeding, to tell his story; again it took the defense to put on the state's witnesses to tell the story. This raises the question: does the state have no interest in putting on a witness who might contribute facts in a case—even if the testimony might show the state's theory to be wrong?

The same question must be asked about the adversary proceeding in light of the testimony of Lieutenant Colonel Pierre A. Finck, one of the three doctors who performed the autopsy on President Kennedy after his death. His testimony, given when he was called as a defense witness, was that the autopsy indicated that the shots that killed the President came from above and behind.

But again, his sworn testimony contradicted the theory of Garrison.

Dymond, anticipating that the state might claim that even the United States Army, for whom Colonel Finck worked, was involved in the conspiracy which Garrison had charged against the FBI, the CIA, and other sundry sources, asked the doctor: "Is this your professional opinion or have you been influenced in any way by the supposed desires or wishes of anyone in government?"

"My opinion is an honest, professional opinion," Finck replied.

Here again, in the adversary system, the district attorney passed up credible evidence which disagreed with his theory that Kennedy was caught in a cross-fire and killed by many conspirators.

The faults in an adversary proceeding are again shown in the instance where Garrison indicated he would call former Texas Governor John Connally as a witness in the assassination trial.

Governor Connally, riding in the car with President Kennedy, was shot at the same time and the Warren Commission concluded, in a bit of high speculation, that the governor was wounded by a bullet which first pierced Kennedy's throat, entering from the rear.

Connally was seriously wounded by the shot. He challenged the Warren Commission's claim that he had been hit by the same bullet that struck the President. But he did not question the direction from which the Commission contended the bullets were fired; he thought the shots came from the rear. He thought Oswald was a lone assassin.

This of course ran contrary to Garrison's idea. And so on February 19, Garrison's office announced Connally would not appear because the Governor was now considered "a hostile witness."

Connally had never sounded hostile when discussing the case with reporters. He had an honest difference of opinion with the Warren Commission about whether he was wounded by a bullet which had first struck the President. But he didn't disagree on other critical questions. He told newsmen he didn't really know what he could add to the case in New Orleans.

"I understand Governor Connally has been giving interviews to television stations, changing testimony he gave the Warren Commission," said Garrison's aide, Alvin Oser, who later was elevated to a criminal court judgeship. "We must now regard him as a hostile witness."

Again, the question is raised: does the prosecution seek only a witness who will agree with its view of the case? Or is there a place for one who would give the truth in an attempt to aid justice? Under the adversary system, as it was practiced in New Orleans, Connally's version of truth was not wanted.

Garrison might contend that it was the duty of the defense to put on proof that helped Shaw; that any testimony that clouded the state's case was not relevant to what the prosecution was trying to prove. Perhaps an argument can be made that the lawyer would waste the court's time by putting on "irrelevant testimony." But what is relevant and what is not? Was Connally's testimony relevant? How about Dr. Finck's? Or FBI agent Frazier's, or Shaneyfelt's? Garrison sought access to the autopsy reports on the President's death, held in the U. S. Archives. On February 14, Judge Charles Halleck, of the District of Columbia General Sessions Court ruled that a Pittsburgh pathologist, Dr. Cyril H. Wecht, who had written articles critical of the Warren Commission findings, should be allowed to see the autopsy reports. Wecht, expected to be called as a witness for the prosecution by Garrison, never was put on the witness stand in New Orleans. Would his testimony have been relevant? Judge Halleck also directed the U. S. Archivist, Dr. James Rhodes, to take the rifle the Warren Commission concluded Oswald used, to New Orleans along with other physical evidence kept in the Archives. Garrison had these items which were surely as "relevant" as much of his evidence. These were never introduced by Garrison as evidence. Garrison's final jury argument was that a massive federal conspiracy had covered up facts. Interestingly, the jury never knew that Judge Halleck had ruled to allow Garrison's subpoenaed pathologist access to the reports. Here again, the adversary system gives to the prosecutor the right to pick and choose evidence which agrees with the state's theory in the case, regardless of what a search for truth would show. Some defense lawyers would be critical of a prosecutor for such action, but would contend that the role would be proper for a defense lawyer whose first duty is to clear the client.

The adversary system can further work to defeat justice in that it encourages each side to find witnesses to bolster its side of the case. There is broad leeway in defining what it takes to qualify as an "expert" witness. In the Shaw trial there had been testimony that the defendant had once signed a register in an airport lounge in the name of "Clay Bertrand." The signature of that name was introduced into the record by a woman who identified Shaw. Then the defense produced an expert witness— Charles A. Appel, Jr., a veteran investigator who had been credited with helping in the conviction of the Lindbergh kidnapper. This witness, an expert in handwriting analysis, swore that it was his opinion that Shaw did not write the signature in the airport book.

Then the prosecution brought its own expert witness who swore that in her opinion Shaw did sign the book. What sort of search for truth is this?

The continuing "expert witness" testimony reached the height of ridiculousness in the psychological experts called in the Sirhan case. Sometimes experts are less than expert. Sometimes lawyers for opposing sides have been known to shop around for the expert witness who will validate a given side of the case. Each expert, as a general rule, is paid to analyze evidence and testify. In the Shaw case, the handwriting expert who testified for the defense said he was consenting to testify not for a fee but because he felt it was his duty, so an "injustice" would not occur. The state's expert in handwriting testified that she was being paid for her testimony—she did not say how much—and that she had been contacted only two days before she took the stand.

What is the jury to presume at this point, after hearing experts who directly contradict each other? And how much depends, not on the expertise of the witness but on how he deports himself on the witness stand, how well he articulates what he knows and how well he is able to withstand cross-examination?

Under the adversary procedure, very often witnesses who have the greatest expertise are poor witnesses.

Finally, the adversary system allows the surprise factor to an unhealthy degree. Charles I. Spiesel, the strange witness from New York, was damaging to Shaw when he gave direct testimony for the state. What would have been the result had Shaw not been able in a very short time to check on his erratic New York background, and determine that he had some highly questionable ideas about the world around him?

The adversary system is dangerous because it makes opposing lawyers generals in war, each anxious to ambush the other; to destroy the case of the other side.

*   *   *   *

What of the power of the court? What of the responsibility of the court?

*   *   *   *

2. *The power and responsibility of the trial judge.* A leading advocate of court reform writes: "A judge is the central figure in a court, the institution in which justice is administered, and a great deal of law reform has to do with the organization, administration, procedures and operations of the courts." [3]

This infers that if there is to be court reform the judges who preside over the organization, administration, procedures and

---

3. Glen R. Winters, executive secretary of the American Judicature Society.

operations of the courts will be required to lead the way in bringing about reformation.

Reviewing the actions and words of Judge Haggerty during the Shaw trial there is little to demonstrate that he had the ability or desire to lead his court toward meaningful reform. His role in the trial in many ways is illustrative of why the court itself sometimes provides an impediment to justice and the search for truth. It is not to say that all, or even most, of Judge Haggerty's rulings were bad or in error, or harmful to the cause of Clay Shaw. After all, Shaw was acquitted. The deeper question is whether Judge Haggerty's presence on the bench was harmful to the cause of justice. In reviewing the case, it seems impossible to conclude that justice was in stable, steady hands when Haggerty took charge of the Shaw trial.

The judge was sometimes ambivalent, sometimes indecisive; at other times, he was overly sure of himself, almost arbitrary. He could be folksy, and then fierce. He would rule in a stern manner which let it be known that he was in control of the case being tried before him. Again, he would declare that he could not control the nature of the case being presented against Shaw. "I cannot tell the state how to run its case," he said. Of course, he could have—and should have. There was an impression of inconsistency in the manner in which he ruled.

And then there was his over-sensitivity about public relations. He went out of his way to show deference to the press and on occasion seemed to take on the demeanor of a movie actor or a press agent for the benefit of the news media. There are some lawyers and judges who feel that publication of the names of jurors is unwise because it subjects them (when they are not sequestered) or members of their families (when they are) to phone calls from persons who might have an interest in illegally influencing the outcome of a case, or from cranks or pranksters. As a rule, newsmen disagree with the prohibition some judges and attorneys would like to impose upon the publication of names of jurors. The argument of newsmen is that jurors are as vital a part of the mechanics of a criminal case as the defendant, the witnesses for state, the presiding judge, the opposing counsel. Names of jurors are not always published in the newspapers but in general the press reserves the right to use the names if it appears to be newsworthy.

Everyone, as a rule, however, acknowledges that most jurors probably prefer privacy. Some judges, mostly in federal courts, seek to bar photographers from the courtroom floor of a courthouse while a trial is underway. This gives jurors relief from having their photographs taken as they walk down the courthouse corridor to and from the trial sessions. Jurors have occasionally had their pictures taken on their way to and from meals—but almost never is the picture posed.

News photographers, it should be understood, deeply resent the restrictions courts place upon them. They feel they have a right to photograph and record whatever the public is allowed to see—in or out of the courtroom. And news photographers were delighted with Judge Haggerty—even though his actions astounded some newsmen.

During the fourteen days of jury selection, the judge had not allowed pictures to be taken of the jurors. But on February 5, an hour after the final member of the panel was chosen, Haggerty appeared at the Rowntowner Motor Inn and presided over a remarkable ceremony at which the jurors were photographed dressed in suits and ties, seated in chairs placed against a backdrop of palms and ferns around the motel swimming pool. The judge darted here and there giving instructions about how the picture-making of his jury should proceed.

He shouted to the jurors: "No one talks to newsmen. I want that understood." A few seconds after that the judge said, "Fire away," and the photographers did. The jurors strolled around the pool for "action shots," then went to lunch.

While he had the newsmen assembled, he took advantage of their presence to make a few small personal points. He had turned down invitations to four Mardi Gras balls, he said. He explained it was all for the good of his court.

"I couldn't be out until 4 or 5 in the morning and then come into court all bright-eyed and bushy-tailed," he said. That quotation and his arrest at a "stag party" some months later give some insight into the personality of the man who presided over the assassination trial against Clay Shaw. As Frank Ritter was to say later: "He is a nice enough fellow—but you wouldn't want him to try your sister."

When the lawyers went at each other in adversary dispute, Haggerty would bristle. At one point he said, "Gentlemen, don't

scream. You'll have me screaming." At times he did. It was a trial
where tensions were high. The lawyers didn't stop screaming—
and occasionally Haggerty would get into yelling matches with
them. With his gavel he always won and so he was at least consistent—and successful—in shouting down opposing counsel. He
was not consistent in many other areas of trial decision. At one
point he arbitrarily excused a prospective juror who had five
small children. "The Mardi Gras parade is coming up and I'm sure
your children will want to see it. I don't think your wife can handle
all those children by herself." How thoughtful. But what if a prospective juror with three children—or without children—wanted to
see the parade?

He excluded from the jury a bank executive who said he had
great confidence in the Warren Report. This meant that this juror
might disagree with Garrison. But he refused to let the defense
ask prospective jurors whether they believed (with Garrison) that
Kennedy died as a result of a conspiracy.

The venireman who said he believed in the Warren Report
was Walter J. Manning, an executive of New Orleans Federal
Reserve Bank. "I have great faith in it," Manning said of the
Commission findings.

"We are not trying the Warren report," the judge responded.
This, as it turned out, was not true. The prosecution proceeded
to try the Warren Report. The other side was forced to defend
many of its conclusions. There were days on end when Clay
Shaw's name was not mentioned as the prosecution sought to attack the Warren Commission findings.

But still Haggerty ruled he could not tell the state how to proceed. When the jurors were chosen, the judge told newsmen:
"I'm glad that game of mental chess is over, the state and defense have been picking these jurors' brains and it finally got so
they were asking if anyone knew cousins of the cousins of the
policemen."

By some standards Judge Haggerty's rules with regard to
courtroom decorum would have been found shocking. For example, he allowed the principals in the case to smoke during trial
and at one point, Russo, the key state witness, sipped from a soft
drink can during his testimony. No doubt this was designed to
make those involved in the trial feel as comfortable as possible.
In a sense, it may have helped. Shaw chain-smoked throughout

the case and no doubt the soft drink gave Russo a feeling of comfort on the stand.

Whether these procedures should be interpreted as running contrary to the Canons of Judicial Ethics—"proceedings in court should be conducted with fitting dignity and decorum"—may be an open question. Many judges would condemn them.

Judge Haggerty, a demonstrative extrovert, was given to colorful—"bright-eyed and bushy-tailed"—statements on and off the bench.

Another incident indicating his concern about his press image came when the judge turned down Dymond's defense motion for a directed verdict of not guilty after all the state's evidence was in. He then recessed court so, he said, reporters could file their stories on his decision—which with all deference to Haggerty was less than earth-shaking. Many out-of-town news reporters had never heard of a judicial officer who went to such lengths to make sure his ruling made the early editions.

If there was ever a moment when Judge Haggerty forfeited his opportunity to move decisively against Garrison's procedures it was at that moment when Dymond asked the judge for a second time to direct a verdict clearing Shaw, rather than have the matter go to the jury.

The judge had heard some of the most outlandish testimony ever presented by a district attorney in a court of law.

There had been Russo, the hypnotized, "truth drugged" witness, confused, contradicting himself, stumbling through answers, weak and subject to disbelief. There had been Bundy, the drug addict who confirmed from the witness stand that he stole to support a dope addiction and whose identification of Shaw and Oswald together supposedly came at the moment when he was preparing to take a shot of heroin. There had been Spiesel, the disturbed man from New York who thought people had been hypnotizing him against his will.

But rather than hold in check or rule out much of this sort of testimony, most of which was shown either on cross-examination or by other evidence to be pure concoction and invention, Haggerty actually at times gave credence to it.

In a circus-like display, perhaps in the spirit of the Mardi Gras carnival time, he took the court and the jury, albeit on Dymond's motion, on a search of the French quarter to try to find a house where Spiesel claimed he had gone to a party with Shaw and David Ferrie.

Spiesel, the judge, the jury, newsmen and spectators flocked to the French quarter while Spiesel tried to find the house where he maintained he saw Ferrie and Shaw together. The search stopped traffic, drew spectators from all over the neighborhood, attracted children on bikes followed by yapping dogs. A frozen-ice vendor hawked his wares. A television cameraman came near blows with another newsman as they shoved for pictures during the "court on the street corner" session.

The entire affair was a parody of a trial and after it was over Spiesel said only that one of the buildings he viewed during his trip was similar to the one where he contended Shaw and Ferrie had been together.

Spiesel was a surprise witness for the prosecution. The defense was caught with a need to find out overnight as much as possible about the man. The defense lawyers contacted sources in New York who discovered that Spiesel was a man who apparently had hallucinations. He thought he was being tortured by various people who disguised themselves as friends and relatives and caused him to suffer "hypnotic illusions." Business competitors, he said, kept turning the lights in his office on and off at inopportune moments. The whole thing had kept him from having "normal sexual relations." Because of all this, he had brought a suit of sixteen million dollars against his enemies, he told Dymond. It was for this sort of witness that Judge Haggerty took his court on a wild goose chase into the French quarter.

There was a moment when the prosecution's tactics finally seemed to wear thin on Judge Haggerty. It came when a policeman, Aloysius J. Habighorst, testified that Shaw, while being booked on the charge of assassination conspiracy, claimed that Shaw used the alias Clay Bertrand.

From the bench, with the jury absent, Haggerty said flatly he didn't believe Habighorst and wasn't going to let him tell his tale to the jury.

"The world can hear it," he said, his voice high-pitched. "I do not believe Officer Habighorst."

But how he could doubt Habighorst and exclude his testimony which was, in fact, weak on its face—and then allow flimsy testimony such as that of Russo, Bundy and Spiesel, is one of the great unanswered questions of the Shaw trial.

The judge seemed to have his greatest difficulty in trying to control the exchanges between the opposing lawyers. Dymond, a forceful, articulate man, was aggressive in his defense of Shaw and challenged the prosecution at every step. Alcock, Garrison's chief assistant, who had to carry the burden of the case when the district attorney "went underground" during the trial, is also a powerful and strong-willed professional prosecutor who did not give an inch.

When Assistant District Attorney Andrew Sciambra was called as a state witness to tell about a memorandum he made on a statement he took from Russo—which he admitted had twenty-six errors and omissions in it—Judge Haggerty was sorely pressed to keep events under control.

Dymond cross-examined Sciambra and the two men were at odds during much of the testimony. Dymond yelled at Haggerty, demanding that Sciambra not give his personal opinions about errors in his memo.

The judge admonished Sciambra. "I agree he should not give his opinion," Haggerty said.

Sciambra, as the record of the trial shows, disregarded these admonitions frequently and injected his opinion about the errors, speaking rapidly and at times in an excited fashion. He talked, for example, about whether he thought certain errors in the Russo memo were important. Each time the defense would challenge an opinion by Sciambra the judge would renew his direction that Sciambra not give his opinion. But a few seconds later, Sciambra would give another interpretation which would elicit another defense objection and another admonition from the judge. At one point when Sciambra was trying to give an answer about install-ing bugging devices in Russo's house, the judge interrupted him twice to halt his statement as improper.

Looking harassed at one moment when the lawyers were railing at each other, the judge explained for the jury: "What is going on here is a lot of legal mumbo jumbo."

Again later in the trial, while the attorneys were raging over whether the Zapruder film of the assassination should be shown the jury, Haggerty yelled: "Wait a minute. Shut up this scream-ing."

Most of the "screaming" by the defense lawyers came during the repeated showings of the Zapruder assassination film which, amazingly, Judge Haggerty allowed to be presented in court eleven times, nine times to the jury. What bearing that film had on any other evidence Jim Garrison dredged up against Shaw is difficult to explain. But this fifty-five-year-old judicial officer with thirteen years on the bench apparently had an idea that the film of Kennedy being slain was relevant to the case against Shaw.

It is no wonder that Dymond was vociferous and loud as he tried to keep the jury from seeing the Zapruder film. He could catch Russo in contradictions—and did. He could cross-examine Spiesel and bring to light his unbalanced personality; he could show that Vernon Bundy was a drug addict; that the signature on the airport register, "Clay Bertrand" was not, according to a handwriting expert's testimony, the handwriting of Clay Shaw.

Through witnesses he would call, Dymond could further tear at the telling weaknesses in Garrison's case. But the defense lawyer knew Shaw was charged with the crime of plotting to murder the President. That charge was in the minds of the jurors. There was simply no way to tell what prejudices or hatreds viewing the bloody, vivid, color film of the brutal death of the President might conjure up in the thinking of the jurors.

And so Dymond bellowed and pleaded with Haggerty not to permit the film to be shown—not once, certainly not nine times to the jury. But Judge Haggerty was adamant. The possibility that the film might create an aura around Shaw in the minds of the jurors, simply because the film was so graphic and terrible, never seemed to occur to Haggerty.

"They can show it a hundred times if they want to," he told Dymond in one exchange.

That statement by a judge in a criminal court says more about what made the Shaw trial a disgrace than any other single event. That a district attorney would try to show the film in this case is disturbing. That the judge would allow it to be shown even once, is a blight on the system of justice.

After the film had been shown the first time, the judge himself volunteered: "If it is requested by the jury, we will show the film again." At one point during one showing, the film was stopped at the most frightening second—the moment the bullet

struck. The indescribably horrible scene was frozen on the
screen.

The state, at times, seemed to be trying to find unique reasons to show the film over. A state witness, Mrs. Mary Moorman,
had taken a picture of the President's car as it passed her in
Dealey Plaza. Another picture taken by someone else showing
where Mrs. Moorman was standing already was in evidence in
the trial.

But the prosecution announced it wanted to re-run the film—
this was the eighth time it had been shown the jury—so that Mrs.
Moorman's location might be ascertained.

"Your Honor," said Dymond, "it's already been shown where
Mrs. Moorman stood. We can see her in this photograph. There
is no reason to run the film again to find that out." But it was run
again—this time some news reporters refusing to look at it.

And while the film was shown again, and again, and again,
the courtroom decorum—what there was of it—evaporated as
witnesses jostled for position, scraped chairs, stood on benches,
whispered "down in front," shushed each other and murmured
"Oh God" aloud for the jury to hear when, on film, the bullets
struck Kennedy.

Frank Ritter, a reporter who has spent his time on the police
beat, covered the ghetto riots, and who has seen his share of
violence, said of the film: "It is the most shocking thing I've witnessed in my life."

An aware, concerned bar should have censured Judge
Haggerty for allowing that movie to be repeatedly shown to a
jury in a case in which a man faced twenty years in prison. His
theory, apparently, was that he could not control the state if it
wanted to over-prove its case. And at least part of that statement
is true: Judge Haggerty could not—or at least would not—control
Jim Garrison's case.

* * * *

3. *The power and responsibility of the district attorney.* It is
difficult to place sufficient blame on Garrison for the debacle at
New Orleans—at the expense of Clay Shaw and the taxpayers
of Louisiana who finance the functions of the courts. Much
already has been said in these pages concerning Garrison's outrageous conduct *prior* to the trial. But the more damning indictment of his deportment is to be found in an examination of what

happened *during* the trial. In truth, he seldom appeared in court. He had broadcast and publicized his claim about the case far and wide prior to the trial. He had been accessible to media representatives prior to the trial.

Now he was elusive. He was not available to reporters. He was hard to find. It is estimated that Clay Shaw saw more of Jim Garrison in the district attorney's office during an interrogation in the hours before Shaw had been charged—almost two years before—than the defendant saw of his prosecutor in court during the six weeks of trial.

The man who had basked in the limelight of publicity now sought the shadows. Why the strange turn-about? Did he realize his case was so sick that it would be rejected? Did he feel that his rare appearances gave more impact to his presence in court as a superstar? Did he fear to hear that many of the weaknesses in the testimony of his witnesses would be so apparent that the prosecution would prefer not to be associated with them? It is impossible to say what motivated Jim Garrison. But whatever it was, it took a jury only forty-seven minutes to reject the arguments Garrison had been making over a two-year period and to clear Clay Shaw of a willful, spiteful prosecution that had no foundation in fact.

When Garrison showed up in court he was not unimpressive. His words were as dramatic as they had been on television, and in *Playboy* magazine. The thrust of his argument was the same: "With David Ferrie now dead and Lee Oswald now dead the state is bringing to trial Mr. Shaw for his role as revealed by the evidence, in participating in the conspiracy to murder John F. Kennedy."

He expounded on his theory that the President had been the victim of a crossfire.

"Furthermore, the state will show that President Kennedy himself was struck by a number of bullets coming from different locations—thus showing that more than one person was shooting at the President. The evidence will show he was struck in the front as well as in the back and that the final shot came from in front of him knocking him backwards in his car."

This was what Garrison said he was going to prove. When the time came to put on the proof to back up his argument to the jury, he ducked out of court and left that job to his assistants.

Still he cannot escape responsibility for the quality of the evidence or the credibility of the witnesses his office summoned to testify. People like Russo, Spiesel and Bundy testified because Garrison wanted to put their testimony on for the jury. There is an axiom of law which provides that the lawyer who puts on the witness and places him under oath vouches for the credibility of the witness. Here are some examples of the testimony Garrison was vouching for: Spiesel testified that he had brought suit for sixteen million dollars against the Pinkerton detective agency, a psychiatrist and various other individuals charging some of the most bizarre allegations in the history of American courts.

He claimed those he sued used "a new police technique" to torture him; that people had disguised themselves as his "friends and relatives" and then passed him quickly on the street; that competitors conspired to ruin his business by tapping his telephone and harassing his customers; that they had stationed someone beside his fuse box to turn out the lights at inopportune moments; that against his will he had been hypnotized by various persons during a period from 1948 to 1964 causing him to have "hypnotic illusions"; that he was prevented by his enemies from having "normal sexual relations." Was this a reliable witness about anything?

The New York accountant, nervous and uncomfortable under a blistering cross-examination by defense lawyer Dymond, seemed near collapse at times late in his testimony.

This was the sort of witness Garrison was asking a jury to believe to send Clay Shaw to prison.

Then there was the testimony of the convicted thief and drug addict, Vernon Bundy, who swore that one day he was out at Lake Pontchartrain and was about to give himself a shot of heroin when he saw a man he swore was Shaw get out of a car and give something that looked like money to a man whose picture he had identified as Oswald. As the man he claimed was Oswald put what he said looked like money in his pocket some leaflets fell out of his pocket.

So, Bundy testified, he proceeded to give himself a shot of heroin and then he was looking for something to wrap his "fix equipment in" and he picked up one of the leaflets. Lo and behold, it had "Help Cuba" or "Free Cuba" or something like that written on it.

He had been a drug addict since he was thirteen years old, he admitted. He denied the statements made by two fellow-inmates that he was lying about what he saw in order to win favors from Garrison.

He was a thief, he admitted on cross-examination: "If I saw something laying around with nobody nearby I picked it up. Sure. To support my habit."

Garrison produced this derelict who admitted under oath that he would steal in order to get dope. If he would steal for dope would he lie in the hope that Garrison would help in his troubles with the law? He said he would not. But even so, could not Garrison, a man whose office was supposed to be committed to finding the truth, see at least as much about the case as lawyers for the defense? Why put on such testimony as this? By the time Dymond finished with his cross questioning of Bundy, the impact of the tale he told about his lakefront sightings had deteriorated.

There was Russo, the state's "star" witness. He maintained he saw Shaw, Ferrie and Oswald having a conversation at a party in Ferrie's apartment. There, he claimed, there was a conversation about "killing the President." That was back in September, 1963, he testified.

This dark-haired, attractive young man sounded plausible, perhaps. But when he was out from under the protective umbrella of the prosecutor's questions his story seemed to fall part. Dymond bore in on the cross-examinations. Russo had heard the conversation in September, 1963—two months before Kennedy was slain. But later, when the district attorney's office talked to Russo about what he knew, he neglected to tell what Oswald said, or at least it didn't show up in a prosecution report of the interview with Russo. He didn't claim he overheard such a conversation about a plot until after the death of David Ferrie, the man he contended talked about killing Kennedy.

Q. "Did this conversation not have every characteristic of a bull session?"

A. "Every characteristic of it."

He testified that after he finally told the story of the conversation, the district attorney gave him "truth serum" and had him hypnotized to help him remember what was said.

Russo, during his cross-examination, acknowledged that he had made these statements to various people:

The Garrison probe was "the most blown up and confused thing I've ever seen."

He "did not know the difference between fantasy and reality."

He wished he "had not gotten involved in this mess."

If Garrison knew what Russo had told the priest about the testimony Russo gave at a preliminary hearing the district attorney "would go through the ceiling."

The conversation he said occurred sounded as if the men "were shooting the breeze."

The alleged conspiratorial conversation did not sound like a legitimate plot, was "vague" in his mind and he could not "truthfully say who said what."

He would have liked to have had a conversation with Shaw to resolve doubts as to whether Shaw was the man he heard talking with Ferrie and Oswald.

He was not sure whether the conversation was about killing Castro or President Kennedy.

Dymond did an excellent job of bringing to the jury the true nature of the man who was testifying against Shaw. Russo was confused, caught in contradictions that made him appear a dishonest witness.

Q. "Didn't you tell (Layton) Martens that you weren't sure they were plotting against Castro or Kennedy?"

A. "A qualified yes. Very qualified."

Q. "Would you answer the question and then you can explain."

A. "Well, okay. I'll say yes and no afterwards. It all depends.

Ferrie talked about Castro too. He liked Castro but he liked Guevara better."

Again Dymond asked him if he made a certain statement.

"I don't know. Maybe. That's hard to say. Perhaps."

He was asked if the person he identified as Oswald—he testified the man had a beard—had any white spots on his beard. "Maybe. I don't think so. There were spots of white."

At least twice, on cross-examination, he became agitated and raced through answers that were jumbled and hard to understand, and the court stenographer had to ask him to slow down.

Finally he was asked: "Did Clay Shaw ever agree to kill the President?"

"No, sir."

Why then had Garrison brought this case and made this man his key witness? Russo's responses were often incredible. But Garrison wanted the jury to believe him.

In discussing David Ferrie on the witness stand Russo described him as "a little crazy" or "screwy" and as "a paradox." Before he left the witness stand many who heard his testimony felt the same way about Russo and some were wondering about Jim Garrison who had based much of his case on what Russo had to say.

Why would Garrison produce Russo or Bundy or Spiesel? Why subpoena FBI agent, Frazier, then not put him on the witness stand as a prosecution witness? Why put FBI agent Shaneyfelt on the witness stand but not ask him the question about his expert opinion on the direction from which the bullets were fired? Why would Garrison not call Governor Connally, who was in the car with Kennedy, after issuing a subpoena for the governor? Why would he not call Doctor Finck, the army physician who was one of those who performed the autopsy on the President?

Finally, why would the district attorney insist on showing to the jury, again and again and again, a film which depicted horrible scenes of bloody murder, when the movie told the jury nothing about the guilt or innocence of the defendant Clay Shaw?

Here was a prosecutor who had stated prior to the trial that various officials of the United States government had worked to destroy evidence and conceal truth; that Oswald was a CIA employee who had tipped off the FBI five days before the assassination; that there were fourteen persons involved in the assassination "plot"; that there were, among others, "a precision team including seven anti-Castro adventurers and members of the para-military right"; that Kennedy was caught in a crossfire; that the CIA, the FBI and the Warren Commission kept facts from the public; that President Lyndon Johnson was "the man who gained the most from the assassination."

These absurd statements, the last a vile slander, were Garrison's buildup to the case against Clay Shaw. In the end Garrison produced as "star witnesses" a confessed liar, a thief, a drug addict, and a psychiatric case.

And when his "evidence" was all given Garrison made a formal statement to the jury in which he only once mentioned the name of Clay Shaw—the man who was on trial facing prison for twenty years.

It was all of this that made the trial of Clay Shaw a search for a lie.

*   *   *   *

For different reasons and in different ways the "trial" of James Earl Ray in Memphis left its own indelible marks on the countenance of justice. In reviewing what occurred in that case there are at least four specific points to be recorded against the manner in which the system of justice functioned.

1. *The court ignored the momentous national concern that resided in the unasked question—who, if anyone, conspired with James Earl Ray?*

This case had been a heavy burden on Judge Battle. His contempt rulings had brought down on his head the ire of his hometown press. He had been constantly needled by Arthur Hanes throughout that lawyer's involvement in the case. William Bradford Huie had bothered him with the notice of intent to publish Ray's "story." Battle had granted a continuance in the case at the "last minute," which caused him even greater mental anguish for additional months. He felt heavy pressures at work upon him; he was to live only a short time after the case was disposed of in his court.

Obviously Preston Battle wanted a simple answer to the case. Foreman's decision to plead Ray guilty and the lawyer's ability to get Ray to agree provided Judge Battle his simple conclusion. A guilty plea would help wash away, Judge Battle thought, the idea that Ray had an accomplice in the killing.

So he thought. But then Ray stood up in court and contested the stipulation by his lawyer and the district attorney who agreed there was no conspiracy. Everybody in the courtroom, but particularly Judge Battle, knew what Ray was contending: there was indeed a conspiracy. There will always be a question as to why Judge Battle did not pursue the matter after Ray's pathetic little peroration. The man had admitted his own guilt and therefore could not have claimed self-incrimination had the judge questioned him at that point on what he meant. At the very least it would have seemed to have made sense for the judge to have directed the district attorney to call Ray immediately after the "trial" before a grand jury to answer questions about what, if any, conspiracy he participated in.

At varying times various sources had supported the conspiracy theory. Initially the federal warrant against Ray charged a conspiracy with a man thought to be his brother; William Bradford Huie believed there was a conspiracy up until about the time Ray changed lawyers; Arthur Hanes believed it even when he was discharged; Percy Foreman said at one point he was proceeding on the theory that someone other than Ray was involved in the killing. He later said it took him fifty long hours to convince himself otherwise. Factors caused many others to believe in a conspiracy long after the case was closed by the FBI. There was the mysterious short-wave radio broadcast immediately after King was shot; there was the statement by Solomon Jones, who saw a hooded man flee the death scene; there was the statement by James Bevel that he knew Ray was a dupe; there were questions about how Ray acquired funds to travel across the country and abroad in his flight. Still Judge Battle would not delve into the matter and dodged the chance to do so with the surmise from the bench that if there were indeed co-conspirators they would not sleep well at night because in Tennessee the statute of limitations never expires in a murder case.

If there were conspirators, it is doubtful they missed much sleep.

There are lawyers who would argue that Battle had no responsibility to concern himself with a question of public policy; that there is no obligation on the courts to deal with matters that are of public concern which go beyond the immediate scope of the litigation directly pending before the court.

It is difficult to maintain that position in this case since Ray was saying in effect *to the judge* that he was guilty, but perhaps somebody was guilty with him. That is where the public policy question is pertinent. Since the court is considered an arm of the law enforcement establishment in this country it would seem incumbent upon the judge to seek to determine whether there was additional evidence available or whether the defendant was trying the court's patience. Ray was one of the few principals in this case who escaped a contempt citation and had he refused to answer Battle after pleading guilty, the judge might have cited him.

2. *The "eleventh hour" change of attorneys from Arthur Hanes to Percy Foreman, without good cause shown on Ray's part, projects the image that criminals are able to use the built-in legal machinery of the system as devices to delay and confound, if not subvert, justice.*

The decision to allow a defendant to change his attorney is purely within the discretion of the judge, in most states of the nation. So it is in Tennessee. Judge Battle allowed it in this case on what seemed to be highly superficial grounds. Ray wrote Hanes a letter saying simply that they had some disagreements. Judge Battle didn't ask what those disagreements were, how they came up, who was in the right or who was damaged. Newsmen learned later that there were two basic disagreements: first, Ray wanted to testify in his own defense; Hanes did not want him to for fear his prior criminal record and the ragged details of what he had done since escaping prison would adversely affect the jury. Second, Ray wanted the case continued; Hanes didn't feel there was any legitimate reason for asking Judge Battle to postpone the case. But in allowing a change in attorneys Battle gave to the defendant what Hanes refused to ask for: a delay.

It might be suggested that Ray was inconsistent in wanting a continuance in his trial while complaining about "torturous treatment" imposed upon him by the cell arrangements where he was confined. But the criminal mind is, if anything, inconsistent in seeking to defeat the aims of justice. And as unpleasant as Hanes contended the cell was for Ray, it was preferable to the antiseptic, maximum security cubicle into which Ray was thrust when he finally arrived at Tennessee State Penitentiary in Nashville. Ray, a professional criminal, wanted a continuance. He got one by employing a new attorney, unprepared for immediate trial. Did Percy Foreman make James Earl Ray a better lawyer than Arthur Hanes? It is impossible to tell. It is an anomaly that Foreman, like Hanes, didn't put Ray on the witness stand in his own defense. Once behind prison bars Ray fired Foreman, as he had discharged Hanes from a jail cell, by letter. He accused Foreman of getting him to plead guilty so Ray would not be able to testify. Ray's contention was that if he had testified it would have spoiled the story Huie was writing for publication in book form, because if he had related events from the witness stand the story would have been in the public domain for every newspaper to publish. Foreman had joined forces with Huie against him, Ray complained. So from the defendant's point of view he was, in retrospect, no more satisfied with Foreman than he had been with Hanes.

In the end, Percy Foreman was to charge $150,000 plus $15,000 in expenses for getting James Earl Ray a life sentence in return for a guilty plea. There is the strong suspicion that Hanes could have done the same thing. And there is the certain knowledge that the public defender, Hugh Stanton—brought into the case when Foreman had Judge Battle declare Ray an impoverished indigent—could have negotiated the same plea, and cheaper. But Judge Battle was not concerned with probing beneath the surface of any questions that confronted him. As he was not interested in asking Ray who conspired with him, or having the district attorney do so, neither was he interested in probing to discover whether Ray and Hanes really had meaningful disagreements. Finally, he did not inquire about Ray's "indigency." Perhaps he feared he might break some legal precedent. Perhaps he simply wanted the case closed. Judge Battle did not mind breaking precedent when it came to handing out contempt citations.

Following the murder of Dr. King some members of the press described Memphis as "a decadent river town." Judge Battle resented this disparagement of his community and after the guilty plea was disposed of he took great pride in a Churchillian declamation from the bench: "Some river; some town," he snorted.

In consideration of the fact that this judge declared a pauper of a man who was able to pay his lawyer $150,000 as a fee, plus $15,000 in expenses, it seems fair to again paraphrase Churchill: some pauper; some judge.

* * * *

3. *The money* Look *magazine and a book publisher made available to Ray for agreeing to "tell his story" through William Bradford Huie threatened the credibility of the system of justice.* How can any defendant with access to more than $150,000 to pay his lawyer be declared indigent by a court of law? Foreman said he spent fifty hours convincing himself that Ray was not involved in a conspiracy. That means he charged $3,000 an hour—if that is all the time he spent on the case. At any rate, $150,000 is a high price for any lawyer to charge to plead a client guilty. Percy Foreman is a superior criminal attorney. But why should a court allow Foreman to charge that sort of fee for the work he did? Perhaps an argument can be made that what Foreman charged Ray was none of Battle's business. That is a lawyer's argument.

When Foreman asked that Ray be declared an indigent he made his fee a matter of court concern.

Ray was quite an indigent. Hanes insisted that he be paid $13,000 in expense money before he turned over to Foreman his files on the case. Finally, the defense investigator Hays filed suit against Ray to get $6,000 he insisted as due him. And Foreman indicated that his fee would have been $400,000 instead of $150,000 if the case had gone to trial.

William Bradford Huie was later to write in his book, *He Slew the Dreamer,* that "every effort I made to pay Ray was defeated." Huie said that by the time Ray pleaded guilty he had advanced $40,000 all of which Ray had signed over to Hanes and Foreman.

Huie recounted that during his first conversation with Foreman, after the change in lawyers, Foreman told him: "Now you know, of course, that I'm depending on you for my fee. So tote that bale, boy! Get to work!"

Huie's view of Ray's guilt or innocence seemed to change as Ray's selection of attorneys changed.

Hanes thought in the beginning that Ray was part of a conspiracy—an innocent dupe in a plot. Huie believed that when Hanes represented Ray and took the inmate's notes to Huie. The writer checked them out and said he was sure a conspiracy had occurred. Thus he planned to entitle his book *They Slew the Dreamer.* "They" referred to Ray and his conspirators. But by the time Foreman took over and finally pursued a different course on the theory that no conspiracy occurred, and Huie began to work with Foreman, the writer had changed his mind about the plot. Foreman may have helped convince Huie that his initial research was wrong; that the story Ray had funneled through Hanes was false. Huie, in his book, claimed he changed Foreman's mind. At any rate Huie substantially altered the final version of the third *Look* article and his book *They Slew the Dreamer* became *He Slew the Dreamer.* Ray was no longer presented to the world through Huie's eyes as a dupe in a plot, but as the sole figure in a heinous racial murder.

It is tragic that the money from publishing "the Ray story" became such a preoccupation in the case. The newspapers told their story daily, offering no inducements to Ray, his lawyers or to witnesses. A magazine following the same procedure would not have created problems. But *Look,* through Huie, bought exclusively of Ray's story. It is interesting to speculate on what would have happened if Hanes had not been fired. Would the original "Ray story" have been published as *They Slew the Dreamer?* Would the magazine have paid for a lie? Did it?

At any rate, the tale the magazine bought at the outset was not the tale it subsequently published and the story Huie checked out while Hanes was Ray's attorney was not the story he wrote when Foreman became lawyer. As Jim Squires commented: "Percy Foreman is a hell of a lawyer. He changed the minds of James Earl Ray and William Bradford Huie—and that did more to expedite the case than if he had changed the mind of judge and jury."

No one can say whether the "true" story was what Huie accepted first, or what he finally wrote—or whether the real truth lies somewhere in between.

In *He Slew the Dreamer,* Huie candidly admits he did a complete turnaround on the conspiracy theory. He also openly acknowledges he published some information Ray gave him, although he knew it to be false. In the first two *Look* articles he published information he knew to be incorrect, which concerned Ray's activities in lesser crimes prior to King's murder. He did this in order to gain Ray's confidence so he (Huie) could get at the "truth" about the slaying, he said.

As it became obvious that Ray's story was valuable property there were others who wanted to try to get it. Tennessee's Commissioner of Corrections, Harry Avery, interviewed Ray once he was behind prison bars and word leaked out that Avery was out to write a book telling the "true" story of James Earl Ray. Thereupon Governor Ellington initiated an investigation into Avery's interviews and subsequently the commissioner was fired.

And there were others who would have paid for an interview with Ray—for publication or broadcast. How does all of this affect the administration of justice? It made Huie more than just another journalist. As the source of Ray's money he became a bankroll for lawyers of the man who admitted he murdered Martin Luther King. The fear remains that money for "a story" tainted decision-making in the Ray case.

*   *   *   *

4. *The contempt actions against the newspaper reporters, a defense lawyer, an investigator for the defense, an FBI agent, an associate of Dr. King and a magazine writer, constitute an unprecedented assault on the traditional concept of freedom of speech and the press. The subsequent failure of the judge to sentence those he had convicted of contempt so that they might immediately appeal his findings and perhaps reverse him, runs contrary to the basic fairness that is supposed to be inherent in the administration of justice in this country.*

What did all this amount to? Arthur Hanes didn't like the conditions under which his client was being held. He said so in court and the judge told him to put it in writing. Hanes had his investigator, Renfro Hays, conduct a study of the jail premises. The two men expressed outrage because the blinding flood lights which lit the cell around the clock made it necessary for Ray to hide his head under a pillow to sleep and the constant eyes of television cameras made it impossible for him even to go to the bathroom without being observed. When reporters asked Hanes and Hays about this they exploded with their protest against the jail conditions. This won each of them a contempt citation from Judge Battle, who didn't want the public to know how Ray was being held because, he said, he thought it might influence potential jurors.

Beyond that, the judge had named a committee of lawyers to advise him on contempt actions with regard to press coverage of the trial. Previously, he had refused to take his committee's advice several times. But when the Memphis newspapers carried the stories quoting Hanes and Hays by Charles Edmundson of the *Commercial Appeal* and Roy Hamilton of the *Press-Scimitar,* Battle moved against the reporters and their sources, lawyer and investigator.

Perhaps the judge thought he was acting with approval of the United States Supreme Court which had castigated the Cleveland news media—particularly the Cleveland *Press,* a newspaper—for its pre-trial coverage of the Sam Sheppard murder case.

But in the Sheppard case the court steered away from recommending contempt against newsmen. The court said in the Sheppard case: "Of course, there is nothing that proscribed the press from reporting events that transpire in the courtroom. But where there is a reasonable likelihood that prejudicial news prior to trial will prevent a fair trail, the judge should continue the case until the threat abates, or transfer it to another county not so permeated with publicity."

Again the court said: "If publicity during the proceedings threatens the fairness of the trial a new trial should be ordered. But we must remember that reversals are but palliatives . . ."

The court went on to say: "The (trial) court's fundamental error is compounded by the holding that it lacked power to control the publicity about the trial. From the very inception of the proceedings the judge announced that neither he nor anyone else could restrict prejudicial news accounts. And he reiterated this view on numerous occasions. Since he viewed the news media as his target, the judge never considered other means that are often utilized to reduce the appearance of prejudicial material and to protect the jury from outside influence. We conclude that these procedures would have been sufficient to guarantee Sheppard a fair trial and *we do not consider what sanctions might be available against a recalcitrant press* [4] nor the charges of bias

---

4. Author's italics.

now made against the state trial judge." The Sheppard ruling, then, steered clear of the "sanction" of contempt.

The reason the Supreme Court thought the trial judge should have continued the Sheppard case, or transferred it to another jurisdiction, was not because the press outside Cleveland published and broadcast *any* news at all about the pending case. That news was disseminated all over Ohio—indeed all over the nation. But the court cited eight specific instances of news in Cleveland which it felt was prejudicial to Sheppard. The Supreme Court felt, for example, that one newspaper, the *Press*, was actually calling for Sheppard's conviction.

But with all of that, the Supreme Court still did not authorize or urge the drastic action of contempt which Judge Battle applied so indiscriminately in Memphis.

The Memphis press was not calling for Ray's conviction. It was merely reporting on a valid criticism of the sheriff, an arm of Judge Battle's court, because of the manner in which a prisoner was held in custody. Actually, the articles did not even criticize Battle, who had approved the method of custodial treatment.

There is a dangerous component in contempt action because it gives to the judge the power to stifle criticism. Suppose the trial judge in a given case was bribed not to proceed against an alleged lawbreaker. Suppose the newspaper in the area is critical of the judge's failure to act. In such a case the judge could and no doubt would exercise the contempt power to cut off criticism of himself.

In a series of cases the Supreme Court commented on the contempt power against newspapers, prior to Sheppard. For instance, in 1941 the court considered two cases at the same time— both involving contempt actions against those exercising the right of free speech and a free press. Judge Battle had found that the stories by the Memphis newsmen represented "a clear and present danger" to the administration of justice. In Bridges versus California and *Times-Mirror* versus Superior Court, Associate Justice Hugo Black wrote an opinion of the court which struck down contempt actions and set out some guidelines for the "clear and present danger" test. He said: "What finally emerges from the 'clear and present danger' cases is a working principle that the substantive evil must be extremely serious and the degree of imminence extremely high before utterances can be punished. These cases do not purport to mark the furthermost constitutional boundaries of protected expression, nor do we here. They do no more than recognize a minimum compulsion of the Bill of Rights. For the First Amendment does not speak equivocally. *It prohibits any law abridging the freedom of speech, or of the press. It must be taken as a command of the broadest scope that explicit language, read in the context of a liberty-loving society, will allow.*" [5]

Justice Black went on to discuss why the trial courts should not have imposed contempt citations.

"Since they punish utterances made during the pendency of a case, the judgments below therefore produce their restrictive results at the precise time when public interest in the matters discussed would naturally be at its height. Moreover, the pen is likely to fall not only at a crucial time but upon the most important topics of discussion. It is therefore the controversies that command most interest that the decision below would remove from the area of public discussion.

". . . The assumption that respect for the judiciary can be won by shielding judges from published criticism wrongly appraises the character of American public opinion. For it is a prized American privilege to speak one's mind, although not always with perfect good taste, on all public institutions. And an enforced silence, however limited, solely in the name of preserving the dignity of the bench, would probably engender resentment, suspicion, and contempt much more than it would enhance respect."

Again, there is the case of Pennekamp versus Florida (1946) in which the publisher and associate editor of the Miami *Herald* were cited for contempt because the newspaper accused a Florida court of being too lenient to criminals. In that case the U. S. Supreme Court said: "Courts must have power to protect the interests of prisoners and litigants before them from unseemly efforts to pervert judicial action. In the borderline instances where it is difficult to say upon which side the alleged offense falls, we think the specific freedom of public comment should weigh heavily against a possible tendency to influence pending cases.

---

5. Author's italics.

Freedom of discussion should be given the widest range compatible with the essential requirement of the fair and orderly administration of justice."

Then there was the case of Craig versus Harney (1946) in which a Texas newspaper, the Corpus Christi *Caller-Times* was cited for contempt because the newspaper failed to "report accurately" a threatened disturbance in the courtroom. In this case Justice William O. Douglas wrote the opinion of the court. He acknowledged that the articles in the *Caller-Times* "did not reflect good reporting . . . but it takes more imagination than we possess to find in this rather sketchy and one-sided report of a case any imminent or serious threat to a judge of reasonable fortitude."

Finally, in Wood versus Georgia, Chief Justice Earl Warren wrote for the court in 1962: "The purpose of the First Amendment included the need . . . to protect parties in the free publication of matters of public concern, to secure their right to a free discussion of public events and public measures and to enable every citizen at any time to bring the government and any person in authority to the bar of public opinion by any just criticism upon their conduct in the exercise of the authority which people conferred upon them."

If Preston Battle thought that the news stories were sufficiently damaging to endanger a fair trial it would have been a simple matter to move the case to Knoxville, Chattanooga, Nashville, or Oak Ridge.

In considering Judge Battle's actions historians will focus on whether the articles which discussed Ray's confinement actually represented a clear and present danger to the administration of justice. Because he would not sentence those found contemptible the U. S. Supreme Court had no chance to rule. The two reporters were making the public aware of how a certain prisoner was being held—not whether the prisoner was guilty or innocent.

At the time the Reardon Committee first made the suggestion that judges use the contempt power, Judge George C. Edwards of the U. S. Sixth Circuit Court of Appeals, decried the report and said that this was not what the Court of Appeals had in mind when it reversed the Sheppard conviction. He pointed out that such contempt power would give to judges the opportunity to silence lawyers and other critics of the court who felt the judicial officer was guilty of arbitrary, capricious or corrupt actions.

Some of the criticism which has been leveled at the press regarding free press and fair trial has been constructive. The press must learn that there are boundaries of reporting and editorial comment that it should not thoughtlessly violate in a given case. But when the press violates those boundaries it would be disastrous for the courts to view a contempt citation as the remedy.

What makes Judge Battle's contempt actions and his refusal to allow an appeal seem ludicrous is the fact that Ray pleaded guilty. Not a single juror was ever asked whether the articles in the Memphis press concerning Ray's incarceration would have affected his attitude in the case. Preston Battle was not a wicked man. In many ways he was a good judge. Lawyers who practiced before him attest to that. No doubt Foreman and Canale would pay him posthumous tributes. But, like so many other jurists, he was insecure and inadequate when confronted by the issues in the case of the State of Tennessee versus James Earl Ray. That is less a criticism of him than condemnation of the system of justice which has not reformed and demonstrates no inherent ability to do so.

*   *   *   *

In Los Angeles the crime charged was the same—political assassination. Again, when it was over there was little to commend the case as any sort of model for justice.

Incidents during the course of this trial sharply strained the fidelity of the system. Five unhappy conclusions can be drawn from this case:

*   *   *   *

1. *The testimony of the "expert witnesses" who spoke about Sirhan's mental problems was turned, by cross-examination, into a string of pitiful contradictions and ambiguities.*

There was no reason for this trial, except to examine Sirhan's mental capacity. His lawyers insisted his mental acuity was diminished. They contended that this entitled him to a sentence less than the supreme penalty. And so the testimony of the psychologists and psychiatrists, produced by both the state and the defense, was fundamental to what the trial was all about. It was, in point of fact, "the case."

There was no question about Sirhan killing Robert Kennedy. He did it. He was observed in the act. The only question was, "why"? The men who had examined his mind were to tell the jury their views about his motives.

Imagine then, the plight of twelve "average" laymen-jurors, many of them unsure about the gains and goals of psychiatry, uncertain even about its validity as a science. Suddenly they are flooded with a wave of testimony filled with professional jargon. Here was some of it: "Jekyll-Hyde personality . . . he finds a symbolic replica of his father in the form of Kennedy . . . so he did to his father, who was Kennedy, what he wanted to do to his father . . . neither side of his personality knows the other side exists . . . psychotic . . . hostile resentful feelings to the maternal figure . . . hate and fear for his father . . . angry demanding dependence on his mother . . . paranoia to a psychotic degree with a schizophrenic process . . . acute and chronic . . . a borderline psychotic . . . paranoid, blaming, suspicious, critical, vulnerable, confused, lacks stamina, unpredictable, scattered, obsessive, compulsive, suicidal, homicidal, has a weak ego, erratic, socially inadequate, anxious, a very ill person . . . descending mental illness . . . psychosis might be underneath . . . ."

This went on for days, by men who agreed that Sirhan was mentally disturbed, but who disagreed as to what degree he was mentally disturbed.

The mauling cross-examinations by the lawyers often made the doctors seem inadequate and unreliable. Also, Dr. Schorr's admission that he had "lifted" from the work of a psychiatrist several key passages which he adopted almost verbatim—but without crediting the source—into his own report on Sirhan, must have smelled of plagiarism to the jury.

A letter by Schorr, written scarcely a month after the assassination, indicated that before examining Sirhan, he had already made up his mind—largely on the basis of articles in *Life* magazine— that the defendant was suffering from a diminshed mental capacity. That letter Dr. Schorr wrote to the defense lawyers, exposed in court by the prosecution, offered his aid in the selection of a "properly attuned" jury. It must have made members of the jury wonder if they had been found "properly attuned," from the psychologist's point of view, before they were found acceptable to the defense.

In considering his testimony on cross-examination, Dr. Schorr comes through as a pathetic figure. But his appearance was only to set the stage for days of confusing statements by the sworn mental experts.

These lay jurors were expected by the defense to accept as valid the techniques of psychological testing of the experts, and then to find the conclusions of the testers sound. This was asking a good deal from jurors who may have never before been exposed to psychiatry or psychology. Some of the testing procedures no doubt impressed the jurors as highly unusual. For example, they were shown a series of slides by Dr. Schorr who demonstrated how he gave the "ink blot" test, known in medical circles as the Rorschach test. Schorr had shown Sirhan ten "standard" ink blots and asked the defendant to give his reactions to them. Sirhan was given blank cards and asked to visualize pictures on them. (He visualized "that arrogant self-assured bastard," Moshe Dayan). He was given blocks and asked to rearrange them to fit patterns. He was given photo strips and asked to put them in sequence. He was hypnotized to get him to talk about things he would not discuss under normal conditions. He was given an overdose of alcohol to see how he would react (he suddenly thought his police guards were Israeli soldiers), since the defense claimed he was drinking when he shot Senator Kennedy.

Some of this probably appeared to be more like a game to jurors than a method of establishing how much mental anguish afflicted Sirhan.

There were some contradictions that emerged as the string of psychiatrists appeared: Sirhan killed Kennedy because he saw the victim as his father, an Arab. But again, he killed Kennedy because he saw in him symbolic manifestations of Arthur Goldberg and Moshe Dayan, both Jews. Sirhan could have malice and could "premeditate" according to one of the expert witnesses, but not on a subject about which he was "obsessed" as he was about Kennedy. Some of the defense psychiatrists said Sirhan's "blackout" after the crime was real. One defense psychiatrist said Sirhan was probably malingering, faking mental illness, therefore, in effect lying, when he indicated immediately after his capture that he could not remember. Still later the same witness testified that when he said this he had not taken into account the severity of Sirhan's mental state. So perhaps he was not faking a memory lapse.

Another of the witnesses testified he believed Sirhan against all the witnesses who testified against him and who gave versions of events contrary to the accounts Sirhan gave of what happened. The experts said Sirhan had above average verbal intelligence, but below average performance intelligence. One of the experts found no brain damage from Sirhan's fall from a horse—but another said he traced the deterioration of Sirhan's mental ability to the time of that fall. One witness testified that Sirhan was not able to cope with the situation when arrested because of mental problems, then listened to tapes and seemed to backtrack on that position even as some jurors listening to the tapes must have concluded that Sirhan sounded as if he were relating to and parrying questions from the police. When Sirhan's lawyers had first argued early in the case that the defendant was mentally ill, the defendant had pounded the table and muttered vicious things about his counsel. But when the chief psychiatrist for the defense, Dr. Diamond, was subjected to a bruising cross-examination by prosecutors who were seeking to show Sirhan was not mentally ill, he again pounded the table and sputtered obscenities against the state's lawyers. Dr. Diamond, who may have had some difficulty getting across his points of mental health testimony, suddenly became a firearms expert (he called Sirhan's gun "a piece of junk . . . no one who knew anything about target shooting or assassinating, for that matter, would use such a gun") as well as an expert on psychiatry. But cross-examination made his testimony as a weapons authority sound as unsophisticated as his testimony as a mental expert seemed incredible to jurors.

There were witnesses on Sirhan's mentality who said they did not believe he would falsify psychiatric tests. There were others who believed he might. There was the chief state psychiatric witness, Dr. Pollack, who said he disagreed with the defense theory about Sirhan being schizophrenic, but agreed that he was paranoid. He insisted that the paranoia was not as serious as the defense thought it was. He saw Sirhan, not as a helpless mental cripple—as the defense attorneys insisted—but as a scheming political assassin. Dr. Pollack disagreed with the defense witnesses whose tests showed Sirhan was "psychotic." But when read a report by him that said Sirhan was psychotic, the doctor said the defendant was, indeed, psychotic. But then he explained that he was not "clinically" psychotic. His entire diagnosis might have been different had he spent more time with

Sirhan, he said. But the defense denied him access to Sirhan when he would not agree in advance of the trial with the defense psychiatrists on Sirhan's condition. He only had twenty-five hours with Sirhan, he said. Apart from the psychiatric testimony, several exotic theories were introduced. For example, it was said that Sirhan practiced "telekinesis"—a belief that mental concentration can influence physical matters; he practiced at "clyclomancy" which he said was "white magic"; he "played around with" thought transference. These were novel ideas to most jurors. Then there was Dr. Diamond describing his own testimony about Sirhan as "absurd, preposterous, highly unlikely, incredible." And finally there were the lawyers in their last arguments attacking the testimony from these experts on the subject of mental deficiency.

Grant Cooper, who headed the team of Sirhan's lawyers wound up stating that he "could have crawled under the table" at some of Dr. Schorr's testimony. He called the San Diego psychologist "the little man in the green suit" and described Schorr's "lifting" of sections of another man's book and putting it into his Sirhan report as "a terrible faux pas which I wish had never happened."

The prosecution was even more harsh with the mental health witnesses on final arguments. Fitts, the assistant district attorney, at one point said: "The psychiatric testimony in this case was, to some extent, not worthy of the respect I had anticipated."

And Compton, who closed the state's argument to the jury, was even more direct and emphatic: "The whole reason for their (the psychiatrists') discipline is finding something wrong with somebody." He described Dr. Diamond: "a walking lie detector, handwriting expert, gun expert . . . anybody who didn't agree with him was a liar."

Finally Compton called upon the jurors to disregard all the testimony from all the psychiatrists and psychologists who had appeared: "I say throw them all out in one big bag," he argued to the jury.

In its total perspective it is interesting that the views of the psychiatrists, who are highly paid professional men, were dismissed in such a cavalier fashion by the jurors. Even the state's psychiatrist didn't think Sirhan should die.

In reviewing the Sirhan trial a doubt arises about the image of men of science who probe the depths of men's minds. While there are exceptions which are dramatized by Dr. Schorr's "faux pas" in copying somebody else's words and offering them in a report under his name, there was overwhelming evidence that Sirhan suffered some mental defects. But so penetrating were the cross-examinations by opposing lawyers, intent upon destroying adverse evidence, that the psychiatrists and psychologists were made to seem asinine. Is it fair to the expert on such an imprecise subject as mental disturbance to subject him to the ridicule that must come to him and his profession in the sort of "search for truth" that is the common occurrence in an adversary criminal proceeding? Is it fair to expect that lay jurors will comprehend the import of such testimony? Must it be the nature of the "search for truth" that expert witnesses testify for the side that pays them? Can the court not do something to provide expert witnesses who would give some independent point of view, other than those views presented by experts paid by one side or the other? Dr. Marcus was a court-paid psychiatrist but he appeared as a witness, subpoenaed by the defense. This meant he was sharply cross-examined by a hostile district attorney, out to disprove his testimony which was damaging to the state's point of view. Dr. Pollack, who testified for the state, was deprived of an opportunity to make a thorough examination of Sirhan. He testified that defense psychiatrists prevented a more thorough examination by Pollack.

A fee of forty dollars an hour had been agreed upon for paying some of the psychiatrists for their work. Pollack, as an example, was paid $10,811 for his services in the trial. This fee was challenged after the trial by a Los Angeles county official, but it was approved after it was reviewed by district attorney Younger who said that the amount was modest and did not cover all the time Pollack spent on the case.

Something is desperately wrong with the administration of justice when ten psychiatrists and psychologists spend so much time and so much tax money presenting their views and the result is that the chief lawyer for the state concludes his argument to the jury by asking that all the expert testimony be thrown out as worthless.

*   *   *   *

2. *The rules for determining mental competence in the*

American criminal courtroom are obsolete, inconsistent, inconclusive and can result in injustice. Standards differ from state to state, leaving an accused guilty in some areas of the country for an act committed in a condition of mind that might be excused in other states. The McNaghton rule which is the standard by which the insanity test is applied in most states dates back to the 1840's when a man named Daniel McNaghton was tried in London for shooting to death Edward Drummond, the secretary to Sir Robert Peel. McNaghton's attorneys pleaded him not guilty by reason of insanity and argued that he was under a delusion that he was being persecuted by Sir Robert, who was then Prime Minister and who had earlier founded the British police force. The court found that McNaghton, because of his delusion, had no control over the act and he was acquitted, by reason of insanity.

The case created quite a stir. Queen Victoria, a few years earlier, had been the target of an assassination attempt by a deranged man and he, too, had been cleared on a defense of insanity.

After the verdict in the McNaghton case the Queen spoke out. She complained that the judges in the McNaghton case and in that of her own would-be killer had "instructed the jury to pronounce the verdict of not guilty on account of insanity whilst everybody is morally certain that both malefactors were perfectly conscious and aware of what they did."

There was an intense debate in the House of Lords, not to mention on the streets and in the pubs of London. A sort of "law and order" atmosphere prevailed. Finally the question of legal sanity was referred by the House of Lords to the fifteen judges of England who were asked to give legal answers to the questions raised by the "insanity" cases. In sum, the judges answered by proposing that in such cases the question for the jury is as follows: at the time of committing the criminal offense did the accused suffer from a defect of reason so that he did not know the quality of the act he was doing, or, if he did know it, did he realize that what he was doing was wrong? In effect, this established the "right or wrong" McNaghton rule which prevails in most jurisdictions in the United States today, more than a century later.

In the United States the rule, which either has been written into law or has become accepted court procedure by virtue of findings of appellate courts, is broadly accepted. However, its application differs from state to state. In California, for example, there is the "diminished capacity" theory which can mitigate an act. In Kentucky, and several other states, there is the "irresistible impulse" theory which holds that while a defendant recognized exactly what he was doing and knew it was wrong, still he was driven by an impulse he could not control to commit the crime. But this theory, like the basic McNaghton rule, dates back a century and a quarter. Tennessee has a law which provides for a method to decide the "present sanity" of a defendant. Upon a petition by the defendant or the district attorney, a pretrial hearing is held, at which time twelve jurors decide the mental competency of the defendant. This procedure is rarely invoked.

In Massachusetts, whenever the sanity of a person accused of crime is called into question, he can be sent to a mental hospital for thirty-five days for observation. During the thirty-five days, he must be examined by two physicians, one of whom should be a psychiatrist. At the end of this period a report is sent to the court recommending trial or treatment.

In New Hampshire, a rule provided by that state's Supreme Court in 1896 provides that if the unlawful act is the product of a mental disease or disorder then a determination is to be made by the jury on the basis of psychiatric testimony.

The Durham rule developed in the federal courts and broadened substantially the "right or wrong" McNaghton rule.

In 1954 Abe Fortas, the Washington lawyer later to serve on the U. S. Supreme Court, accepted court appointment as lawyer to appeal the conviction of an indigent housebreaker named Monte Durham. Fortas' arguments resulted in the U. S. Court of Appeals for the District of Columbia adopting the rule which held that an accused was not criminally responsible "if his unlawful act was the product of mental disease or defect." This case resulted in various other jurisdictions beginning to break away gradually from the old McNaghton rule—but led to more chaos and confusion as to what is "legal" insanity and what is not.

In 1960 the American Law Institute proposed a change for courts in the rule to be applied. The proposal was worded this way: "Mental disease or defect excluding responsibility. (1) A person is not responsible for criminal conduct if at the time of such conduct as a result of mental disease or defect he lacks substantial capacity either to appreciate the criminality of his conduct or to conform his conduct to the requirements of the law. (2) The term 'mental disease or defect' does not include an abnormality manifested only by repeated criminal or otherwise antisocial conduct."

But this rule is a long way from accepted procedure in the courts of the land. The confusion over what is legal insanity in criminal cases is going to continue and grow until those who preside over the courts and those who practice in them recognize that justice is not going to be served by rules which confound jurors and procedures that encourage the humiliation of those who practice psychiatry.

Either psychiatry has a legitimate role to play in the system of justice, or it has not. At this point in history only a few lawyers would seek to exclude psychiatry, as Sirhan's prosecutors did, from relevancy to a criminal trial. But if the role of psychiatry has a place in the search for justice those who practice that specialty of medicine need to be called upon to help lawyers and judges find some procedures which seek to serve the administration of justice.

It is ironic that the search for justice—in this case a search for a modern, scientifically sound, legally acceptable rule of law—is centered almost exclusively in the structure of the organized bar. The search has largely excluded consultation and advice, much less direction, by experts from the field of psychiatry. And this historically has been the case. No psychiatric help was sought by the judges of England one hundred and twenty-five years ago when they established the McNaghton rule—although even then there were men of medicine probing the human mind to try to determine why men act and react as they do.

In 1966, Judge Irving R. Kaufman of New York, sitting on the U. S. Second Circuit Court of Appeals, wrote an opinion in a case involving a convicted narcotics pusher. His ruling sought to modify previous doctrines set down on the question. Judge Kaufman called for the psychiatrist to give to the court an objective report considering the social and psychological background of the defendant, as well as his mental state at the time of the crime. This puts the burden on the judge to act on whether the defendant is mentally irresponsible for the crime, or whether he should stand trial. It was Kaufman's opinion that the Durham rule labels defendants as "psychotic" or "paranoid" and at the same time gives the psychiatrist too much of a role in determining questions that should be reserved for the judge.

Some psychiatrists feel the best role for them to play is to advise the court at an "in chambers" hearing in the presence of opposing lawyers. Some lawyers, even those most interested in court reform, still prefer to trust the common sense of the jury to decide on the question of mental competence in criminal cases.

*   *   *   *

3. *Sirhan's personal demeanor in court—pounding the table, blurting out obscenities and vulgarities, shouting at the judge, upbraiding the court for unfairness, hissing slurs at prosecutors, arguing with his own counsel—was the first clear manifestation of a phenomenon that was to recur with disturbing frequency in the months to follow, threatening the system.*

At one point Judge Walker warned that the court would have to gag and handcuff Sirhan and to physically restrain him from his vituperative outbursts at the defense table. As the trial progressed Judge Walker found it was not necessary, in his judicial discretion, to handcuff and gag Sirhan, although there were times when the court officers had to physically force him to keep his seat.

No one realized it at the time, but Sirhan's antics were the first of a series of similar situations wherein the behavior of defendants in criminal cases became a threat to the established order and procedure of the administration of justice.

In October, 1969, Bobby Seale, the Black Panther leader, was on trial along with seven other militants who were charged with conspiracy to incite riots at the 1968 Chicago Democratic National Convention. Seale, a young, black revolutionary, pursued Sirhan's pattern of courtroom activity, except that he was more deprecative of Judge Julius Hoffman, who presided over the trial of "the Chicago Eight," than Sirhan was of Judge Walker.

Judge Hoffman, who came to be satirized by young militant radicals across the nation as "Julius the Just," resorted, after several of Seale's shouted expletives, to having Seale shackled and gagged. He had called Hoffman "a fascist dog" and "a lying pig." At one point, Seale struggled free from his gag and again disrupted the proceedings, whereupon court officers had to restrain him. "Don't hit me in my nuts," he screamed as he was held by officers.

Shortly thereafter Seale was held in contempt on Judge Hoffman's findings that on sixteen separate occasions over a three-day period the defendant had been guilty of "contumacious conduct." He sentenced Seale to four years in prison—three months for each of the sixteen separate acts—and separated his trial from that of his seven co-defendants.

Even after Seale departed court and the trial proceeded, Judge Hoffman felt the actions of the other defendants and their lawyers were threatening to the administration of justice. In February, 1970, after the jury found five of the seven guilty of crossing state lines to incite riots at the 1968 convention, and acquitted them of conspiracy to plot the Chicago violence, the judge then held the two lawyers for the "seven," William Kunstler and Leonard Weinglass, in contempt of his court, giving Kunstler a four-year sentence in prison and Weinglass a twenty-month term. The cases all were appealed.

The action against Seale, binding and gagging him, after several days of "contemptuous" activity in court, must have had some impact on the jury observing the case. What, it might legitimately be asked, is the effect on a co-defendant when the court binds and gags an accused such as Seale? Did putting Seale in shackles adversely affect the rights of any of the other defendants? What if Seale had not shrugged free of his gag and had gone all through the trial, seated before the jury, bound and gagged? Would that have affected his rights to a fair trial? Some courts have held such action is within the discretion of a judge, faced with threats to his power to preside. In a later trial in 1970, Charles Manson, the cult leader from California, was removed to an annex courtroom where the trial was broadcast after his outburst in court offended the trial judge's view of proper decorum.

In Sirhan's case, what effect did the mere threat to bind and gag him have on the jury? And unrelated to the evidence, what did his outbursts have to do with the final decision of the jury to execute him? Was his activity so unruly that the jurors became angered at him? It is impossible to read the minds of jurors. Perhaps the appellate courts will not try—although in the

Sheppard case the Supreme Court "read the minds" of the jurors who convicted Sheppard and found that although they swore they would not be influenced by the pre-trial publicity, they were in fact influenced by it.

The U. S. Supreme Court held in April, 1970, that the trial judge has the power to control unruly defendants by citing them for contempt, removing them from the courtroom or shackling and gagging them. The court's decision was instigated by William Allen, a Chicago man accused of robbing a bartender of two hundred dollars. Allen, at his trial, had told the judge, "You're going to be a corpse," and flung his court-appointed lawyer's files to the floor. After repeated warnings, Allen was expelled from the courtroom and convicted of armed robbery. He later petitioned the federal district court for relief on grounds he had been denied his right to confront his accusers. But the Supreme Court, in its ruling, laid down the doctrine that a defendant who makes the progress of his trial impossible has effectively waived his constitutional right to confront the witnesses against him and can reclaim that right only when he is willing to behave in court.

Another question already being raised by defense lawyers challenges whether the trial judge at whom "contemptible actions" are directed should be the judge who rules on contempt.

Two weeks after the "Chicago Seven" cases ended, there came to trial in New York thirteen members of the Black Panther party, charged with a series of bombings there. Again, there was disorder as the defendants interrupted the proceedings, talking loudly among themselves and shouting in a chorus.

"All power to the people," they cried in unison at one point before Judge John Murtaugh adjourned court and abruptly recessed the hearing. The trial would not proceed, he said, until he received written notice from the defendants which would include "an unequivocal assurance that the defendants are now prepared to participate in a trial under the American system of justice."

Lawyers for the thirteen said they had urged their clients to conduct themselves in a manner that conformed to established courtroom decorum, but that the group of Panthers had not heeded this counsel. Nonetheless the lawyers said they would prepare a "careful" appeal—as careful as Judge Murtaugh's pronouncement, at least—to the higher courts.

All of this poses a new sort of threat to the administration of justice and points up the inability of the system to cope with this new attack. There are several constitutional questions to be constructed from all of this: the right of the accused such as Sirhan to be judged fairly on the issues, unrelated to his personal behavior, his vocabulary or his personality, the point of his sanity aside; the rights of co-defendants in a case such as the trial of the Chicago Eight where the actions of one defendant, and the gagging and binding of him, may damage the other seven; the rights of the thirteen Panthers to a "speedy trial" when the judge has decided he will not try them until they assure him they will act in accord with established standards of the administration of justice.

The highest court in the land sooner or later is going to have to face up to all these legal and constitutional conundrums, but what sort of guidelines will come from them? It might be a simple matter to agree with Judge Hoffman or Judge Murtaugh—and forget it—if the case would never arise again. It would be an easy matter to side with Judge Walker—and forget it—except that Sirhan faces death and there may always be a doubt as to whether the jury might not have given him a life sentence, rather than deciding he should be executed, if he had behaved himself in court.

There is every indication in the present "violent society" that there will be additional demonstrations further challenging the system. Perhaps it may be determined that it would have been better to have held Seale in contempt the first day he disturbed court, rather than allow him to build up sixteen separate offenses over several days; perhaps it would have been advisable for Judge Walker to have held Sirhan in contempt on the theory that in the face of such antics the jurors could not possibly have given him a fair trial; perhaps it would have been a wiser course for Judge Murtaugh to have cited all thirteen Panthers for contempt, rather than insist that they conform to the rules of decorum before they are tried.

There will always be the danger that defendants in the future will use such tactics to block the measured flow of the stream of justice. A defendant such as Sirhan, particularly, faced with a death penalty, could continually disrupt the proceedings until he had thwarted what is accepted as the due end of justice. Others, revolutionaries by nature and determined to impede the established order of government in any way possible, could use upsetting tactics such as those employed in these cases simply to prove that the system of justice doesn't work in America. And so, what started with the Sirhan case was destined to become a plague on the house of justice, and was to emphasize again the house was in desperate need of remodeling.

* * * *

4. *The decision of District Attorney Evelle J. Younger to check with the U. S. Department of State to determine what effect the disposition of the Sirhan case might have on foreign affairs in the Middle East, suggests that the administration of justice could be subverted if foreign policy dictated that such was the "wise" course.*

Here was a defendant who had shot down in cold blood a candidate for the U. S. presidency. Ultimately, a jury would decide that he should go to the gas chamber for that offense. But District Attorney Younger, before the trial, contacted federal officials in Washington, presumably to find out if his prosecution of this capital offense would get in the way of anything the State Department had in mind.

Younger sounded more like a state department bureaucrat than a vigilant prosecutor when he said: "I made it convenient for appropriate officials in the government—the present administration—to express an opinion to me. They declined and made no comment."

But what if they had made comment? What if they had said that to try Sirhan would have made matters difficult in stabilizing the conflict between Arabs and Israelis in the Middle East? Would that have impeded the just prosecution of the trial? A similar question was raised in the Ray case when Mrs. King was asked whether she would object to the accused slayer receiving less than the death penalty. In Sirhan's case, the Kennedy family apparently was not asked about it in advance, but after Sirhan was sentenced to death Senator Edward Kennedy, brother of the slain victim, speaking for his family, asked that Sirhan's life be spared.

It is possible that every case of political assassination could have foreign policy overtones.

In the Shaw case foreign policy was affected, in that the attitude of Cuban refugees was brought up and into the open. In the Ray case, because the defendant was apprehended in a foreign land and because King was an idol of millions around the world the impact on foreign policy was considerable. And in the Sirhan matter the foreign policy issue was even more pertinent, because a Middle East crisis was approaching and extremely perilous as Sirhan went to trial.

All of this seems to suggest that American justice in a court of law could be subordinated to issues ranging from personal whims to national policy—hardly the desired image of a court system seeking truth.

*   *   *   *

5. *Judge Walker, by "leaking" to a* Los Angeles Times *reporter the news that Sirhan was planning to plead guilty, subverted justice, if the standards of the Sheppard ruling are applied to the California assassination trial.*

Superior Judge Arthur L. Alarcon issued orders to lawyers and interested parties not to discuss the Sirhan case. But in Los Angeles Judge Walker himself violated the rule. He told the reporter Sirhan planned to plead guilty. No doubt the judge told Ron Einstoss, of the *Los Angeles Times,* what he knew to be the truth at the moment he spoke to the newsman: Sirhan was considering a guilty plea. The Los Angeles newspaper reporter said later that he had confirmed the same story from another source before Walker verified it to him. But of course, Sirhan decided against entering a guilty plea. Thus the newspaper, while jurors were still at their homes, and some several hours before they were to be sequestered, broke the story which turned out to be in error.

In retrospect it is difficult to understand why the newspaper decided to run the story with the sort of front page play it received. Other newspapers in the country, faced with the same decision, might have done the same thing. For example, *The New York Times,* with information diametrically opposed to that received by the *Los Angeles Times,* ran a front page story saying that Sirhan would *not* plead guilty. Would the New York newspaper have run the other story had it found—as the *Los Angeles Times* did—that Sirhan planned to enter a guilty plea?

There probably is an excellent warning here for newspapers

to heed: until a plea is entered in court a defendant has the option of changing his mind. He may agree with his lawyers, his lawyers may work out a deal with the state to accept a lesser sentence in return for the guilty plea, the trial judge may be informed of this and approve of it informally out of court—but when the accused comes into court he must concede *then* that he is guilty. If he does not, no deal previously agreed to, even sanctioned by the court, can be made. What then is the advantage in a newspaper risking that a defendant will change his mind overnight? Obviously, as the *Los Angeles Times* found, there is none.

News about court cases is sometimes treated by the press in the same way hot "scoops" were treated in the days of yellow journalism. There is something about a reporter getting the story and having it published—or broadcast—*first,* that has a sort of "in-trade" prestige.

But when a man's freedom hangs in the balance there is every reason to temper enthusiasm with caution. Here the credibility of a great newspaper was gambled on a vital matter of justice. But the guilt or innocence of a defendant—even a defendant whose sanity and stability are in question—is not something that needs to be treated as a three-alarm fire by industrious newsmen.

The *Los Angeles Times* had an "unimpeachable source" if there was one—the trial judge himself. It is fair to say that the judge should never have spoken to the reporter about the case. But once he did the manner in which the story was written and the place in the paper it was played became critical decisions because a jury was still at large. And the decision on a plea—even if reached—could be reversed by the defendant, as indeed it was. Had Sirhan entered a plea of guilt no charge could have been made that the news story was "overplayed." The *Times* found sadly that even a judge can be fallible.

*   *   *   *

Throughout the Sirhan case there were questionable points which seemed to cross-track the other two assassination trials. As in the Ray case, there was a writer, Robert Kaiser, who got "exclusive" rights to the story of Sirhan and members of his family. In addition, after the trial Sirhan was paid by NBC to go on television and "tell his story." But there was a difference in the way it happened in Los Angeles and the way it occurred in Memphis. In Los Angeles the entire matter of publicity was "post trial." This took away the element of controversy over pre-trial publicity. It would be improper to suggest that a defendant who has been the victim of pre-trial publicity by the prosecution—as Shaw was, for example—should be debarred from answering the charges. But when the matter is handled as it was in the case of Ray and Huie those who tell the story and those who have it published must expect that their versions will be suspect as the product of journalistic mercenaries.

The issue of jury service came up again. In California, jurors are paid five dollars a day. Persons whose occupations would be adversely affected by jury service are excused. Doctors, teachers, and "keepers of alms houses" are automatically excused under the statute. In New Orleans jurors were not paid until recently and the judges dismissed any on whom jury duty would work an undue hardship. In Tennessee all "householders or freeholders" who are called who are otherwise qualified—regardless of profession or business—must serve. Some are excused as hardship cases, at the discretion of the court. Sirhan's claim that his rights were adversely affected because there were no poor people on the jury seems a ludicrous legal claim since Kennedy's basic political appeal was with the poor. But the larger and more valid question is whether the jury should be a representative cross-section of community life so that the defendant has some opportunity to get a good chance to find "a jury of his peers." When segments of the population are excluded by virtue of their vocations, the administration of justice is the poorer.

The question of film evidence was raised again in Los Angeles. The judge allowed still pictures of Kennedy, taken after the shooting, but he disallowed moving pictures of his "victory" speech taken a few minutes before he was slain. It would have been prejudicial to Sirhan to show such an emotion-packed film, the judge said. But still, in New Orleans the jury had seen on nine separate occasions what must be the most emotion-packed picture on film: the death of President Kennedy.

In the Shaw case Garrison had given key witnesses lie detector tests. The results were not shown to the defense lawyers. In Los Angeles lie detector tests were given some witnesses and those tests were made available to the defense so that lawyers could attack the credibility of state witnesses.

In Memphis the judge would not allow closed circuit television so that interested newsmen might view the court proceedings. In Los Angeles the judge allowed closed circuit television for reporters seated in a courtroom annex, which raises another question: If it is acceptable for reporters to view trial proceedings, why should not the public at large be allowed to view the same thing on TV at home? Ultimately the courts will have to confront this question and provide a logical answer to taxpayers who, after all, pay for the operation of the courts.

The length of sequestered jury service needs to be considered by court reformers. It is not fair to separate a juror from family and business ties for five or six weeks—as happened in two of these three cases. Nor does it make much sense to go through the mockery of a jury trial—as was the case in Memphis—where the jurors are told what they are to do: nod agreement with a verdict and a sentence and let the case end in a matter of minutes.

Again, there was the question of whether a defendant has a right to fire his lawyer. Sirhan stood in open court and tried to fire his but the judge would not allow it. Ray fired Hanes from his jail cell, by letter, without announced cause and the judge allowed it.

Sirhan stood in open court and told the judge he wanted to plead guilty, but the judge would not let him do it. In Memphis, Judge Battle heard Ray plead guilty and hastily dispatched him to prison without taking time to explore whether Ray had some additional information to give the court or the grand jury.

And the contradictions and conflicts and coincidences go on and on, befogging the judicial environment.

2.

"An indefinable something is to be done,
in a way nobody knows,
at a time nobody knows when,
that will accomplish nobody knows what."
Thomas B. Read

It is impossible to develop a set of meaningful and lasting recommendations for reforming the administration of criminal justice in the United States on the basis of what happened in New Orleans, Memphis and Los Angeles. Decades of laxness, lethargy and legalism have piled fault on top of fault and only extensive study and dramatic action can cure the sickness in the system. The cure is not likely to come.

Developments at New Orleans, Memphis and Los Angeles are symptomatic. And it is possible to look at these three sensational cases and mark, on the basis of what happened in them, some clearly defined inadequacies in criminal justice in this country.

The weaknesses brought into focus by these three cases need to be corrected. Here are eight specific suggestions:

1. **There should be some uniform method of selecting judges and prosecutors.** Samuel I. Rosenman, then president of the Association of the Bar of the City of New York, said in 1964: "Let us face this sad fact: that in many—far too many—instances the benches of our courts . . . are occupied by mediocrities. Men of small talent, undistinguished in performance, technically deficient and inept."

What he says of judges is also true, in many cases, of prosecutors. Part of the problem with the system is that in most states judges and district attorneys are elected by popular vote. There are no requirements that potential judges, prosecutors, or public defenders have any background record or expertise in the field of the office to which they seek election.

The judge may never have entertained the slightest interest in serving on the bench before he runs for the office. The district attorney need never have prosecuted a case, nor need the public defender ever have defended one, to qualify him for election.

If the candidate has an attractive, politician's manner, if he is a vote-getter, he can be a judge, prosecutor or defender. No one investigates the candidate's competence or integrity. No question is raised by any agency—unless the political opposition makes it a campaign issue—about whether the candidate is qualified. No investigative office delves into the background, private interests, and financial holdings, of the candidates in most situations.

Often in the recent past questions of scandal have haunted presiding judges. In Oklahoma, Tennessee, New York, Illinois, and elsewhere judicial officers have left the bench in disgrace. And the shadow has even fallen across the bench of the Supreme Court of the United States.

But the possible dishonesty of judges and attorneys did not come up during the trials of Shaw, Ray and Sirhan. Aside from the party-going of Judge Haggerty in New Orleans, revealed in lurid detail some months after the Shaw trial, all of the judges seemed to be unmarred by any taint of scandal.

Still, there was a feeling on the part of all three reporters who covered these trials that, to differing degrees in each case, the question of judicial competence was a problem. Looking at these three trials as the yardstick, these reporters did not feel any of the three judges measured up to what might be described as excellence. Judge Walker in Los Angeles seemed adequate. The measure of excellence in Memphis and New Orleans left a good deal to be desired.

As far as the prosecutors are concerned, the worst example of what the system can produce was seen in New Orleans. The rating of the two prosecutors in Memphis and Los Angeles moved upward from the low point in Garrison's case in New Orleans. And yet Garrison was re-elected shortly after the end of the Shaw trial. And Judge Haggerty, removed as a result of a post-Shaw trial "scandal" announced he would run again.

The judge, and to a greater degree, the prosecutor, have partial control of the destiny of defendants. It is obvious that the political process must occasionally tempt those who preside and those who prosecute—even as financial reward tempts the defense attorney. It is not healthy to leave a defendant's case, particularly a sensational case where community emotions may be high, in the hands of a district attorney or judge when they may have an election coming up. The temptation to play politics with justice in such cases is simply too great to be entrusted to the judge and district attorney. A few states provide a judge must run on his record—not against another political opponent. This system, which originated in Missouri where court vacancies are filled by the governor of the state who acts on recommendations made by a panel of three lawyers and three laymen, would seem to hold far more protection for the system of justice than leaving the judiciary emersed in competitive politics.

But since widespread adoption of the Missouri plan seems years away in most states, and since even in states where this plan works there is no set standard of qualifications or competence of those who are named, there needs to be established some procedure to give immediately to the new judicial officer, and to the prosecutor just in office, a complete, if brief, course of instruction on how to perform the duties of office. And attendance needs to be mandatory. Periodically, there needs to be a required refresher course for judges and prosecutors.

A system that has no provision for requiring judges and district attorneys to know what their business is about, is no system at all. The federal system of selecting judges, which calls for an extensive background investigation by the FBI, a searching examination by the ABA, an investigatory hearing before the U. S. Senate judiciary committee and the regular regional judicial conference to discuss problems in the administration of justice, is by far preferable to the political method of selecting judges in most of the fifty states.

The public has a right to expect that a workable system of justice will provide magistrates and prosecutors who are, at the very least, qualified to perform their duties in court. This system makes no attempt to meet that public expectation.

2. **There should be some new method of investigating and, when justified censuring or disciplining prosecutors, defense lawyers and judges who, during the course of trials, engage in actions that undermine justice.** So often lawyers who are questioned about inadequacies in the system contend that it is not procedures or precedents but the caliber of individuals in positions of power who cause the system to break down. Still, the system in most of the fifty states has no continuing method of moving

against these individuals whose inadequacies cause the system
to fail.

The idea that local lawyers or bar associations will ade-
quately investigate or properly discipline judges, district attorneys
or even defense lawyers, is ludicrous. Local bar members want
to get along with presiding judges, prosecuting attorneys and
their fellow lawyers. They don't want trouble. And they do not
want to damage further the image of their profession by calling
attention to the faults of those who work in the courts. As a result
nobody investigated Jim Garrison for his outrageous performance
in New Orleans in the case against Clay Shaw; nobody challenged Judge Haggerty for his poolside photography session for
the Shaw jury; nobody questioned Percy Foreman's $150,000 fee,
charged for settling a case which could have been resolved by
a freshman lawyer three months out of law school; nobody inside
the system challenged Judge Battle or his Memphis "bar committee" for the press contempt citations or Judge Battle's refusal to
sentence the reporters so that they might appeal his action and
possibly have it overturned; nobody questioned whether the arrangement William Bradford Huie had with lawyers of James Earl
Ray took unfair advantage of the client; nobody challenged Judge
Walker for his "leak" to newsmen regarding a possible guilty plea
in the Sirhan case.

The lawyer's theory is simply that if any one of these incidents interferes with the administration of criminal justice only
the rights of the defendant are damaged and he has a right of
appeal. The idea that justice, the public interest or the interest of
the defendant is amply served by the process of appeal is falla-
cious. Many interim bad actions of a judge, prosecutor or defense
lawyer are never raised as points of appeal. And these actions
continually tear at the stability of the system of justice.

A year after the president of the American Bar Association
spoke out questioning Garrison's handling of the Shaw prosecution and implied that there might be a local investigation of
Garrison, there had been no investigation. Shaw had been acquitted, so he had no right or reason to appeal. He then faced a
new charge: perjury. No local lawyer or bar association spoke
out against Garrison. He managed to be re-elected after the trial.
And so, once again, the administration of justice which needs a
high degree of professionalism to maintain a high degree of

efficiency and public confidence, is left to the whims of politics. It is necessary to have some national agency or authority made up of laymen as well as lawyers, to whom individuals can complain about individual actions which hurt the cause of justice. If appeals are pending, an investigation might have to be put off so that an inquiry and public censure would not interfere with the appeal. But investigations need to be made on a continuing basis; and intelligent censure, if no more than a public, published report of criticism, should become a reality. Since such a national agency or authority is not likely to be organized, it would be helpful if ad hoc groups could develop at the local level—lawyers and laymen who would organize committees to serve outside the bar associations as watchdogs on the administration of justice. Law schools could provide the impetus for such local organizations. Such groups are not likely to be organized. Confidence in the system will continue to suffer while nobody criticizes or censures the criminal courts or those who preside over or practice in them.

3. **There should be a critical re-examination of the adversary system and a de-emphasis of the conflict aspect that comes from lawyers on opposing sides in criminal cases putting to use any extreme courtroom trick in order to try to win a victory.** The brutal clash of wills of opposing lawyers often cannot be intelligently handled by those judges who fit Samuel Rosenman's description—"mediocrities."

A look at the adversary system in New Orleans will lead some lawyers to argue that this ability of an opposing counsel to hit back in behalf of Shaw saved the defendant from a possible prison term of twenty years. But such an argument simply gives to Garrison the right to use his techniques in order to try to win. The other extreme of what the adversary system should not produce is found in the case in Memphis where the prosecutor, the defense lawyer and even the judge seemed to join hands in a sort of "love feast," the purpose of which was to get a settlement in behalf of James Earl Ray on a plea of guilty. Here the adversaries were non-adversary and the judge seemed happy with that in order to get a crime "solved" and in order to "save" the good name of his home town.

In Los Angeles the best examples of the weaknesses of the adversary system became evident: witnesses for opposing sides became caught up in the proceedings and themselves became adversaries. The psychiatrists and psychologists for state and defense became advocates themselves for the lawyers who put them on the witness stand, and one of them actually lifted another man's writings and adopted them as his own in order to better articulate his advocacy point of view. The result was that a lay jury heard "expert" testimony that directly clashed with and contradicted other "expert" testimony.

Lawyers and judges need to recognize and admit to themselves and the public that the criminal trial, under the adversary system, is *not* a search for truth. It makes mistakes. The society that accepts such a system must be willing to accept the mistakes that will flow from the system. This does not mean that the adversary system should be abolished in favor of the "inquisitorial system" which is practiced in most of Europe. In that system there is an interim pre-trial procedure handled by a public official, a *juge d'instruction*, who serves as an impartial seeker of truth with the responsibility to gather evidence for both sides and make a determination as to whether a case should be prosecuted.

In this way many cases are resolved without trial by this interim investigator-administrator. In the United States and England the grand jury function preempts much of the role of the *juge d'instruction*. In many jurisdictions the district attorney himself is expected to wash out many cases in which he does not have ample evidence to proceed.

The inquisitorial system assumes that the *juge d'instruction* will be a seeker of truth and will not develop a "policeman complex" or see his role as a paid public official who needs to curb or control crime. In placing its faith in a grand jury and then a trial jury the system in the U. S. builds in a safeguard that relies on ordinary citizens, not paid officials of government, to decide on a defendant's guilt.

A glance at the transcript of the 1966 "inquisitorial system" trial of the Russian writers Andrei Sinyavsky and Yuli Daniel, smuggled out of the Soviet Union and published in the United States [6] is fair warning that a nation drifting toward heavier reliance on supporting the authority of government does not need to think of abandoning citizen safeguards that exist under the jury system. Despite the impact of violence in America on citizens

6. **On Trial,** Max Hayward, editor, New York: Harper & Row, 1966.

who serve on juries, there is still evidence from the time of John Peter Zenger to the trial of Clay Shaw that jurors are willing to stand up against arbitrary governmental power. For all its weaknesses the adversary system, which ultimately places its trust in a citizen-jury, seems more suited to the nature of this nation than the inquisitorial system.

This does not mean that the adversary system must be left as it is. It must be constantly re-examined. There are defense lawyers who legitimately worry about a too-close relationship existing between the judge and the prosecutor whose office is down the hall. They worry that the grand jury, in some states appointed by the judge, is serviced by the district attorney. They fear this builds a sort of psychological bridge between the prosecutor and what should be a neutral judge.

If the adversary system is to endure it will have to rely most on a strong judicial officer who is, more than anything else, an impartial arbiter. There is and must be no tie or mutuality of interest between the prosecutor and the judge simply because they are both paid by the state. It must have seemed to the defense in the New Orleans trial that there was at least some sort of mental identity of purpose between the prosecution and Judge Haggerty when it came time to show the Zapruder film over and over to the jury. In that case the judge's repeated declaration that he could not stop the state from "over-proving" its case must have seemed to Shaw and his lawyers an open judicial invitation to Garrison's men to try to over-prove their case.

There may be no way to stop a judge from being swept away by the eloquence of a lawyer. But judges need to be reminded constantly that when such a thing happens justice may suffer. No one can tell what indigent defendant in Memphis may have suffered from lack of counsel because Percy Foreman convinced Judge Battle that James Earl Ray was an indigent who needed not only Foreman's talents but the public defender's help. It is hard to imagine what valid contribution the Memphis public defender made to the settlement of the case of James Earl Ray, who happened to have access to thousands of dollars to pay Foreman for representing him. Judge Battle's "neutrality" in this case could more aptly be described as partisanship for a guilty plea.

The adversary system was not really at work in Memphis, but it was in New Orleans, where shouting matches between the opposing lawyers became the rule; and in Los Angeles, where it produced days of worthless and contradictory testimony on Sirhan's mental competence which led the prosecutor finally to ask the jury to forget it all.

The system whereby an independent lawyer has the right to argue his case before a jury of his client's peers has safeguards that should not be given up lightly, even to those who argue that there is a direct tie between the inquisitorial system and the lower crime rate in nations where it is practiced. Still, while the adversary system has advantages which fit more comfortably with the sort of freedom the United States enjoys, it cannot be allowed to languish as "the best" system, as many lawyers insist.

In practice in many jurisdictions in this country it is not an asset to the cause of justice. Its over-emphasis on victory, not truth, encourages phony "play-acting" by criminal lawyers on both sides and puts immense burdens on judges, who too often are unable to cope with them. The inability or unwillingness of the prosecutor to exercise judgment on many cases that should not be prosecuted clogs court dockets and hampers the system. The unavailability of court managers to help the judge keep the process of justice moving smoothly now seriously damages the functioning of the system. The adversary system as it too often operates invites vicious conflict and malicious outbursts which do a disservice to justice. A court of law is not a jungle and survival should not be dependent upon which lawyer is the fittest. The violent nature of the struggle as it now is must be toned down. And there must be balance in the reform: the "deal" in Memphis is not the answer. Justice, not to mention truth, requires an end to the circuses that the adversary system produced in New Orleans and Los Angeles.

4. **Plea bargaining should be sharply curtailed and more strictly supervised.** The gigantic logjams that exist in court procedures, caused by a mountainous backlist of untried cases, puts heavy pressure on those in the courts to try to barter for case settlements.

Too often this has the effect of bartering justice.

The prosecution wants a guilty plea. The defense lawyer is looking for a quick, light sentence for his client. The judge wants to clear cases from his court docket.

In the James Earl Ray case there seemed to be an unspoken,

accidental conspiracy to dispose of the matter without trial. This typifies the other extreme from the violence that is typical of the adversary court trial. The difference between Ray in Memphis and Shaw in New Orleans is a difference of extremes. While the adversary system must be softened in nature, so must the tendency be curtailed to quick-settle rather than try cases.

When there is an overemphasis by the court and district attorney on clearing cases from the docket, and the lawyer for the defense can be enticed into a mood supportive of that overemphasis, justice will be the loser.

In Memphis the matter of the Ray settlement was worked out behind the scenes and acted out in court, with the approval of Judge Battle. In Los Angeles the plea bartering was going on backstage when the judge inadvertently leaked word of it all to the press and a news story—which could have been prejudicial— got in the way of the system. The judge himself, in Los Angeles, had refused to personally agree to a settlement that excluded the death penalty.

Again, there is no consistency in procedure from state to state. While the evils of a Garrison operating within the framework of the adversary system are obvious, the evils that attach to what occurred in Memphis and to a lesser degree in Los Angeles, are no less real.

Somehow courts must move to strike a balance between extremes and adopt procedures that are workable and acceptable.

Since plea bargaining involves life and liberty it is a vital source of concern in any effort to reform the system. Because it is a reform that depends upon lessening court loads and crowded dockets the prospect that it will become a reality is remote.

5. **There should be a more sensible role provided the "expert witness" in criminal cases.** Too often in the present context each opposing side employs an "expert" to testify on such questions as handwriting, weapons, bullets and legal sanity. Each side seems to have no difficulty in getting an expert who will express a point of view contrary to the point of view of the expert employed by the other side. There is a strong suspicion that the expert whose testimony is the most believable to the average juror is not always the witness who actually knows the most about handwriting

or bullet characteristics, but the witness who has the best court-room demeanor, the best voice, bearing and personality. If there are experts who can shed light on a contested point, would not justice be better served if the court employed them to make a finding which would then be subjected to limited cross-examination? This would not bar either side from bringing in other experts. But their testimony would be seen by the jury for what it is: that of a hired gun.

In the sensitive and delicate area of "legal sanity" where psychiatric or psychological testimony is required, some special steps need to be taken to make sure that assaults on intelligence, such as those that occurred at Los Angeles, are not permitted.

The courts need to consider how they can best find what truth, or to be more precise, what valid opinions, psychiatry has to offer on a given case without allowing this important evidence to be prostituted or negated by the turbulent nature of the present adversary system.

Much of the evidence offered in Los Angeles was the honest and highly intelligent testimony of men who had given their best professional efforts to try to resolve questions about Sirhan's competence. To give such men the final judicial word would be a mistake. But to subject their tenuous findings in a highly technical field to the sort of badgering cross-examination that comes from the hostile adversary environment of a criminal trial, may rob the cause of justice. The courts need to move in firmly, with common sense and authority, to get valid, competent testimony, ruling out that of men whose actions establish them as charlatans or paid lackeys for one side or the other. Once the expert testimony is offered, under the protective authority of the judicial officer, cross-examination should be controlled and restrained. If mental experts are then called to provide hired gun testimony, these witnesses would be fair game for cross-examination. The best psychiatrist in the world may be the worst criminal court witness in the world. His testimony is valuable. But under harsh cross-questioning it can be made worthless. A system that supports the destruction of such testimony in search of "justice" needs correction.

It is important that the system of justice move immediately to find some degree of intelligent uniformity as it discards the McNaghton rule in favor of some other standard. McNaghton is obsolete. The Durham rule obviously is not an adequate substitute because it often makes a judge of the psychiatrist. But whatever the sanity rule, the courts need to recognize that present procedures which encourage opposing lawyers to hire experts to give "their side," on the theory that the best expert is also the best witness, is defective and defeats the aim of justice.

6. **The contempt power recommended by the Reardon Committee in its "free press and fair trial" study should be stripped from the hands of judges.** Judge Battle demonstrated the inadvisability of it. His actions cut off press discussion of a case where conspiracy was a viable possibility. Judge Battle's contempt action mocked Justice Reardon's theory that the contempt power was in fact a weapon to discipline lawyers and police officers who talked too much about cases pending in court. The contempt citations by the judge against the media were a raw attempt at prior restraint of news publication. This was extreme action, precipitated by news stories which were critical of the manner in which a prisoner was being incarcerated by the state. The refusal of Judge Battle to sentence the reporters so they might appeal his ruling was arbitrary and unnecessary and compounded the injustice. That the contempt citations were recommended by a committee of lawyers is no explanation of his action, but actually further offends justice. The influence of the recommendations of Justice Reardon's committee can perhaps best be gauged for effectiveness by the application in each of these three cases. Each of the three judges established press guidelines. Judge Haggerty ignored the opportunity to use the Reardon recommendations to discipline Garrison. In truth, he didn't need the Reardon report to control the district attorney. He simply was not strong enough to use his authority against a strong public personality like Garrison. Battle, armed with the Reardon report, became a judicial martinet. Judge Walker violated the spirit of his court's guidelines, and the spirit of the recommendations of the Reardon committee by leaking information himself to the press.

Already there are some defendants who are appealing criminal convictions contending in principle that the courts, in imposing press restrictions, violated their right to a public trial.

What is needed is more balanced application of law in the system of justice. Bar association reports which encourage an imbalance and instability hurt the system. The Reardon report hurts the system.

7. **The death penalty should be abolished.** James Earl Ray pleaded guilty to murdering Martin Luther King. Sirhan Sirhan was found guilty of murdering Robert Kennedy. It makes no sense for a system of justice to execute one man for the crime of first degree murder while another man is imprisoned for the rest of his life for an identical crime.

8. **There should be a national system of justice to somehow parallel and complement, but still be independent from, the federal system of justice.** Archibald Cox, the former Solicitor General of the United States, has theorized that Congress, by implementing Article 5 of the Fourteenth Amendment, could enact a national code of criminal procedure that would bind the state courts.[7] While it may be argued that constitutionally Congress has the power to take such action, Professor Cox is the first to admit that politically such a course is out of the question at this point in history.

Still the administration of justice in the fifty states must find some way to move toward uniformity or there will soon begin to develop broad public disfavor with the manner in which the system functions. National reform must bring to bear far more than lawyer-interest representation because so much more is involved in the administration of justice: police, parole officers, prison officials, the public—all have as much at stake in the way justice functions in the fifty states as the lawyers who are before the bar or the judges who are on the bench. *How such a national system representing such diverse groups could come into being, how it could be financed, how it would function is not a matter to be seriously considered. Like most of the other needs set out above, this one too will go unmet.*

Much of what has been said in these pages represents an indictment of lawyers for weaknesses in the system of justice. In fairness, a mood for reforming the administration of criminal justice began to grow among leaders of the organized bar during the decade of the 1960's. Late in the decade it became fashionable in high circles of the American Bar Association to talk about correcting "the system."

---

7. Cox, "The Supreme Court 1965 Term"; Foreword, **Harvard Law Review** (1966), p. 91.

Many influential lawyers felt that statistics demonstrated convincingly a direct connection between inadequacies of the system of justice and the increasing crime rate. Crowded court dockets, static sentencing techniques, sloppy pardon and probation procedures all played a part in the way criminals were handled by society—and in the way they, in turn, have mishandled society.

Many leaders in the bar felt that court procedures had become obsolete, outdated and irrelevant. Chief Justice Warren Burger of the U. S. Supreme Court, asks, "Is it not a paradox that, except in details, a civil or criminal trial today . . . is essentially the same as in Daniel Webster's time? With slight briefing on how to move to exclude evidence Webster could step into any courtroom in America and be quite at home."

The Chief Justice suggests that "many lawyers have come to accept this philosophically and many have simply surrendered to 'the system.' "

He warns: "The public will not."

Many concerned lawyers know the image of their profession has not been good and some suspect it has been damaged by the inability of the courts to deal with the criminal threat to the nation during the last two decades. A comprehensive survey conducted in 1960 by the Missouri bar with funds furnished by Prentice-Hall Publishing Co., showed that most people interviewed rated lawyers below bankers, teachers, preachers and doctors in "general reputation." Only thirty-five percent of those interviewed thought lawyers were honest and truly dedicated to their profession. Nearly fifty-seven percent of those asked felt that lawyers created lawsuits unnecessarily and about forty percent thought lawyers overcharged for their services. Almost twelve percent of those who used lawyers said the legal business was solicited by the attorney himself: a violation of the Canons of Ethics of the profession. Those who had personally used the services of lawyers did express confidence in their personal attorney, but their view of the legal profession as a body was not favorable.

The same general view of lawyers was documented in a less extensive poll conducted at about the same time in Los Angeles with one notable addition: in the California survey, conducted by a single attorney, most of those interviewed said they thought criminal lawyers distort the truth and produce false evidence to aid defendants charged with crimes.

There has been a mountain of empirical data gathered in recent years on the problems of law enforcement and criminal justice: the Brown Commission, which is the National Commission on Reform of Federal Criminal Laws; the Miller Commission, or the President's Commission on Crime in the District of Columbia; the Katzenbach Commission, or the President's Commission on Law Enforcement and the Administration of Justice; the Kerner Commission, or the National Commission on Civil Disorder; and the Eisenhower Commission,[8] or the National Commission on Causes and Prevention of Violence. All of these bodies have completed extensive studies and research on the problems in the administration of criminal justice. However, in many ways their findings are not unlike those of the Wickersham Commission named by President Hoover to study the same general area about forty years ago.

Congress has now moved into the business of trying to improve "the system" and has created the Law Enforcement Assistance Administration which received appropriations of $60 million in its first year, 1968.

From the point of view of the lawyers, the most serious "reform" effort is the American Bar Association's Project on Minimum Standards for Criminal Justice.

More than sixty lawyers, judges and law professors have been working through various ABA "project" committees, to formulate new standards for criminal justice. The considerations stretch all the way from pre-arrest practices to post-conviction procedures. These committees have relied on a wealth of courtroom experience, extensive staff research and widespread consultations with other attorneys, judges, police officials, parole experts, and others. By early 1970 the project had published a dozen reports and another four were in various stages of production.

With all of this material and more at hand some lawyers are likely to say, and sincerely believe, that reform of "the system" is just around the corner. The leadership of Chief Justice Burger may cause some to say, in good faith, that reform is already here.

It is not, in fact, anywhere in sight.

---

8. Headed by Dr. Milton Eisenhower.

In August, 1954, Earl Warren, then Chief Justice of the Supreme Court, in a speech dedicating the ABA Center in Washington, said: "As lawyers, we know better than most other people that there are defects in our administration of justice . . . we are sensitive to the fact that technicalities, anachronisms and lack of uniformity in the law still beset us in the ascertainment of facts and that haphazard methods of appointment of judges, inadequate court organization and loose courtroom practices too often cause delay, confusion, inefficiency and consequent justifiable expense."

Sixteen years later it is almost as if the former Chief Justice had not spoken. The first director of the Law Enforcement Assistance Administration, Charles H. Rogovin, said in a speech to an ABA group in August 1969: "In some states felony defendants wait as long as two years before going to trial because of a shortage of judges, inadequate administrative procedures by the courts, and—in some cities—because of a shortage of court reporters.

"There are states," Rogovin said, "which do not require justices of the peace or magistrates to be attorneys. One state said its justices of the peace hold court in pool rooms. Many judges have staffs not large enough to operate the corner grocery store."

A year later Justice Burger seemed to think some progress was being made in moving the bar to action.

In the first "state of the judiciary" speech delivered to the ABA convention in St. Louis August 10, 1970, he recited the list of existing problems and made some specific recommendations for reform. Then he said: "The price we are now paying and will pay is partly because judges have been too timid and the bar has been too apathetic to make clear to the public and the Congress the needs of the courts. Apathy, more than opposition, has been the enemy, but *I believe the days of apathy are past.*"

Justice Burger pointed out in his address that the ABA had been warned in 1906 by Dean Roscoe Pound that justice could not function in the twentieth century with nineteenth century methods and machinery.

Despite his awareness of the enormity of the problem Justice Burger seems to offer optimism when he says he believes "the days of apathy are past."

Perhaps he has worked so long and so hard seeking to effect reforms that he wants to believe success is about to come to the system. There is no evidence of it.

Chief Justice Burger questioned a 1969 ABA meeting in Dallas: "Is it inevitable that all the mechanisms for resolving legal issues should be immune from change? Frankly I do not know the answer. But I do know that the patience of the American people with the processes of litigation is wearing thin."

To his credit, the Chief Justice has tried to lift the organized bar from its lethargy. He served as the second chairman of the ABA project on criminal reform. He has spoken out repeatedly in speeches urging the reform of criminal justice. He has documented the need for some of it as he has talked of the project on minimum standards. But the idea that this well-intentioned and costly ABA "project" will solve the crying problems of the administration of criminal justice is unrealistic.

Most lawyers know there is a sharp discrepancy in viewpoints existing at two levels of the organized bar: the inner-circle of leadership of the ABA on one hand and the lawyer in actual courtroom practice in cities and towns and county seats on the other. The court system in the fifty states is not run by the ABA. It is operated at the local level. It was pointed out earlier in these pages that there is no one system of justice in the nation. There are fifty-one systems: the federal court system and the system in the fifty states.

From state to state, and frequently from jurisdiction to jurisdiction within a given state, the methods of pursuing justice differ. In Louisiana nine jurors can convict and sentence a defendant. It takes twelve to sentence and convict in Tennessee. In some cases it may require twenty-four jurors to sentence and convict in California. In the federal courts and in forty states the jury convicts and the judge sentences.

Pay for witnesses and for jurors—and in fact for judges—is not consistent from state to state. In almost every situation, the pay is low for the responsibility involved.

As laws in different states differ regarding court procedures, so do rules in different courts differ. And so does crime punishment differ from state to state. Gambling, abortion, liquor sales and prostitution are looked upon differently in various states. In Virginia a young man was sentenced to twenty years in prison in 1969 for possessing marijuana. In neighboring North Carolina students were given suspended sentences for the identical crime. There are 300,000 certified lawyers in the United States and about 225,000 in actual practice. The 130,000 members of the ABA may represent a consensus of bar thinking in principle. Practice is something else again.

It will be up to local lawyers, local bar associations, local and state legislative bodies and local courts to bring about whatever reform comes from the ABA "project."

Chief Justice Burger has touched on the problem of implementation in speeches to the ABA about the project recommendations. He says: "Some states must establish such procedures by legislation. In some it may be done directly by rules promulgated by the highest court. In others it may be done by a rulemaking process which involves concurrence of the judicial branch and the legislative branch, with the judiciary having the responsibility for proposing rules of procedure."

In other words each of the fifty states will have to engage in the slow, painful process of getting these recommended standards into actual operation in the state courts and all its jurisdictions. These minimum standards are not going to be adopted uniformly across the country. There will be a long period while some "model laws" are drafted. These will be proposed in some legislatures. Some lawyers in the states will disagree among themselves about the value of the proposed changes. State and local bar associations will be expected to push for these changes and some bar leaders may seek to lobby them through the legislative bodies. Some of them will be amended by the local legislative bodies. In other states and other jurisdictions an effort will be made to short-circuit the legislature and bar leaders will try to have the recommendations, or some of them, built into the rules of courts. Some lawyers, because of apathy or because of opposition, won't help push the proposals and some may work covertly to defeat them.

Over the years the charge has been made that this system of criminal justice, from the bail-bond point to the post-conviction point, is a "rich man's law." The U.S. Supreme Court took steps during the 1960's to correct some of the inequities, and the result was that "Impeach Earl Warren" signs were posted all across the nation.

The introduction to the published report of the ABA project

study for providing defense services to criminal indigents shows some recognition at the ABA's higher levels of the need to end the idea of the "rich man's law." It says: "Over the past quarter century or more, we have become increasingly aware of infirmities in our system of administering criminal justice which have rendered the standard of 'equal justice under the law' more a hope than a universal reality."

The report goes on to recommend that it is incumbent upon the system to provide to the indigent defendant not just a lawyer, but a lawyer of "substantially equal skill and experience" to the lawyer for the prosecution.

For two decades there has been a movement, pushed by many leaders of the ABA, to start public defender programs in communities across the land. There has been substantial resistance to this among elements of the local bar in many communities. Some lawyers have felt the creation of a public defender office infringes on the potential income of those who practice in criminal court. In recent years the public attitude has begun to grow in some areas that such public defender offices, paid for by tax funds, in effect "coddle criminals."

But the efforts to provide public defender offices have had a positive effect. As Fred P. Graham points out in his book *The Self Inflicted Wound,* the number of public defender offices increased from 75 in 1961 to more than 300 in 1968. During the same period the amount spent through these offices increased from $2.6 million to $21.4 million.

Still, well over half the court jurisdictions in the nation have no such offices. The federal government and some state courts have adopted the policy of providing direct pay to lawyers who defend indigents—and in general this has been more popular with local practicing attorneys than the establishment of public defender offices. To a "law and order" oriented public, it is still "coddling criminals."

But, as Graham points out, the increase in indigent defense procedures has created substantial problems for the courts: "People who would have pleaded guilty before did not; motions that would not have been filed before were; appeals that would have been finessed were filed . . . Suddenly the system had to digest a rich mix."

Now the ABA is acknowledging formally that a "rich man's

law" runs against the concept of "equal justice under the law." But as the need to erase the "rich man's law" image grows, the related problem of providing courts that can handle the increased volume of the "poor man's law" is also going to grow. Reform action produces counter-action and confusion mounts. Even if the ABA project recommendations could be immediately and universally adopted in every state there is a real question as to whether the suggestions contained in some of the reports are worthwhile or whether they will actually reform weaknesses in the system. Of all the project work, by far the most noted and controversial is the report of the Reardon committee on the subject of free press and fair trial. It is, to say the least, a lawyer's report with lawyer-like recommendations. Efforts by the Reardon committee to reach an accord with responsible representatives of the press failed because the bar committee members held the view that the courts needed the contempt power to restrain newsmen who circulate information about pending criminal cases. News executives maintained that such power was pernicious and ran against the First Amendment "free press" guaranty. Some members of the ABA group, including Justice Reardon, contended that the contempt power was needed, not to discipline newsmen, but rather to give the courts more opportunity to discipline lawyers, policemen and court officers who gave out statements to news media about a pending case. Newsmen feared the power would be used as a prior restraint on the press and Judge Battle's handling of the Ray case made their worst fears reality. And so it can be anticipated the other project reports by other ABA committees will be less than definitive statements on what justice really means.

It can be expected, since many of the ABA's proposed changes involve delicate constitutional questions, that there will be test cases taken up on appeal to try to establish some guidelines to conform with or put down the recommended procedures. In short, the legal hodgepodge that now surrounds criminal trials in the fifty states, the shadow of which could be seen in New Orleans, Memphis and Los Angeles, can be expected to magnify during that period when an effort is made to integrate the ABA recommendations into the mainstream of justice. Retired Supreme Court Justice Tom Clark agreed to take on the difficult job of seeking to have the proposals implemented across the land. His will surely be a tiring and frustrating job. His willingness to take it on should earn for him the universal thanks of ABA members. But a mere recitation of the titles of some of the bar project reports—electronic surveillance, speedy trial, pretrial release, defense services—presages the sort of conflict that will exist inside the bar when it tries to universally reform the system. The result can be practically predicted: true reform won't come.

In any case, it is an error to suggest that reform of criminal justice should be left to the lawyers alone. For one thing, the prime motivating force that gets lawyers into courts is that it is their business; it is how they earn a living and provide for their families.

In principle, the organized bar favors oiling the machinery of the court system in order to cut down on the backlog of cases which delay criminal trials for years in some jurisdictions. In practice, the criminal lawyer may believe that the best interest of the client who pays him is served by the delay that comes from the court machinery grinding slowly. Two books published in recent years, *The Trouble With Lawyers* by Murray Teigh Bloom [9] and *The Lawyers* by Martin Mayer [10] document the degree to which the dollar interest dominates the lawyer's involvement in his pratice. This fact of a lawyer's life mocks the over-emphasis most members of the bar place on their "public interest" role in society. The individual lawyer's conflicting roles as money maker and court reformer are obvious.

And the conclusion is just as obvious; more interests should be concerned with reforming the system than those making their money in the courts.

But the mercenary motives of lawyers aside, so much more than the judge, the prosecutor, the defense lawyers, is woven into the defective cloth that blindfolds justice.

Police are involved; professional bondsmen are involved; jail and prison personnel are involved; parole and rehabilitation officers are involved. Most of all, the public—those who pay for the administration of justice—is involved.

The eight suggestions listed above are not recommendations

9. Simon & Schuster (1968)
10. Harper & Row (1966)

that would come from the organized bar as the most important considerations in reforming justice in America. Nor can they be accurately described as recommendations that represent the thinking of "the press." The authors are four independent journalists and they speak only for themselves. In sum, their suggestions grew out of a close observation of three sensational criminal cases, all of which put "justice" under the microscope of public scrutiny. In general they are a plea to bring national consistency to the manner court officials are investigated, trained, appointed, and disciplined, and to bring some semblance of national order that will make the "system of justice" both a system and just.

The lawyers call it a "system of justice." A report to the National Commission on the Causes and Prevention of Violence by the Task Force on Law and Enforcement, calls it a "nonsystem of justice." This report says that the police, the courts and the rehabilitation agencies frequently work at cross purposes.[11]

"It is commonly assumed that these three components—law enforcement (police, sheriffs, marshalls) the judicial process (judges, prosecutors and defense lawyers) and corrections (prison officials, probation and parole officers)—add up to a 'system' of criminal justice. The system however is a myth." [12]

The report goes on: "In the mosaic of discontent which pervades the criminal process . . . each sees his own special mission being undercut by the cross-purpose frailties or malfunctions of the other . . . To the extent that they are concerned about other parts of 'the system' police view courts as the enemy. Judges often find law enforcement officers themselves violating the law. Both see correctional programs as largely a failure. Many defendants perceive all three as paying only lip service to individual rights." [13]

What is wrong with the criminal system of justice?

"Mechanisms for introducing some sense of harmony into

---

11. Ramsey Clark, in **Crime in America** writes: "We cannot wait for the courts to point the way to justice. All agencies and institutions must exercise initiative in the quest.

12. Dr. Milton S. Eisenhower, Chairman, **The Rule of Law: An Alternative to Violence** (A Report to the National Commission on the Causes and Prevention of Violence), Aurora Publishers, 1970, p. 266.

13. Ibid., p. 268.

the system are seldom utilized. Judges, police administrators and prison officials hardly ever confer on common problems. Sentencing institutes and familiarization prison visits for judges are the exception rather than the rule. Neither prosecuting nor defense attorneys receive training in corrections upon which to base intelligent sentencing recommendations.

"Nearly every part of the criminal process is run with public funds by persons employed as officers of justice to serve the same community. Yet every agency in the criminal process in a sense competes with every other in the quest for tax dollars. Isolation or antagonism rather than mutual support tends to characterize their intertwined operations. And even when cooperative efforts develop, the press usually features the friction, and often aggravates it.

"One might expect the field to be flooded with systems analysts, management consultants and publicly-imposed measures of organization and administration in order to introduce order and coordination into this criminal justice chaos. It is not."

In the late 1960's young people across the nation began to express their disillusionment with most of the institutions of society and of government. It included assaults on the administration of criminal justice, the best example of which is probably the biting criticism youth leveled at Judge Julius Hoffman after the trial of the Chicago Seven. Most of this youthful condemnation of the society was rejected by older people in the nation. The lack of support for government institutions did not spread across that segment of the population which had come to be known as "the silent majority."

There was no indication that it would affect middle class adults who were older and unwilling to endorse revolutionary changes in the established institutions of government.

But with crime affecting so many in the land—including most of those in the "silent majority"—there is a real danger that in at least one area, the administration of criminal justice, the disenchantment of the young will spread. In the late 1960's the beleaguered police were the heroes of middle America. As the nation fails to subdue the threat of crime this attitude can be expected to change and the ineffective policeman may become society's scapegoat; but he is only one of the scapegoats. He may be joined by judges, prosecutors, defenders, and all who are caught in the web of the system.

Chief Justice Burger in one of his speeches in August 1969 asked: "If we do not solve what you call the problems of criminal justice, will anything matter very much?"

His answer is so obvious he did not bother to state it: nothing will.

New Orleans, Memphis and Los Angeles, and the reaction of the bar and society at large to these cases, seem to indicate in a frightening way that nothing will.

BIBLIOGRAPHY

Bloch, Herbert A., editor. *Crime in America.* New York: Philosophical Library, Inc., 1961.

Bloom, Murray Teigh. *The Trouble with Lawyers.* New York: Simon and Schuster, 1968.

Borkin, Joseph. *The Corrupt Judge.* New York: Clarkson N. Potter Co., 1962.

Clark, Ramsey. *Crime in America.* New York: Simon and Schuster, Inc., 1970.

Egerton, John. *A Mind to Stay Here.* New York: The Macmillan Company, 1970.

Eisenhower, Milton, chairman. *The Rule of Law: An Alternative to Violence.* Task Force Report to the National Commission on the Causes and Prevention of Violence. Nashville: Aurora Publishers, Inc., 1970.

Epstein, Edward Jay. *Inquest.* New York: The Viking Press, Inc., 1966.

Friendly, Alfred, and Ronald L. Goldfarb. *Crime and Publicity.* New York: Twentieth Century Fund, 1967.

Garrison, Jim. *A Heritage of Stone.* New York: G. P. Putnam's Sons, 1970.

Graham, Fred P. *Self Inflicted Wound.* New York: The Macmillan Company, 1970.

Graham, Hugh Davis, and Ted Robert Gurr, editors. *The History of Violence in America.* New York: Praeger, 1969.

Hayward, Max, editor. *On Trial: The Soviet State versus Abram Tertz and Nikolai Arzhak.* New York: Harper and Row, 1966.

Houghton, Robert A. *Special Unit Senator.* New York: Random House, 1970.

Huie, William Bradford. *He Slew the Dreamer.* New York: Delacorte Press, 1970.

Jones, Penn, Jr. *Forgive My Grief.* Midlothian, Texas: The Midlothian Mirror, Inc., 1966.

Kaiser, Robert Blair. *RFK Must Die.* New York: E. P. Dutton and Company, Inc., 1970.

Kaplan, John, and Jon R. Waltz, *The Trial of Jack Ruby.* New York: The Macmillan Company, 1965.

King, Coretta. *My Life with Martin Luther King, Jr.* New York: Holt, Rinehart and Winston, Inc., 1969.

Kirkwood, James. *American Grotesque.* New York: Simon and Schuster, Inc., 1970.

Mayer, Martin. *The Lawyers.* New York: Harper and Row, Publishers, 1966.

Reardon, Paul C., and Clifton Daniel. *Fair Trial and Free Press.* Washington: American Enterprise Institute for Public Policy Research, 1968.

St. John-Stevas, Norman. *Life, Death and the Law.* Bloomington: Indiana University Press, 1961.

U.S. President's Commission on the Assassination of President Kennedy. *Report of the President's Commission on the Assassination of President John F. Kennedy.* Washington: U.S. Government Printing Office, 1964.

INDEX

414

415